# THE SCARECROW AUTHOR BIBLIOGRAPHIES

1. John Steinbeck (Tetsumaro Hayashi). 1973.
   See also no. 64.
2. Joseph Conrad (Theodore G. Ehrsam). 1969.
3. Arthur Miller (Tetsumaro Hayashi). 2nd ed., 1976.
4. Katherine Anne Porter (Waldrip & Bauer). 1969.
5. Philip Freneau (Philip M. Marsh). 1970.
6. Robert Greene (Tetsumaro Hayashi). 1971.
7. Benjamin Disraeli (R.W. Stewart). 1972.
8. John Berryman (Richard W. Kelly). 1972.
9. William Dean Howells (Vito J. Brenni). 1973.
10. Jean Anouilh (Kathleen W. Kelly). 1973.
11. E.M. Forster (Alfred Borrello). 1973.
12. The Marquis de Sade (E. Pierre Chanover). 1973.
13. Alain Robbe-Grillet (Dale W. Frazier). 1973.
14. Northrop Frye (Robert D. Denham). 1974.
15. Federico Garcia Lorca (Laurenti & Siracusa). 1974.
16. Ben Jonson (Brock & Welsh). 1974.
17. Four French Dramatists: Eugène Brieux, François de Curel, Emile Fabre, Paul Hervieu (Edmund F. Santa Vicca). 1974.
18. Ralph Waldo Ellison (Jacqueline Covo). 1974.
19. Philip Roth (Bernard F. Rodgers, Jr.). 2nd ed., 1984.
20. Norman Mailer (Laura Adams). 1974.
21. Sir John Betjeman (Margaret Stapleton). 1974.
22. Elie Wiesel (Molly Abramowitz). 1974.
23. Paul Laurence Dunbar (Eugene W. Metcalf, Jr.). 1975.
24. Henry James (Beatrice Ricks). 1975.
25. Robert Frost (Lentricchia & Lentricchia). 1976.
26. Sherwood Anderson (Douglas G. Rogers). 1976.
27. Iris Murdoch and Muriel Spark (Tominaga & Schneidermeyer). 1976.
28. John Ruskin (Kirk H. Beetz). 1976.
29. Georges Simenon (Trudee Young). 1976.
30. George Gordon, Lord Byron (Oscar José Santucho). 1977.
31. John Barth (Richard Vine). 1977.
32. John Hawkes (Carol A. Hryciw). 1977.
33. William Everson (Bartlett & Campo). 1977.
34. May Sarton (Lenora Blouin). 1978.
35. Wilkie Collins (Kirk H. Beetz). 1978.
36. Sylvia Plath (Lane & Stevens). 1978.
37. E.B. White (A.J. Anderson). 1978.
38. Henry Miller (Lawrence J. Shifreen). 1979.
39. Ralph Waldo Emerson (Jeanetta Boswell). 1979.
40. James Dickey (Jim Elledge). 1979.
41. Henry Fielding (H. George Hahn). 1979.

42. Paul Goodman (Tom Nicely). 1979.
43. Christopher Marlowe (Kenneth Friedenreich). 1979.
44. Leo Tolstoy (Egan & Egan). 1979.
45. T.S. Eliot (Beatrice Ricks). 1980.
46. Allen Ginsberg (Michelle P. Kraus). 1980.
47. Anthony Burgess (Jeutonne P. Brewer). 1980.
48. Tennessee Williams (Drewey Wayne Gunn). 1980.
49. William Faulkner (Beatrice Ricks). 1981.
50. Lillian Hellman (Mary Marguerite Riordan). 1980.
51. Walt Whitman (Jeanetta Boswell). 1980.
52. Jack Kerouac (Robert J. Milewski). 1981.
53. Herman Melville (Jeanetta Boswell). 1981.
54. Horatio Alger, Jr. (Scharnhorst & Bales). 1981.
55. Graham Greene (A.F. Cassis). 1981.
56. Henry David Thoreau (Boswell & Crouch). 1981.
57. Nathaniel Hawthorne (Jeanetta Boswell). 1982.
58. Jean Genet (R.C. Webb). 1982.
59. August Derleth (Alison Morley Wilson). 1983.
60. John Milton (Michael A. Mikolajczak). 1983.
61. Algernon Charles Swinburne (Kirk H. Beetz). 1982.
62. George Washington Cable (William H. Roberson). 1982.
63. Christine de Pisan (Edith Yenal). 1982.
64. John Steinbeck (Tetsumaro Hayashi). 1983.
    See also no. 1.
65. John G. Neihardt (John Thomas Richards). 1983.
66. Yvor Winters (Grosvenor Powell). 1983.
67. Sean O'Casey (E.H. Mikhail). 1985.
68. Tennyson (Kirk H. Beetz). 1984.
69. Floyd Dell (Judith Nierman). 1984.
70. R.C. Hutchinson (Robert Green). 1985.
71. Charlotte Perkins Gilman (Gary Scharnhorst). 1985.
72. Maxwell Anderson (Alfred S. Shivers). 1985.
73. Theodore Dreiser (Jeanetta Boswell). 1986.
74. Ezra Pound (Beatrice Ricks). 1986.
75. Robert Bly (William H. Roberson). 1986.
76. Edward Albee (Richard Tyce). 1986.
77. Robinson Jeffers (Jeanetta Boswell). 1986.
78. Edward Bellamy (Nancy Snell Griffith). 1986.
79. Studies on Clarín (David Torres). 1987.
80. Edwin Arlington Robinson (Jeanetta Boswell). 1988.
81. Antonio Buero Vallejo and Alfonso Sastre (Marsha Forys). 1988.

# Edwin Arlington Robinson and the Critics:

A Bibliography of Secondary
Sources with Selective
Annotations

by

# JEANETTA BOSWELL

*Scarecrow Author Bibliographies, No. 80*

The Scarecrow Press, Inc.
Metuchen, N.J., & London
1988

Library of Congress Cataloging-in-Publication Data

Boswell, Jeanetta, 1922-
    Edwin Arlington Robinson and the critics.

    (Scarecrow author bibliographies ; no. 80)
    Includes indexes.
    1. Robinson, Edwin Arlington, 1869-1935--
Criticism and interpretation--Bibliography.
I. Title. II. Series.
Z8748.37.B67 1988 [PS2719.R526] 811'.52    87-32324
ISBN 0-8108-2076-5

Dedicated to the Memory of
Professor Thomas Hill McNeal,
the best of Robinson teachers
in 1945

# CONTENTS

Preface               vii

THE BIBLIOGRAPHY               1

Index of Coauthors, Editors, and Translators       277

Subject Index               279

# PREFACE

## Edwin Arlington Robinson, 1869-1935

Perhaps one of the things an E.A.R. fan likes to do best (after having read and understood the poetry) is simply to quote "good" lines. Never has a poet been so eminently quotable and not once resorting to clichés, trite expressions, or folksy humor. Take for instance:

> "We cannot know how much we learn
> From those who never will return...."

> "God siays himself with every leaf that flies...."

> "...a slowly freezing Santa Claus
> Upon the corner, with his beard and bell."

> "...we thought that he was everything
> To make us wish that we were in his place."

> "Time swings a mighty scythe, and someday all your peace
> Goes down before its edge like so much clover...."

Admittedly, one is inclined to go on and on! The poetry reflects the author's exceptional literary education: Greek and Roman literature, Shakespeare, Milton, the English Bible, later English literature, American literature. This literary background expresses itself in an overwhelming use of allusion, and his reader has to know or be willing to learn as much as Robinson himself. For a great many readers (and good ones at that) this is asking too much, and so Robinson loses ground in favor of simpler poets.

It is not difficult to make an argument for Robinson that he may well have been the spokesman for most of the 20th century. His poetry reflects an acute awareness of the times he lived through --the violence, the heyday of madness in the 1920's with their tinsel glitter, the crushing poverty of the 1930's, the foreshadowing of the long dark night of World War II. Had he lived with us in the 1980's, as the century begins to exit, Robinson might have written an updated version of "The Man Against the Sky." Although written nearly three-quarters of a century ago, the poem would need few changes to bring it into the present, and hardly any change to remind the reader of our ever-present threat of nuclear holocaust: "A world on fire ... with nothing on it for the flame to kill...."

It is difficult to make any worthwhile generalization about the criticism of Edwin Arlington Robinson. Only recently has he been "studied" in an objective, analytical fashion. Earlier criticism leaned too far in the direction of adulation or denial, and seldom said precisely what Robinson's poetry was all about. Perhaps Robinson will not attain the position of "greatest poet," but his reputation will remain closely aligned with the poetry itself, "very solid."

It is always a pleasure to acknowledge those who have been of tremendous help in these endeavors. Such is the case for all the studies listed in the "Subject Index" under the heading "Bibliographical Studies." Of particular note is Nancy Carol Joyner's 1978 Reference Guide to Robinson; Richard Cary's fine editorial work in general, and the four special issues of the Colby Library Quarterly in 1969, Robinson's centennial birthday. At a personal level, many friends and well-wishers helped in various ways: my assistants Tanya Simmons and Karen Wilson; my brother who made sure books were returned to the library on time; the interlibrary loan staff at the University of Texas in Arlington; the library at Colby College that so willingly supplied copies of many a Robinson article.

A word is needed to honor an undergraduate course I took over forty years ago: the first "single" author course I had. It turned out to be a good one and was the herald of many more to come. I am glad that the subject matter did not wear thin in that semester, and I came to the end with still more Robinson to cover than had been covered.

# THE BIBLIOGRAPHY

1 ANONYMOUS (listed chronologically). "Review of The Torrent and the Night Before." Time and the Hour, 4 (December 26, 1896), 10-11.

2 "Review of The Torrent and the Night Before." Bookman, 4 (February, 1897), 509-510. Those who read this and have any liking for poetry will read on to the end. Some of the verses we do not care for, especially the long poem at the end. There is true fire in his verse, and there are the swing and the singing of wind and wave and the passion of human emotions in his lines; but his limitations are vital. His humor is of a grim sort, and the world is not beautiful to him, but a prison-house. In the night-time there is weeping and sorrow, and joy does not come in the morning.

3 "Review of The Torrent ...." Literary World, 28 (August 7, 1897), 260.

4 "Review of The Children of the Night." Nation, 66 (June 2, 1898), 426. Among all the new American poems, there is no question as to which is entitled to praise. Robinson's book is a work of small variety, yet the work is deftly and thoroughly done within that plot of ground, and packs even his sonnets with such vigor and creative imagination that the whole story is told. He writes of men and women, not of external nature, and uses the latter only as the Greeks did, for a setting, not a theme, which is the better way.

5 "Review of Captain Craig." Nation, 75 (December 11, 1902), 465. Calls Robinson one of the most promising "of our younger poets, one who has not yet mastered his own powers, and has to follow his muse for a time, not direct it. His very singleness of mind sometimes defeats itself and leaves his meaning unconveyed." He brings marvelous color and music into his verse when at his highest point. This book is likely to be passed unnoticed by all indolent readers, and with impatience by those who are a little more careful; but those more careful still will revert to it again and again, and wish health, fortune, and encouragement and still further development to one who could write it.

6   "A New Poetry: Review of Captain Craig." Independent, 55
    (February 19, 1903), 446-447.

7   "Topics Uppermost." New York Times Saturday Review of
    Books, August 19, 1905. P. 537.

8   "The President as a Critic of Poetry." Current Literature, 39
    (October, 1905), 388-389.

9   "Review of The Children of the Night." Dial, 39 (November
    16, 1905), 314. President Roosevelt has recently gone out
    of his way to recommend the poems of Robinson and this new
    edition is the natural consequence. This time the presiden-
    tial lightning has struck in the right place, for Robinson's
    work has never got half the attention it deserved. This
    volume includes "The Torrent" and "The Night Before,"
    which poems gave a title to the author's first public venture.

10  "Recent Poetry: Volumes of Minot Savage, Edwin Arlington
    Robinson." New York Times, November 25, 1905. The mood
    is usually serious, and quite removed from the sweet sadness
    of one who invokes grief as an adjunct to his verse. The
    numerous poems of religious feeling are the product of a
    wholesome faith. They are nearly always individual, and
    show little tendency to echo poets of a larger gift which too
    often is the hallmark of the minor poet.

11  "Review of Children of the Night." Critic, 47 (December,
    1905), 584. Does not dispute the President's good word
    about this work, but suspects that he has not kept up with
    the flood of American minor verse. If he had done so, he
    would think twice before applying the word "genius" to Rob-
    inson, notwithstanding the author's simplicity and good faith.

12  "Review of Children of the Night." Nation, 81 (December 21,
    1905), 507. No minor poet of the day is less indebted to
    poetic conventionalisms than Robinson, or more securely him-
    self. One of the most characteristic and striking of Robin-
    son's gifts is his way of coining musical and suggestive
    names for his poetic characters, each a perfect symbol and
    almost a poem in itself. Something of the same haunting in-
    dividuality pervades all of Robinson's work, and makes it,
    even when least poetic, of a curious vividness.

13  "Review of Children of the Night." Review of Reviews, 33
    (January, 1906), 122.

14  "Review of Town Down the River." Nation, 92 (January 5,
    1911), 11. Lists Robinson's volume, along with ten or twelve
    others as "Recent Verse." Quotes from "Calverly" to illus-
    trate the mood of nostalgia and the vain regret for the

impermanence and fleetingness of the individual, the creature
of a hapless and haunting memory.

15  "Three Poets of the Present:  Edwin Arlington Robinson and
    Town Down the River."  New York Times, 6 (February 12,
    1911), 79.  The book reveals a distinctly individual point
    of view and manner of feeling--something expressive of a
    small group more than of humanity at large.  At times a
    rare beauty shines through the words.

16  "Good American Poets."  Independent, 70 (March 2, 1911),
    468-470.  Includes remarks on Town Down the River.  Re-
    gards Robinson's latest volume as "good" poetry, but agrees
    with Richard Le Gallienne that there are perhaps more good
    poets in the world at this moment than there have ever been
    before in its history.

17  "Review of Town Down the River."  Literary Digest, 42 (March
    4, 1911), 424-425.  There is always a hidden something in
    the lines--each poem has a lyric secret.  We may add that
    at times his style is too cryptic and occasionally the meaning
    dives into complete obscurity and does not reappear again
    for several stanzas.

18  "Review of Town Down the River."  Outlook, 98 (June 3, 1911),
    245.  Robinson is quietly himself; he is neither a reactionary
    nor a rebel; he steers clear of the commonplace and escapes
    the strain of a deliberate and painful effort to be original.

19  "Edwin Arlington Robinson."  The Sunday Journal (Minneapo-
    lis), November 3, 1912.  P. 5.

20  "Review of Edwin Arlington Robinson by Herman Hagedorn."
    New York Times Review of Books, December 1, 1912.  P.
    747.

21  "Edwin Arlington Robinson."  Outlook, 105 (December 6, 1913),
    736.  Is a general comment with some focus on The Children
    of the Night.  Robinson is the most individual of American
    poets, combining intensity of thought and feeling with a
    curious simplicity of expression which sometimes baffles even
    his most ardent admirers.  The words he uses are the words
    of ordinary speech, put together sometimes in cadences that
    seem close to prose, yet their half-hidden rhythm conveys to
    the attentive ear much of the story and most of the underly-
    ing emotion.

22  "A Difference of Opinion:  Van Zorn."  Independent, 80 (Octo-
    ber 26, 1914), 141.  Quotes the publisher who says "the
    story here is humorous and dramatic.  The reader's attention
    is held by the technique of playwriting.  His comedy scores

heavily both for the brightness and cleverness of its dialog
and for its ingenious and thought-provoking plot." The reviewer says, "we cannot agree with the publishers on any
of these points."

23  "Playbooks: Van Zorn." New York Times, November 15, 1914.
    P. 499. This play lacks substance not because, quite liter-
    ally, it is not all there.

24  "Review of Van Zorn." Nation, 100 (February 18, 1915), 205.
    This play depends for its interest almost entirely upon the
    development of character. It contains very little action,
    but is not without emotional crises. It is enriched with a
    variety of carefully wrought detail and dialogue, and much
    philosophic humor. On the printed page with the author's
    notes, it is drama, but one cannot envision its being acted.
    In general it is original and clever.

25  "Review of The Porcupine: A Drama in Three Acts." Cleve-
    land Open Shelf, October, 1915. P. 93. A drama of a
    hopeless domestic entanglement, rather remarkable in its
    characterizations but hazy and ineffective in the working
    out of its plot.

26  "The Bristling Wife: A Review of The Porcupine." The Eve-
    ning Sun (New York). November 13, 1915. P. 9.

27  "Review of The Porcupine." Drama, 6 (February, 1916), 156-
    157.

28  "Current Poetry: The Man Against the Sky." Literary Di-
    gest, 52 (March 18, 1916), 738. Prints several poems from
    Robinson's volume, and says that this poet has been gov-
    erned by the principle that "the proper study of mankind
    is man." The heart of man, the mind of man, the soul of
    man--are the things that exclusively interest him. Robin-
    son states questions rather than answers them; he exhibits
    humanity, but does not attempt to explain it. He has been
    called a realistic poet, but he is an artistic and creative
    one, whose portraits are illumined with genius. He has
    been called the greatest American poet of our time.

29  "Review of The Man Against the Sky." North American Re-
    view, 203 (April, 1916), 633. There is thought here, not
    merely mood--and with it a sense of the exaltation that
    comes of successful intellectual striving. But the expres-
    sion is also a matter of expression. There is a certain
    difficulty, almost amounting to obscurity, in the longest and
    most important poem in the volume--the title poem. Each
    cleanly sculptured phrase challenges attention. This poetry
    does not merely lull and narcotize; it makes thought musical.

30  "Fine Artistry and Power of Interpretation:  The Man Against
    the Sky."  New York Times, April 2, 1916.  P. 121.
    Robinson's attitude toward life is the Russian attitude--the
    attitude of Dostoevsky.  He is intent on pointing out the
    good in evil.  He is the subtlest of the subtle and has been
    called the portrait painter of the soul.

31  "Mr. Robinson's New Poems:  The Man Against the Sky."  Out-
    look, 112 (April 5, 1916), 786-787.  In this work Robinson
    maintains that curious attitude of impartiality towards his
    characters which has done so much to give him his peculiar
    and enviable position in American letters.  His characters
    are always strangely independent.  He puts them on the stage
    of his poetry or his plays, and there they work out their
    own destiny unhampered by their creator.  Their sins, their
    virtues, whims and foibles are matters for neither praise nor
    blame, but for analysis and exposition.  Yet the reader is
    very conscious of Robinson's own personality and point of
    view.

32  "Review of Van Zorn."  Bruno's Weekly, April 22, 1916.  P. 12.

33  "Review of The Man Against the Sky."  Review of Reviews, 53
    (May, 1916), 632.  The material in this book is simple, di-
    rect lyricism, so effortless as to seem magical, and possess-
    ing more insight into the kingdom of the mind than the work
    of any other American poet.

34  "Review of The Man Against the Sky."  American Library Asso-
    ciation Booklist, 12 (June, 1916), 419.  There are somewhat
    over twenty poems in this volume, each a work of distinc-
    tion.  With the exception of "Ben Jonson Entertains ...,"
    which should be counted as one of the tercentenary tributes,
    the themes are modern.  The treatment is modern too in its
    deceptive simplicity.  A number of the poems are reprinted
    from periodicals.

35  "Review of The Man Against the Sky."  Dial, 61 (July, 1916),
    61-63.  This volume does not disappoint:  it contains real
    creations in character, like those of dramatist or novelist,
    and it represents a further interesting study in the problem
    of making diction at once colloquial and poetical.  The title
    poem stands at the end of the volume, and is a kind of final
    mystical character study of a nameless man who becomes--
    from being seen on a clearly outlined hill-top, descending to
    some unknown place--a type of Man himself.

36  "Review of The Man Against the Sky."  Athenaeum, December,
    1916.  P. 593.  These verses are typical of the good-class
    magazine or periodical, satisfactory in many ways, but never
    inspiring.  "The Gift of God" is one poem which rises above
    the level of its fellows.

37  (Signed D.L.M.)  "The Arthurian Legend in New Guise:  Mer-
    lin."  Boston Transcript, 3 (March 31, 1917), 9.  His peo-
    ple are as strongly individualized and speak as naturally as
    though their author had been putting them into a novel in-
    stead of into a narrative poem of medieval setting.  This
    brings their problems much closer to the reader.  Robinson
    has always been placed by critics among the few of our real-
    ly great poets.  He is a very complete master of his art.

38  "Poets Who Adhere to Rhyme:  Merlin."  Review of Reviews, 55
    (June, 1917), 660.  The state of the modern world is subtly
    symbolized in this fine poem, which has amazing beauty of
    texture and ventures a new philosophy.

39  "Notable Books in Brief Review:  Merlin."  New York Times,
    August 26, 1917.  P. 313.  It is not a great poem, though
    its failure is not intrinsic in its subject.  The subject sim-
    ply betrays more openly than a modern one certain defects
    in the author.  He has neither the singing magic of the old
    school nor the swift egotistic vitality of the new.  He is a
    respectable poet, but he is heavy.

40  (Signed S. Y.)  "Review of Merlin."  New Republic, 12 (Sep-
    tember 29, 1917), 250-251.  It is pleasant to take up Merlin
    and read as one reads mere poetry.  It is clear at once that
    the style, and often the quality, are very like Tennyson's.
    In Robinson there is more smoothness, more expected pro-
    portions, leisure, and fluency than in much of Robinson's
    previous work, and less of that effect of rather trenchant
    rhythm, of brusque acumen and passionate shrewdness, and
    of a kind of analytical excitement for the mind, that have
    made a distinguishing quality in his poetry.

41  "Review of Merlin."  Catholic World, 106 (November, 1917),
    255.  On the whole, in spite of Robinson's literary power,
    we prefer the terrors of "mid-Victorian morality" and the
    symbolism of the Idylls of the King.

42  "Review of Merlin."  American Library Association Booklist, 14
    (January, 1918), 121.  Robinson has retold the story of
    Arthur, Merlin, and Vivian, altering the outlines of the
    traditional tale very little, but reading new meanings into
    the situation.  He has chosen for the time of his narrative
    the eve of the downfall of Arthur's court.  Merlin, after the
    ten years spent with Vivian in Broceliande, has returned
    with the purpose of again lending Arthur his counsel, but
    in thinking out the problem he comes to see that he must
    turn back without seeing the king, leaving him to the fate
    he has prepared for himself.

43  "Appreciation of the Poetry of Edwin Arlington Robinson."

Scribner's Magazine, 66 (December, 1919), 763-764.  Those
of us who are fortunate enough to know him and his work
can fully appreciate how great has been his contribution to
the literature of his country.  He is essentially and above
all else American, and at the same time cosmopolitan and of
every country and age, as all great poets must be.  There
has never been a master poet who depended for his name
less on any individual poem.  Poem after poem comes to mind,
and in each instance such painstaking toil and refining of
words.  Robinson writes and rewrites, chooses and eliminates;
every word that is eventually printed has been weighed and
considered over and over again, not once but many times.

44  "A Poet's Birthday."  New York Times,, December 21, 1919.
    P. 5.

45  "A Poet's Birthday."  Outlook, 123 (December 24, 1919), 535.
    Robinson's influence has been much wider than the constantly
    growing circle of his readers.  He has influenced to a very
    great extent the content and form of modern American poetry.
    It is unfortunate that most of these have caught such a small
    share of his understanding of the real spirit of his art.  The
    influence of Robinson is more widely acknowledged today than
    at any time in the past decade, and his place seems surer
    today than at any time during the past fifteen years.  As he
    celebrates his fiftieth birthday, he has received no applause
    which has not been deserved, nor published a single line
    which was not wrought with a devotion comparable to the
    devotion of those who builded in stone the faith and hopes of
    the Middle Ages.

46  "A Poet's Birthday."  Literary Digest, 64 (January 10, 1910),
    32-33.  Reviews a number of remarks that critics have re-
    cently made to commemorate Robinson's fiftieth birthday, most
    of which were made with an air of solemnity.  Among those
    who noted the poet's birthday were Vachel Lindsay, Louis V.
    Ledoux, Amy Lowell, Bliss Perry, and a great many others
    of varying persuasions.  This critic says in conclusion:
    "never was there a poet who depended less on any individual
    poem.  In writing of Mr. Robinson verse after verse comes
    into one's head, and the temptation is strong to continue
    quoting poem after poem" (quoting the anonymous writer in
    Scribner's Magazine).

47  "Review of Selected Letters of Thomas S. Perry."  New York
    Herald Tribune Books, 6 (February 23, 1920), 17.

48  "Review of Lancelot."  Dial, 69 (July, 1920), 103.  All the fam-
    iliar characters are present--somewhat unfamiliar in their halt-
    ing, introspective speech.  The verse moves with dignity and
    attains at times even a detachable beauty, and yet the memorable

lines are comparatively few--for this author.  Beneath the
surface of the well-known story one feels, however, the quiet
current of the allegory that must have been the motive for a
return to this legend.

49  "Review of Lancelot."  Cleveland Open Shelf, October, 1920.  P.
     86.

50  "Review of Three Taverns."  Springfield Republican, October 7,
     1920.  P. 10.  Robinson's verse, as always, flows with limpid
     purity, but his quaintly compounded vocabulary and his in-
     tellectual penetration compel the closest attention to his pages.
     Readers who have the patience or the agility to follow Robin-
     son are not meanly rewarded.  His fondness for portraying
     the complex facets of character in an oblique light and by
     means of inscrutable hints and sinuous innuendoes has led
     him to further workings of the dramatic monologue.

51  (Signed G. C. F.)  "Somber as the Time:  The Three Taverns."
     Grinnell Review, 16 (January, 1921), 332.  It is a somber
     book.  The title poem, a monologue by Saint Paul just before
     he enters Rome, is somber and polished to a high dark sheen,
     and the bitter tang of it remains in the memory long after
     reading.

52  "From Lancelot to Steeplechasing:  Lancelot and The Three Tav-
     erns."  Outlook, 127 (January 12, 1921), 67-68.  Lancelot is
     a vital contribution to the literature which has sprung from
     the Arthurian legends.  Robinson's poem moves swiftly and
     surely to its allotted end.  As a narrative there are no flaws
     in its construction, but its supreme beauty lies in its analysis
     of character and motive.  Of the second volume, one might
     say it is a poor choice to introduce Robinson to someone not
     already familiar with the poet.  Little of the old magic is
     here, although the intellectual appeal overmasters at times
     the poetic.

53  "Edwin Arlington Robinson's Dime Novel:  Avon's Harvest."
     Bookman, 53 (May, 1921), 248.  Avon's Harvest is less dif-
     ficult than much of Robinson, and it is more moving.  In
     American literature, surely, there is no more powerful drama-
     tic poem.

54  "Review of Avon's Harvest."  Grinnell Review, 16 (June, 1921),
     455.  This is not an easy book to read, and it will not be
     popular.  But it deserves, and we believe it will get, its own
     place in the more serious of American narrative poetry.

55  "Review of Avon's Harvest."  Dial, 71 (August, 1921), 243.  At
     first glance seems a barren tale of hatred and corroding fear
     with melodramatic snatches of ghostly demons and lurid

obsession. But the melodrama is tempered by unerring character analysis, by a searching portrayal of the subtle interplay of two personalities whose clash is invisible and persistent even though they are separated by endless miles of
land and sea. Robinson has written better poems and this
last product is marred by the defects of his peculiarly intimate method. His effort to evade the cliché, one feels, has
become like Avon's fear, something of an incubus and the
result often is a series of absurd locutions.

56 (Signed W. W.) "Insight and Epithet." John O'London's Weekly,
    6 (December 17, 1921), 364-365.

57 "Review of Collected Poems." Literary Digest, 71 (December 24,
    1921), 38. As a poet Robinson has never made concessions,
    either in subject matter or in form; he is in tradition, yet
    out of it; he is fanciful yet profound; he is realistic, yet a
    mystic. He has fervor, yet philosophic stability. We are
    glad, in this collected series, to be able to judge Robinson
    under one roof, so to speak. All lovers of poetry will be
    pleased to own all his poetry, so conveniently bound.

58 "Authors' Club Hails Poet: E. A. Robinson." New York Times,
    January 27, 1922.

59 "Robinson as a Poet Born Ahead of His Time." Current Opinion,
    72 (April, 1922), 525-527. Reviews a number of critical esti-
    mates of Robinson, but concentrates on several reviews and
    comments by Amy Lowell, who seems to have a particular un-
    derstanding and insight to the poet. Her remarks, covering
    over a decade of commentary, are principally high in praise.
    Although Robinson's poetry and Amy Lowell's poetry are un-
    related, the critic-poet does feel that he spoke for an age,
    the age to come.

60 "Yale Bestows Academic Honor." New York Times, June 22,
    1922.

61 "An American Poet." The Outlook (London), 50 (August 26,
    1922), 243. Review of Collected Poems.

62 "An American Poet: Review of Collected Poems." (London) Times
    Literary Supplement, October 12, 1922. P. 639. Reprinted
    in Allan Angoff, ed. (1954), pp. 354-356.

63 "An American Bard and the British Reviewers." Living Age
    (Boston), 315 (October 28, 1922), 244. Robinson was rec-
    ognized long ago by most Americans who love poetry as a
    writer of great originality and distinction, but few English
    critics have been sufficiently acute to discern his true rank.
    England will have none of him, although the critics have made

up their minds with a very slight acquaintance. What will the English critics say when they read the Complete Poems? Is the English critical mind, once formed, made up forevermore? Or will it change?

64 "American Poet's Verse Most Enduring in English Literature the Past Year." National Magazine, 51 (November, 1922), 285.

65 "Contemporary American Poetry: Edwin Arlington Robinson." Bookman, 57 (March, 1923), 107-108. Consists of a brief biographical preface followed by excerpts from four other critics. Of late Robinson has been much honored: the Pulitzer prize, an honorary degree from Yale, and much recognition of his fiftieth birthday. He is definitely not a part of the furor of current literary life, as his work is not comparable with most of the surface journalistic writing of present-day America.

66 "Progress of the Philosophical Art of Edwin Arlington Robinson: Roman Bartholow." New York Times, March 25, 1923. P. 3. Robinson moves his pawns with a mordant certainty. Life flares through them, and it is life itself which the poet pictures. His characters are never ends in themselves; they are always aspects of life as a whole.

67 "Tragedy: A Review of Roman Bartholow." New York Herald Books, April 8, 1923. P. 14.

68 "Edwin Arlington Robinson's Somber Muse: Roman Bartholow." Current Opinion, 74 (May, 1923), 549-550. This poem is one of Robinson's greatest. Here is life, he says in effect, and there is no special moral to be drawn from it, either for good or evil. It is equally useless for us to lift up our hands in despair about this scheme of things or to accept it wholeheartedly. Rather it should be observed carefully. It will be found of intense psychological interest.

69 (Signed F. M. L.) "New Books and Old: Roman Bartholow." Independent, 110 (May 12, 1923), 319. This reviewer says: "I confess that I quite lost my way in the metaphysical mazes of Roman Bartholow. The lines scan, the sentences construe, and there is an air of meaningfulness, but what the whole signifies I cannot divine."

70 "A Circumscribed Triangle: Roman Bartholow." Bookman, 57 (June, 1923), 450-451. In this story of three souls torn by love, Robinson is exceedingly faithful to the gods of obscurity. This narrative contains some of the loveliest lines Robinson has written. It also contains more of his curious inverted structures, more of his verbal tentatives. He is the great poet of the subjunctive mood. There are four characters

who move curiously through a sort of allegorical House of
Love.  It is also a House of Mirrors, a crystal maze in which
the reader can grasp only vaguely the image of Robinson's
actual thought.

71  "Review of Roman Bartholow." North American Review, 217
    (June, 1923), 862-863.  If one takes the poem apart and
    looks at the pieces, the only poetic quality one can discover
    is intellectual vigor in imaginative expression.  The author's
    characteristic intensity, his almost marvelous power of con-
    densation are here.  But the work has so many unbeautiful
    features that one is repelled.  While there is no muddling of
    the thought, there is real obscurity.  The phraseology is by
    turns pseudo-Shakespearian, glaringly commonplace, truly
    poetic, or endlessly tenuous and abstract.  Yet when all has
    been said, one must concede that the cumulative effect of
    this poem is great.  Each development of feeling or character
    contributes to the next.  The poem, despite its curious arti-
    ficiality, is somehow lifelike and real.  A vigor not only in-
    tellectual but emotional pervades it.  And it is not easy to
    forget.

72  "Review of Roman Bartholow." New York World, June 24, 1923.
    This is a story of a triangle gone sour, so to speak.  Lover,
    husband, and woman all appear to walk and talk as if stricken
    with the palsy.  It is time the poets quit talking about these
    New Englanders who have not enough courage or animal force
    to look a sin between the eyes.

73  "Mr. Robinson's New Poem:  Roman Bartholow." (London) Times
    Literary Supplement, January 9, 1924.  P. 6.  The style, as
    a vehicle for a long poem, is too contentedly prosaic:  it
    swoops on the banal with too keen a satisfaction, as though
    it were necessarily an artistic triumph to capture a colloquial
    expression in a line of verse.  None the less the poem is
    woven in one piece, spun from a mind aware of itself and of
    deep issues, and it is as a whole that it must be regarded.

74  "Edwin Arlington Robinson Sets Down the Career of a 'Penitent
    Hercules': The Man Who Died Twice." New York Times,
    March 23, 1924.  P. 10.  The blank verse in which this poem
    is composed, is musical and restrained, and yet revelatory of
    the most delicate and difficult aspects of the human mind.
    There is perhaps not so much color (in the pictorial sense),
    but here Robinson is the musician in poetry.  The interrela-
    tion of the arts is not so apparent at first glance as it is
    with a little study.  But attention will show that he is reti-
    cently doing just those things that many of our younger poets
    attempt so loudly and so feebly.

75  "Review of The Man Who Died Twice." (London) Times Literary
    Supplement, September 18, 1924.  P. 582.

76  "Edwin Arlington Robinson." Our World Weekly, 2 (March 4, 1925), 205.

77  (Signed J. R. S.) "Review of Dionysus in Doubt." Boston Transcript, 6 (April 4, 1925), 2. In this work Robinson has made an estimate of life without once trailing the white garment of poetry in the often muddy puddle of preaching. It is gratifying to have Robinson to come forward with so much new material in his best manner. All the brilliance, preciseness, restraint, soberness of his best work of former days is here.

78  "Sidney Howard Play Wins Pulitzer Prize." New York Times, April 27, 1925. P. 19.  Refers to Howard's play They Knew What They Wanted. Article also includes reference to Robinson's poem The Man Who Died Twice, also a winner.

79  "Work That Won Prizes Founded by Pulitzer." New York Times, May 3, 1925. P. 11.

80  "Review of Dionysus in Doubt." Time, 5 (May 4, 1925), 12.

81  "New Books in Brief Review: Dionysus in Doubt." Independent, 114 (May 16, 1925), 563.  This volume will not add appreciably to the already adequate recognition of Robinson as a poet of ideas and technique. The poem from which the volume takes its name is a rather labored diatribe on the blindness and folly of the poet's native land. It is reasonably good satire, though crabbed and wordy in the saying--and that is all.

82  "Review of Dionysus in Doubt." Dial (Chicago), 79 (September, 1925), 261.  Best poetry in volume has nothing to do with Dionysus or Demos. The best is found in the poetry "under the shadowy elm-trees of Tilbury Town in the polished figures which are his puppets, cold, austere, unbreakable, like red and white chess-man, moved by hushed fingers in puritan sleeves across a board of walnut-wood."

83  Edwin Arlington Robinson. New York: Macmillan, 1927. 35 pages.  Contains tributes by Cestre, Redman, and Morris, among others.

84  "Review of Edwin Arlington Robinson by Ben Ray Redman." Poetry, 29 (January, 1927), 229.  This book should do much to foster a more general appreciation of Robinson, who unfortunately does not appeal to a popular audience because his poetry requires hard work to read. Yet the book is not confined to such an elementary purpose; because it lacks superficiality and is generous in detail, its brevity is an achievement, and its almost journalistic legibility admirable.

85  "New Books in Brief Review: Tristram." Independent, 118
    (April 23, 1927), 448.  The fine strain of irony which is so
    strong a factor in Robinson's work runs through Tristram
    to heighten the effectiveness of its three-cornered tragedy.
    The verse, strong and pungent, gains its ends without re-
    course to conceits of archaic idiom, yet the tale loses none
    of its heroic flavor thereby.  It will surely rank with the
    best of Robinson's work.

86  "Review of Tristram." Time, 9 (May 23, 1927), 38-39.

87  "Robinson, Edwin Arlington." Literary Digest, 93 (May 28,
    1927), 28, 33.  Quotes a good passage from Tristram, saying
    a taste of it may be enough to lead to the whole work.
    Quotes a number of critics, all of whom think the poem is of
    excellent quality.  The story is over a thousand years old,
    yet young as long as the world lasts.  Robinson's poem is
    alive in every line.  The lapses are few and far apart, and
    should not be used to criticize the poem.

88  "Review of Tristram." Dial, 83 (August, 1927), 174.  In the
    love and death of Tristram and Isolt, Robinson finds another
    narrative vehicle well adapted to the poetic conveyance of
    his irony and dignity, his concentrated insight, and his fine
    emotional force.  The reader, however, may feel that the
    work is more drawn out emotionally than it need be.  It ap-
    pears not to possess the continuous intensity of scene and
    line which one associates with Mr. Robinson's earlier works.
    A reader may wonder if there has not been in this case a
    slight deficit of fire.

89  "Mr. Robinson's Tristram." (London) Times Literary Supplement,
    September 22, 1927.  P. 640.

90  "The Nation's Honor Roll for 1927: Literature." Nation, 126
    (January 4, 1928), 4.  Refers to Tristram, a book that proves
    that poetry can be both good and popular.  Does not go
    further in comment or analysis.

91  "Books in Brief: Collected Poems." Nation, 126 (February 8,
    1928), 169.  These five small volumes supply a want that has
    become great since Robinson added so many poems to the canon
    established by the Collected Poems of 1921.  Everything is
    here and in attractive form.

92  "E. A. R. Wins Pulitzer Prize: Tristram." New York Times,
    May 8, 1928.  P. 4.

93  "Review of a Collected Robinson: Five Volumes of the Verse."
    Boston Transcript, 5 (June 23, 1928), 4.

94  "Edwin Arlington Robinson."  Wilson Bulletin, 3 (November,
     1928), 326.

95  "Editorial Staff."  Book League Monthly, 1 (November, 1928),
     1.

96  "Review of Sonnets."  Saturday Review of Literature, 5 (No-
     vember 24, 1928), 412.  This series contains nothing new
     for students of Robinson, but they will like having his own
     special contribution to the writing of the sonnet in English
     here compacted to its own essence, stringent but cordial.

97  "Review of Sonnets."  Springfield Republican, December 13,
     1928.  P. 10.  This volume will permit the reader to study
     in a convenient form the technique of one who has used the
     sonnet form as effectively and pointedly as any contempo-
     rary poet.  The earlier sonnets (they are printed chrono-
     logically), though good enough, do not show characteristics
     to be found in the later ones--a crisp incisiveness of dic-
     tion, a cryptic sense of the complexity of human relations
     and emotions, an almost Meredithian preoccupation with the
     mystery and frustration of human existence.

98  "Review of Cavender's House."  Outlook and Independent, 151
     (April 24, 1929), 668.  Because it marks a departure from
     medieval moods, Cavender's House is exceptionally interest-
     ing.  And because the new narrative is written in the same
     peculiarly individual blank verse, shows the same intellectual
     interest in emotional values and has the same essential qual-
     ity of objective introspection, the transition from Tristram
     is accomplished easily and naturally.  This work is uniquely
     Robinson.  Indeed, this story of a murderer's conscience is
     in many ways its author's best poetry.

99  "Review of Sonnets."  Dial, 86 (May, 1929), 436.  Nowhere is
     Robinson more the individual than in his sonnets.  In the
     collection of 80 selections, written over a period of 30 years,
     there are some that are gnarled, but all are filled with sap,
     and about a dozen are remarkable among the sonnets written
     in our time.  The reading of the collection leaves an impres-
     sion that one had read a narrative poem.  They are not
     fourteen line meditations, but each one represents some ac-
     tion taken, and effort made to bring warmth and light into
     a place of twilight and chill.

100  "Review of Sonnets."  Poetry, 34 (May, 1929), 114-115.  Scope
     of book covers 1880's to 1928, but does not show any great
     change in style or in his "general opinions of man and his
     world."  His method is better suited to the long narrative
     or to characterization rather than to the form of poem which
     requires, above all, organic richness and eloquence.  However,

his acid wit and sometimes his lavish beauty show that he
has brought a real contribution to sonnet literature, and
the present volume is convenient in telling just how much
it is worth.

101   "Books in Brief: Cavender's House." Nation, 128 (May 8,
      1929), 567. Reviewer thinks that the new narrative must
      take a minor place among the many that Robinson has writ-
      ten. It is far better than most living writers could have
      made it, but does not compare with Tristram, which sug-
      gests that the author is happiest when dealing with persons
      already created by history or legend. Cavender and his
      wife are "whole new cloth," and the weave is frequently
      limp and tenuous.

102   (Signed W. E. G.) "Review of Cavender's House." The Chris-
      tian Century, 45 (May 8, 1929), 618. There really is no
      story, except a mere theme, conveyed by hints and indirec-
      tions which gradually piece together into a pattern. Such
      story as there is might have been taken from the records of
      a criminal court or from the headlines of a tabloid newspa-
      per: a love too possessive, too jealous, a crime of violence,
      etc. Only an artist of the greatest ability could develop
      from this somber theme so much of beauty and handle it
      with so much emotional and verbal restraint, yet with such
      profound comprehension. If the theme is somber, the poem
      itself is luminous with insight, imagery and terse felicity of
      phrase.

103   "EAR Gets Medal for Poetry." New York Times, November 15,
      1929. P. 32.

104   "Robinson, Poet, Sixty Years Old." New York Times, Decem-
      ber 23, 1929. P. 9.

105   "Review of Cavender's House." (London) Times Literary Supple-
      ment, August 21, 1930. P. 666.

106   "Review of The Glory of the Nightingales." Time, 16 (Septem-
      ber 22, 1930), 64.

107   "Review of The Glory of the Nightingales." Outlook, 156 (Sep-
      tember 24, 1930), 145. A newspaper clipping could have told
      the tale with more succinctness; a state drama with less ter-
      rific accumulation and monotony; nobody but Robinson and
      his almost diabolical form could have piled up the terrible
      weariness and horror of vengeance and disgrace as he has
      done.

108   "Review of The Glory of the Nightingales." Springfield Repub-
      lican, October 19, 1930. P. 7ff. The poem is a sustained

achievement of thought, wherein the motives of two men,
one the doer, the other the recipient of evil, are presented
as an epitome of human beings facing their spiritual opportunities.  The execution is sustained in flexible and fluent
verse, which partakes of the abstractness of the theme, yet
does not lack occasional flashes of aphoristic condensation.

109  "Review of The Glory of the Nightingales."  Pittsburgh Monthly
       Bulletin, 35 (November, 1930), 82.

110  "The Old Master:  Review of Matthias at the Door."  Time, 18
       (October 12, 1931), 71.  Never a writer of spectacular
       verse, Robinson's natural inclinations toward subtle state-
       ment, his growing preoccupation with the psychological
       niceties of tragic states of mind have quieted his writing
       more and more.  In Matthias you will be struck gasping by
       no mighty lines.  But if you read closely you may note many
       a pithy phrase.  Tall, thin, baldish, spectacled, with a
       mustache partly concealed by his hypersensitive mouth,
       Robinson never talks about his own poetry, never criticizes
       other people's, wouldn't read in public for a million dollars.
       He loves to read detective stories, does not know whether
       he is a great poet or not but says he has never consciously
       injured anyone.

111  "Review of Matthias at the Door."  Pittsburgh Monthly Bulletin,
       36 (December, 1931), 86.

112  "Einstein Is Terse in Rule for Success:  Five Notables Give
       Advice:  Edwin Arlington Robinson."  New York Times,
       June 20, 1932.  P. 17.

113  "Review of Matthias at the Door."  (London) Times Literary Sup-
       plement.  September 22, 1932.  P. 665.

114  "Review of Nicodemus."  Time, 20 (October 10, 1932), 44.
       Of the eleven poems in this volume, seven are reprinted
       from magazines.  Like many a matured poet before him,
       Robinson turned to Biblical and historical themes.  Most of
       them are written in Robinson's familiar, intricately lucid
       blank verse.  Unlike his colleague, Robert Frost, Robinson
       has at times warmed his publisher's heart by proving popu-
       lar.  His Tristram sold 85,000 copies, is still quietly on the
       move.  Tristram readers may not all want a copy of Nico-
       demus, but Robinson readers will.

115  "Shorter Notices:  Nicodemus."  Nation, 135 (October 26, 1932),
       407.  This is a series of philosophical, ironic portraits of
       men who, in moments of illumination, talk in monologue or
       to another of the idealism in apparent failure.  Here is all
       of Robinson's wisdom--the inevitable technique and power

that are always his--and here is the same philosophy--that
beyond failure lies a kind of spiritual glory if the failure is
due to man's search for light.  The book gives us nothing
new, but it gives us more of the spirit and subtle interpretation of Robinson himself.  Every poem in the new volume fits exactly into the scheme of Robinson's art and philosophy.

116  "Poetry That Is Not Song: Nicodemus."  Christian Century,
     49 (November 2, 1932), 1347-1348.  Robinson's reputation
     is now too secure either to require defense or to admit de-
     nial.  He is no songster, and makes no concession to beauty
     except in its most austere and intellectual forms.  He is at
     his best in long narrative poems, or extended monologues,
     in which he has time and room to turn things over and de-
     velop his ideas with some deliberation.  He often seems to
     be seeking with almost painful anxiety for the proper word
     or phrase; and he does not always find it.

117  "Review of Nicodemus."  Pittsburgh Monthly Bulletin, 37 (De-
     cember, 1932), 78.

118  "Review of Nicodemus."  (London) Times Literary Supplement,
     No. 1611, December 15, 1932.  P. 966.

119  "Review of Talifer."  Time, 22 (October 16, 1933), 59.  This
     work marks another notch in Robinson's descent into poetic
     old age.  The bare outlines of his story are filled in not
     with detailed narrative but with long conversations....
     Handled by a poet less gifted with quiet discernment and
     a pithy irony which makes extended comment unnecessary,
     Talifer would be quite empty of significance.  But Robinson,
     though his lines now lack poetic fire, retains a sure and
     practiced technique, a shrewd discernment that radiates
     light if not heat.

120  "Two American Poets: Talifer."  (London) Times Literary Sup-
     plement, February 1, 1934.  P. 72.

121  "Robinson Presents His Twenty-Third Book of Verse: Amar-
     anth."  Newsweek, 4 (September 29, 1934), 39.

122  (Signed by W. M. L.).  "Review of Talifer."  English Journal,
     23 (October, 1934), 677.  Honest, solid Talifer, seeking
     "peace" turns from the earthly Althea to Karen, passionless
     brain--a "fish-Venus."  Robinson, contrary to his usual
     treatment, has shunted the tragic stream of "time and
     events" in this triangular narrative through the rational
     mind of Dr. Quick, hard-drinking poet-pathologist, who
     counsels wisely and brings happiness to the deserving pair.
     Most optimistic of Robinson's long poems, Talifer shows no

falling-off in surgical analysis of character or in subtle, pungent, dialogue.

123  "Review of Amaranth." Time, 24 (October 1, 1934), 62. Like other Robinson narratives, Amaranth is a tale of moral issues. This time the scene is set in a shadowy town not unlike a New England intellectualization of Hell. It is the place to which those are condemned who inhabit "the wrong world," preachers who should have been lawyers, businessmen who should have been artists. The principal figure is a painter who escaped from the "wrong world" by becoming a pump manufacturer, then somehow relapsed. Escaping from suicide and other tempting modes of flight by the mysterious figure of Amaranth, the painter watches him overtake the other inhabitants, eventually winning his release from the accursed obsession.

124  "Review of Amaranth." English Journal, 24 (February, 1935), 173. This is a gently chastening story of (and to) those people whose vanity and ambition have made them misfits, people who in stubborn delusion inhabit the world they want rather than that for which they are fit. It is the tragedy, sympathetically treated, of those who choose to be doctors, lawyers, and artists, instead of what they were meant to be, bakers, clerks, and plumbers. A not unworthy addition to Robinson's list of fine narrative poems.

125  "Robinson's Illness, Death, and Will." New York Times, April 4, 5, 6, 7, 8, 9, 20, 1935. "EAR is Very Ill: Physicians Give Up Hope," April 4, p. 21. "EAR Near Death," April 5, p. 19. "EAR, Poet, Is Dead at 66," April 6, p. 15. "Robinson Funeral," April 7, p. 40.

126  "Edwin Arlington Robinson Dies as Friends Sit by Bedside." New York World Telegram, April 6, 1935. P. 14.

127  "Edwin Arlington Robinson, Pulitzer Prize Poet, Dies Here." New York Herald-Tribune, April 6, 1935. Pp. 1-3.

128  "Robinson, Poet, Dies in New York." Boston Transcript, 1 (April 6, 1935), 4.

129  "Edwin Arlington Robinson, Noted Poet, 65, Taken by Death." Chicago Herald-Tribune, April 7, 1935.

130  "Sonnets on the Death of Edwin Arlington Robinson." Chicago Herald-Tribune, April 13, 1935.

131  "Obituaries: Edwin Arlington Robinson." Publishers' Weekly, 127 (April 13, 1935), 1520.

132   "Edwin Arlington Robinson." Time, 25 (April 15, 1935), 72.
      An obituary, which gives a few relevant details of Rob-
      inson's life.  Once established as a top-flight craftsman,
      austere, cerebral and passionate, he continued to live
      frugally and obscurely, doing much of his writing in a Man-
      hattan attic near the East River and at the MacDowell Col-
      ony in New Hampshire.

133   "Edwin Arlington Robinson." Nation, 140 (April 17, 1935), 434.
      Article is a review of Robinson's poetry, following his death
      in 1935.  While he lived he did nothing to ingratiate any
      conceivable public.  He refused to toss us the customary
      information about his personal self, but the very poetry he
      gave us to read in twenty volumes was agnostic in temper
      and austere in tone.  What his excellence was another age
      will be in the best position to say.  This particular moment
      is the poorest of all moments for defining the virtue destined
      to be associated with his name.  The most that can be done
      is to record the impression he has so far made.

134   "The Excellent Career." Commonweal, 21 (April 19, 1935),
      694, 708-709.  To Robinson Life was a chance to write verse.
      At the beginning this required a heroic act of faith, since
      poverty and obscurity kept nothing they could reveal from
      this young man.  The fact that he eventually triumphed may
      have been due to good luck.  His first book was remark-
      ably fine poems, but it was sufficient foundation upon which
      to base hopes for a brilliant career.  And despite the num-
      erous reservations any critic will feel compelled to make,
      there is no doubting that Robinson is the only name in this
      generation who has anything like the ring of Browning or
      Tennyson.

135   "Edwin Arlington Robinson." Modern Literature, 3 (May 1-14,
      1935), 9.

136   "On the Robinson Memorial." Poetry, 46 (August, 1935), 293.
      See entry 140 for continuation.

137   "Edwin Arlington Robinson." New York Times, August 31,
      1935.

138   "Edwin Arlington Robinson." Modern Literature, 4 (September
      15-30, 1935), 12.

139   "Poet's Corner: Edwin Arlington Robinson." Newsweek, 6
      (November 16, 1935), 47.  Review of King Jasper.

140   "News Notes: On the Robinson Memorial," [continued] Poetry,
      47 (December, 1935), 172-173.  Comments further on the
      memorial tablet which is to be placed, with seats and suitable

planting, in the outer court of the public library of Gardiner, Maine. The fund is not yet complete, and contributions may be made to Poetry or to the National Bank of Gardiner.

141  "A Modern Allegory." editorial. (London) Times Literary Supplement, January 31, 1936. P. 58.

142  "Prince of Heartachers: Edwin Arlington Robinson." London Times Literary Supplement, February 1, 1936. P. 91. Review of King Jasper.

143  "Edwin Arlington Robinson." Library Journal, 61 (February 15, 1936), 138.

144  "Robinson Memorial." Publishers' Weekly, 129 (February 22, 1936), 895.

145  Edwin Arlington Robinson Memorial. Gardiner, Maine: privately printed, 1936.

146  Academy Notes and Monographs, No. 95 New York: American Academy of Arts and Letters, 1939. Tributes to Robinson.

147  "Faith of E. A. Robinson: Review of Selected Letters." (London) Times Literary Supplement, No. 2012, August 24, 1940. P. 412.

148  "Poetry Album: Edwin Arlington Robinson." Scholastic, 39 (October 13, 1941), 22.

149  Edwin Arlington Robinson at Colby College. Waterville, Maine: Colby College Library Press, 1944. 4 pp.

150  "He Saw the Gleam of Lancelot: Edwin Arlington Robinson, 1869-1935." Senior Scholastic, 46 (April 2, 1945), 17.

151  "Your Town: Your People ('Mr. Flood's Party')." Senior Scholastic, 48 (May 13, 1946), 23.

152  "Vanity's Impatient Ear." Time, 49 (January 6, 1947), 96, 98. Comments on biography by Yvor Winters. Winters admits that in many of Robinson's poems there is a frosty New England eccentricity, "an intellectualism that is clever rather than perceptive, and reduces his dry rhythm to a jingling parlor verse." Winters's comparisons of Robinson with other poets are crisp and do not overlook the tragic possibilities.

153  "Edwin Arlington Robinson." The New Yorker, 20 (February 8, 1947), 98-99. Review of biography by Yvor Winters.

154 "Living Poems." New York Herald Tribune Books, May 11,
      1947. P. 35. Review of biography by Yvor Winters.

155 "Edwin Arlington Robinson." United States Quarterly Booklist,
      3 (March, 1947), 14. Review of biography by Yvor Winters.

156 (Signed M. N. O.) "Robinson's Sonnet: 'Oh For a Poet.'"
      Explicator, 5 (May, 1947), item 21. Brief note is a query:
      "Am I correct in reading the poem as unconscious irony?"
      Thinks a comparison with first printing of poem in 1894,
      and a clearing up of the allusion in closing lines could de-
      cide the problem.

157 "Untriangulated Stars: A Review." (London) Times Literary
      Supplement, #2403, February 21, 1948. P. 111.

158 "Untriangulated Stars: A Review." United States Quarterly
      Booklist, 4 (March, 1948), 39.

159 "Poet in America: Review of Untriangulated Stars." Time, 51
      (March 8, 1948), 110, 112. In the life and work of Robin-
      son there are plenty of signs that he never got what he was
      after. His poetry is racked by tension between its tightly
      controlled, dry surfaces and a subterranean shouldering
      towards something grander and more universal than he was
      able to express. Almost his only friend as a boy was Harry
      de Forest Smith, whose letters are now made public for the
      first time. Though not in themselves great letters they are
      a fascinating, often extremely moving record of the youthful
      travail of an American poet. Readers of this book may real-
      ize some of the suffering, the agony and the terrible con-
      sumption of human resources that go to make a poet in
      America.

160 "Untriangulated Stars: A Review." Wisconsin Library Bulletin
      (Madison), 44 (April, 1948), 82.

161 "News Notes." Poetry, 74 (May, 1948), 122. The Library of
      Congress has announced the acquisition of a collection of
      E. A. Robinson manuscripts from the estate of Louis Le-
      doux, who was a close friend of the poet for many years.

162 (Signed by J. Z.) "Edwin Arlington Robinson." More Books:
      Bulletin of the Boston Public Library, 23 (December, 1948),
      387-388. Review of biography of Emery Neff.

163 "Edwin Arlington Robinson: A Biography by Ellsworth Bar-
      nard." Bulletin from Virginia Kirkus' Bookshop Service,
      (New York), 19 (December 15, 1951), 721.

164 "American Poet." Time, 59 (February 11, 1952), 100, 102.

Review of biography by Ellsworth Barnard. In his critical
study Barnard scans the poet's lines closely, deliberately
scants the poet's life. His book is the poorer for it, for in
Robinson's case one of the clues to what he is driving at
is knowledge of what he was driven by. When Barnard is
not busy unraveling the poet's knottier lines, he sees Robinson pretty much the way Robinson saw himself: as an
idealist in philosophy, a traditionalist in verse form, a
liberal humanist in spirit. He called himself an optimist,
and refused to call the world "a prison house," but instead
a kind of spiritual kindergarten, where millions of bewildered infants are trying to spell God with the wrong blocks.
Robinson picked up quite a few wrong blocks himself, but
also enough right ones to spell American poet.

165   "Edwin Arlington Robinson." The United States Quarterly
        Booklist, 8 (June, 1952), 131.

166   "Edwin Arlington Robinson." The United States Quarterly
        Booklist, 10 (December, 1954), 500. Review of biography
        by Edwin S. Fussell.

167   "A Traditional Poet." London Times Literary Supplement, No.
        2794 (September 16, 1955), 539. Review of biography by
        Edwin S. Fussell.

168   "'Torrent' No. 27 Located." Colby Library Quarterly, 4 (Feb-
        ruary, 1956), 95. At the time of compiling the Jubilee Cen-
        sus of Robinson's The Torrent and The Night Before (Feb-
        ruary, 1947), Copy No. 27 was listed, as the one which
        Robinson had given to John W. Marr in January 1897. This
        copy had passed on to other hands and was unavailable.
        After ten years the long-lost copy has turned up, and is
        now in Philadelphia in the Library of the University of
        Pennsylvania.

169   "Where the Light Falls: A Review." Virginia Quarterly Re-
        view, 41 (Summer, 1965), xc. Work by Chard Powers
        Smith. This volume fills a long-felt need for a balanced se-
        lection of Robinson's poems. Unfortunately the editor died
        before the book was published, and some errors still re-
        main. The introduction by James Dickey is excellent in it-
        self, but is probably less authoritative than the one Profes-
        sor Zabel would have written had he lived. The volume
        contains 120 separate poems, of which about 50 are son-
        nets. The representation would have been better balanced
        if at least one long poem could have been included, but a
        defensible choice would have been difficult. A good selec-
        tive bibliography of works on Robinson is appended.

170   "Where the Light Falls: A Review." Choice, 2 (September,

1965), 390. Work by Chard Powers Smith. Book begins
and ends as a personal memoir of the author's friendship
with Robinson which lasted eleven years at the MacDowell
Colony. The memoir is interrupted to include two other
sections, a brief one on Robinson's thought and beliefs and
a biographical section that covers more than half the book.
Smith is concerned chiefly with the aspects of Robinson's
life which have been largely ignored or inadequately covered
by others. He draws heavily on other published material
and some on family records which have not hitherto been
made public. The most striking aspect of Smith's book is
his heavy reliance on Robinson's poetry in interpreting the
events of his life.

171  "Selected Poems: A Review." The Booklist, 62 (December 15,
     1965), 392. This lengthy portrait by a close friend com-
     bines reminiscence with analysis, biography with literary
     interpretation in a reconsideration of the character and
     achievement of this major American poet. An ardent dis-
     ciple, Smith brings an attention and appreciation that only
     love can beget and consequently produces a portrait that
     is intimate, profound, and precise. His book is a lasting
     contribution to our knowledge of the man behind and in the
     works of this great American poet.

172  "Selected Poems: A Review." Virginia Quarterly Review, 42
     (Winter, 1966), xviii. Brief Mention.

173  "Selected Poems: A Review." American Literature, 37 (Janu-
     ary, 1966), 521. Included in "Brief Mention" column. Says
     the volume is a greatly needed selection which is well chosen,
     with an Introduction by James Dickey which should be imme-
     diately displaced by an essay from the hand of someone who
     really knows Robinson's work.

174  "Edwin Arlington Robinson: A Poetry of the Act: A Review."
     Virginia Quarterly Review, 44 (Winter, 1968), xxiii. Work
     by W. R. Robinson. The purpose of this book is to "asso-
     ciate" Robinson with his proper contemporaries. The dis-
     cussion of Robinson seeking out the true and the believable,
     and recording that search in his poetry, is the sustenance
     of the work. What is most affecting is that Robinson's work
     embodies this search is demonstration that answers could be
     found. This volume is a treatment which makes a reading
     of the poems in itself an adventure.

175  "Edwin Arlington Robinson: A Critical Introduction: A Re-
     view." American Literature, 39 (January, 1968), 591. Work
     by Wallace L. Anderson. Included in "Brief Mention" sec-
     tion. Says the book is "a competent, brief survey, accom-
     panied by a selective bibliography which lists unpublished
     dissertations as well as published works on the poet."

176  "Edwin Arlington Robinson:  A Critical Introduction:  A Re-
     view."  Choice, 5 (June, 1968), 480.  Work by Wallace L.
     Anderson.  Provides the most readable and useful introduc-
     tion to Robinson, the man and the poet yet published.
     Against a background of Robinson's personal experience
     and philosophy and of period developments in literature
     and thought, Anderson discusses Robinson's career and
     contribution as poet, with interpretive analyses of the best
     short and medium-long poems and three of the long narra-
     tive poems.

177  "Robinson's Letters to Edith Brower:  A Review."  Publishers'
     Weekly, 194 (July 1, 1968), 48-49.  These letters begun in
     1897 when Edith Brower worked for a New York literary
     agent office, span thirty-three years.  They reveal Robin-
     son as sensitive, withdrawn, gloomy but grateful to be able
     to unburden himself to an admiring stranger.  For us they
     are interesting for their many literary sidelights and judg-
     ments.

178  "Robinson's Letters Are Published."  Boothbay Register, Au-
     gust 29, 1968.  P. 1.  Review of Letters to Edith Brower.

179  "Edwin Arlington Robinson:  A Poetry of the Act:  A Review."
     Choice, 5 (September, 1968), 779-780.  Work by W. R.
     Robinson.  This work is intended for the advanced student
     or scholar.  Robinson achieved a "modern" poetry, influ-
     enced by a number of contemporaries, William James, White-
     head, Santayana, etc.  In two important chapters, "The
     Alienated Self" and "Man As He Actually Is," the dualism
     of self vs nature and self vs society remain unresolved.
     Despite some confusions of terminology and a tendency to
     repeat and to overstate the argument, this is a challenging
     new look at the philosophic implications of Robinson's poetry.

180  "Harvard Press Publishes Book of Robinson."  Morning Senti-
     nel, October 4, 1968.  P. 7.  Review of Letters to Edith
     Brower.

181  "Edwin Arlington Robinson."  The Booklist, 65 (November 15,
     1968), 344.  Review of Letters to Edith Brower.

182  "Robinson's Letters to Edith Brower:  A Review."  Virginia
     Quarterly Review, 45 (Winter, 1969), xxx.  In this corre-
     spondence Robinson airs his estimates of other writers and
     his convictions about literature.  Although characterized,
     like his poems, by impeccable restraint, the letters disclose
     Robinson's personal warmth as well as his "almost intolerable
     isolation," his brand of Yankee humor as well as his anxiety
     about failure, his profound modesty as well as his profound
     commitment to his art.  Mr. Cary's detailed and valuable

notes complement the text to convey an intimate impression
of one of America's finest poets.

183  "Robinson's Letters to Edith Brower:  A Review."  American
     Literature, 40 (January, 1969), 594.  This collection con-
     tains 189 previously unpublished letters by Robinson cover-
     ing the years 1897 to 1930.  In two appendixes appear
     Edith Brower's "Memories of Edwin Arlington Robinson" and
     her critical appraisal of The Children of the Night, this
     latter originally published in the Wilkes-Barre Times for
     December 20, 1897.  Many of the poet's letters are of great
     biographical value, and the careful editing of Mr. Cary
     helps to make the volume a consequential addition to the
     store of information about Robinson.

184  "Colby Volume Honors Poet Robinson."  The Morning Sentinel,
     December 15, 1969.  P. 6.  Review of collection edited by
     Richard Cary.

185  "Appreciation of Edwin Arlington Robinson."  American Litera-
     ture, 42 (May, 1970), 271.  Review of collection edited by
     Richard Cary.  Included in "Brief Mention" column.  To
     celebrate the hundredth anniversary of Robinson's birth,
     the editor has selected essays to give "a diversity of criti-
     cal methods and ideological approaches."  He has included
     only essays first published separately and not collected by
     the author.  The authors include Harriet Monroe, Floyd
     Stovall, Frederic Ives Carpenter, Hyatt Waggoner, Yvor
     Winters, Charles T. Davis, and Louis O. Coxe.

186  "Edwin Arlington Robinson:  Centenary Essays."  American
     Literature, 42 (November, 1970), 426.  Notice of collection
     edited by Ellsworth Barnard.

187  ABERCROMBIE, Lascelles.  "Review of King Jasper."  Modern
     Language Notes, 52 (March, 1937), 218-220.  King Jasper
     should have been one of the most interesting of the blank-
     verse narratives, for it is done with all Robinson's skill and
     subtlety and expatiating nicety, and its theme is a version
     of the world's very present sense of the instant and formi-
     dable future--a version in terms of the most modern actual-
     ity.  Yet it hardly turns out to be what it promises to be.
     There is no diminution of power; natural manner has not
     set in a fixed and facile habit.  Yet our interest is baffled
     by the fact that so much has to be surmised which ought to
     have been made especially clear.  It puts before us a series
     of intricate psychological situations; and we have to make
     out as best we can, the story out of which they arise and
     to a very large extent the persons concerned in them.

188  ADAMS, Léonie, ed.  "The Ledoux Collection of Edwin Arlington

Robinson Letters." Quarterly Journal of the Library of
Congress, 7 (November, 1949), 9-13.

189   ADAMS, Richard P.   "The Failure of Edwin Arlington Robinson."
Tulane Studies in English, 11 (1961), 97-151.   Long, well-
documented article based upon a clearly defined theme.   Most
critics agree that Robinson was, or could have been, a great
poet, yet some believe that he failed in some measure to
achieve the greatness of which he was capable.   The solution
which Adams suggests is that Robinson was potentially a
great romantic poet, but was bluffed out of greatness except on a few occasions, by the inordinate popular prestige
in his time of mechanistic materialism.   The failure was of
nerve rather than intellect.   Robinson recognized the conflict, and placed himself in the camp of those who established
the romantic tradition.   But his morale was bad, and therefore he failed to realize either the strength of his own position or the weakness of the opposing one.

190   ADLER, Elmer, ed.   Breaking into Print.   New York:  Simon
& Schuster, 1937.   Reprinted Freeport, N.Y.:  Books for
Libraries Press, 1968.   "The First Seven Years," by Edwin
Arlington Robinson, pp. 161-170.   Article first appeared in
Part IV, The Colophon, December, 1930.   Remembers Chil-
dren of the Night, written nearly 40 years earlier, published in 1897.   About 1889, he says, he realized "that I
was doomed, or elected, or sentenced to life, to the writing
of poetry.   There was nothing else that interested me, and
I was rational enough to keep the grisly secret to myself."
His first book was The Torrent and the Night Before (1896),
printed in 312 copies which cost him $52.00.   Perhaps 30 or
40 went to friends.   The others went into the "unknown."
In 1897 most of these poems and new ones were published
in Children....   Robinson says:  "My incurable belief in
what I was doing made me indifferent alike to hostility or
neglect."

191   ADLER, Jacob H.   "Robinson's 'Gawaine.'"   English Studies
(Amsterdam), 39 (February, 1958), 1-20.   As employed by
Robinson, Gawaine is practically a new creation.   Except
for the titular heroes and their respective heroines, he is
Robinson's most fully realized Arthurian character.   And
he is vital to the structure, unity, and significance of the
poems.   Yet treatment of Robinson's Gawaine seems as a
rule to have been not only casual but largely unsympathetic.
This paper is based on three points:  (1) Robinson's Gawaine is a new character, a real young man, basically admirable; (2) his character has provided a man who can assist in the plot in many directions and thus keep the group
of important characters down to manageable limits; (3)
Gawaine's own story is significant and interesting, and is
an important element in unifying the three Arthurian poems.

192  AIKEN, Conrad.  "The Poetry of Edwin Arlington Robinson."
     Freeman, 4 (September 21, 1921), 43-46.  Review of Avon's
     Harvest.  We prefer to believe that Robinson does not in-
     tend his reader to take this volume as weightily as many of
     his other things.  It is a ghost story, and a fairly good
     one.  One wonders whether it would be unjust to see in this
     work, as one often sees in an artist's less successful work,
     a clearer indication of Robinson's faults and virtues than
     might be palpable.  It is not so easy to explain why Robin-
     son should so superlatively succeed once, and not again.
     In this work he seems to lack "energy," there is no breadth
     here; it is the closer and narrower view in which Robinson
     excels, and it may well be this that led him into simplifica-
     tion and the "hint and gleam" may take the place of the
     richly extensive.  These are not the virtues on which to
     build in long form: they are stumbling-blocks in the long
     narrative poem, since if they are allowed free rein they
     must render it fragmentary and episodic.

193  _____.  "The New Elizabethans:  Robinson's Collected
     Poems."  Yale Review, 11 (April, 1922), 632-636.  Robin-
     son's work included in article dealing with a half-dozen or
     more recently published books of poetry.  Is easily the best
     thing published during the winter, but no great clamor went
     up over this, and the applause has not been unanimous even
     among fellow-poets.  It is agreed that Robinson is the best
     of contemporary American poets, but the matter is not dis-
     cussed very generously.  No contemporary English poet has
     his insight into character, his intellectual beauty, his ex-
     quisite sense of form.

194  _____.  "A Letter from America."  London Mercury, 5 (June,
     1922), 196-198.

195  _____.  "Review of Tristram."  New Republic, 51 (May 25,
     1927), 22.  Calls this work a "courageous venture" into the
     Arthurian legend, for the third time, and perhaps here to
     the best effect.  All of Robinson's work sounds like Robin-
     son, and this is no exception.  His method is half way be-
     tween the creating of a tapestry and a psychological treat-
     ment of the characters.  Robinson has given to his poem
     great beauty of design, and that it contains many pages of
     extraordinary loveliness and tragic force goes without say-
     ing.

196  _____.  "Review of Sonnets."  Bookman, 68 (January, 1929),
     576.  Comment appears in a review of five poets, in which
     the reviewer points out the great dissimilarity of modern
     poetry, and suggests that the contemporary poet is in a
     sense a lost man.  Of Robinson he says:  "One reads them
     with a genuine pleasure and with a feeling that one's mind

is being employed; but one fails, afterward, to remember
them particularly. They are just a little colorless."

197 _____. "Review of Cavender's House." Bookman, 69 (May,
1929), 322-323. The theme is such a one as Henry James
or Hawthorne might have used for a long short story:  a
man who has murdered his wife, in a panic of jealous suspicion, argues the case with his conscience, which takes
the form of his wife's ghost, and this is the poem. As a
whole it is skilfully managed, but one comes away from it
feeling a little empty-handed. The piece becomes monotonous and cloying; and by reminding one so forcibly of all
the other conversations in all his other poems, the two
present protagonists become unbelievable.

198 _____. "Edwin Arlington Robinson." (London) Times Literary
Supplement, October 14, 1955. P. 605.

199 _____. "On Edwin Arlington Robinson." Colby Library
Quarterly, 4 (February, 1956), 95-97. Brief comments to
deny what an English reviewer said of Robinson in the
1930's. This reviewer had said that Robinson rejected
"much of the folly of his contemporaries," and in turn was
rejected by them. Aiken cites Amy Lowell and Louis Untermeyer to illustrate that Robinson early established a stable
reputation which hardly wavered for his entire life. Furthermore, one may point to the single fact that Robinson received the Pulitzer Prize three times for his work.

200 _____. "Three Reviews," in A Reviewer's ABC. New York:
Meridian Books, 1958. Reprinted as The Collected Criticism
of Conrad Aiken from 1916 to the Present. New York: Oxford University Press, 1968. Pp. 333-346. Also reprinted
in Murphy (1970), pp. 15-28. Three reviews as listed:
Review of Avon's Harvest (1921); Review of Collected Poems
(1922); Review of Tristram (1927). Deals mainly with poems
from the Arthurian cycle:  Merlin, Lancelot, and Tristram.
Robinson's method lies halfway between the tapestry effect
of Morris and the melodrama of Wagner. Its chief excellence
is an excellence of portraiture, and he particularly excells
in his portraits of women. Merlin was not so good as Vivien,
nor Lancelot as Guinevere; and in Tristram it is again true
that the heroines are much more sharply and sympathetically
realized than the hero. For the full-length portraits of the
two Isolts, one can have only the biggest praise. In Isolt
of the White Hands especially, Robinson has created a figure
of extraordinary loveliness and pathos, deeply moving.
Sometimes Robinson loses himself in a maze of inversions
and parentheses. This elaborate obscurity, with its accom-
panying absence of tactile qualities in the language and of
the ruggedness in the blank verse, too frequently makes

these pages hard and unrewarding reading. It is the more
regrettable as Robinson has given to his poem great beauty
of design. And that it contains many pages of extraordinary loveliness and tragic force goes without saying.

201 _____. "Three Meetings with Robinson." Colby Library
Quarterly, 8 (September, 1969), 345-346. Does not discuss
the poetry, but limits himself to the subjects of the title.
Aiken first met Robinson at Camp Merryweather in Maine.
On this occasion, Aiken says he proceeded to discuss the
subject of the skylark in English poetry--being all of a
brash seventeen. Robinson visited Aiken in Sussex about
1923. Two days later they went to Canterbury, on an
"alcoholiday." Sometime after Aiken gave a detailed report
of this last meeting to someone who published a good deal
of it. Robinson replied that he didn't like it to be said
that he drank. And this was the last letter Aiken ever
had from the poet. They saw each other in passing, and
Robinson was always cordial, but they were not friends
any longer.

202 ALDEN, Raymond M. "Review of The Man Against the Sky."
Dial, 61 (July 15, 1916), 62-63. This sort of workmanship
is highly significant to those interested in the poetic art,
as showing how all the effects of directness, veracity, and
individuality can be obtained not only without losing the
sense of beauty but--what is especially pertinent to our
generation--without losing the sense of form.

203 ALLEN, Don Cameron, ed. The Moment of Poetry. Baltimore:
Johns Hopkins Press, 1962. "Surroundings and Illumina-
tions," by John Holmes, pp. 4-26. Robinson, passim.
Critic here says: "I come to attention before the Robinson
shelf: the line of his own published verses, narrative
poems, and, alas, plays, is still much longer than all the
books yet written about him as man and poet. Any poet
whose manners, rhythm, and vocabulary are so pervasive
as to stain the style of anyone who touches him is dangerous, and Robinson is just such a poet. Here is a poet who
seeks life with honor, for himself and us. Robinson re-
corded failures in the search."

204 ALLEN, Gay Wilson. American Prosody. New York: American Book, 1935. Robinson, passim. Robinson not treated.

205 ALLEN, Hervey. "The Poetry of Edwin Arlington Robinson."
Reviewer, 4 (October, 1923), 56-58. Article is a review of
the book by Lloyd R. Morris, which Morris calls an "essay"
to express the appreciative attitude of the Authors' Club of
New York for Robinson's volume of Collected Poems that received from the club the award of the most significant book

of 1921. This work is far more than an "essay," it is a
complete and incisive critical treatise of the poetry of Robinson, the first and only adequate exposition of his work
as a whole. The book is written with a scholarly but living
style.

206  ALLEN, James L., Jr. "Symbol and Theme in 'Mr. Flood's
     Party.'" Mississippi Quarterly, 15 (Fall, 1962), 139-143.
     It is generally agreed that Robinson's work is very uneven
     in quality. Had he written more poems like "Mr. Flood's
     Party," in which statement of theme is skillfully implemented
     with patterns of symbol and metaphor, his right to designa-
     tion as major and modern might be more generally agreed
     upon than it has been in the years since he lived and wrote.
     This is one of Robinson's most successful short pieces.
     Had he written more consistently in this mode and avoided
     his drift toward an abstract and somewhat arid speech, as
     one critic called it, he might perhaps be more generally
     considered as equal to his fellow regionalist, Robert Frost,
     in both stature and modernity.

207  _____. "Edwin Arlington Robinson:  Poet or Versifier?"
     English Record, 14 (February, 1964), 9-15.  The dual pur-
     pose of this article is to suggest that when Robinson was
     genuinely poetic he was so sometimes almost as much by
     chance as by design and, second, that his works make ex-
     cellent tools for illustrating the essential difference between
     poetry and verse.  The truly dedicated reader of Robinson
     will object to the first purpose, since the general trend has
     been to become eulogistic and superlative.  As for illustrat-
     ing the difference between poetry and verse because of its
     now poetic, now prosaic qualities, there arises the more
     scholarly and academic question of why a writer's work
     should run poetically hot and cold.  Reading some of the
     more colorless and literal passages makes one tend to agree,
     that Robinson had a natural drift toward an abstract and
     somewhat arid speech.

208  ALTMAN, Louise Knutson.  "The Technique of Edwin Arlington
     Robinson and Robert Frost."  Ph.D. diss., University of
     Washington (Seattle), 1929.

209  AMACHER, Richard E.  "Robinson's 'New England.'"  Explica-
     tor, 10 (March, 1952), item 33.  Sees the poem as largely
     an ironic attack on the "patronizing pagans," the outsiders
     with their condescending attitudes and criticism of New Eng-
     land morality.  Such outsider opinion is erroneously based
     on the assumption that New Englanders were subject to "an
     emotional and moral frigidy," largely because of their cold
     climate and religious heritage.  Robinson's poem, however,
     denies all this and holds such opinion up for ridicule.

210 ANDERSON, Charles R., general ed. <u>American Literary Mas-</u>
     <u>ters</u>. New York: Holt, Rinehart, and Winston, 1965. "In-
     troduction" to Edwin Arlington Robinson, by Carl F.
     Strauch, Vol. 2, pp. 507-516. Consists of 23 Robinson
     poems with annotations, pp. 516-561; reading suggestions
     and biography, pp. 561-563.

211 ANDERSON, Hilton. "Robinson's 'Flammonde.'" <u>Southern</u>
     <u>Quarterly</u>, 7 (January, 1969), 179-183. Article is a care-
     fully worked out explanation of Robinson's poem as an alle-
     gory, if not an outright depiction, of Christ. The details
     are convincing: the name "Flammonde" suggests "light of
     the world"; the character is not ambitious for power or
     material success. He was interested in others, not himself.
     Good deeds that Flammonde performed parallel acts in
     Christ's life. The poet concludes with an expression of
     Christian faith and hope for the future world. More than
     half of the article is devoted to a reprinting of Robinson's
     poem.

212 ANDERSON, Wallace L. <u>Edwin Arlington Robinson: A Critical</u>
     <u>Introduction</u>. Boston: Houghton Mifflin, 1967. Also in
     paperback, Riverside Studies in Literature, 1968. Contains
     bibliography, pp. 155-165. Consists of 175 pages with in-
     dex and selective bibliography. Text is organized in six
     chapters: 1. The Poetic Context; 2. Background and
     Early Influences; 3. Toward a Philosophy and Poetics;
     4. 1906-1935: A Summary; 5. Robinson's Poetry: Char-
     acteristics and Illustrations; 6. Achievement and Perspec-
     tive. Excellent over-all study. Does not aim to be schol-
     arly, but informal for the average intelligent reader. Is a
     combination biographical-critical study designed to provide
     "an introduction to Robinson the man, his growth and de-
     velopment as a poet, his major work, and his relationship
     and contribution to modern American poetry."

213 _____. "Edwin Arlington Robinson's 'Scattered Lives.'"
     <u>American Literature</u>, 38 (January, 1967), 498-507. Article
     is a discussion of the "sketches or prose tales" which Rob-
     inson called <u>Scattered Lives</u>. The body of sketches is no
     longer extant, but some fragments and titles have been re-
     covered from letters which Robinson wrote to Harry de
     Forest Smith. "These literary bones do not enable us to
     reconstruct the skeleton of any one of the sketches, but
     as a group they clearly reveal Robinson's original concep-
     tion." This volume, if indeed it were published, was prior
     to the first book of poetry, <u>The Torrent and the Night Be-</u>
     <u>fore</u>.

214 _____. "The Young Robinson as Critic and Self-Critic,"
     in Barnard, ed. (1969), pp. 68-87. Quotes early passages

from Robinson, 1897 and 1913, which underscore a critical
position that Robinson held throughout his life: great poetry
is individual, contemporary, and timeless. The poetry of the
future, like that of the past and the ever-moving present,
would be part of a dynamic tradition, constantly extended
and modified by individual poets striving to present in artistic form something about the human condition. What additional characteristics great poetry would have other than its
quality of magic, Robinson did not say. But it would be unmistakable, in the long run. This is the kind of poetry Robinson tried to write, and it was the long run he counted on.
In his own mind he knew what he was looking for.

215 APP, Austin J. "Edwin Arlington Robinson's Arthurian Poems."
Thought, 10 (December, 1935), 468-479. No matter how noble
the author, agnosticism and fatalism never can yield inspiration, build character, or give a wholesome explanation of life.
They are negative and cannot yield a positive value. And
above all things, the least capable of inspiration, whether
good or bad, is agnosticism, for it is of its nature merely indifferent. And this is what one regretfully has to say of
these Arthurian poems: they have no real philosophy, no
wholesome, no significant meaning, they do not give us ideals,
they do not help us live--they are in purpose at best merely
indifferent. The brilliance of their style, the excellence of
their blank verse make them the most noteworthy Arthurian
productions in American literature. If they had more substance, and a real meaning, they would be as great as some
critics like to call them--great enough to be for all time rather
than an age.

216 ARVIN, Newton. "Some Recent Books of Poetry." Atlantic
Monthly, 144 (July, 1929), 20. Includes comments on Cavender's House. Regards this poem as better than some of
Robinson's more recent adventures in domestic tragedy. Although it creates levels of ambiguity, it is not obscure.
Robinson's use of "house" imagery is astounding and is
matched only by that of Henry James.

217 _____. "About Poetry and Poets: A Review of King Jasper."
New Republic, 85 (January 8, 1936), 252-263. This last long
poem by Robinson and the prose preface by Robert Frost are
two remarkable documents, full of disappointing implications.
Jasper is more interesting than most of the long narratives
of Robinson's later years; the language and the verse themselves have color and speed. But the intellectual cementation
makes Robinson seem like the poet of some alien people. There
is a cant of skepticism, a complacency of the pessimist, as
well as their opposites, and it is profoundly disappointing to
see distinguished minds succumbing to them.

218 _____ . "The Letters of Edwin Arlington Robinson:  A Samp-
ler." Colby Library Quarterly, 16 (1980), 51-62.  Quotes
from what is believed to be the earliest extant letter, January 1882, and Robinson's last letter, March, 1935, twelve days
before his death.  Between these two letters Robinson wrote
thousands of others.  Most of the originals are scattered
across the country in sixty or more libraries, some in the
hands of private collectors, a few are inaccessible.  More
than 4,000 have been preserved, and of these about one-sixth
have been published.  Article names and discusses the significant publications of Robinson's letters:  Selected Letters
(1940), Untriangulated Stars (1947), and Letters to Edith
Brower (1968).  Generally the collected letters will establish
a more detailed and accurate chronology of Robinson's life
and work.  They will also establish a more accurate reading
of letters previously published.  They will be helpful in as-
certaining the dates of composition and publication of some
of his poems, and gives a fuller picture of the man and his
world.

219 ANGOFF, Allan, ed. American Writing Today:  Its Independence
and Vigor. London:  Times Literary Supplement Press, 1954.
Reprinted New York:  New York University Press, 1957.  Review of Collected Poems, pp. 354-356.  Reprinted from The
Times Literary Supplement, October 12, 1922.  The collected
volume represents the work of about thirty years in nearly
600 pages and argues for a fair though not extraordinary flu-
ency.  Robinson is not a writer from whom one can quote
readily.  His happiest effects, pictorial as well as verbal, are
too intimately bound up with the poem to permit separating
them alive.  His work lingers in the memory like something
observed, something experienced in reflection; not less real
but less insistent than the direct impact of the poetic giants.

220 AUSLANDER, Joseph.  "Robinson Indignant:  Dionysus in Doubt."
New York World, April 26, 1925.

221 _____ , and Frank Ernest Hill, eds.  The Winged Horse Anthology. New York:  Doubleday Page, 1927.  "'Under Steam and
Stone,' Robinson," pp. 405-407.  At once lovers of poetry
proclaimed Robinson one of the finest of our living poets.
Since then he has become even more important.  He has written successfully a great variety of poems, and all with fine
art.  He has explored the tortured minds and souls of men,
turning into poetry our growing knowledge of the subconscious.  Robinson has made a poetic language of his own, taking the casual American speech about him and giving it a firm
literary form, with many of its weaknesses refined, and much
of its strength intensified.

222 _____ . "A Posthumous Poem:  Review of King Jasper." North

American Review, 241 (June, 1936), 375-376. Thinks the
readers of this work will remember the Introduction by Robert Frost much longer than they will remember Robinson's
poem. This Introduction is at once a generous and penetrating tribute and an important contemporary testament of poetic faith. Does not feel that King Jasper adds anything to
Robinson's stature as a philosopher or a poet, but neither
does it subtract from that stature. The poem as a whole suffers from a "certain weariness." The delineation blurs, the
action lags, the language misses fire, and grows wordy.

223  AYO, Nicholas. "Edwin Arlington Robinson and the Bible."
     Ph.D. diss., Duke University, 1966. DA, 27 (1966), 469A-
     470A. Begins by pointing out that no book-length study of
     Robinson and the Bible has been done, nor has a long article
     been done (see below, later, by Ayo). The many references
     to the Scriptures are noted in the Collected Poems, but the
     emphasis is on a small number of poems, and biblical charac-
     ters. In conclusion it is established that Robinson knew a
     great deal more about the Bible than is generally recognized,
     and is the single most extensive literary source in his poetry.
     To appreciate more fully Robinson's poetry demands some
     knowledge of how deep his roots reached into the fertile soil
     of the English Bible.

224  _____. "Robinson's Use of the Bible." Colby Library Quar-
     terly, 8 (March, 1969), 250-265. Reprinted in Cary, ed.
     (1969), pp. 263-275. Article is based on the dissertation
     listed above. Whatever else the Bible might be, Robinson ap-
     preciated it as great literature. In each of his Biblical poems,
     he capitalizes on dramatic elements in its source story. With
     a keen eye for a situation amenable to successful poetic treat-
     ment, he picked out of the Bible stories the crucial moment,
     the turning point, the painful moment of truth. These Bibli-
     cal narratives, which most readers take seriously, always tend
     to create tension, and Robinson takes advantage of the situa-
     tion. Even so the major Biblical poems were by no means an
     unqualified success. These poems became too analytical, and
     there was little attempt at a bold synthesis of ideas or images.
     They lacked color and vitality, and even their didactic suc-
     cess was often achieved at the cost of being overly abstract.
     Even so, they deserve more acclaim than they have yet re-
     ceived.

225  BAKER, Carlos. "Robinson's Stoical Romanticism, 1890-1897."
     New England Quarterly, 46 (March, 1973), 3-16. Article shows
     that Robinson was not the "pessimist" he was often called. He
     called himself a fatalist, but continued to assert that he was
     in truth an optimist. He typically rejected many subjects
     sometimes associated with Romanticism, but he never rejected
     a certain form of Idealism, namely that life and the universe

did have a meaning, although it might be obscure to man,
and that the world is not a "prison house" but a kind of
spiritual kindergarten where millions of bewildered infants
are trying to spell God with the wrong blocks.

226 _____. "'The Jug Makes the Paradise': New Light on Eben
Flood." Colby Library Quarterly, 10 (June, 1974), 327-336.
Robinson did not really regard Eben Flood as disreputable.
He often confessed to a liking for "the old man," and at the
time of its publication (1920) thought it was the best thing he
had done. The poem was published almost on the eve of the
Volstead Act, which began Prohibition.... It is possible that
the jug he used in his lonely upland carousal contained hard
cider, rather than whiskey, as is commonly supposed.

227 BANKS, Theodore Howard, Jr. "Review of Cavender's House."
The Cardinal, 4 (June, 1929), 29-31.

228 BARBOUR, Brian M. "Robinson's 'Veteran Sirens.'" Explicator,
28 (November, 1969), item 20. Sees the poem as controlled
by the unifying symbol of Ninon, the famous French courtesan,
who lived from 1620-1710, and was loved by nearly everyone
of any pretension at court. The irony centers about the fact
that Ninon herself battled age successfully, living past ninety
without forfeiting her diadem. Hence she solved the problem
that threatens the "veteran sirens" or aging prostitutes of
Robinson's poem. The poem is a contrast between Ninon and
these women as they face the problems of loss of beauty and
loss of hope; she did not lose.

229 BARNARD, Ellsworth. Edwin Arlington Robinson: A Critical
Study. New York: Macmillan, 1952. Reprinted New York:
Octagon Books, 1969. 311 pages with notes and index. In
eight chapters, it does not contain much biography. In conclusion, quotes about King Jasper, Robinson's last poem.
A last word on the last poem is that Zoe (Jasper's daughter)
is clearly not only knowledge but also beauty and love. Perhaps the main reason why she fails to convince us of her hu-
manness is not merely that she is a symbol but that she symbolizes so much--everything that justifies and ennobles human life. She embodies the synthesis that poets have always
dreamed of, in which reason, affection, and the sense of
beauty are combined, and in which man may achieve complete
self-realization.

230 _____. "Where the Light Falls: A Review." American Literature, 37 (January, 1966), 497-498. Work by Chard Powers
Smith. Comments on the style and structure of the work,
which is part criticism, part memoir. The biographical details
are perhaps doubtful. But the notion that Robinson would
have used them so literally is not only at odds with his

abnormal reticence and his concern for his own and other's
privacy, but denies his strongest claim to greatness--his
dramatic power as a dramatic poet. It does not contribute
to--it is in fact destructive of--a just estimate of Robinson's
work. And it distracts the reader's attention from the substantial contributions to such an estimate that Mr. Smith <u>does</u>
make.

231 _____. "Edwin Arlington Robinson: A Poetry of the Act."
American Literature, 40 (May, 1968), 244-245. Review of
biography by W. R. Robinson. The book as a whole is open
to serious criticisms. For one thing there is carelessness in
names and quotations. The style is often abstract and poly-
syllabic, the writing is at times unintelligible. Content of
work is based on thesis that Robinson could not accept an
aggressive "materialism" or a defensive "idealism," but had
to find a compromising solution.

232 _____, ed. Edwin Arlington Robinson: Centenary Essays.
Athens: University of Georgia Press, 1969. Contains the
following items (original except Levenson): "'Of This or
That Estate': Robinson's Literary Reputation," by Ellsworth
Barnard, pp. 1-14; "The Strategy of 'Flammonde,'" by Wil-
liam J. Free, pp. 15-30; "'The Man Against the Sky' and the
Problem of Faith," by David H. Hirsch, pp. 31-42; "The
Book of Scattered Lives," by Scott Donaldson, pp. 43-53;
"The Metrical Style of E. A. Robinson," by Robert D. Stev-
ick, pp. 54-67; "The Young Robinson as Critic and Self-
Critic," by Wallace L. Anderson, pp. 68-87; "Robinson's
Road to Camelot," by Charles T. Davis, pp. 88-105; "The
Transformation of Merlin," by Nathan Comfort Starr, pp.
106-119; "Imagery and Theme in 'Lancelot.'" by Christopher
Brookhouse, pp. 120-129; "A Crisis of Achievement: Robinson's Late Narratives," by Jay Martin, pp. 130-156; "Robinson's Modernity," by J. C. Levenson, pp. 157-174 (printed
from Virginia Quarterly Review, 44, Autumn, 1968, pp. 590-
610); "Tilbury Town Today," by Radcliffe Squires, pp. 175-
183. (Each item is listed and discussed in regular alphabetical sequence.)

233 _____. "'Of This or That Estate': Robinson's Literary Reputation," in Edwin Arlington Robinson Centenary Essays, ed.
Barnard (1969), pp. 1-14. Robinson's ascendancy during the
twenties is in sharp contrast to the harrowing and at times
almost hopeless struggle for recognition during the first two
decades of his poetic career. The main cause of this rejection
seems clear enough. What Robinson and Frost were trying to
do was to bring poetry back into touch with life, to take it
out of the drawing room, out of the realm of hearts and flowers, and onto drab small town streets and dusty country roads;
to tell the stories of humdrum and even sordid lives and show

that these were after all the lives of human beings; and to
tell these stories in the real language of men.

234 _____. "Edwin Arlington Robinson," in Fifteen Modern Amer-
ican Authors: A Survey of Research and Criticism, ed. by
Jackson R. Bryer. Durham: Duke University Press, 1969.
Pp. 345-367. Revised and brought up to date in Sixteen
Modern American Authors New York: Norton, 1973. Pp.
473-498. Work is carefully surveyed and presented as a
"Bibliographical Essay." It is arranged in the following categories: I. Bibliography; II. Editions; III. Letters and
Manuscripts; IV. Biography; V. Criticism. Items are presented with running commentary, which is hardly ever evalu-
ated, but rather descriptive. The documentation is given in
abbreviated form (no publishers, pagination, volumes, etc.),
but any item can be found with the information that is given.

235 _____. "The Man Who Died Twice: A Review of Biography by
Louis O. Coxe." Hartford Studies in Literature, 3 (1971),
154-156. The present work is one of the best books yet written about Robinson. The approach is in general chronological, permitting the critic to weave together the factual, the
intellectual, and the creative strands of Robinson's career.
This plan, though obvious, is rewarding in the case of Robinson who was a product of the nineteenth century background,
with a twentieth century existence. The style is lively, informal, sometimes subtly or not so subtly abrasive. Robinson
was never an "in" poet. Hence the critics who have chosen
to write about him have done so not from policy but from conviction; and in the long run this is what counts.

236 BARNEY, Virginia. "Review of Talifer." North American Review,
237 (January, 1934), iv. Written with beauty of expression
and depth of feeling.

237 BARRY, James D. "Robinson's 'Firelight.'" Explicator, 22 (November, 1963), item 21. This poem exemplifies skillful use of
the Petrachan sonnet to express irony of situation, the phenomenon that appearances belie reality, a reality character-
istically less pleasant than appearances would suggest. To
climax his account of the inability of people to communicate
with one another, Robinson adds that the wife's lover would
be her possession if he had known of her feelings for him.
But for the characters it is now too late for change. It is
better to live on in the illusory light than to bring forth the
dark reality which would overpower this light. Better a
quivering firelight than no light at all.

238 BARSTOW, James Stewart. My Tilbury Town. New York: privately printed, 1939. Pamphlet, 11 pages.

239 BARTLETT, Phyllis. Poems in Process. New York: Oxford
University Press, 1951. Robinson, pp. 104-106. Probably
no modern American poet can be studied more thoroughly in
manuscript than Robinson. Dispersed in collections are to
be found manuscript versions of what appear to be nearly all
of his poems, some of them running through every stage of
composition. He dated his manuscripts, usually at the beginning and end, and sometimes along the way. He was exceptionally neat, and he probably composed by ear; this habit,
together with the fact that he never forced himself, would
account for the remarkable approach to final accuracy in his
first drafts.

240 BATES, Esther Willard. Edwin Arlington Robinson and His
Manuscripts. Waterville, Maine: Colby College Library
Press, 1944. Monograph, No. 11, 32 pages. This writer says:
"He told me that he was perhaps, two hundred years in advance of his time, indicating in brief half-statements, with
pauses in between, that his habit of understatement, his absorption in the unconscious and semi-conscious feelings and
impulses of his characters were the qualities in which he was
unlike his contemporaries. He said he wondered if he wasn't
too dry, too plain, if he wasn't overdoing the simple, the
unpoetic phrase."

241 BATES, James M. L. "Robinson's Letters to George Burnham."
Colby Mercury, 7 (May, 1942), 93-94. Comments briefly on
his experience of transcribing the personal letters of Robinson to his friend George E. Burnham. These letters do not
have the literary interest of Robinson's letters to Edith Brower, but their personal side reveals a great deal: Robinson's
reluctance to be of any trouble to his friends, his joy in their
good fortune, occasional humorous and extremely personal
touches. This article does not include any texts of the letters.

242 BATES, Robert Chapman. "Edwin Arlington Robinson's Three
Poems." Yale University Library Gazette, 8 (October, 1933),
81-82. This brief note was written on the occasion of the
Yale Library receiving a copy of this book by Robinson.
The first poem is a deleted fragment of "Lancelot," here published for the first time; the other two poems were published
in 1891, in the Harvard Advocate. Each poem shows variants
from the original printing, for the proof reading was far from
carefully done for Three Poems. It is a poor, thin little book;
but it is rare enough. It also contains the first published version of some fine poetry deleted by the author from a great
poem.

243 _____. "The Robinson Gift." Yale University Library Gazette,
17 (October, 1942), 33-35. Begins with a general review of
materials which the Yale Library has acquired on Robinson.

The latest addition is a considerable group of books and
manuscripts presented by Mr. Lucius Beebe. Valuable though
the books and manuscripts are, the heart of the collection is
the forty-one letters from Robinson to Beebe, running from
1924 to the end of 1931. Almost none of them fails to show
some spark of the wry, shy light of the writing shining
through it. They are practical, reasonable letters, matter-
of-fact, always a trifle aloof, with here and there a flash, a
glint of the inward fire. They are letters of a great poet after he had written all his great poetry. They show us a sad
and somewhat lonely Robinson, for all he knew he was "dean
of American poets."

244  BAUM, Paul F. "Review of Collected Poems." South Atlantic
        Quarterly, 29 (April, 1930), 208-210. Review summarizes
        some of the major poems contained in the 1,000-page collec-
        tion. Comments and evaluations are uniformly positive, and
        it is clear that the reviewer regards Robinson's massive work
        as a gigantic contribution to American literature.

245  BAUMGARTNER, Alfred. "Das Lyrische Werk Edwin Arlington
        Robinson's." Ph.D. diss., Mainz University, 1952. In Ger-
        man.

246  BEACH, J. W. Concept of Nature in Nineteenth Century English
        Poetry. New York: Macmillan, 1936. "Victorian Afterglow,"
        pp. 522-546. Robinson, pp. 538-539. The word and concept
        of nature are scarcely to be found in Robinson. He does have
        a good deal to say of the general hopelessness of our spiritual
        state, and expresses the Tennysonian view that unless we sur-
        vive death there is no point or value in life.

247  BEACH, Stewart. "Review of Tristram." Independent, 120
        (January 21, 1928), 68. Seemingly without meaning to, Rob-
        inson has discovered that verse--all verse, any verse--affords
        readiest expression to ideas which he has found good, where
        others of his contemporaries have striven to breathe a divinity
        into their mortal thoughts which should make these worthy of
        their lines. With Tristram Robinson has at last convinced a
        wary public that it is as natural, for him at least, to think in
        poetry as to think up to poetry. He has touched an immortal
        beauty with the color of a simple and honest mortality. It is
        in this that his genius lies.

248  BEATTY, Frederika. "Edwin Arlington Robinson as I Knew Him."
        South Atlantic Quarterly, 43 (October, 1944), 375-381. Arti-
        cle is a sketch by someone who knew Robinson at the Mac-
        Dowell Colony. Everyone knows something of the poet Robin-
        son, but this writer feels that she "had a special privilege in
        knowing--even slightly--the genuine, kindly man, Mr. Robin-
        son." He did not like to be treated as a celebrity, and almost

never talked about himself or his poetry. He enjoyed conversation, however. He also enjoyed detective stories and
played a poor game of billiards or pool. Perhaps his two
dominant qualities were integrity and his kindness. He was
absolutely honest, both with other people and with himself.
His honesty apparently made him independent.

249 BEDELL, R. Meredith. "Perception, Action, and Life in The
    Man Against the Sky." Colby Library Quarterly, 12 (March,
    1976), 29-37. This poem secured Robinson's reputation in
    1916. The title poem which was a conscious attempt to phi-
    losophize, has maintained a tenuous popularity. The popu-
    larity of the poem seems mistakenly based on its reputed tone
    of despair. Robinson maintained that he was an optimist and
    that a careful reading of his work would show this to be true.
    Although an artists' intention is not always reflected in the
    finished product, this poem does seem to reinforce the mes-
    sage that Life is for the strong, for those who can face real-
    ity even though it brings pain, because it is the pain itself
    which may prompt change--the essence of life.

250 BEEBE, Lucius Morris. Edwin Arlington Robinson and the Ar-
    thurian Legend. Cambridge: privately printed by Samuel
    Marcus Press, 1927. Pamphlet, 30 pages, later included in
    entry below.

251 _____. Aspects of the Poetry of Edwin Arlington Robinson.
    Cambridge, Mass.: Dunster House Bookshop, private print-
    ing, 1928. Consists of 110 pages. Bibliography of primary
    sources by Bradley Fisk. Text is brief, 67 pages, but deals
    specifically with a number of poems, mostly those that later
    became very familiar. In conclusion, Beebe says: "He is the
    most modern of contemporary American poets, without excep-
    tion, both in theme-treatment and in philosophy, although his
    best poetry is not intimate and trivial, after the present
    fashion, but epic, the poetry of world destinies and world
    cataclysms. Humanity is to him a symbol of unhappy im-
    potence, protestant against the silver shears of destiny, yet
    inevitably compelled by a faint, insistent world voice along
    the ways of its manifold dooms."

252 _____. "Robinson Sees Romantic Strain in Future Verse."
    New York Herald Tribune, December 22, 1929. P. 19.

253 _____. "Dignified Faun: A Portrait of Edwin Arlington Rob-
    inson." Outlook and Independent, 155 (August 27, 1930),
    647-650, 677. Reviews Robinson's career from 1905 when the
    best known book reviewer in America--President Theodore
    Roosevelt--discovered Children of the Night to the present
    by which time Robinson's reputation had increased over a
    thousand times. Some of the recollection is based on the

author's recollection of the summers at Peterborough, where
Robinson did most of his best work, producing a work on the
average of every other year. In spite of his extreme devotion
to his craft, there is in him friendliness and loyalty as enduring as the New England hills whence he derives. Behind the
interpreter of cosmic and abiding values is the human being
with a warm sympathy for human failings and a profound understanding of human and fallible genius.

254 _____, and Robert J. Bulkley, Jr. A Bibliography of the
Writings of Edwin Arlington Robinson. Cambridge, Mass.:
Dunster House Bookshop, private printing, 1931. 59 pp.

255 BEECH, Johnstone. "Review of Nicodemus." Churchman, 146
(October 15, 1932), 5. The book is sad--not only in the
poems themselves, which are far from gay--but because the
critic (who after all is only a reader) thinks of an artist who
once poured forth a vital, breathing song for all the world to
hear and feel, now using his same instrument to play vague
fanciful things which are never fully formed and cannot live.

256 BEEDE, Martha Frances. "The Dramatic Elements in the New
England Characterizations of Frost, Robinson, and Amy
Lowell." M.A. Thesis, Ohio State University, 1929.

257 BEERS, Samuel G. "A Poet for Pastors." Religion in Life, 12
(Summer, 1943), 421-430.

258 BENET, William Rose. "Robinson in Retrospect: Collected
Poems." New York Evening Post, February 11, 1922.

259 _____. "Review of Collected Poems." Literary Review, February 11, 1922, p. 409. He is the supreme psychologist
among the poets of America. His collected poems are a mine
of first-hand experience greatly shared.

260 _____. "Poetry Ad Lib: A Review of Roman Bartholow."
Yale Review, 13 (October, 1923), 161-165. Comments on
Robinson's poem in article covering several volumes of poetry.
Calls Roman Bartholow "Robinson at his most ruminative,"
and finds it dull. As to content, it is a closely knit psychological novel, but there is also too much circumlocution. The
book is hard to read, but Robinson "remains the greatest living poet of America."

261 _____. "Escort to Leviathan: Review of Tristram." Outlook,
146 (June 1, 1927), 158. It may not be the best of his Arthurian poems, but it is the most human of them all, a poem with
few faults, and above everything, showing an increase of
emotional power over the work even of his youth. This last
is an astonishing phenomenon.

262 _____ . "Round About Parnassus (title of column)." Saturday
Review of Literature, & (September 20, 1930), 142. Includes
comments on The Glory of the Nightingales. Does not regard
this as one of Robinson's best, but it is a good example of
his psychological probing. Robinson's protest to the contrary,
he is similar to Browning, except that he never slips into
Browning's sentimentality. Perhaps not so "masculine" Robinson nevertheless wields his pen with as much sang froid as
any tower executioner wielded his ax.

263 _____ . "Two Veterans: Nicodemus." Saturday Review of
Literature, 9 (November 5, 1932), 224. He is as sage and
as subtle as ever. And his maintenance of a high level of
writing is no less than marvelous when one takes into consideration the amount of work he has done. This is one of Robinson's lesser works, though it is a dignified book; and were
it a new poet who stepped forward with such a presentation
of thought so mature, we should probably become excited.
As it is, having established for Robinson a cruelly high
standard, we can only say "This is not Robinson's best."

264 _____ . "Round About Parnassus: Amaranth." Saturday Review of Literature, 11 (February 23, 1935), 508. Particularly
admires this latest work Amaranth. At a time when most
poets would be practically through writing, or else repeating
themselves, Robinson accomplishes something peculiarly his
own yet different from much of his work. In spite of its presentation of the miscast, it is anything but a "tired" poem.
It has energy, remarkable imagination, and a subtle humor--
deeply ironic though its implications are--that in a man of
less achievement would have confounded the critics.

265 _____ . "The Phoenix's Nest: The Death of Robinson." Saturday Review of Literature, 11 (April 13, 1935), 628. Few
enough of us can boast a life of such single purpose, or a
life so thoughtful of friends.... This was a great man who
moved through our hasty and greedy world, with its ill-
considered judgments. He could afford to bide his time.
When one thinks how long he has been writing before his
country's recognition came to him, one recognizes the irony.
But it did come at last, in full measure, and his life has closed
under the laurel, which was never better awarded.

266 _____ . "Edwin Arlington Robinson." Forum, 93 (June, 1935),
381. Critic says, "I have known no man except my own father
more thoughtful of the feelings of others. For both were wit-
ty men, and neither with ever a trace of malice. Both were
somberly agnostic, with a residuum of faith more valuable,
because of their life-long investigation of the truth, than all
the church services that ever were held. Both men possessed
the mental integrity nothing could move." Robinson left behind

him a body of superb work that is a great inheritance to future generations in America.  Whatever may come to pass in
this country, such work will remain "a rampart to the mind."

267 _____.  "Contemporary Poetry: King Jasper."  Saturday Review of Literature, 13 (November 16, 1935), 18.  As the last
work of one who had dedicated a long life to poetry and had
worked more assiduously at his craft than most artists, failing now and again--never in the wielding of a style that is
one of the most saliently individual of our time in literature;
but sometimes in the significance of what he had to say--as
the last work of such a man, this narrative seems to be of
extraordinary directness and vitality.  Its characters are
really symbols, but they are symbols significant of our era.

268 _____.  "The Phoenix's Nest."  Saturday Review of Literature,
16 (May 22, 1937), 19.  Contains a letter from Howard G.
Schmitt regarding textual changes in Amaranth.  Apparently
a good many readers of the poem were somewhat confused.
As a result Robinson had written the publisher asking them
to make the change.  The fact that the new line is added
actually makes the 1937 Collected Poems a first edition.

269 _____.  "Perfect Artistic Integrity."  Mark Twain Quarterly,
2 (Spring, 1938), 10.  As an example of the artistic integrity
of a man of letters, Robinson was perfect.  His style of writing in poetry was unique.  As a friend, he was warmly human,
with unusual charity for others, and a delightful dry humor.
Some of his best short poems will never be equalled in their
kind.  One of the greatest treasures of American literature
exists in his collected work.  He was one of the sanest people
who ever moved among us.

270 _____, and Norman Holmes Pearson, eds.  Oxford Anthology
of American Literature, 2 vols.  New York:  Oxford University Press, 1938.  Robinson, pp. 1112-1128.  Prints about
fourteen short poems and two long selections, "Ben Jonson
Entertains a Man from Stratford," and "The Man Against the
Sky."  In the "Commentaries" section Robinson is called "the
man who stripped poetry of the florid diction typical of the
late nineteenth century and turned it toward straight-forward
and hard speech."  Increasingly he became fixed upon the
idea that man must stand in darkness in order to see the light,
and with this perhaps Puritan heritage he was always content.
When he turned to the composition of the long narratives, he
appeared to be confused between the provinces of the novel
and of poetry.  Little narrative verse is successful unless it
moves through the force of highly charged emotion.  This,
unfortunately, Robinson's psychological narratives never did.

271 _____.  "The Phoenix's Nest." (title of column) Saturday Review

of Literature, 26 (February 20, 1943), 18-20. Contains commentary on "The Meaning of 'The Whip'" by Ben Ray Redman.
Calls it a lucid explanation of the poem by which we were baffled, not to say buffaloed. Quotes at length from the critic
Redman.

272 _____. "The Phoenix's Nest." Saturday Review of Literature,
26 (April 17, 1943), 54. Continues discussion of "The Whip."
Content of this article is the discussion by Carl J. Weber of
"The Whip." This study appeared in the Colby Mercury for
November, 1938. It was Robinson's first popular success.
Its popularity made him wonder whether it could really be
the good poem he thought it was. "What have I written here,
a little Longfellow poem?" he asked himself with dry humor.

273 _____. "The Phoenix's Nest: Survivals." Saturday Review
of Literature, 30 (January 18, 1947), 32. Continues discussion of "The Whip," the obscure poem by Robinson which
Yvor Winters comments on in his brochure on Robinson.
Winters admits that he does not understand the poem, but
furnishes an explanation by Don Stanford, a young Western
poet.

274 _____. "The Phoenix's Nest: A Ride in the Subway." Saturday Review of Literature, 30 (March 8, 1947), 48. Includes
comments on "The Whip," in Yvor Winters, Edwin Arlington
Robinson (1946). Article is largely a letter from Winters,
whose comment on Robinson's poem initiated the inquiry.
Winters remarks that the "interpretation is interesting" and
may be right, but cannot share the conviction that it is absolutely and necessarily right.

275 BERMAN, Ruth. "Edwin Arlington Robinson and Merlin's Gleam."
Eildon Tree: A Journal of Fantasy, 1 (1976), 16-19. Includes
Tristram, Merlin, and Lancelot. In Merlin, Lancelot, and
Tristram Robinson takes on the ambition of dealing directly
with one of these ideal worlds, the Arthurian one, using it
as a symbol of his own world, as deeply faulty as it is beautiful. Robinson's Arthurian poems are not strictly fantasy--he
is not interested in the fantasy elements of the stories--but
anyone who is interested in the Arthurian cycle should find
Robinson's version fascinating.

276 BERRYMAN, John McAlpin. "Note on Edwin Arlington Robinson."
Nation, 141 (July 10, 1935), 38. Consists of a six-line poem
in which Robinson is characterized: "He was forever walking/
A little north/To watch the bare words stalking/Stiffly forth,/
Frozen as they went/And flawless of heart within without
comment."

277 BERTHOFF, Warner. "Robinson and Frost," in The Ferment of

Realism: American Literature, 1884-1919. New York: The
Free Press, 1965. Pp. 263-272. Reprinted in Murphy, ed.
(1970), pp. 117-127. For poetry the important consequences
of the renewed impulse toward realism in this rising generation were formal and stylistic. It is hard now, after the ex-
perimental novelties and triumphs of another half-century,
to imagine the indifference of established critical taste around
1900 to the kind of poetic language Edwin Arlington Robinson
and Robert Frost had begun teaching themselves to write in.
It is also hard to imagine how unsure they themselves could
be as to when in fact they had achieved what they wanted,
in Robinson's case the "sense of reality" which he had found
in no poet of his time so much as in the prose of Hawthorne
and Thomas Hardy.

278 BETSKY, Seymour. "Some Aspects of the Philosophy of Edwin
      Arlington Robinson: Self-Knowledge, Self-Acceptance, and
      Conscience." Ph.D. diss., Harvard, 1942. Summary in
      Harvard University Summary of Theses, 1943-1945. Pp. 457-
      460.

279 BEVINGTON, Helen. "Edwin Arlington Robinson." South Atlan-
      tic Quarterly, 51 (July, 1952), 468. Review of biography by
      Ellsworth Barnard. There is painstaking attempt to interpret
      anew the man and his poetry. From it we derive two views,
      that Robinson is a foremost poet worthy of the most exhaus-
      tive and continued study that critics can apply to him, and
      that the poems themselves present such a real difficulty, be-
      cause of their admitted obscurity, that the reader must be
      led by the hand if he is to reach an awareness of their mean-
      ing. These chapters deal with the poetics, with the barriers
      which exist to an understanding of the poems, with the or-
      ganic form. They inquire the meaning of the remarkable
      characters Robinson invented. They discuss the verities and
      values which he found in life, the religious and philosophical
      views which gave stature to his poetry.

280 BIERK, John Cashion. "Edwin Arlington Robinson as Social
      Critic and Moral Guide." Ph.D. diss., Northwestern Univer-
      sity, 1969. DA, 30 (1970), 2997A-2998A. This study estab-
      lishes the relationship of Robinson's idealist philosophy to
      his social criticism; and, then, through a detailed analysis
      of a selected body of his poetry, traces his developing role
      as a social critic and a spiritual, moral guide. From 1897 to
      1935 Robinson dramatized his refusal to capitulate to Material
      domination, believing that Man is capable of greater goals
      than worshipping a deity of Money, and economic success.
      The poetry examined indicates how committed Robinson was
      to the dual role of social critic and moral guide, and demon-
      strates a continuity in his poetry not before properly under-
      stood nor carefully analyzed.

281  BISHOP, John Peale. <u>Collected Essays</u>, edited with Introduction
      by Edmund Wilson. New York: Scribner's, 1948. "Intelli-
      gence of Poets," pp. 263-269. Article includes a review of
      <u>Collected Poems</u> by E. A. Robinson, first published in <u>Vanity
      Fair Magazine</u>, January, 1922. From the first Robinson has
      written in a style which is at once clear and evasive, stark
      but indirect. He begins by a direct statement which is no
      sooner made than qualified, or after a suggestion of dark
      hints he surprises us with an epigram. Standing before his
      characters, with one hand he snatches away a mask and with
      the other casts a veil. His right hand knows perfectly well
      what his left hand is doing, but there are times when the
      reader is too confused by the swiftness of his movements to
      know what has been revealed.... His interest lies in those
      men and women who belong neither to success nor to failure.
      He is a pessimist with whom there remains a doubtful hope.
      He has eaten his bread alone and knows that it is bitter; he
      trusts that it may be yet the best nourishment for a man's
      soul.

282  BLACKMUR, Richard P. "'Verse That Is to Easie.'" <u>Poetry</u>, 43
      (January, 1934), 221-225. Review of <u>Talifer</u>. There is a
      kind of competence about Robinson's verse which in another
      era might have seemed rich and a model, rather than thin
      and to be escaped. Even today it can be admired, in reminis-
      cence. It is not ambitious; neither is it smug in its modesty.
      Its emotional content is not great; neither does its rhythmical
      texture require much emotion. The reader is not led astray;
      neither is he left to himself. The verse scans, easy and as-
      ured, both in subject and meter; and it has most of the nega-
      tive virtues of sound versification. <u>Talifer</u> is a series of con-
      versations, with a certain amount of transitional descriptive
      stage-direction, which together present a fable of modern
      love and the basis of human relationships.

283  BLAIR, Emily Newell. "For Those Who Love Poetry: <u>Tristram</u>."
      <u>Good Housekeeping</u>, 85 (December, 1927), 208-209. He is a
      writer to "understand." This is not easy because what he
      has to say is not simple, is not easily said, is, perhaps, not
      clearly apprehended. On this problem even the greatest see
      through a glass darkly, but the fact that they peer and,
      peering, catch glimpses of things not visible to us who are
      content with reflections and shadows, is what differentiates
      the major writers from the minor. His works are among those
      which must be studied, explained, discussed. The legend of
      Tristram has been used by poets for over a thousand years,
      but now Robinson has taken this instrument and by his use
      of certain scenes and emphasis of certain motives and omission
      of others, has created a Tristram of his own.

284  BLANCK, Jacob. "News From the Rare Book Sellers." <u>Publishers'</u>

Weekly, 141 (May 23, 1942), 1923-1924. Reports that during
his 'teens Robinson contributed certain juvenilia to Golden
Days (and possibly other magazines) under the pseudonym
"1812." A page by page search of Golden Days was made,
but no such contribution was found, and no contribution from
Gardiner, Maine, was found. It is possible, that since the
magazine conducted a number of puzzle clubs, that only a
small percentage of the riddles and puzzles sent in was ever
published.

285 _____. "News From the Rare Book Sellers." Publishers' Weekly, 152 (November 22, 1947), B354. Reports that the Robinson
collection by the late Lewis M. Isaacs and his wife has been
presented to the New York Public Library. The manuscript
portion includes over 600 pages in Robinson's holograph.
The collection of the published works is complete and contains
first editions of all of Robinson's books; virtually all of the
books are inscribed. The collection will be put on exhibition
at the library early in 1948.

286 _____. "Edwin Arlington Robinson," in Bibliography of American Literature, 7 vols. New Haven: Yale University Press,
1955-1983. Vol. 8, in production, planned for Fall, 1989.
Vol. 7 completed under the editorship of Michael Winship and
Virginia Smyers, after Professor Blanck died in 1974. Vol. 8
to be completed by Michael Winship. E. A. Robinson not represented in any of this work.

287 BLANKENSHIP, Russell. American Literature as an Expression
of the National Mind. New York: Henry Holt, 1931. Edwin
Arlington Robinson, pp. 583-588. Robinson is a bleak, spare
writer of gray moods. Hopes and aspirations are tumbled
about by transcendent forces that, if they are not actually
malignant, are senseless and blind. If there is ordered power
in the universe, it conceals the order and reveals only
strength. But before he comes to the final renunciation
something holds him from the final gesture. There is a
vaguely defined Light or Gleam that keeps the philosophy
from turning unbearably bitter.

288 BLOOM, Harold. "Bacchus and Merlin: The Dialectic of Romantic Poetry in America." Southern Review, 7 (January, 1971),
140-175. Reprinted in Harold Bloom, The Ringers in the
Tower: Studies in the Romantic Tradition. Chicago: University of Chicago Press, 1971. Pp. 291-321. Article includes
a great many authors besides Robinson. In the Introduction,
Bloom says: "In what follows I propose to examine four first
volumes of American poetry as part of a personal critical
quest after the governing dialectic I sense in our poetry's
central tradition, our version of Romanticism." These volumes
include Robinson's The Torrent and the Night Before (1896),

which he later calls "one of the best first volumes in our poetry." At least three of these poems were never surpassed,
and all of them are memorable. They prophesy Robinson's
finest later lyrics and suggest the affinity between Robinson
and Frost that is due to their common Emersonian tradition.

289 BOGAN, Louise. "Tilbury Town and Beyond." Poetry, 37
(January, 1931), 216-221. Review of Collected Poems (1927)
and The Glory of the Nightingales (1930). Comments on the
works which are included in Collected Poems, and shows how
Robinson has steadily been gaining scope and depth. His
talents were early fixed in their mold, announcing their power
and drawing their limits. The Glory of the Nightingales repeats a theme and elaborates an obsession. In spite of his
limitations, Robinson stands in our literature a figure of un-
doubted strength. His mask has many times betrayed him,
yet the spirit, from the first, has set him free. He told the
hard truth, told it early, with intelligence and in form. His
audience, finally, is large and worthy of him.

290 _____. Achievement in American Poetry, 1900-1950. Chicago:
Henry Regnery, 1951. Robinson, pp. 19-22. Reprinted in
paperback, Regnery Gateway edition, 1962. Robinson, pp.
15-19. His own nature was sensitive without being rich; he
inherited the laconic speech and the dry sense of humor of
the New England townsman; and his bent was toward realism.
Through a long series of trials and errors he finally evolved
a poetic style and point of view. Robinson's reaction to
events and his conclusions concerning human life and destiny
continued to be based on the idealism of his youth, to which
was added a simple variety of agnosticism and stoicism.

291 BOIE, Mildred. "Review of King Jasper." New England Quarterly, 9 (March, 1936), 154-156. In this work Robinson gave a
last expression to his quiet, patient meditation upon men and
women and the forces in them that made them feel, think, and
act as they do. It was a last expression (he stayed alive until it was corrected and handed to the publisher), but not a
final one, for in the isolated quiet of his own mind he knew
that there are few things that can be dogmatically proclaimed
final. In him and in this last poem, as in Jasper, the king,
there was rather "a calm and overwhelming recognition of ir-
revocable changes."

292 _____. "Edwin Arlington Robinson: A Biography." New England Quarterly, 12 (June, 1939), 390-393. Review of Hagedorn's biography. In other less sympathetic hands this biography might have become a sensation; in Hagedorn's, it is
primarily, for all its concrete retelling without shirking of
the cloudy or bitter parts of the doings and lack of doing in
Robinson's life, a study of the contradictions of a poet's mind.

Everything is made subordinate to that end--the history and character of his family, the sensitive tracing of Robinson's loneliness as a child, the reserve of his mother, the tragedy of his older brother--a brilliant doctor who became a drug addict--Robinson's growing sense of failure, his intellectual restlessness which drove him to endure poverty and lack of recognition--all these are told as they relate to his poetry and his mind.

293 BOIS, Jules. "Edwin Arlington Robinson." Revue Bleue, June 15, 1926. In French.

294 _____. "Le Poète Américain de la conscience: Edwin Arlington Robinson." Revue Politique et Littéraire, 66 (June 16, 1928), 369-374.

295 BOMPARD, Paola. "Un gran precursore di Spoon River: Edwin Arlington Robinson doganiere del Pessimismo." La Fiera Letteraria (Rome), 36 (September 7, 1962), 4. In Italian.

296 BONAWIT, Dorothy. "A Critique of Edwin Arlington Robinson's Use of the Tristram Legend with Reference to Bedier and Malory and to the Rest of Robinson's Works." Columbia University, 1932, M.A. thesis.

297 BOONE, Esther. "Robinson's Matthias at the Door: A New Variant." Serif, 8 (1971), 31. Is a note describing an edition of this work at Kent State Library unlike the description of any other bibliographical reference to the poem.

298 BOOTH, Philip. "He Survives His Popularity: Review of Selected Poems of Edwin Arlington Robinson." Christian Science Monitor, February 24, 1966. P. 7. Robinson survives both the fluctuations of literary fashion and his own limitations in this collection. His poetry is important because it is an early record of people intuitively rebelling against both the restraints of Puritanism and the dehumanizing forces of a world well on the way toward becoming wholly materialistic. Yet there was in Robinson, and remains in his poetry, a remarkably stubborn refusal to examine, to resolve, or to judge the complex causes of his characters' (and his own) frustrations.

299 BOYCE, Neith. "Books and Men: Van Zorn." Harper's Weekly, 60 (February 6, 1915), 131. Thinks this one-act play in prose is a triumph in expression of a novel kind. The people talk as people actually do talk--saying anything but what they are thinking or what really concerns them. And in some way the real drama of their relations to one another, their characters, desires, destiny pierce through the spoken word--the trivial, irrelevant and incompetent word that we all speak,

especially when we might say something interesting. The
play is a masque or masquerade, the sort we are all playing
every day, with more or less meaning!

300  BOYNTON, Percy H. A History of American Literature. New
York: Ginn & Company, 1919. "The Later Poetry," pp.
462-466. As a craftsman Robinson has won distinction by
his simple, direct realism. He employs for the most part the
old iambic measures, a sentence structure which is often
conversational, and a diction which is severe in its restraint.
There are few "purple patches" in his poetry, but there are
many clear flashes of incisive phrasing. His work is like a
May day in his own seacoast town--not balmy, but bracing,
with lots of sparkle on the blue, and the taste of the east
wind through it all.

301  _____. "American Authors of Today: Edwin Arlington Robinson." English Journal, 11 (September, 1922), 383-391. In
any complete survey of contemporary American literature
would be included discussions of poetry, fiction, the drama,
and the essay--both general and critical. As for Robinson,
the article begins with a biographical note, and continues
with a discussion of the poet as an emphatic illustration of
the fact that modernity in art does not depend on strangeness or newness. His subject matter has no word of modern
movements in it. The residents of his Tilbury are apparently
men and women of today, but the qualities that make them
humanly alive are constants in human life.

302  _____. Some Contemporary Americans: The Personal Equa-
tion in Literature. Chicago: University of Chicago Press,
1924. Robinson, pp. 16-32. Article begins in 1891, when
clearly it was the passing of the best-known Victorian poets.
New poets were coming onto the scene, but most of them
passed away almost as quickly. Robinson is an emphatic illustration of one who did not. The residents of Tilbury town
are men and women of today, but the qualities that make them
alive are constants in human life. It is not surprising that
the "art for art's sake" crowd has had much to say about
Robinson.

303  _____. Literature and American Life. Boston: Ginn and
Company, 1936. Robinson, pp. 800-805. Few constants in
Robinson's poetry are more insistently recurrent than his
disregard for the world of getting and spending, and his
contempt for the usual measure of success. Yet his contempt
for the rewards of success is not a contempt for life or a disillusionment. Robinson invented no new measures and de-
parted from no old ones. And it is a matter of record, that
although ignored for fifteen years, the appearance of a new
work by the Robinson of later years eventually became a
literary event of prime importance.

304 _____. "Review of Collected Poems." New Republic, 91 (July
      21, 1937), 314-315. Calls it a "portentous volume," and says
      the only thing lacking is Robert Frost's Introduction to King
      Jasper. There is not much to be said of it, except that as a
      job of book-making it is less attractive than its contents de-
      serve. But there is a great deal still to be said about Robin-
      son as a poet.

305 BRADDY, Varnelle. "The Arthurian Poems of Edwin Arlington
      Robinson." Emory University, 1933. M.A. thesis.

306 BRADFORD, Gamaliel. The Letters of Gamaliel Bradford, 1918-
      1931, edited by Van Wyck Brooks. Boston: Houghton, Mif-
      flin, 1934. Robinson, p. 342 et passim. Contains six letters
      to Robinson in which he comments on Robinson's work, gen-
      erally and specifically. In 1930 Bradford says: "I cannot
      help being struck with the similarity of what we are trying
      to do, in very different fashions. I heartily sympathize with
      your passion for probing the dark corners of souls, and I
      also profoundly envy you your gift for using poetry to that
      end.... I admire your skill in handling the medium also. It
      is extraordinary, the flexible, sinuous adaptiveness with
      which you make that blank verse cling to the tenuous move-
      ment of those shadowy souls."

307 BRAHMER, Mieczyslaw, Stanislaw Helsztynski, and Julian Krzy-
      zanowski, eds. Studies in Language and Literature in Honour
      of Margaret Schlauch. Warsaw: Panstwowe, 1966. Reprinted
      New York: Russell & Russell, 1971. "Edwin Arlington Robin-
      son and the Arthurian Tradition," by John H. Fisher, pp.
      117-131. Article discussed under Fisher.

308 BRAITHWAITE, William Stanley. "America's Foremost Poet."
      Boston Evening Transcript, May 28, 1913.

309 _____. "Van Zorn: A Three-Act Comedy." Boston Evening
      Transcript, November 14, 1914.

310 _____. "Edwin Arlington Robinson: A Personal Sketch."
      Cornhill Booklet, 4 (December, 1914), 90-91.

311 _____. "A Poet as a Dramatist: The Porcupine." Boston
      Evening Transcript, December 24, 1915. In his new play
      Robinson again shows his power in the deft handling of char-
      acter. The action is deep, so deep that the mind has got to
      dive beneath the surface to feel it. It is a tragedy that
      arouses a deep sense of pity. The well-meaning attempts of
      one man to straighten out the lives of others precipitates the
      tragedy from the beginning.

312 _____. "The Man Against the Sky." Boston Evening Tran-
      script, February 26, 1916.

313 _____. "The Year in Poetry." <u>Bookman</u>, 45 (June, 1917),
429-430. Review of <u>The Man Against the Sky</u>. His mood and
quality have been consistent from the beginning, and this
poem shows them developed more profoundly and to more
prophetic issues. He has advanced from presenting the character of the individual to interpreting the destinies of mankind. Some poems seem designed to "console humanity with
what he knows."

314 _____. "<u>Lancelot</u>: The Arthurian Legend in Poetry." <u>Boston
Evening Transcript</u>, 3 (June 12, 1920), 9. In this narrative
Robinson not only proves by reason of thought and substance
his position as the greatest of all living American poets, but
also by the supreme consciousness and evocation of beauty.

315 _____. "A Poet Approaches Human Mystery: <u>The Three Tav-
erns</u>." <u>Boston Evening Transcript</u>, 3 (September 11, 1920),
9. The substance of the longer poems in this book is more
profoundly grounded in Robinson's philosophy of human nature and experience than in any of his other poems. Even in
the shorter poems we find this power distilled until almost
achingly the meanings break through a speech that is simplified to a bareness of figure or illusion. Take the poem "The
Mill" and say if a tragedy could be so mercilessly told with
the economy of speech by any other living poet.

316 _____. "A Poetic Tale of Consuming Mystery: <u>Avon's Har-
vest</u>." <u>Boston Evening Transcript</u>, 4 (April 2, 1921), 6.
In this work one meets with one of the most appalling revelations of the terror complex in modern literature. Robinson
has given this simple idea a tragic embodiment that makes a
powerful appeal to the imagination. Avon's monologue strives
to explain a lifetime of fear, hatred, and vengeance.

317 _____, ed. <u>Anthology of Magazine Verse for 1926</u>. Boston:
B. J. Brimmer, 1926. 897 pages. "Poetry of New England,"
by Jessie B. Rittenhouse, pp. 12-16.

318 _____. "William Stanley Braithwaite Remembers Edwin Arlington Robinson." <u>New Letters</u>, 38 (Fall, 1971), 153-164. Reviews Robinson's career from a personal perspective, with
many details having to do with manuscripts and the inclusion
of such in Braithwaite's many anthologies. This piece was
found in the papers of Braithwaite, and will be included in
Philip Butcher, ed., <u>The Writings of William Stanley Braith-
waite</u>, to be published by the University of Michigan Press
in 1972.

319 BRANNON, Nelle Viola. "The Legend of Tristram in the Works
of Hardy, Masefield, and Robinson." Ph.D. diss. University
of Nebraska, 1931.

320 BRASHER, Thomas L. "Robinson's 'Mr. Flood's Party.'" Explicator, 29 (November, 1971), item 45. Is a discussion of
"Roland" in stanza 3, and an argument that the reference is
to Browning and the theme of "Childe Roland to the Dark
Tower Came" more than to Charlemagne's famous champion,
the hero of Chanson de Roland. Robinson's Roland is truly
alone, and all of his actions are those of defiance in the face
of certain death. At the end of Charlemagne's Roland, there
are those to lament bitterly. There is no one left to mourn
the approaching lonely deaths of Eben Flood and Childe Roland at the foot of the Dark Tower.

321 BREGY, Katherine. "Review of The Glory of the Nightingales."
Catholic World, 132 (February, 1931), 626-627. This work
does not reach either the singing heights nor the wounding
depths of his Tristram, yet it is one of the best of those
quiet domestic tragedies which so much of his work has incorporated.... As usual Robinson's telling of the story is
deeply psychological; with the pitiful psychology of groping
men, physically and mentally almost too tired to ask questions,
certainly too tired to wait for answers. This sense of lassi-
tude is accentuated by the chorus of the lapping sea--the
waves themselves longing for rest. A unity of past and
present and even future is suggested by the memory of the
woman whose death has taken the love of two men with her
into eternity.

322 _____. "Review of Matthias at the Door." Catholic World, 134
(February, 1932), 634-635. This work is a grim door leading
to tragedy--and Matthias is not very vital either in his earlier
egotism or his later, somewhat hazy, regeneration--nor are
the other characters whose lives, and particularly deaths,
react upon him. There are moments when Matthias' false wisdom falls suddenly and breaks like glass on a stone floor.
But in the main Robinson's art seems a little weary. At any
rate, readers who have thrilled to Tristram will never again
be content with any such dreary psychological study as this
year's harvest.

323 _____. "Edwin Arlington Robinson." Catholic World, 175
(July, 1952), 319. Review of biography by Ellsworth Barnard. The biographer is determined to rescue his subject
from undeserved neglect. The poet himself was not a very
vivid personality. His philosophy of God and man was rather
vague, so that his most poetic moments were in the interpretation of Arthurian themes than in the long realistic studies of
contemporary people. But certainly his verse-novels gave
something unique and memorable to the Newer American Poetry
movement.

324 BRENNER, Rica. Ten Modern Poets. New York: Harcourt Brace,

1930. Robinson, pp. 83-115. When Robinson first began to write, poetry in America had fallen into a decline. People were writing pale imitations of earlier poets, elaborating fancies and conceits, intrigued more with manner than with subject. Into this heavy, stifled air, Robinson came as a fresh breeze. His poetry was definitely his own, individual, original, and modern. At the same time Robinson must not be considered a leader of the "new poetry." Whatever his influence has been, he has never had any conscious connection with any group. He did not feel hampered by old verse forms, but molds them to his own use. Nor is he a rebel. He looks beneath the world of change for the lasting and permanent influences and finds them in man's own character. He uses little local color, and removes his men and women from a definite setting.

325 BRETON, Maurice le, ed. With notes. Anthologie de la poésie américaine contemporaine. Paris: Editions Denoel, 1948. Robinson, pp. 40-41. Poems in English; notes in French.

326 BRIEN, Dolores. "Edwin Arlington Robinson's Amaranth: A Journey to the 'Wrong World.'" Research Studies (Washington State University), 36 (June, 1968), 143-150. Reviews the critical reception of Robinson's last poem to be published in his lifetime, and finds that it was not always so favorable. There are sufficient reasons for this response, but despite its apparent deficiencies, there are at least three reasons why the poem is worth a close reading: (1) Within a carefully constructed narrative, Robinson creates a dream world which adumbrates the theatre of the absurd. (2) The poem, written at the close of his life, represents the culmination of Robinson's thinking on the artistic vocation and on his own in particular. (3) The major theme, self-knowledge and self-acceptance, is not a new one for Robinson, but his ambivalence in dealing with the theme in Amaranth is perhaps one way of assessing his achievement as poet.

327 BROOKHOUSE, Christopher. "Imagery and Theme in Lancelot," in Barnard, ed. (1969), pp. 120-129. Reviews sources for Robinson's poem, and points up differences and similarities in sources. Robinson's own vision in Lancelot, where he brings us not just up to but beyond the destruction of Arthur's world, is of a private, spiritual salvation. This answer may have been what attracted Robinson to the Arthurian material. Robinson reduced Arthur to a very imperfect king and a very imperfect man, and reduced the scope of the story to concentrate on Guinevere and Lancelot, both human and imperfect, both in part morally responsible for the end of Camelot, but who find a private salvation in withdrawal from the material world, endurance, and spiritual vision beyond the garden of this life.

328 BROOKS, Van Wyck. New England: Indian Summer, 1865-1915.
New York: E. P. Dutton, 1940. Robinson, pp. 491-499,
and "Pre-War Years," pp. 522-546. Robinson personified
winter. He carried to New York an aura of blight, desola-
tion, decay, and defeat. His view of the world was wintry--
so was his life--and his style and his personality were bleak
and bare. Had there ever been a poet who loved life less or
found so little joy in the turning of the seasons? Robinson
was "master chilly." There was something starved and cold
about him, as if his clothes were too scanty and his blood
were too thin, as if the Maine wind had invaded his marrow.
Taciturn, shy as an owl, diffident, lonely, he could establish
relations with others only by drinking; yet everyone con-
fided in him, for he was the most sympathetic of men.

329 _____. Opinions of Oliver Allston. New York: E. P. Dutton,
1941. Robinson, pp. 116 et passim. Later he seems to have
considered the question of riches and poverty. Was it not
still possible to "live on a crust"? Robinson had done so,
and a few others might do so; and, while this could not be
asked of any man, any successful attempt to do so was bound
to clear the air.

330 _____. Chilmark Miscellany. New York: E. P. Dutton, 1949.
Robinson, pp. 245-261. Mostly biographical details in which
is embodied a character sketch. His probing, questioning,
doubting mind was the mind of a new generation, and his
portraits, even the sonnets, were little novels. He had reacted against facile jingling. He had sought for the spoken
phrase, for the neat and plain; and if his style was too prosaic, if it was too bare and cold, it was hard, it was clear
and it was honest. Robinson eschewed the nebulous, the
blurred and the vague, as he abhorred the fatuous and the
stereotyped. In short, in a poetical world of baker's bread
and confectionary, Robinson brought forth real bread again.

331 BROSNAN, Thomas J. "Edwin Arlington Robinson." Connecti-
cut Teacher, 5 (June, 1938), 3-4, 6.

332 BROWN, David. "Some Rejected Poems of Edwin Arlington Robinson." American Literature, 7 (January, 1936), 395-414.
In 1897 most of the poems contained in The Torrent and the
Night Before (1896) were published under the title of The
Children of the Night. Two poems were omitted, and later
in 1921 in Collected Poems, twelve had been rejected from
The Children.... Later two others were cut. Robinson did
not have occasion to tell the story of these rejections. Yet
this story is an interesting one to reconstruct, because it has
significance in revealing forces at work in his development
as a poet. The mere amount of his editing of the first two
volumes makes a review of its nature worth attention.

333 _____ . "Edwin Arlington Robinson Later Poems." New
England Quarterly, 10 (September, 1937), 487-502. Reprinted in Cary, ed. Appreciation ... (1969), pp. 43-54.
The response to the narrative poems of Robinson which appeared after Tristram was chilly. The poems were praised,
but usually with a hovering air of disappointment or un-
easiness. The enormous success of Tristram has blinded
critics, if not to the true value of the later poems, at least
to their significance in Robinson's career. It is still too
early to predict the measure of permanence which these
poems will enjoy in relation to the earlier ones. Robinson
himself rarely felt disposed to justify a particular work, or
even to judge it, in terms of such finality. Although it is
too early to judge the relative permanence of these later
volumes, it is possible to accord them a closer critical attention than they have received.

334 _____ . "A Note on Avon's Harvest." American Literature,
9 (November, 1938), 343-349. The purpose of this note
is to correct an error, which has considerable currency,
concerning Robinson's intentions with respect to Avon's
Harvest. All of the poet's revisions are not equally notable.
In this work, for example, the revisions were not occasioned
by a change in ideas which was the result of the passage
of time. These revisions were made in response to the reviewers of the story: they had made a mistake in their
reading of the poem, and Robinson revised it to take care
of the error. But the interesting fact is that he revised
in such a way as to legitimate the reviewers' interpretation
rather than to correct it. A reconstruction of what happened is not without significance.

335 BROWN, Edmund R. "A Master of Thought and Speech: Review of The Man Against the Sky." Poetry Journal, 5
(March, 1916), 82-89. Sees this volume as a real advance
in Robinson's career, but is more impressed with some of
the shorter poems than with the title poem. In particular,
"Ben Jonson Entertains..." is a masterpiece of accuracy,
interpretation of Shakespeare, and use of language. Robinson is direct, modern, and creates at once a simplicity
of language and complexity of thought.

336 BROWN, John. Panorama de la littérature contemporaine aux
Etats-Unis. Paris: Librairie Gallimard, 1954. Robinson,
pp. 260-261.

337 BROWN, Maurice F. "Moody and Robinson." Colby Library
Quarterly, 5 (December, 1960), 185-194. Moody was interested in Robinson from 1898. From the time they met, in
1899, until Moody's death in 1910 they shared an important
friendship, related to the careers of both. It is difficult

to understand why Moody might have been interested in
knowing Robinson: differences in their characters and
poetic aims are so striking they would seem to make any
kind of friendship impossible. Moody was spontaneous and
emotional, while Robinson tended to be quiet and self-
conscious. Robinson's sensitivity to the potential misery
and the quiet ironies of human experience were balanced
by Moody's buoyant enthusiasm and his love of the grand
and dramatic.

338 BROWN, Rollo Walter. Next Door to a Poet. New York: D.
Appleton-Century, 1937. 97 pages. This little book pro-
fesses to be nothing but a memoir--"the memoir of a friendship." Brown lived "next door" to Robinson in the summer
of 1923, the summer Robinson spent in England, in the
MacDowell Colony in New Hampshire. At first Brown had
stayed in Robinson's apartment, but then he moved. They
became good friends, although it is difficult to say just
how far Robinson ever went in his friendships. In 1934,
the last time Brown saw Robinson, he remembers the clear-
cut profile, the dark gray suit, the slouched hat, which
is so much of the permanent image Robinson makes.

339 _____. "A Letter from R. W. Brown about Edwin Arlington
Robinson." Mark Twain Quarterly, 2 (Spring, 1938), 14,
24. Written in response to a request that he contribute
something to the special issue on Robinson. Brown says:
"I see with even greater clarity his readiness to give time
to others. Always he seemed to have the manuscript of
some young poet or novelist in his room or studio. But I
still think of him more than his work. Death has a strange,
sure way of enabling us in the end to detach a man's work
from him and see it somewhat as a stranger would. But
E. A. was a powerful personality, and the mention of his
name brings him, rather than his poetry, to mind still."

340 _____. "Mrs. MacDowell and Her Colony." Atlantic Monthly,
184 (July, 1949), 42-46. Article is an appraisal of Mrs.
MacDowell, and Edwin Arlington Robinson is mentioned as
one of the writers who stayed at her Colony. The Colonists
had great diversity of interests, and they had their own
self-disciplined excellences. Merely to watch them move off
after breakfast, in their own freedom, in their own way,
to an uninterrupted period of work that each one could make
as long or as short as he liked, was to catch something of
the whole purpose of the Colony and know the atmosphere
of creative work that it had come to possess.

341 BUCHAN, Alexander M. "The First Citizen of Tilbury Town."
St. Louis Post-Dispatch, April 25, 1937. P. 4H.

342  BUCKALEW, Anne.  "Review of Selected Letters."  Daily Times
     Herald (Dallas), March 3, 1940.  Part 3, p. 16.

343  BUDD, Louis J.  "Robinson's Letters to Edith Brower:  A Re-
     view."  South Atlantic Quarterly, 68 (Summer, 1969), 430-
     431.  Those who appreciate Robinson's almost cryptic verse-
     portraits will enjoy these letters as snapshots from his own
     mirror.  Initiates will watch out for his sly role-playing, but
     anybody can have a smiling time by taking him literally, as
     when he announced that his aching teeth gave him "lessons
     in idealism every day."  Both Robinson's humor and dedica-
     tion to poetry were inveterate, as the last letter in this
     volume shows.  He closed by worrying if he would have
     "an idea in his head," the next time he tried to work and
     by hoping:  "Perhaps there will be one or two."  There
     always were.

344  _____.  "Edwin Arlington Robinson Unbends for Academe."
     Colby Library Quarterly, 16 (December, 1980), 248-251.
     Article is an account of the friendship and interviews which
     Robinson extended to A. Gayle Waldrop, a graduate student
     in journalism at Columbia University, and Professor Albert
     Shipp Pegues who was then Chairman of the Department of
     English at Southern Methodist University.  The details of
     the interview are recorded by Waldrop in a letter addressed
     to Dr. Jay Hubbell who at the time was editing his book An
     Introduction to Poetry, which was published in September,
     1922.  The record of this visit is further evidence that per-
     haps Robinson was not quite so reticent and aloof as some
     of his friends made him out to be.  In this interview Robin-
     son commented on some of his poems that still interest us
     and confided his opinion of several of his popular contempo-
     raries.

345  BUNKER, Robert.  "Edwin Arlington Robinson."  New Mexico
     Quarterly, 17 (Autumn, 1947), 382-383.  Review of biogra-
     phy by Yvor Winters and In Defense of Reason, also by
     Winters.  Article mostly deals with In Defense of Reason
     with numerous comments on Winters's criticism of poetry.
     Thus the book is relevant to Robinson's poetry.  Winters's
     criticism of much poetry is brilliant, but ultimately narrow
     in concept and range.  In the Robinson volume, Winters
     analyzes with great insight the techniques, and some unfor-
     tunate formulas, of a poet whose "moral" concepts did indeed
     dictate the forms of his successes and the shells of his
     lengthy failures.  The successes and the shells of his lengthy
     failures.  The volume, with extensive specific references to
     the Collected Poems, is invaluable to the appreciation of
     Robinson.

346  BURKHART, Charles.  "Robinson's 'Richard Cory.'"  Explicator,
     19 (November, 1960), item 9.  One can treat it as no more

than an exemplum, and it lends itself to several clichés so
easily that it may seem merely to point a prosaic and tritely
ironic moral and to lack all richness of implication. Without
quite dismissing the obtrusive didacticism of the poem, however, one can find an organic scheme which enhances the
interest of it and enlarges its intention. The entire poem
is built upon the use of contrasts which support the fundamental contrast between the splendid appearance of Richard
Cory's life and the harsh reality of whatever disease of the
soul led him to end it.

347  BURLINGAME, Roger. Of Making Many Books. New York:
     Charles Scribner's Sons, 1946. "Poetry," pp. 248-275; in-
     cludes commentary on Robinson. Comment consists largely
     of discussion of Robinson's poetry that went on between
     John Hays Gardiner, professor of English at Harvard, who
     wrote Pitts Duffield, then on the editorial staff of Scrib-
     ner's. This was in 1900. In the long run Scribner's did
     not accept Robinson's manuscript. It was not until after
     President Roosevelt took a lively interest in Robinson that
     Robinson was admitted to the Scribner fold. Roosevelt was
     regarded as an able statesman and as a literary appreciator
     if not a critic.

348  BURNS, Winifred. "Edwin Arlington Robinson in the Hands
     of the Reviewers." Poet-Lore, 48 (Summer, 1942), 164-175.
     Robinson's search for a public was a long and painful one.
     However, he did not cease to write steadily, eagerly. His
     principal concern was to cut away the ornaments and arti-
     ficialities of the poetic language he had inherited. The
     nearer he came to breaking with tradition, the surer he
     was to fail in any worldly sense. From first to last he did
     not cease to suffer from the critics' blundering judgment.
     He was sensitive to the shafts which came his way after
     every new publication. The years did not ease his agony
     and even the success of Tristram carried with it the bitter-
     ness of the misunderstanding heart, the hypercritical mind.

349  BURTLESS, Anna Catherine. "An Analysis of the Epic Poetry
     of John Gneisenan Neihardt, Alfred Noyes, and Edwin Ar-
     lington Robinson with Respect to the Immortal Line." Lin-
     coln: University of Nebraska, 1928. M.A. thesis.

350  BURTON, David H. "Christian Conservatism in the Poetry of
     Edwin Arlington Robinson." Ph.D. diss., Georgetown Uni-
     versity, 1953.

351  _____. "Theodore Roosevelt and Edwin Arlington Robinson:
     A Common Vision." The Personalist, 49 (Summer, 1968),
     331-350. In 1905 the president had liked what he had read
     of Robinson, and when he learned of the poet's dire financial

need, provided a position for him. A comparison of Roosevelt's public mind and that portion of Robinson's work which can be termed "socio-historical" poetry can but underscore that the president and the poet had much more in common than an incidental relationship. It was a kinship drawing heavily on the American sense of mission, a feeling for its high destiny rooted in the national consciousness and manifested in its national history.

352        . "The Intellectualism of Edwin Arlington Robinson." Thought, 44 (Winter, 1969), 565-580. Article is a thorough discussion based on the thesis that the present-day general disillusionment is not just an isolated phenomenon, but dates from the late 19th century. Because he was so thoroughly American, Robinson is an especially valuable source of insight. He wrote at length of the paradoxes in the American experience that yielded misgivings, and of the contradictions that time and events have worked to make the profound issues of America today. The composition and juxtaposition of elements in the poet's thoughts convey an urgency of crises, just as his indigenous quality renders his soul-searching analysis relevant.

353        . "Robinson, Roosevelt and Romanism: An Historical Reflection of the Catholic Church and the American Ideal." Records of the American Catholic Historical Society of Philadelphia, 80 (March, 1969), 3-16. Article is based upon the premise that the Catholic Church has never had a totally favorable role in American life and affairs. The average non-Catholic regards it as foreign, slightly to be distrusted, and somewhat alien to the American concepts of individual freedom. Robinson himself was not a Christian believer, either Catholic or Protestant, but he did respect the loyalty with which men held to the Church, and he was always interested in the life and teachings of Jesus. President Roosevelt held very similar views, with Christianity, social Darwinism, and everything else subordinated to his intense love of country and his passionate devotion to its republicanism. He was not much interested in theology, but was committed to its social ethics.

354        . "Edwin Arlington Robinson's Idea of God." Colby Library Quarterly, 8 (December, 1969), 280-294. Reprinted in Cary, ed. (1969), pp. 276-288. Robinson's attraction to the God of his fathers and the ethical values that inhered in the ancient religion was inimical to his philosophical awareness and the instruction of science. This contention remained a feature of his poetry, unresolved quite as much as it continued unresolved in the larger context of the American mind. Without this conflict Robinson would be less interesting as a poet, and less important as an

intellectual whose keenness to enjoy both the assurances of
a scientific world and the reassurances of the old faith was
an important detail in the larger canvas of American thought.

355 _____. "Edwin Arlington Robinson and Christianity."
Spirit, 37 (1970), 30-35. In the poetry of Robinson ex-
tremes meet; the spiritual collides with the scientific, and
belief with doubt. Robinson possessed an enormous sympathy for mankind, yet he allowed enough of his characters
to end in defeat or failure to gain a reputation as a poet
of despair; he was attracted to the God of the Testaments
and tradition, but never accepted Him. As Robinson is
read today, much of his fascination and meaning lies in the
ambiguity of his poetic response to the perplexities of
twentieth-century man.

356 _____. "Edwin Arlington Robinson and Morris Raphael
Cohen." Colby Library Quarterly, 14 (1978), 226-227.
Robinson enjoyed a wide variety of friends, many of them
distinguished, as in the case of Theodore Roosevelt. Many
of them, however, were fellow artists, especially at the
McDowell Colony. Cohen was among the latter. Although
of vastly different backgrounds, Cohen greatly admired
Robinson's poetry, particularly the Arthurian poems which
he advocated to Justice Oliver Wendell Holmes in 1927. It
is not known if Robinson was aware of Cohen's extreme
argument on the value of his poems.

357 BURTON, Richard. "Review of Town Down the River." Bell-
man, 9 (December 24, 1910), 1646.

358 _____. "Robinson as I Saw Him." Mark Twain Quarterly,
2 (Spring, 1938), 9. Article recalls three meetings with
Robinson, the first of which was at the famous Literary
Colony at Peterborough, N.H. This was the most memorable
meeting with Robinson living that summer in McDowell's
cabin, still furnished with the musician's piano. Burton
says: "We happened to sit in it at sunset time, and I shall
never forget looking through the great tree trunks to see a
Wagner-like, dramatic moment in Nature, the afternoon
shadows glorified by a spangled, high-lit western sky. It
was exactly like a stage scene out of the Niebelungen."

359 BUTCHER, Fanny. "Edwin Arlington Robinson Presents New
Book of Poems: Nicodemus." Chicago Tribune, October 22,
1932. P. 10.

360 CAMBON, Glauco. The Inclusive Flame: Studies in American
Poetry. Bloomington: Indiana University Press, 1963.
"Edwin Arlington Robinson: Knight of the Grail," pp. 53-
78. "The Grail" is the ever-receding boundary of human

experience, the furthermost term of any quest, Kant's
"Highest Good." It could also be taken to signify the
American dream, the propelling vision of the Pilgrim Fathers, of the pioneers, of the later immigrants, the continuous challenge of a reality that refuses to be confined within
a definitive horizon. Robinson was a true knight of the
Grail, born either too late or too soon, forever confronting
in his quietly heroic isolation the perilous ordeal of a quest
for the ultimate experience, the "inclusive flame" that would
either destroy or remake the unappeased seeker.

361  CAREW, Harold D.  "A Poet to His Friends: Review of Se-
     lected Letters."  Pasadena Star-News, March 16, 1940.

362  CARLSON, C. Lennart.  "Robinsoniana."  Colby Mercury, 6
     (December, 1939), 281-284.  Commentary on the Robinson
     materials which are held by the Maine State Library, largely
     due to the incentive and interest of the late Henry E. Dun-
     nack, librarian.  In addition to autographed copies of his
     books and a variety of clippings relating to Robinson, the
     collection includes a number of letters.  Most of the letters
     are addressed to Mr. Dunnack by way of reply to requests
     for copies of his works for the library.  A few of the other
     letters are addressed to Robinson's friend, the late Dr.
     Alanson Tucker Schuman, a Gardiner physician.  All of
     these date from 1907 and are of a highly personal character,
     revealing Robinson in the mood for pleasant confidences,
     amiable humor, and serious advice.

363  CARPENTER, Frederic Ives.  "Tristram, the Transcendant."
     New England Quarterly, 11 (September, 1938), 501-523.
     Reprinted in Cary, ed. (1969), pp. 75-90.  Begins with a
     general review of early criticism of Tristram, which most
     critics agreed was different from Robinson's earlier narra-
     tives.  All at once he seemed to have abandoned the intel-
     lect for the emotions, to have given up morality for passion.
     Yet closer examination indicates that it is in line with the
     other two Camelot poems, and is the third and final type
     of love as explored in these three poems.  Tristram trans-
     cends the world of time, and affirms that the greatest real-
     ity is that which follows death.

364  CARY, Richard.  "Robinson's Notes to His Nieces."  Colby Li-
     brary Quarterly, 5 (December, 1960), 195-202.  Based on
     65 notes, few over a page in length, which Robinson wrote
     to his three nieces, Ruth, Marie, Barbara, over the years
     1912-1935.  There emerge from these brief, unstudied mes-
     sages--to greater degree and acuity than in the biographies
     --at least five integral qualities of Robinson's character:
     his instinctive, unobtrusive generosity to his own family;
     his fundamental modesty and self-effacement; his sober wit

and moderated pessimism; his absolute dedication to the
writing of poetry; his consistent solicitude for others.  The
manuscript of these notes is in the Colby College Library.

365 _____.  "In Memoriam:  Edwin Arlington Robinson."  Colby
Library Quarterly, 5 (December, 1960), 169.  Robinson was
preoccupied with the surviving of his work for 25 years.
It has now been 25 years since his death, and we now know
he was a poor prophet.  In the first place, his works never
"died" to the point of having to "begin to live again."  In
the second, he is most positively not "extinct."  His fame
has pulsed steadily through several shifts in literary taste
since his time.  Editions of his books and critical commentary have appeared with abounding regularity.  Inclusion of
certain poems in anthologies have given them a familiar place
and made them indubitable short classics of American literature.

366 _____.  "Robinson on Moody."  Colby Library Quarterly, 6
(December, 1962), 176-183.  Begins with reference to article
by Maurice Brown in which it was shown how different these
two poets were.  Their tastes, philosophies, influences, etc.
impelled notably disparate views of the world.  Yet there
also inhered enough fundamental similarities to draw them
together eventually (perhaps in subconscious league against
philistinism) and to bring their literary objectives into closer
alignment.  An air of superficiality may appear to invest
some of these similarities, but the motivating drive beneath
them strongly testifies the common personality of the buoyant midwesterner and the taciturn down-easter.

367 _____.  "Robinson on Browning."  Victorian Newsletter, 23
(Spring, 1963), 19-21.  Robinson never published a poem
about Browning, and there is no evidence that he ever
wrote one.  He refers to Browning just once, yet was never
able to shake off the label of "American Browning."  A number of critics have advanced the idea.  Robinson was always
on the defensive when he was compared with Browning, and
always denied that there was any similarity.  The truth is
that Robinson read Browning in his youth, referred to him
in some of his early letters.  As Robinson grew older and
more sure of himself, this antagonism toward the English
poet lessened, and Robinson resigned himself to be "like
Browning to the end of my days."  Robinson believed himself to have an affinity with Heine, and complained that no
one had ever mentioned that.

368 _____.  "Edwin Arlington Robinson as Soothsayer."  Colby
Library Quarterly, 6 (June, 1963), 233-245.  Reprinted in
Cary, ed. (1969), pp. 200-209.  Robinson often yearned to
cut through the veils of the future and preview the "mintage

of Eternity." There is no record that Robinson ever dab-
bled in any of the occult sciences, yet there was a touch
of the mystical in his early claims to divination. These intuitive flashes accord with his sympathy for Emerson's concept of the poet as seer. In his poems after 1900, the flow
of the future takes on a cyclic appearance. Time is represented as a continuous holocaust in which old ways dissolve
in flames as the new rise from among the ashes. Inherent
in this endlessly repetitive scheme is man's tragic inability
to alter his destiny. In so purposive a universe the well-
springs of prophecy are fed from more determinable areas
than the purely visionary....

369 _____. "Robinson Bonanza." Colby Library Quarterly, 6
(June, 1963), 262. Refers to 54 letters of Robinson to
Arthur Davis Variell. These letters have been added to
the already more than 900 holograph letters by the poet.
A school chum of Robinson's in Gardiner, Maine, Variell
fared into the world and soared to international fame. For
his work in medicine, Dr. Variell was knighted by several
nations and accorded an imposing array of honorary orders,
military ranks, and diplomas. Years later Robinson and
Variell ran into each other again. These letters range from
August 1922 to September 1929.

370 _____. "Robinson on Dickens." American Notes and
Queries, 2 (November, 1963), 35-36. Consists of excerpts
from three letters to Edith Brower--August 7 and 26, 1928,
February 24, 1929--in which Robinson expresses his views
on Dickens, favorably.

371 _____. "The Library of Edwin Arlington Robinson: Addenda." Colby Library Quarterly, 7 (March, 1967), 398-
415. Article is an "addenda" to the 1950 publication The
Library of Edwin Arlington Robinson, compiled by James
Humphry, III, then librarian of Colby College. His com-
pilation consisted of 372 books, and was complete at the
time. Over the years 173 additional books have accrued,
and are now listed. Some of these books belonged to the
Robinson family library, and since Robinson himself did not
make a practice of writing his name in and marking his
copies of books, it is sometimes difficult to know exactly
what his relation to the book might have been.

372 _____. "'Go Little Book': An Odyssey of Robinson's The
Torrent and The Night Before." Colby Library Quarterly,
7 (December, 1967), 511-527. Begins with 1896 when Robinson published his little book on his own, 312 blue paper-
bound pamphlets, 44 pages. Over the years the copies of
this little publication were wafted to the four corners of the
world. After Robinson became well known or famous, copies

of this first publication became very valuable, rising in
price from about 17¢ per copy that Robinson paid for them,
to the more than $1000 which a stray copy would bring to-
day. Robinson would have watched this spiral with mingled
satisfaction, repugnance, and suppressed amusement.

373 _____. "Torrents Come in Driblets." Colby Library Quarterly, 7 (December, 1967), 548. From 1947 to 1956 the
editor, Mr. Carl J. Weber, pursued elusive copies of Torrents.... This short note documents five copies of the
work which have not hitherto been docketed. Two of these
copies have specific locations, but the whereabouts of the
others is unknown.

374 _____, ed. Edwin Arlington Robinson's Letters to Edith
Brower. Cambridge, Mass.: Belknap Press of Harvard,
1968. Consists of 189 letters, pp. 13-202. Introduction
identifies the subject of the letters, most of which are about
Robinson's poems. In an Appendix, Edith Brower writes
"Memories of Edwin Arlington Robinson," and a review of
Children of the Night. She always believed in Robinson,
and theirs was a relationship unclouded by sentimentality.

375 _____, ed. Appreciation of Edwin Arlington Robinson:  28
Interpretive Essays. Waterville, Maine: Colby College
Press, 1969. 356 pp. of reprinted material. "On Rereading-
ing Robinson," by Archibald MacLeish, pp. 3-5; "The
Arthur of Edwin Arlington Robinson," by E. Edith Pipkin,
pp. 6-16; "Tilbury Town and Camelot," by Edna Davis
Romig, pp. 17-37; "Robinson as Man and Poet," by Harriet
Monroe, pp. 38-42; "E. A. Robinson's Later Poems," by
David Brown, pp. 43-54; "The Optimism Behind Robinson's
Tragedies," by Floyd Stovall, pp. 55-74; "Tristram the
Transcendent," by Frederic Ives Carpenter, pp. 75-90;
"E. A. Robinson and the Cosmic Chill," by Hyatt Howe
Waggoner, pp. 91-104; "The Shorter Poems of E. A. Robin-
son," by John R. Doyle, pp. 105-116; "The Pernicious Rib:
E. A. Robinson's Concept of Feminine Character," by Lou-
ise Dauner, pp. 117-133; "Religious and Social Ideas in the
Didactic Work of E. A. Robinson," by Yvor Winters, pp.
134-146; "'Here Are the Men...': E. A. Robinson's Male
Character Types," by Richard Crowder, pp. 147-163; "E. A.
Robinson: The Lost Tradition," by Louis O. Coxe, pp.
164-177; "Does It Matter How Annandale Went Out?" by
David S. Nivison, pp. 178-190; "Image Patterns in the Poetry of Edwin Arlington Robinson," by Charles T. Davis,
pp. 191-199; "E. A. Robinson as Soothsayer," by Richard
Cary, pp. 200-209; "E. A. Robinson's System of Opposites,"
by James G. Hepburn, pp. 210-224; "E. A. Robinson's Poetics," by Lewis E. Weeks, Jr., pp. 225-242; "Robinson's
'For a Dead Lady': An Exercise in Evaluation," by Clyde

L. Grimm, pp. 243-252; "Robinson's Impulse for Narrative,"
by J. Vail Foy, pp. 253-262; "Robinson's Use of the Bible,"
by Nicholas Ayo, pp. 263-275; "E. A. Robinson's Idea of
God," by David H. Burton, pp. 276-288; "Formulation of
E. A. Robinson's Principles of Poetry," by Robert D. Stevik,
pp. 289-300; "The Plays of Edwin Arlington Robinson," by
Irving D. Suss, pp. 301-314; "The Octaves of E. A. Robin-
son," by Ronald Moran, pp. 315-321; "E. A. Robinson's
Yankee Conscience," by W. R. Robinson, pp. 322-334; "He
Shouts to See Them Scamper So: E. A. Robinson and the
French Forms," by Peter Dechert, pp. 335-345; "The World
Is ... a Kind of Spiritual Kindergarten," by Paul H. Mor-
rill, pp. 346-356.

376    _____, ed. Colby Library Quarterly, 4 issues of 1969 devoted to Robinson on his 100th Birthday. Also makes contribution to Robinson scholarship as indicated in the articles
listed below.

377    _____. "Robinson's Books and Periodicals." Colby Library
Quarterly, 8 (March, 1969), 266-277. This is Part I of the
Series which will follow. Colby College has the most exten-
sive and at the same time the most personal collection of
Robinsoniana in existence. The following categories are
represented: Books by E. A. Robinson (9 pages of article);
Proof Sheets of Books by Robinson; Robinson in Periodicals.

378    _____. "Robinson's Books and Periodicals." Colby Library
Quarterly, 8 (June, 1969), 334-343. This is Part II of the
inventory. Whereas Part I consisted mostly of published
material by Robinson, this installment catalogs material of
other sorts: Books by Others, Inscribed by Robinson;
Periodicals, Inscribed by Robinson.

379    _____. "Robinson's Books and Periodicals." Colby Library
Quarterly, 8 (September, 1969), 399-413. This is the third
part of the series, and consists of only two parts: Books
by Others and Inscribed by Others; Periodicals, Inscribed
by Others. All the items are of established association with
Robinson--most of them are books given to Robinson by
friends or fellow authors. Books which he received and
passed along to friends without mark of the transition, are
not included.

380    _____. "Robinson's Manuscripts and Letters." Colby Library Quarterly, 8 (December, 1969), 479-487. This article
is an inventory of Robinson manuscripts and holograph letters in the Colby College Library. This includes four of
his book-length poems and over 1,000 letters, the largest
extant collection. The article is arranged in sections: I.
Manuscripts by E. A. R.; II. Manuscripts about or to

E. A. R.; III. Letters by E. A. R.; IV. Letters to
E. A. R.; V. Letters about E. A. R.

381      _____. "Additions to the Robinson Collection, I." Colby
         Library Quarterly, 9 (September, 1971), 377-382. Is an
         update of the four articles published in 1969. The items
         are arranged in the following categories: Books by Robin-
         son; Proof Sheets of Books by Robinson; Books by Others,
         Inscribed by Robinson; Books by Others, Inscribed by Oth-
         ers; Periodicals, Inscribed by Others; Robinson Manuscripts,
         by Robinson; Manuscripts About or to Robinson; Letters by
         Robinson; Letters to Robinson/Letters about Robinson.

382      _____. "Additions to the Robinson Collection, II." Colby
         Library Quarterly, 10 (June, 1974), 385-388. Brings the
         listing of Colby College Library holdings on Robinson up to
         date. It is arranged according to the following: Books by
         Robinson, inscribed by Robinson. Books by Others, in-
         scribed by Robinson. Books by Others, inscribed by Others
         for Robinson. Robinson Manuscripts and Letters: Manu-
         scripts by Robinson; Manuscripts About or to Robinson;
         Letters by Robinson; Letters about Robinson.

383      _____. "Mowry Saben about Edwin Arlington Robinson."
         Colby Library Quarterly, 9 (March, 1972), 482-497. Sub-
         ject is a youth, whom Robinson met in the Fall of 1891 when
         both were freshmen at Harvard. What they had in common
         was love of literature, and a magnet that drew them together
         and sustained their relation over the next forty-four years
         to Robinson's death. And beyond, for Robinson remained in
         Saben's memory an indestructible image which he often evoked
         with mismatched feelings. Refers to four items that Saben
         wrote about Robinson: an obituary and two reviews for
         The Argonaut, and a brief piece for the Colby Mercury.
         (Items listed under Saben.)

384      _____. "The First Publication of Edwin Arlington Robinson's
         Poem 'Broadway.'" American Literature, 46 (March, 1974),
         83. This note is offered as a correction to Edwin S. Fus-
         sell who presented this poem as "unpublished" when he found
         a manuscript copy in the Robinson collection at Harvard.
         This error was repeated by William White in 1971. In fact
         the poem was printed in the New York Evening Sun on No-
         vember 15, 1918, in Don Marquis' daily column without Rob-
         inson's knowledge until after it was printed.

385      _____. "Robinson's Friend Arthur Davis Variell." Colby
         Library Quarterly, 10 (June, 1974), 372-385. Robinson had
         a rather wide variety of friends, each one more or less iso-
         lated from the others, and never brought together by Rob-
         inson, "esteeming each for his private and exceptional

essence." Arthur Davis Variell was one such friend whom
Robinson grew up with in Gardiner, Maine, and who turned
up again in 1922. Fifty-three letters and one postcard by
Robinson to Variell--from August 14, 1922 to September 23,
1929--are in Colby College Library. Only one copy of a letter and one telegram by Variell survive. Variell lived until
1940, but their friendship seems to have broken off rather
suddenly in 1929.

386 _____. "'The Clam-Digger: Capital Island': A Robinson
Sonnet Recovered." Colby Library Quarterly, 10 (December, 1974), 505-511. Article includes a poem, not hitherto
attributed to Robinson, which appeared on April 26, 1890,
in The Reporter Monthly (a four-page literary supplement
of the Kennebec Reporter). The poem bears no signature
other than "R." Although this signature may cause some
lingering doubt as to its author, the burden of evidence,
circumstantial and internal, favors including it as Robinson's.

387 _____. Early Reception of Edwin Arlington Robinson: The
First Twenty Years. Waterville, Maine: Colby College
Press, 1974. 321 pages of early reviews. Scope of book
is 1896-1916. Seventy items of this period have been listed
in the Hogan-White bibliographies, but now about 90 addition items have been uncovered, and full texts are printed
in Cary's volume. Appraisals of Robinson's two plays are
excluded.

388 _____. "The First Twenty Years of Edwin Arlington Robinson
Criticism: A Supplementary Checklist." Resources for
American Literary Study, 4 (1974), 184-204. Is a listing of
90 sources of early reviews and articles from 1896 to 1916
when Robinson emerged into relative fame with the publication of The Man Against the Sky. Five items are listed at
the end which could not be totally verified. The first 90
items were not listed in Hogan's bibliography (1936) or in
William White's Supplementary work (1971).

389 CESTRE, Charles. "L'Oeuvre poétique d'Edwin Arlington Robinson." Revue Anglo-Américaine, 1 (April, 1924), 279-294.
In French.

390 _____. "Edwin Arlington Robinson: The Man Who Died
Twice." Revue Anglo-Américaine, 2 (June, 1925), 464-466.
In French.

391 _____. "Edwin Arlington Robinson: Dionysus in Doubt."
Revue Anglo-Américaine, 2 (August, 1925), 560-562. In
French.

392 _____. "Edwin Arlington Robinson's Treatment of the

Arthurian Legend." <u>Bryn Mawr Alumnae Bulletin</u>, 5 (November, 1925), 5-15.  Reprinted in Cestré, <u>An Introduction to Edwin Arlington Robinson</u> (1930), Chapter 3, pp. 67-118.

393 _____.  "Amy Lowell, Robert Frost, and Edwin Arlington Robinson." <u>Johns Hopkins Alumni Magazine</u>, 14 (March, 1926), 363-388.

394 _____.  "Le Tristram d'Edwin Arlington Robinson." <u>Revue Anglo-Américaine</u>, 5 (December, 1927), 97-110; 5 (February, 1928), 219-228.  In French.

395 _____.  "Edwin Arlington Robinson: <u>The Sonnets</u>." <u>Revue Anglo-Américaine</u>, 6 (April, 1929), 377-378.  In French.

396 _____.  "Le Dernier Poème d'Edwin Arlington Robinson: <u>Cavender's House</u>." <u>Revue Anglo-Américaine</u>, 6 (August, 1929), 489-507.  In French.

397 _____.  <u>An Introduction to Edwin Arlington Robinson</u>.  New York: Macmillan, 1930.  230 pages.  Consists of Introduction and six parts:  A Modern Classic; Poetry of Emotion and Reflection; Treatment of the Arthurian Legend; Interpretative and Dramatic Poetry; Humor; and Psychology.  In the Introduction, Cestré says:  "Robinson, as poet, deserves to be styled a modern classic, because he combines in harmonious union the old-time qualities of intellectual acumen, broad humanity, universal appeal, decorum, sense of proportion, and art of composition, with powers more recently developed as means of literary expression:  imaginative coloring, sensuous richness, suggestive foreshortenings, and word melody....  A survey of his work yields the impression of wealth of vision and felicity of technique, together with a concern for what is most human in man: preference for the general, subordination of sensation to sensibility and of sensationalism to sense, propriety and reserve."

398 _____.  "Edwin Arlington Robinson: <u>The Glory of the Nightingales</u>." <u>Revue Anglo-Américaine</u>, 8 (February, 1931), 271-273.  In French.

399 _____.  "Récit, drame et symbole chez Edwin Arlington Robinson." <u>Revue Anglo-Américaine</u>, 9 (June, 1932), 405-413.  In French.

400 _____.  "Review of <u>Nicodemus</u>." <u>Revue Anglo-Américaine</u>, 10 (February, 1933), 48-49.  In French.

401 _____.  "Edwin Arlington Robinson, artiste dans les jeux de l'humour et de la fantaisie." <u>Revue Anglo-Américaine</u>, 11 (February, 1934), 246-251.  In French.

402 _____ . "Avec Edwin Arlington Robinson dans l'inferno de
l'art." Revue Anglo-Américaine, 12 (April, 1935) 323-328.
In French.

403 _____ . "Edwin Arlington Robinson: Maker of Myths."
Mark Twain Quarterly, 2 (Spring, 1938), 3-8, 24. Discusses the stages by which Robinson expressed his moral
concern for the influences which human beings exert on
each other, some being strong, and warping or at least re-
tarding the mental faculties of others. Keen psychological
analysis was at the basis of his tragic tales. Later he became less interested in strangeness of behavior, and more
interested in the consequences it has in a man's life. His
narratives came to be built with less psychological analysis
and were built on moral scrutiny. His stories create their
own mythology, our daily problems, our immediate suffer-
ings, fears, misdeeds and expiations.

404 _____ . "Edwin Arlington Robinson." Etudes Anglaises
(Paris), 3 (July-September, 1939), 304-305. Review of
Hagedorn's biography.

405 _____ . "Edwin Arlington Robinson." Etudes Anglaises, 8
(April-June, 1955), 181. Review of biography by Edwin
Fussell.

406 CHANT, Mrs. Elsie Ruth (Dykes). "The Metrics and Imagery
of Edwin Arlington Robinson as Exhibited in Five of His
Blank Verse Poems." University of New Mexico, 1930,
M. A. Thesis.

407 CHILDERS, William C. "Edwin Arlington Robinson's Proper
Names." Names: Journal of the American Name Society, 3
(December, 1955), 223-229. The names Robinson bestows
upon his characters are as unforgettable as the characters
themselves. His choice of original and unusual sounding
names adds much to the enjoyment of his poetry, but sometimes they are much more than picturesque choices. Robinson borrows appropriate names from persons, real or fic-
tional. Some names are susceptible of punning interpreta-
tions. Through the choice of a name Robinson often artfully
betrays a character's motivation or behavior in a poem.
Perhaps the most interesting of Robinson's names are those
in which he reveals his punning instinct.

408 _____ . "Amaryllis." Explicator, 14 (February, 1956), item
34. Refutes the interpretation that this poem is an expression of the bereavement and the loneliness of old age which
is a characteristic theme in Robinson's poetry. Believes
there is more to the poem than this and sees the name
"Amaryllis" as standing for the totality of poetry, the old

man as a representative of poets in isolation, and the grave
as the destiny of isolated poetry. By giving the poem a
pastoral setting and using the classical allusion of "Amaryllis" Robinson has dramatized his belief that poetry had become isolated and eccentric, and divorced from life will die.

409  CHRISTENSEN, Claude Hansen. "The Tristram Story in Edwin
     Arlington Robinson's Tristram." University of Chicago,
     1928. M.A. thesis.

410  CIARDI, John. How Does a Poem Mean?  Boston:  Houghton
     Mifflin, 1959. "Mr. Flood's Party" (pp. 738-739) is in-
     cluded in section "Poems for Study." Of Robinson's poem,
     Ciardi says, "...it presents an incident and character in
     great detail. Old Eben Flood, drunkenly singing, becomes
     a specific and unforgettable person. Yet his very name is
     a pun--Eben Flood, ebb 'n flood, the going and the coming
     tide. Of what? Of life, and feeling, of the old order and
     the new, of the world that changes out from under a man
     leaving him silly and tragic and lovable and lost--all that
     and more, to the last ripple at the last edge of the pool at
     whose center this sort of thought waits."

411  CLARK, Beulah B. "Edwin Arlington Robinson:  A Biographi-
     cal and Critical Study." Columbus:  Ohio State University,
     1925. M.A. thesis.

412  CLARK, Harry Hayden, ed. Major American Poets.  New York:
     American Book, 1936. Robinson, pp. 938-947; selections
     pp. 755-778. Prints a dozen or more familiar poems by
     Robinson, including several sonnets and the long poem "The
     Man Against the Sky." Notes consist of Chronology, a se-
     lective bibliography, general notes, and commentary on each
     separate poem. Most of the commentary is quoted from works
     about Robinson.

413  _____. "The Poet as Critic." CEA Critic, 30 (February,
     1969), 3. Review of Letters to Edith Brower. Beyond the
     oddity of the revelation of Robinson's peculiar personality,
     the letters will be useful to the scholar in supplementing
     evidence about the poet's reading and literary preferences,
     even if his theory of literature is not entirely consistent.
     Robinson may have shown humility about his personal life,
     but his aesthetic standards were high. Miss Brower was a
     Presbyterian spinster, twenty-one years older than Robin-
     son, who had done much to infuse him with confidence dur-
     ing his dreary early years. He credited her with propelling
     him toward further quests of his profoundest self.

414  CLARK, S. L. and Julian N. Wasserman. "'Time Is a Casket':
     Love and Temporality in Robinson's Tristram." Colby Library

Quarterly, 17 (June, 1981), 112-116. Discusses the love
theme of Tristram, in which the hero is in love with Isolt
of Ireland, the wife of King Mark, and is himself married
to "Isolt of the White Hands," the Queen of Tintagel. The
structure of Robinson's poem gains its conflict in that it is
a study of love within a frame of time--past, present, or
future--and a love that exists outside the frame of time,
that of Tristram and Isolde, for whom "love is to live for
ever," after death has effected their release and given them
a peace in which they are done with time.

415  CLEMENS, Cyril (ed. of special Robinson issue). "Edwin Ar-
     lington Robinson: 1869-1935." Mark Twain Quarterly, 2
     (Spring, 1938), 1-2. Brief, introductory remarks for this
     special issue of the Mark Twain Quarterly. Mark Twain and
     Robinson did not know each other; they passed but once,
     and someone pointed out to Robinson who the older writer
     was.

416  _____. "Robinson Collection at Gardiner, Maine." Ibid.,
     p. 18. Comments on the seven years of work by friends
     and students of Robinson who undertook to build this col-
     lection. It was started in 1930 by Robinson himself who
     sent seven autographed books in reply to a request for his
     approval of such a plan. Among those most dedicated to
     this project was Mrs. Laura Richards, who contributed,
     among other things, a letter from Robinson to a "Mr.
     Berry," then editor of the Gardiner Journal which had
     printed one of Robinson's poems January 31, 1924.

417  CLIFTON, Linda J. "Two Corys: A Sample of Inductive
     Teaching." English Journal, 58 (March, 1969), 414-415.
     Article is based on an analysis of the poem by Robinson
     and the song by Simon and Garfunkel. No real decision
     was reached as to which one "was better," in fact, the
     study was not designed to reach that conclusion, but rather
     to show that they are different. Students themselves con-
     cluded that the character in the poem was much more sym-
     pathetically presented, but on the other hand the music ac-
     companying the other version gave mood and coloration to
     the character and was also enjoyable.

418  COFFIN, Robert P. Tristram. New Poetry of New England:
     Robinson and Frost. Baltimore: Johns Hopkins University
     Press, 1938. Reprinted New York: Russell & Russell, 1964.
     Robinson, pp. 25-50 et passim. Being a major poet, Robin-
     son writes of a wider country than the small cluster of New
     England states. Most of his longer poems are set far back
     in distant times and places, or they are acted out in a
     peculiarly generalized locality where particular landmarks
     are hard to identify. His geography is a geography of a

gray place, and the trees and houses often have no individuality or style of leaf or architecture. Yet his thinking
is peculiarly a New Englander's, and his characters, though
often as faceless as dreams, are New Englanders in their
brains and their hearts.... Some of them stand on rotting
wharves and look down at evil, dead waters where ships do
not ride any more. The water fascinates them, and they
cannot take their eyes away, and they think of the end of
things. Voices often call them from the grave, and tell them
the one way to peace.

419  _____. "A Poet Who Was Less Than His Poems." Yankee
(Dublin, N.H.), 5 (June, 1939), 4-5. Review of Hagedorn's
biography.

420  COLLAMORE, H. Bacon. Edwin Arlington Robinson, 1869-1935:
A Collection of His Works from the Library of Bacon Collamore. Hartford, Conn.: Hawthorne House, 1936. Most of
the items are now part of the Robinson collection at the
Colby College Library.

421  _____. "Robinson and the War." Colby Library Quarterly,
1 (March, 1943), 30-31. Comments on the one letter to
Edith Brower in which Robinson speaks of the war. This
letter is dated June 2, 1918, in which Robinson says "I
ought to be driving a mule in France." In 1914 the poet
had sent Miss Brower a copy of the poem "Cassandra,"
which had first appeared in the Boston Evening Transcript,
on December 21, 1914, and certainly can be read as an
"anti-pacifist" commentary.

422  COLTON, Arthur W. "Edwin Arlington Robinson." New York
Evening Post, Literary Review, 3 (June 23, 1923), 781-782.
Review of Collected Poems. What other volume of collected
poems of any other modern poet has as much in it as this?
"Ben Jonson Entertains..." is as good an example as any.
If this is not Shakespearean talk, it is very near it, and to
come so near the inimitable is no simple matter. "The mis-
chievous half-mad serenity" which Ben Jonson noticed is
noticeable in more than one of Robinson's own characters.

423  COLUM, Mary M. "Poets and Their Problems." Forum, 93
(June, 1935), 343-344. His was a great poetic talent, but,
as with many poetic talents, the work produced by it was
not of a kind that could easily be traded for bread. The
values of the work of the mind and the spirit cannot be
gauged in that way, and it is time that we awoke to that
fact. Robinson's poetry was an expression of the civilization of this country; it was a pillar in the foundations of
this country's culture.... The funeral of this man whose
name will be remembered was not as it should have been--

something that represented the country. In France his
funeral would have been organized officially, with all rites
and ceremonies, to let people understand how they honored
the products of the spirit and the making of a civilization.

424  COMMAGER, Henry Steele. "Traditionalism in American Poetry."
     The Nineteenth Century and After, 146 (November, 1949),
     311-326. Long article in which Robinson and several other
     figures are discussed. Remarks on Robinson are essentially
     the same as those in Commager's book The American Mind
     (1950). Robinson was the poet of doubt, but doubt requires
     the existence of belief. He was the poet of failure, but
     failure implied some standard of success.... It is signifi-
     cant that the most profound of American poets of the twen-
     tieth century should have been so preoccupied, obsessed
     even, with failure, frustration, desolation and death.

425  _____. The American Mind. New Haven: Yale University
     Press, 1950. "The Traditionalists," pp. 141-161. His was,
     above all, the tragic muse; sadness and compassion permeate
     all his lines. He was a Calvinist who yielded occasionally
     and reluctantly to the lure of Transcendentalism and then
     returned penitently to brood on the depravity of man, the
     inscrutability of God or of fate, the necessity of suffering
     and defeat. Man's fate, as Robinson read it, is forever
     tragic; he cannot avoid that fate but he can ennoble it by
     acquiescence, by fortitude, and by loyalty to some ultimate
     truth, some gleam, some vision, some light--the terms ap-
     pear again and again and are interchangeable.

426  CONKLING, Grace Hazard. "Review of Dionysus in Doubt."
     North American Review, 222 (September-November, 1925),
     159-160. The four dialogues, distinguished as they are in
     condensed style and dramatic detail, fail to admit the reader
     to any closer acquaintance with his philosophy than is found
     in other books of his. In the sonnets, on the other hand,
     the reader may feel a new poignance, as of violins with
     muted strings.

427  CONNER, Frederick William. Cosmic Optimism: A Study of
     Evolution by American Poets etc.... Gainesville: Univer-
     sity of Florida Press, 1949. Robinson, pp. 365-374. Robin-
     son retained traces of the underlying philosophy of the cos-
     mic doctrine and a notable tinge of its fundamental hopeful-
     ness. His belief was not simply that things would turn out
     well for himself or his group but that somehow justice was
     inherent in the nature of things and would one day right
     the scandalously overset balances of the present. He felt
     the "coming glory of the Light" but he avoided saying that
     he could tell what it is or show it to another or demonstrate
     its necessity. An optimism of a kind must certainly be

granted to Robinson, but he was too painfully aware of the
ills of the world to accept the easy rationalizations of the
evolutionary faith.  He was an optimist in spite of what the
world had to show, not because of it.

428   CONRAD, L. H.  "The Critics' Poet:  A Study of Edwin Ar-
      lington Robinson."  Landmark, 15 (January, 1933), 23-26.

429   CONVERSE, Florence.  "Review of Collected Poems."  Atlantic's
      Bookshelf (February, 1922).  Not since William Vaughn
      Moody's poems and dramas were collected in the definitive
      edition after his death, has there been a more important
      and distinguished contribution to American verse than this
      latest volume, the fruits of thirty years.

430   COOK, David M. and Craig G. Swauger, eds.  The Small Town
      in American Literature:  A Casebook Anthology.  New York:
      Dodd, Mead & Co., 1969.  Robinson, pp. 83-88.  Chapter
      is entitled "People of Tilbury Town," and consists of a brief
      introduction and 8 well-known poems from The Children of
      the Night (1897).  All of these "children" are failures, but
      in Tilbury Town they have dignity and distinction, for each
      is regarded as an individual and significant human being....
      It is the "little man" of the lower middle class whom Robin-
      son has immortalized, the farmer, the lumberjack, the crafts-
      man, the drifter.  The despair of the people of Tilbury
      Town was Robinson's own despair.  He was most of the time
      financially insecure, lonely, and depressed.  He is now rec-
      ognized as a major American poet, and depended greatly on
      his friends for a means of living.

431   COOK, Howard Willard.  Our Poets of Today.  New York:
      Moffat, Yard, 1923.  Robinson, pp. 18-30.  Is a running
      commentary on Robinson interspersed with long, full-length
      quotations of poems by Robinson.  It was with the publica-
      tion of "The Man Against the Sky" that Robinson achieved
      one of the finest things he has yet done.  This was in 1916.
      Here, with all the genius that is his own, he has crammed
      into a minimum space some colossal verse....  With the pub-
      lication of Collected Poems in 1921, Robinson achieved one
      of the most noteworthy events in contemporary American
      poetry.  Here is presented under one cover the work of a
      poet who has been generally acknowledged as the most fin-
      ished and settled of the poets alive in America today and
      one who has won a high and permanent place in American
      literature.  It is a great book--this volume, by a man whose
      genius grows rather than bursts full force upon the student.

432   COOPER, Frederic Taber.  "A Golden Gargoyle:  Avon's Har-
      vest."  Publishers' Weekly, 99 (April 16, 1921), 1236.  He
      has woven lines of lingering, haunting horror, and he is

at his best when he is most simple. The powerful memorable lines are almost monosyllabic.

433  COPELAND, C. T.  "An Appreciation."  Mark Twain Quarterly,
     2 (Spring, 1938), 16.  Copeland says: "I knew Robinson
     very little, but I hoped to know him better.  And on the
     very evening when he had to be taken to the hospital in
     New York he started out 'to call on Copey.'  While he was
     in the hospital he said to someone, 'When I get well and
     get back to Cambridge we must go to see Copey.'"

434  COURNOS, John.  "Biography of Robinson Recalls Tour of
     Pubs."  New Haven Sunday Register, October 23, 1938.
     Part 4, p. 5.  Review of Hagedorn's biography.

435  COURTNEY, Winifred F., ed.  The Readers' Adviser: A Guide
     to the Best in Literature, 2 vols.  New York:  Bowker,
     1968, 11th edition.  Robinson, p. 196, Vol. 1.  Tremendous,
     scholarly compilation of materials designed for students' re-
     search and librarians to use in ordering for the library.
     Lists bibliographical aids, dictionaries, encyclopedias, etc.
     Good chapter on "Modern American Poetry," Vol. 1, pp.
     189-240, which includes E. A. Robinson.  In this Robinson
     receives adequate representation, but the editor says "For
     the time being at least, Robinson seems somewhat in eclipse."

436  COUSINS, Natalie A.  "Gardiner's Poet."  Colby Mercury, 6
     (February, 1940), 285-288.  Reviews Robinson's life in
     Gardiner, Maine, a life that never was happy there.  He
     was generally alone, and what friendship he enjoyed was
     sporadic.  No one seemed to understand him, and he kept
     to himself.  he went to Harvard in 1891, and left Harvard
     in 1893.  He tried life once again in Gardiner, upon the
     death of his father, but left in 1897, saying "Gardiner and
     its people have no charms for me."  He went back for two
     days when his brother Dean died, again when Herman died,
     and in 1925 to receive the Doctorate of Letters from Bowdoin
     College.  He lived most of his life in New York City with
     summers spent at the McDowell Colony.  In April 1935 he
     died in New York, by then famous and more than justified
     for his one-track pursuit of poetry....  In October 1936
     on Gardiner's city common, a monument was unveiled to the
     poet.  The inscription was written by Laura Richards.  Her-
     mann Hagedorn spoke at the dedication.

437  COWAN, S. A.  "Robinson's 'Lost Anchors.'"  Explicator, 24
     (April, 1966), item 68.  Article is principally an answer to
     Jenkins' interpretation of the poem (see April, 1965), which
     Cowan regards as careless and avoids the simplest and most
     obvious meaning, specifically that the anchors were made
     ready for use.

438  COWLEY, Malcolm. "Edwin Arlington Robinson." New Repub-
         lic, 82 (April 17, 1935), 268-269.    Written after Robinson
         died in 1935.   He was the only American poet who devoted
         his whole career to writing verse and refused every oppor-
         tunity to capitalize on his reputation, who never wrote maga-
         zine articles or mystery novels or memoirs, or edited anth-
         ologies, etc.... He tried to convey the meaning of life by
         writing poems in bare, straightforward Yankee speech, about
         the men, the women, and the flowers he had lived among
         since birth.  His two high virtues, dignity and honesty,
         ended by interfering with each other.  The honesty caused
         him to write poems that were sometimes undignified and
         prosaic; the dignity forced him to lead a restricted and im-
         poverished life, and thereby cut him off from the world of
         his time.

439  _____. "Edwin Arlington Robinson:  Defeat and Triumph."
         New Republic, 119 (December 6, 1948), 26-30.  Article is
         an overall review of Robinson's career, beginning with his
         first publications which were largely ignored and concluding
         with comments on the recently published biography of Rob-
         inson by Emery Neff, which he finds to be an excellent work
         but deficient in its analysis of Robinson's poetry.  In con-
         clusion, Cowley also thinks too much has been derived from
         Hagedorn's biography of Robinson.

440  _____. After the Genteel Tradition:  American Writers,
         1910-1930.  Carbondale:  Southern Illinois University
         Press, 1964.  Robinson, pp. 28-36, by Malcolm Cowley
         (first appeared in 1937).  New edition edited by Harry T.
         Moore.  Essay on Robinson similar to article in New Repub-
         lic, 1935.  See above.

441  COX, Don Richard. "The Vision of Robinson's Merlin." Colby
         Library Quarterly, 10 (December, 1974), 495-504.  The task
         of reworking an existing legend always poses a problem to
         the creative artist.  The legend presents a frame, the nar-
         rative structure becomes a kind of constant and the central
         issue becomes a matter of the writer's interpretation of the
         material.  Robinson is concerned with why Arthur's kingdom
         falls, not whether it will fall....  Of his three long Arthur-
         ian poems, Merlin is the one most original in its character-
         izations, and also the one least dependent on original sources
         for its narrative line.  It is in the matter of Merlin's "en-
         trapment" which most interests Robinson, and in which he
         diverges largely from his sources.  Robinson's Merlin, al-
         though he is a rational man, goes willingly to his fate,
         neither tricked nor seduced, and free to leave Vivian when-
         ever he pleases--an addition to the legend which originates
         with Robinson.

442   COX, Hyde, and Edward C. Latham, eds. Selected Prose of
      Robert Frost. New York: Holt, Rinehart, Winston, 1966.
      Reprints "Introduction" to King Jasper (1935), pp. 59-67.
      Comments on the endless number of ways poetry has tried
      to be new, but Robinson stayed content with the old-
      fashioned way to be new: for forty years it was phrase
      on phrase on phrase, and every one for the closest de-
      lineation of something that is something. Any poet, to
      resemble him in the least, would have to resemble him in
      that grazing closeness to the spiritual realities. The style
      is the man. Rather say the style is the way the man takes
      himself; and to be at all charming or even bearable, the way
      is almost rigidly prescribed.

443   COXE, Louis O. "Mr. Barnard's Robinson: C+." Poetry, 81
      (December, 1952), 187-191. This work, according to Coxe,
      raises some pertinent issues and clears away some miscon-
      ceptions; he avoids the emphasis on the poet's life that tends
      to show Robinson as a martyr. He has covered the ground
      of extant Robinson criticism; he makes as good a case as
      can be made for the long narrative poems, and most of all
      he does not plague the reader with theories. Yet a serious,
      informed, purposeful book like this should come out better;
      despite all the very real virtues we can be grateful for, the
      book follows the tradition of Robinson studies and has little
      to say about the nature of the poetry or about the quality
      and scope of Robinson's gift.

444   _____. "Review of Tilbury Town, etc., edited Lawrance
      Thompson." Poetry, 84 (April, 1954), 108-111. Thinks the
      present volume of Selected Poems fills a great need, and
      may replace the enormous Collected Poems. On the other
      hand, the editor's organization leaves out a great many
      poems that should not have been omitted. Some of the In-
      troduction also seems irresponsible, and out of touch with
      the real subject of Robinson. Overall, this work would have
      profited if the editor had not been too arbitrary in his meth-
      od of selection and comment.

445   _____. "E. A. Robinson: The Lost Tradition." Sewanee
      Review, 62 (Spring, 1954), 247-266. Includes discussion
      of "The Clerks," "The Gift of God," and "Eros Turannos."
      Reprinted in Enabling Acts, Pp. 7-26. Also reprinted in
      Cary, ed. (1969), pp. 164-177, and in Murphy, ed. (1970),
      pp. 60-76. Discusses the reason for Robinson's decline and
      thinks that much of the neglect has derived from the decep-
      tively old-fashioned appearance it presents and from the
      very stern cosmology out of which the poetry arises. The
      texture of the poetry is of a sort we are not used to; the
      subject-matter can be misunderstood. Above all Robinson's
      technique lends itself to abuse so that very often the reader

may not detect that under an apparently calm surface many
forms are in motion.

446 _____. E. A. Robinson. Minneapolis: University of Minnesota Press, 1962. University of Minnesota Pamphlets on
American Writing, No. 17. 48 pages. Adequate for no
more than it undertakes. Author regards Robinson as one
of greatest in American literature, and says: "...he had
a consummate mastery of versification and rhetoric, he could
pile on the colors with the best of them, and he had the in-
ventiveness to treat the mind with symbol and intellectual
puzzle. He indulged these capacities from time to time, the
latter most frequently, but not until his later years did he
allow them to assume the upper hand. All of Robinson's
best work is the product of a sensibility that was on guard
against fraud, that concerned itself with making into form
what vision had discovered."

447 _____. "Edwin Arlington Robinson," in Six American Poets,
ed. Allen Tate, with introduction. Minneapolis: Pp. 45-81.
University of Minnesota Press, 1969. Reprint of item listed
above.

448 _____. Edwin Arlington Robinson: The Life of Poetry.
New York: Pegasus Publishers, 1969. Is not a duplicate
of 1962 book. Consists of about 200 pages, with index and
bibliography. In 10 chapters: I. Critics, Biographers
and Readers; II. Person, Place and Thing; III. Steps to
the Great Place; IV. The Town Down the River; V. Down
and Out; VI. The Man Against the Sky; VII. A Digression
on Obscurity; VIII. The Downward Years, 1916-1927; IX.
Of Pits Before Him and Of Sands Behind; X. The Poet as
Modernist. In the "Preface" Coxe says: "The limitations
in education, upbringing, taste and whatever that we note
in the man and his work simply describe that man and that
work, or one aspect of them; they do not explain nor present an alternative. I hope this book may help to define an
approach to that poetry, making it more accessible."

449 _____. "Essays on Poet Robinson Cover a Wide Spectrum of
Opinions." The Boston Globe, January 26, 1970. P. 13.
Review of collection edited by Ellsworth Barnard.

450 CRANE, Milton. "Creators of 'Walden' and 'Tristram.'" Saturday Review of Literature, 31 (November 13, 1948), 12-13.
Review of biography by Emery Neff. The biography of
Robinson presents a profound and sensitive understanding
of one of America's most extraordinary poets. It was at
once Robinson's misfortune, and his glory to have come to
maturity in a barren era for poetry. His generation produced only one other poet, Robert Frost, of the first rank.

Virtually self-trained, he began almost without warning and
without volition to write poetry of hard brilliance and deceptive simplicity--and paid for his devotion with a life of poverty, relieved by occasional gifts from patrons and interrupted by exhausting labor at jobs unsuited to him. Mr.
Neff has achieved rare success in blending three distinct
elements in his book: a biography of Robinson, a critical
account of Robinson's poetry and thought, and a literary
history of the reception of Robinson's work, both here and
abroad.

451  CRAWFORD, John. "Success and Failure in the Poetry of Ed-
     win Arlington Robinson." Rendezvous, 5 (Spring, 1970),
     27-29. Robinson's poetry reveals that his interest lay in
     the failures and misfortunes of life.... He accepts failure
     as an experience which is unavoidable; he insists that tri-
     umph is temporal and final defeat inevitable. The conviction
     that success is followed by failure appears so frequently in
     his poetry that it becomes a common theme in the longer
     poems and a common expression in the shorter ones. How-
     ever, one should not conclude that Robinson finds nothing
     worthwhile. Dismay will do no good; one should accept life
     as it is failures and all....

452  CROWDER, Richard H. "Three Studies of Edwin Arlington Rob-
     inson: His Male Character, His Emergence, and His Con-
     temporaneous Reputation." Ph.D. diss., State University
     of Iowa, 1945.

453  _____. "'Here Are the Men': Edwin Arlington Robinson's
     Male Character Types." New England Quarterly, 18 (Sep-
     tember, 1945), 346-367. Reprinted in Cary, ed. (1969),
     pp. 147-163. Well-documented study of the subject, both
     from primary and secondary sources. Critics have agreed
     that Robinson's method in general is to seize upon a situa-
     tion, usually at its most telling moment, and to subject to
     minute examination the characters therein enmeshed. From
     first to last, the number of his portrait studies is large
     enough to satisfy a very exacting scientist. This study
     proposes to look at characters as representatives of specific
     psychic attitudes toward life. These attitudes are based on
     the classification by Eduard Spranger, the German psychol-
     ogist, who gives six divisions: the theoretic, economic,
     aesthetic, social, political, and religious. To this may be
     added the sensual man.

454  _____. "'An Old Story.'" Explicator, 4 (December, 1945),
     item 22. The obscurity of the second quatrain disappears if
     we interpret the stanza backwards, as in the following: (4)
     a critic praised Robinson, (3) the poet was envious because
     the critic was praised and not the poet, (2) the critic showed

the poet that he was suffering from jealousy, (1) the poet
is doubly chagrined, by the jealousy itself and by the clarity of the critic in proving that it was jealousy (or envy)
and not a righteous anger.  The conclusion is that in praising the critic's remarks, the readers were naturally support-
ing and commending the poet.

455 _____.  "The Emergence of Edwin Arlington Robinson."  South
Atlantic Quarterly, 45 (January, 1946), 89-98.  Begins with
the status of American poetry when Robinson appeared on
the scene, attracting little notice and seemingly lost in the
vast mediocrity of the period.  Critical opinion was usually
grounded in what the critics were accustomed to find in the
poetry of the time.  It was not until 1912 that Robinson began to emerge as a major American poet, thanks largely to
the so-called "Little Renaissance" fostered by Poetry:  A
Magazine of Verse and the efforts of Harriet Monroe.  Robinson's first highly acclaimed volume was The Man Against
the Sky (1916).

456 _____.  "Edwin Arlington Robinson's Craftsmanship:  Opinions of Contemporary Poets."  Modern Language Notes, 61
(January, 1946), 1-14.  Article is a well-documented survey
of criticism from 1916 to 1937.  Among the poets referred
to are Amy Lowell, Harriet Monroe, Robert Frost, Allan
Tate, Babette Deutsch, etc.  In conclusion, it should be
pointed out that most of the poets missed the excellence of
Robinson's verse.  They complained of the paucity of concrete imagery in his poems; they regretted the lack of mu-
sicality, the coldness of diction.  They found fault with
Robinson's obscurity.  In short they were commenting more
upon their own concepts of poetry than that which was contained in Robinson.

457 _____.  "'The Sheaves.'"  Explicator, 4 (March, 1946), item
38.  During the summer wheat appears to be a permanent
part of nature, its mind being manifest in its "yielding to
the change assigned."  It appears to be a part of a transcendental concept of all-inclusive mind, perhaps that defies
analysis.  Yet the wheat is harvested for a price.  The
last two lines are ironic, for convention forbids our associ-
ating material gain with poetic "girl with golden hair."

458 _____.  "'For a Dead Lady.'"  Explicator, 5 (December,
1946), item 19.  It has been thought that the poem was
written to Robinson's mother, but this seems unlikely since
the woman in the poem is seen as a "flirt."  Flirtation does
not concern itself with children.  On the other hand, Robinson did go unnamed for the first six months of his life,
and he nearly always felt unwanted in the circle of his family.  "The laugh that love could not forgive ..." may be a

line of quiet resentment at being something of an outsider.

459 **_____** . "Edwin Arlington Robinson's Camelot." <u>College
English</u>, 9 (November, 1947), 72-79. Reviews the scholarship concerning Robinson's three "Camelot" poems, and
thinks it is time to re-consider the three problems posed
by each of the poems, not in a chronological order, but
observing them as a group. Article concludes with a good
bibliography of articles on these three poems, but the article does not add any new conclusions of its own.

460 **_____** . "'Luke Havergal.'" <u>Explicator</u>, 7 (November, 1948),
item 15. Supports the theory that the poem is related to
the fad for melancholia, private symbol, fascination with
suicide and decay then current in France and England at
the time of its composition. If all this is true it is difficult
to agree with a more ingenious interpretation offered by
Mathilde Parlett in June, 1945.

461 **_____** . "Edwin Arlington Robinson's Symphony: <u>The Man
Who Died Twice</u>." <u>College English</u>, 11 (December, 1949),
141-144. In addition to being known through the best of
his short poems, college students should be introduced to
the long narrative, and <u>The Man Who Died Twice</u> is perhaps
the most excellent example of this. Several critics have
rated it the best or among the best of Robinson's long narratives. Various qualities would make it of interest to students: it is short enough to let the structure be compre-
hended without confusion, and yet not so short that the
reader is unable to get the feel of body in it. There is
also ample room for the development of a moral theme. The
poem divides itself into an introduction and conclusion and
four main parts, each of which is dominated by a certain
definable mood.

462 **_____** . "Robinson's 'The Field of Glory.'" <u>Explicator</u>, 8
(February, 1950), item 31. There is no evidence to suppose
that Robinson intended this to be a portrait of the son of
Jacob and Leah, although on one occasion the poet says that
Levi "is unheroic, virtually witless, and totally miscast--a
misfit in a materialistic world." he says there are many men
like him in the world. The poem seems to be a part of
Robinson's never-ending criticism of materialism. He is saying once again that if this materialistic life on earth is all
the story, we had better beget no more children, indeed
commit suicide. The first five stanzas recount the incident
in which Levi cannot go to war and be a hero, but must
stay at home and support his mother. The mother is the
instrument by which he loses his faith, becomes unloved,
forgotten, and rejected as useless.

463 _____. "'The Man Against the Sky.'" College English, 14
(February, 1953), 269-276. Is a detailed analysis of the
poem by outlining the general play, examining the development of ideas, and facing down the stubbornly obscure passages, and trying to see what the poem really says, how
well it says it, and how important are the things said....
Though the poem is mostly in negative, or at any rate in
questioning form, Robinson does indicate some tenets of a
positive creed: Man can live a meaningful life, at his own
level of achievement and belief. The general inconclusive-
ness is, however, the meaning of the poem, the principal
dilemma of the twentieth-century. Its questioning structure
is the structure of our day. Its discursiveness is born of
the faith that man is unwilling to pretend to total security
in the deceptive exactitudes of science.

464 _____. "Edwin Arlington Robinson." Modern Language
Notes, 70 (November, 1955), 537-539. Review of biography
by Edwin S. Fussell. This work traces the complex influences which Robinson's reading had on his poetry. From
all available sources he determines what reading interested
Robinson and then examines the poetry to discover how
Robinson was indebted to that reading. A concluding chapter contends that Robinson and Eliot, though not in sympathy, both felt the necessity of relating their work to their
literary heritage ... the book is quite readable. It is built
on often penetrating insight and proffers a rich addition to
our knowledge of Robinson.

465 _____. "Edwin Arlington Robinson and the Human Condition." Lecture delivered on October 26, 1959, under the
auspices of The Gertrude Clarke Whittall Poetry and Literature Fund, in Washington, D.C., at the Library of Congress. Content is essentially the same as 1961 article listed
below.

466 _____. "Robinson's Talifer: The Figurative Texture."
Boston University Studies in English, 4 (Winter, 1960),
214-247. When this poem was published the critics feared
for the poet's future reputation and for the critics themselves
if they held Talifer up blindly as typical of Robinson's best.
The poem did not receive good reviews, but may be a good
deal better than was first assumed. Length and simplicity
surely cannot be held against a poem, and the judgment of
dullness is often a matter of personal taste. For some readers Talifer shows within the framework of realism symbols
and recurrent metaphors which give the poem a thicker
texture, lift the characterization above the banal, and contribute to an expansiveness which permits exercise of what
is called the poet's ironic humor. What the critics have not
done is observe the revealing allegorical link between the

names of the characters and their functions, the relationship of the times of year to the plot, and especially, the
prevalence and import of certain recurring images.

467 _____. "Edwin Arlington Robinson and the Meaning of Life."
Chicago Review, 15 (Summer, 1961), 5-17. To link Robinson with modern-day Existentialists is to make a dangerous
leap. He rightly regarded himself as poet, not philosopher,
and he would have turned away in disgust at the suggestion
that he was a follower of any dialectical system, but it must
be made clear at the outset that at the center of Existentialism is individuality, unwillingness to subscribe to any system and an avowal that a set creed of any sort is inadequate
and stultifying. A man must "follow his own light." At any
rate, a case can be made for relating much of Robinson's
poetry to the ideas by which the so-called Existentialists try
to explain and maybe comfort man. That the poet may never
have even heard the word existentialism and yet centered
his work in many instances about that point of view would
give substantial support to the validity of these more sys-
tematic thinkers.

468 _____. "Redemption for the Man of Iron." Personalist, 43
(January, 1962), 46-56. Article is a discussion of Talifer,
which appeared two years before Robinson's death. It is
based on a simple plot: a man betrothed to a fine girl
breaks off the engagement and marries another young woman
who disappoints him. Through the intervention of a friend,
the man is freed and finally is happily married to the first
girl. It is a pattern which Robinson used many times--
alienation, suffering, and recovery. In other characters
the theme of born again is illustrated, unlike those who are
permanently lost. Talifer, whose name means "worker of
iron" is a demonstration of the eternally haunting problem
of error, consequence, and recovery.

469 _____. "Edwin Arlington Robinson and the Garden of Eden."
Colby Library Quarterly, 7 (December, 1967), 527-535.
Robinson was basically a romantic poet, though with important reservations. One of his pervading themes is mutabil-
ity, colored by intuitional idealism. In communicating this
concept, he used the Eden myth, whether directly from the
Bible or through Milton.... Much can be done to show this
myth at work. A program for study may be suggested:
Miltonic influence; use of characters, symbols, and situations
of the Bible story; and the poet's additions and final position.

470 _____. "Robinson's Reputation: Six Observations." Colby
Library Quarterly, 8 (March, 1969), 220-238. Article is a
survey arranged in six parts as follows: (1) Robinson's
popularity according to the sale of his books, which seems

to have peaked around 1927. (2) A thin but steady stream
of doctoral dissertations has been flowing from the univer-
sities. (3) Comments on Robinson by fellow poets. (4)
Recognition abroad, and particularly in England. (5) Books
devoted entirely to Robinson, before 1936 were scarce; has
not done too well since then. (6) In the periodicals of the
last thirty years, there has not been an oversupply of Robinson essays, but there is some slight indication that Robinson may come into a "revival."

471 _____. "Robinson's Tristram and the American Reviewers."
Colby Library Quarterly, 16 (June, 1980), 123-132. Is an
excellent review of the sales records of Tristram, which was
probably the all-time poetic best-seller. Certainly it sold
more than any other book by Robinson. Article is also a
summary study of reviews of this work: a record of 86
American reviews, four reviews in England, one two-part
review in France by Charles Cestré. "This paper is based
on 39 American reviews from Savannah to Seattle, Chicago
to Dallas, Boston and New York to San Francisco." Article
concludes with a good bibliography of the reviews. Conclusion is that most of the reviews were awash with adulation. Labels moved from the noblest long love poem in
American literature to the equal of any other narrative poem
in English. Some critics were moderate in their praise and
cautioned readers to enjoy the poem and let time and events
award a final ranking.

472 CROWLEY, John W. E. "Edwin Arlington Robinson and Henry
Cabot Lodge." New England Quarterly, 43 (March, 1970),
115-124. The relationship of Theodore Roosevelt on the career of Robinson is well known, yet the friend of Roosevelt,
Henry Cabot Lodge, has never been studied in relation to
the poet. The most important material in this influence is
the Robinson-Lodge correspondence, which dates from 1909
until Lodge's death in 1924. These letters reveal that the
two men were devoted to each other's work. Robinson came
to cherish Lodge's good opinion and came to regard him as
a friend as well as a patron. What may be surprising is
Lodge's recognition of Robinson's talent. Because of Lodge's
distinguished career in politics, his parallel success as a
man of letters has been obscured. The Lodge-Robinson relationship grew in part from mutual psychological dependency.
In light of his son's failure (refers to George Cabot Lodge,
who died in 1909 at a very young age) to attain popular
success as a poet, Lodge understood Robinson's need for
sympathy and encouragement. In turn, Robinson sustained
Lodge's hopes for the eventual recognition of his son's poetry.

473 CUNNINGHAM, J. V. "Edwin Arlington Robinson: A Brief

Biography." Denver University Quarterly, 3 (Spring,
1968), 28-31. Reprinted in The Collected Essays of J. V.
Cunningham. Chicago: Swallow Press, 1971. Pp. 375-378.
Also reprinted Atlantic Brief Lives, ed. Louis Kronenberger
and Emily M. Beck. Boston: Atlantic Monthly Press, 1971.
Pp. 646-647. Toward the end of his life he concluded: "As
lives go, my own life would be called a rather fortunate one."
Most commentators have not thought so, but it seems true.
He died of cancer at sixty-five.... He was decent, reticent, likable, and contrary--he himself called it selfish. He
was not going to work for a living. He would do nothing
but write poetry, except at times prose fiction or drama for
their economic potentialities. But in this he failed; prose
was not his language. And unsuccessful prose he ultimately
transmuted to poetry.

474 DALY, James. "The Inextinguishable God." Poetry, 27 (October, 1925), 40-44. Review of Dionysus in Doubt. Two
poems in this collection are based on the human triangle, a
theme that Robinson always found fascinating. In both he
proves again his power of deft characterization and psychological insight. In the sonnets wisdom pulses. Some of
them are tragic, some cryptically ironic, some dramatic; but
there is beauty in all of them. As for the two long poems
featuring Dionysus, they are uninspired, laborious social
tracts in iambic pentameter. Nowhere does it rise to the
level of poetry. The sincerity of Dionysus in Doubt and
the high courage of its intention, the acuteness of its perceptions are admirable, but for all its profundity of motive,
never quite comes alive.

475 DANIELS, Mabel. "Robinson's Interest in Music." Portland
Sunday Telegram (Maine), April 21, 1935. Also published
in New York Times, April 21, 1935. Reprinted in Mark
Twain Quarterly, 2 (Spring, 1938), 15, 24. The great
poet's love for music was only second to his love for poetry.
Wherever he might have been, if any music was to be performed, he was the first to take his seat among the listeners. Invariably he chose a high-backed rocking chair, and
leaning his elbow on the broad arm, and shading his eyes
with one hand, sat silent and absorbed and was the last to
leave.... Of classical composers Brahms, Wagner, and Verdi
were his favorites. A Brahms symphony would pull him away
from anything, but for the modern school he had little use.
He never tired of commenting on the extraordinary genius
of Wagner, and greatly admired MacDowell.

476 _____. "Edwin Arlington Robinson: A Musical Memoir."
Radcliffe Quarterly, 46 (November, 1962), 5-11. Reprinted
in Colby Library Quarterly, 6 (June, 1963), 219-233. Article is an informal account of the author's association with

Robinson on musical grounds. She first met Robinson in
1914 at a Festival of Music at the MacDowell Colony, and
knew him all the way to near his death in 1935. The author
says: "The longer I knew Robinson, the more apparent it
became that he had a passionate love for music second only
to his love for poetry. He confessed in his shy way that
he had played the clarinet in his youth, but aside from this
he must have had an inherent love of the art. Whenever
good music was to be performed, he was the first to take
his seat among the listeners, the last to leave."

477  DAUNER, Margaret Louise. "Avon and Cavender: Two Chil-
     dren of the Night." American Literature, 14 (March, 1942),
     55-65. Throughout his work Robinson uses certain symbols,
     or characteristic images, among which is the image of the
     Light, with its opposite image, the Night. These images
     appear in the earliest poems and in the latest. This article
     analyzes and describes two of the most genuine "children of
     the night"--Avon (Avon's Harvest), and Cavender (Caven-
     der's House), both late poems. These two men are creatures
     of the Night of ignorance, passion, overgrown pride. Both
     are blind dwellers in a world more basically moral than their
     sealed vision may discern.

478  _____. "Vox Clamantis: Edwin Arlington Robinson as a
     Critic of American Democracy." New England Quarterly, 15
     (September, 1942), 401-426. Much of his poetry depicts the
     varied tragedy attendant upon our mortal and personal er-
     rors. But some of it, concerning not personalities but soci-
     eties, forecasts a world "blown to pieces," analyzes a coun-
     try of "short-sighted Sampsons," warns that definitely "it
     can happen here." The predictions of a poet, the predica-
     tions of history--a few years lie between. Robinson may
     come to be considered the greatest moralistic voice of his
     poetic generation. He looks beyond the chaos which he so
     vividly anticipates, to an indictment of materialism and
     equalitarianism as seeds of social disorder--which must be
     eradicated if chaos is not to become infinite.

479  _____. "The Pernicious Rib: Edwin Arlington Robinson's
     Concept of the Feminine Character." American Literature,
     15 (May, 1943), 139-158. Reprinted in Cary, ed. (1969),
     pp. 117-133. The problem of feminine characterization and
     its implications is particularly interesting in Robinson's po-
     etry, both because of its biographical overtones and because
     of its importance in any attempt at adequate comprehension
     of his art. The tragic-quality prevails in the bulk of Rob-
     inson's narratives, and at least eight of the long poems are
     based on the relationships of men and women as basic motives
     for tragedy. From a study of these eight works (Merlin,
     Lancelot, Tristram, Cavender's House, Roman Bartholow,

Matthias at the Door, Talifer, and King Jasper), emerges
the composite figure, Woman. She knows man's nature and
can beguile him, she is sensitive to the inevitably cruel
Fate of love, she is often futile, hopeless, cynical.

480 _____. "Studies in Edwin Arlington Robinson." Ph.D. diss.,
State University of Iowa, 1944.

481 _____. "Edwin Arlington Robinson and His Manuscripts."
Modern Language Quarterly, 6 (September, 1945), 361–362.
This is not a scholarly book. Yet it is consistently, if ob-
liquely, revelatory of the enigmatic poet, hence valuable for
the Robinson specialist, as well as for the general reader.
Based on many years of contact with Robinson, it does provide leads which are more than usually suggestive. It is a
welcome and authoritative addition to Robinsoniana. Its very
modesty is no small part of its charm, and certainly no fair
indication of its value.

482 _____. "Edwin Arlington Robinson." American Literature,
19 (May, 1947), 189–191. Comment on biography by Yvor
Winters. Its virtues lie in many complex details, its limitations in what appear to be some basic misconceptions and
negligences. It is a clever technical analysis of the texture
and structure of Robinson's poetry, from the short lyrics
to the long narratives. The plan is sound, the intention
"creative rather than academic." The difficulty is that
"creativity" has become so internal, so self-centered, not
to say self-righteous, that the book bristles with debatable
points.

483 _____. "Edwin Arlington Robinson." New England Quarterly, 20 (September, 1947), 427–428. Comment on biography
by Yvor Winters. One wonders why Mr. Winters chose to
operate upon a poet whose temperament and intention are so
disparate from his own. Every work of art demands its own
critical technique; the critic cannot justly apply a ready-
made, authoritarian set of standards to any work of art.
Winters is so preoccupied with his dissection of the long
narrative poems, that he has yet to discover the basic implications of the poems.... Here is a great flashing of razor-
edged critical blades. But this work will probably not either
materially increase Robinson's intelligibility to older readers,
or induce much new reading.

484 _____. "Review of Untriangulated Stars." American Literature, 20 (March, 1948), 78–80. The editor has allowed Robinson to speak largely for himself. In a brief introduction,
the editor has drawn together main lines of Robinson's
thought, cogently emphasizing qualities rather than external
facts, although facts are also present. The correspondence

is arranged according to the pre-Harvard years, the two
years at Harvard, the four following years in Gardiner,
and the years up to 1905 when Robinson was in New York
City.... A comprehensive first-person portrait of the man
emerges, and for a poet for whom we have far too scanty
a knowledge, this is a valuable addition.

485 _____. "Review of Untriangulated Stars...." New England
Quarterly, 21 (March, 1948), 111-114. The letters are not
only a psychograph of Robinson, the poet. They are also
another significant testimonial to the Artist in America, as
they suggest antiphonally Robinson's firm refusal to compromise with the literary fashions of the period, and his
resultant long probation. Thus, they are a symbolic unit,
not only for Robinson scholars and enthusiasts, but for anyone concerned with the creative effort in a materialistic culture. These letters are addressed to Harry de Forest
Smith, 1890-1905.

486 _____. "Edwin Arlington Robinson: A Biography by Emery
Neff." New England Quarterly, 22 (March, 1949), 111-113.
Theoretically we do not question the determined and scrupulous effort to comment upon early every poem that Robinson
wrote. But in this popular-sized volume, is obviously impossible. The result is a catalogue-like listing of innumerable poems, with a line, or a sentence or two of commentary,
unfortunately reminiscent of a student's "cram-book." This
new work leans heavily upon Hagedorn's biography, as it
leans upon the assistance of Robinson's friends and colleagues, who remain devoted to his memory. For the reader
the result now is too often a feeling of "old stuff": one has
encountered much of this before.

487 _____. "Two Robinson Revisions: 'Mr. Flood's Party,' and
'The Dark Hills.'" Colby Library Quarterly, 8 (June, 1969),
309-316. Revisions in Robinson are scarce, usually consisting of omitting a line or two or a short group of lines.
When he does make changes, he moves toward greater logical and metaphorical unity, a more sensuous and flexible
rhythmic movement, and greater universality. In a character portrayal, details tend to become more tightly integrated,
to create a stronger confirmation of the character.... Two
poems which reveal some of these gain are those above,
which in their final forms are regarded as among Robinson's
most expert utterances.
    Article continues with a point by point comparison of the
early and final versions of the two poems.

488 DAVENPORT, William H. "Edwin Arlington Robinson." The
Personalist, 34 (April, 1953), 206. Review of biography by
Ellsworth Barnard. The number of people equipped and

disposed to approach this new study of Robinson must be
small indeed.  Barnard makes little effort to win over his
small potential by popularizing his material....  The author
is almost too thorough in documentation.  It is written with
restraint and sober appraisal, leaving little to quibble about.

489  DAVIDSON, Levette J.  "Lazarus in Modern Literature."  Eng-
       lish Journal (College edition), 18 (June, 1929), 462-463.
       Robinson's poem first appeared in The Three Taverns (1920).
       His interpretation of the experience of Lazarus is in harmony
       with much modern thinking.  Many calmly accept the testi-
       mony of the senses or even disregard the dissolution of the
       body in the grave, in order to conjure with the central
       problem--what lies beyond?  Upon one's answer depends
       one's philosophy.  Robinson, the poet, finds no solution
       unless it be in the mysterious figure of the Master, who
       looked "as if he knew."

490  DAVIS, Charles T.  "The Poetic Drama of Moody, Robinson,
       Torrence, and MacKaye, 1894-1909."  Ph.D. diss., New
       York University, 1951.

491  _____, ed.  Selected Early Poems and Letters of E. A. Rob-
       inson.  New York:  Holt, Rinehart, and Winston, 1960.
       Rinehart edition.  Consists of 238 pages, mostly poetry;
       the letters are to Harry de Forest Smith.  From the Intro-
       duction, the editor says:  "Far too little has been written
       of Robinson's early achievement as a poet....  The odd
       fact about Robinson is that he began, in a sense, as a
       mature poet, almost immediately conscious of his artistic
       goals and aware of his own powers and weaknesses.  The
       Robinson of 1901 was a mature poet who had broken away
       completely from the intellectual standards of his contempo-
       raries.  Recognition came slowly, but he was shortly known
       as a great poet of the new century."

492  _____.  "Image Patterns in the Poetry of Edwin Arlington
       Robinson."  College English, 22 (March, 1961), 380-386.
       Reprinted in Cary, ed. (1969), pp. 191-199.  Most critical
       comment on Robinson fails finally to do justice to Robinson's
       poetic practice, the discussion often restricted to the light
       and dark figures of his verse.  The approach to Robinson's
       imagery has been too rigid, often philosophical rather than
       literary.  From the beginning Robinson has relied heavily
       upon a few carefully chosen figures, but these have great
       importance because they give concrete status to the abstract
       variables of his verse....  One of Robinson's important
       claims to being a modern poet rests upon his imagery.  What
       is modern is his emphasis, the tendency to organize the ref-
       erences into systems, the ability to use the image at depth,
       with a sense of discrimination and nuance.

493 _____. "Robinson's Road to Camelot," in Barnard, ed.
(1969), pp. 88-105. Robinson had his reasons for selecting
Merlin, Lancelot, and Tristram as characters and rejecting
Galahad, out of his affection for the imperfect man, figures
who can achieve only partial or temporary success in a hos-
tile or indifferent world. There was nothing in Robinson's
experience to sustain a perfect Galahad who achieved a direct and total vision of the mysterious vessel of God--the
Holy Grail.... Much source study has been expended on
trying to establish influences on Robinson's Arthurian
works, most of it without value. He, of course, knew the
basic literature--Malory, Tennyson--but mostly the creations
are his own. Robinson's Arthurian poems are an extension
of his earlier work. Man is shackled by the weakness of
his own nature, by selfishness, indifference and stupidity,
limitations that create a twilight world more akin to death
than life....

494 _____. "Edwin Arlington Robinson: A Poetry of the Act."
English Language Notes, 6 (March, 1969), 226-228. Review
of work by W. R. Robinson. This work is a study of the
philosophical context of Robinson's poems, and as such it
fills a gap in the scholarship of this poet and has unques-
tioned value. The approach is a hard one to deal with and
the author does not quite succeed, although his book is far
more valid than the one by Estelle Kaplan in 1940. There
are some specific mistakes in scholarship, yet the main fault
lies in the fact that the poems are not adequately discussed.

495 _____. "Edwin Arlington Robinson." American Literature,
42 (January, 1971), 588-590. Article is a review of two
books about Robinson, by Louis Coxe and Hoyt C. Franchere. An approach to Robinson is not easy to come by, as
these two studies demonstrate. it is no accident that the
best criticism of Robinson's work is to be found in specialized limited studies. In this instance Coxe's book does little
to advance the Yvor Winters's critique of Robinson, and the
Franchere work, in attempting to classify Robinson's poems
by theme, is even less satisfying.

496 DAVIS, William V. "'Enduring to the End': Edwin Arlington
Robinson's 'Mr. Flood's Party.'" Colby Library Quarterly,
12 (June, 1976), 50-51. Article is a commentary on the allusion to "Roland" in the third stanza, and the suggestion
that perhaps this is not the single most important allusion
in the poem. He is referring to the twice mentioned "Auld
Lang Syne" and "enduring to the end." The poem is exceedingly complex with those intimate expressions of the
bereavement and the loneliness of old age. Among Robinson's contributions to this thematic development, none is
more graphic, more fully realized than "Mr. Flood's Party."

497  DECHERT, Peter. "Edwin Arlington Robinson and Alanson
     Tucker Schumann: A Study in Influences." Ph.D. diss.,
     University of Pennsylvania, 1955. DA, 15 (1955), 822-823.
     The subject of this study is one that is not generally known.
     It is based on the existence of a large quantity of manuscript
     poetry by Schumann, which is now in the Gardiner Public
     Library. Robinson wrote of his indebtedness to Schumann,
     and thus a study of Schumann's techniques, attitudes, and
     subjects was prepared and compared to similar aspects of
     the early work of Robinson. The results were informative:
     Robinson adopted many of Schumann's techniques in the
     sonnet; he acquired a view of what and who the poet should
     be; and he was influenced philosophically.

498  _____. "'He Shouts to See Them Scamper So': Edwin Ar-
     lington Robinson and the French Forms." Colby Library
     Quarterly, 8 (September, 1969), 386-398. Reprinted in
     Cary, ed. (1969), 335-345. Reviews what several biograph-
     ers have said about Robinson and the French forms. His
     handling of the forms was competent enough, but the matur-
     ing Robinson found the jingle-effects of French form struc-
     ture to be at cross-purposes with the increasing seriousness
     of what he had to say.... From his experiences with the
     French forms and from his other early practice, Robinson
     had developed and honed the ability to express himself eas-
     ily and to the point in structured verse. The shape of his
     early verse was no longer congruent with the shape of his
     thoughts.

499  DERLETH, August. "Old Voices and New." Voices: A Journal
     of Poetry, No. 177 (January-April, 1962), 62. Review of
     Selected Early Poems and Letters.

500  DEUTSCH, Babette. "A Sophisticated Mystic." Reedy's Mirror,
     26 (March 22, 1918), 166-167.

501  _____. "A New Light on Lancelot." Poetry, 16 (July, 1920),
     217-219. One of the chief distinctions of Robinson is his
     mingling of two strains: a Puritan austerity, and a discern-
     ing tenderness. It is perhaps natural that at a time when
     men grope for refuge from a broken world, Robinson should
     find his in a retreat to the dim Arthurian fields. But it is
     equally characteristic that his retreat has in it no shadow
     of surrender. He recreates the disillusion, the desolation,
     and the pain of our own period in the tragedy of this half-
     forgotten legend. He dramatizes the griefs of the medieval
     characters in such a way as to make them our contempo-
     raries, and he presents their time as an age wherein men
     wronged each other and helplessly hurt each other in ways
     no different from our own.

502 _____. "A Poet's House of Life: Cavender's House."
Ibid., 6 (April 21, 1929), 1-2. His poem not only exhibits
Robinson the poet, with his shrewd drawing of men and
women, his power to evoke atmosphere, his gift of music,
but also Robinson the man, with his dry humor, his essential seriousness, his philosophy of resigned if sorrowful agnosticism.

503 _____. "With No Less Wisdom: Matthias at the Door."
Ibid., 8 (October 4, 1931), 7. His later work seems, by
comparison with the earlier, not rich and deep and resonant
enough. it is evident that this poem adds practically nothing
to what Robinson has said equally well elsewhere. But wisdom is not less wisdom for not being novel, and to have expressed it as persuasively as he has done here is no small
thing.

504 _____. "Talifer: A Jamesian Novel in Verse." Ibid., 10
(October 8, 1933), 8. So removed are the persons of this
narrative from the modern mind that their history affords a
total escape from the present as does the most placid of
Henry James' fictions. The narrative runs smoothly and
there is enough suspense, but the reader is left with no
reason ever to return to it. What one misses chiefly in this
work is Robinson's fine psychological insight....

505 _____. "The Hands of Esau: A Review of Nicodemus."
New Republic, 72 (October 5, 1932), 213-214. Neither in
form nor in matter has Robinson made a departure from the
work upon which his reputation is established. This is of
no great moment, but one could wish that in traveling the
old road he had discovered more of the old beauties. Too
many of these poems are inferior to his best; and of poets
who have wrought finely one is continually asking their
best.

506 _____. This Modern Poetry. New York: W. W. Norton,
1935. Robinson, pp. 103-107. Much of the comment is directed toward a comparison of Robinson with Hardy, both
of whom are "bearers of tradition." Robinson's elaborate
fictions are but a more roundabout way of presenting the
forlorn characters of The Children of the Night, and of re-
iterating the melancholy wisdom which is there set down....
Robinson saw enough of starved, diseased, misshappen
lives to need a dose of stoic bitters ever so often, yet his
verse keeps recurring to some vague ultimate "Light." His
poetry dwells upon man's plight in a world where death is
the sole certainty and change the one enduring fact....

507 _____. Poetry in Our Time: A Critical Survey of Poetry in
the English Speaking World. New York: Holt, Rinehart,

& Winston, 1952. "Glove of a Neighborhood," pp. 55–78.
Revised edition, 1963, pp. 59–84. He deserves consideration
because his best work is finely representative of traditional
poetry, because in a few pieces he evoked as no poet had
previously, a landscape with figures familiar to his fellow
Americans.... Robinson was incapable of the savage realism he praised though he reiterated the need to look truth
in the face. It is honest, serious work, and represents
"the application of ideas to life."

508 D'EVELYN, C. "Review of Tristram." Springfield Republican,
    August 7, 1927. P. 7ff. It is a bold thing to retell a
    story so rich already in notable tellings. A well-known
    theme must be handled masterfully or not at all. Robinson
    has not let the reader down. He has proved equal to the
    test imposed by so famous a theme. He has restated its
    essential values, leaving the story romantic still, but roman-
    tic in terms intelligible to the present.

509 DICKEY, James. "Edwin Arlington Robinson: The Many
    Truths," from the Introduction to Selected Poems of Edwin
    Arlington Robinson, edited by Morton D. Zabel. New York:
    Macmillan, 1965. Reprinted in Murphy, ed. (1970), pp.
    77–94. Also reprinted in Modern American Poetry: Essays
    in Criticism, edited by Guy Owen. Delano, Fla.: Everett/
    Edwards, 1972. Pp. 1–20. It is curious and wonderful that
    this scholarly, intelligent, childlike, tormented New England
    stoic, always hungry for the nameless, always putting in the
    reader's mouth "some word that hurts your tongue," useless
    for anything but his art, protected by hardier friends all
    his life, but enormously courageous and utterly dedicated
    should have brought off what in its quiet, searching, lab-
    orious way is one of the most remarkable accomplishments
    of modern poetry. Robinson has done what good poets have
    always done: he has forced us to re-examine and finally to
    re-define what poetry is--and so has enabled poetry itself
    to include more, to be more, than it was before he wrote.

510 _____. Babel to Byzantium: Poets and Poetry Now. New
    York: Farrar, Straus, & Giroux, 1968. Robinson, pp.
    209-230. Reprinted New York: Octagon Books, 1973.
    Reprints essay first published in 1965 as "Introduction"
    to Selected Poems ... edited by Morton D. Zabel.

511 _____. "The Poet of Secret Lives and Misspent Opportun-
    ities." New York Times Book Review, May 18, 1969. Pp.
    1, 10. Review of biography by Louis O. Coxe.

512 DOMINA, Lyle. "Fate, Tragedy, and Pessimism in Robinson's
    Merlin." Colby Library Quarterly, 8 (December, 1969),
    471-478. Reviews other criticism which has remarked on

Robinson's trilogy, including <u>Merlin</u>, and objects to the
conclusion that the three poems taken together make a statement on Fate, Tragedy, and Pessimism.  This article examines just the poem <u>Merlin</u> and undertakes to show that
the question of fate, the nature of Merlin's love affair with
Vivian and Merlin's spiritual defeat, and the whole question
of pessimism.  When one considers the complexity of Robinson's Arthurian poems, one is convinced that <u>Merlin</u> is
neither the most pessimistic nor the tragedy of falling away
from wisdom; the idea that Merlin ended in spiritual defeat
appears equally untenable.  Merlin finds a salvation which
transcends whatever there may be of personal failure in his
love affair with Vivian.

513  DONALDSON, Scott.  "The Alien Pity: A Study of Character
     in Edwin Arlington Robinson's Poetry."  <u>American Litera-</u>
     <u>ture</u>, 38 (May, 1966), 219-229.  Does not see Robinson as
     a "dramatic" poet, but rather as "a storyteller, a narrative
     rather than dramatic poet."  The stories are told by indi-
     rection, by inference, by suggestion.  Never in his best
     work does Robinson yield to the temptation of the omnisci-
     ent narrator and <u>tell</u> us what to think.  The sound and
     sense of the poetry gives us clues, but the author is not
     obtrusive.  The technique is the opposite of dramatic in
     that Robinson leaves as much to the reader as he possibly
     can....  At the end of each story, the reader derives an
     insight into character.  Often it is tenuous, delicate, and
     uncertain, principally because Robinson refuses to turn his
     poetry into paraphrase.

514  _____.  "The Book of Scattered Lives," in Barnard, ed.
     (1969), pp. 43-53.  Discusses <u>Town Down the River</u> which
     Robinson referred to as a book of <u>Scattered Lives</u>, dealing
     with a group of incomplete geniuses he met and drank with
     in New York City.  These friends, or ones like them, come
     flickering to life, with customary Robinson indirection in a
     group of poems centered around a saloon called Calverly's.
     They go no more to Calverly's, and four old companions
     who used to go there are now dead.  The situation offers
     limitless possibilities for bathos, but Robinson redeems with
     his craft what might have been merely sentimental reminis-
     cence.  So reticent in his own relationships, Robinson in-
     vested love and compassion in those characters who make
     up his book of scattered lives.

515  _____.  "Books: Amplification."  <u>Harper's Magazine</u>, 241
     (September, 1970), 9.  See article by Irving Howe.  Ob-
     jects to Howe's remark that the 1969 centennial of "Robinson
     passed without a murmur of public notice," and proceeds to
     list various activities and publications which occurred in
     that year.  Comments specifically on the collection of new

essays which were edited by Ellsworth Barnard. While it
may not have been a celebration admirers of Robinson might
have hoped for, it constitutes something on the poet's behalf.

516 _____. "Robinson and Music." Colby Library Quarterly,
     16 (June, 1980), 63-72. Robinson's appeal is to the ear
     rather than the eye. Not that he aims for or achieves the
     musicality of a Lanier or a Poe. His voice carried a sub-
     tler tune. And yet his poetry sounds. Refrains from na-
     ture and the music of the spheres serve throughout to em-
     body image and convey metaphor, to abet characterization
     and lend structure. In individual poems as in entire vol-
     umes, music was rarely far from Robinson's thoughts. He
     used melody, for example, to make personal, philosophical,
     and political comments.

517 DONOGHUE, Denis. Connoisseurs of Chaos: Ideas of Order
     in Modern American Poetry. New York: Macmillan, 1965.
     "Edwin Arlington Robinson, J. V. Cunningham, Robert
     Lowell," pp. 129-159. In Robinson's case there was a
     resolution of a kind, and it is to be found in the long
     poems. Indeed the difference Robinson's heroic narratives
     and the shorter poems, length apart, is that the legends
     offered him a release from the furies of reason and passion:
     sometimes a new dawn, sometimes an apocalyptic flame, of-
     ten a gleam, a Light. In the short poems, the poems of
     circumstance, there was often no way out. The Arthurian
     legends, halfway between time and eternity, gave him a
     visionary gleam that he could not find on earth and would
     not posit there.... He wanted to give his characters room
     to move, and he thought he could not do so in the modern
     poetic world....

518 DOWNING, David Claude. "The Poetry of Edwin Arlington
     Robinson: A Critical Re-appraisal." Ph.D. diss., Univer-
     sity of California (Los Angeles), 1977. DA, 38 (1978),
     6129A. His singular career provides a touchstone for un-
     derstanding the course of early twentieth-century poetry.
     In six chapters, the first two describe Robinson's relation
     to the "Genteel Tradition," and the so-called "poetic ren-
     aissance" of 1912. Chapter three discusses Robinson as a
     new England Poet, and Chapters four, five, and six examine
     the poet's psychological portraits, with a study of the prin-
     cipal sources from which he drew his poetry--traditional
     and classical materials, and perhaps above all the Bible.
     All of his works demonstrate Robinson's lifelong search for
     enduring values in an era of "dynamics and dollars."

519 DOYLE, John R. "The Shorter Poems of Edwin Arlington Rob-
     inson." Bulletin of the Citadel, 6 (1942), 3-18. Reprinted

in Cary, ed. (1969), pp. 105-116. What position Robinson
will take in American literature is difficult to say, but it
seems certain that he will hold a secure place among our
true poets.... Throughout his writing years he tackled
boldly the problems of the unlovely side of life, proclaiming
the unnoticed, pointing condemnation at the surface observation of most people. He attempted to make his language
the servant of his thought, and at its best it has more
density than that of most contemporaries. He tried to write
that which was of himself, his age, and the heritage of humanity.

520 DOYLE, Justin J. "The Poems of Edwin Arlington Robinson."
University of Rochester, 1927. M.A. thesis.

521 DRINKWATER, John. "Edwin Arlington Robinson." Yale Review, 11 (April, 1922), 467-476. Also in Fortnightly Review, 111 (April 1, 1922), 649-660. Reprinted in The Muse
in Council: Being Essays on Poets and Poetry. New York:
Houghton, Mifflin, 1924. Pp. 248-262. English publication
London: Sidgwick & Jackson, 1925. Pp. 186-201. Also
reprinted in A Book of Essays, edited by B. C. Williams.
New York: Houghton, Mifflin, 1926. Pp. 127-137. First
written on the occasion of Robinson's 50th birthday, it is
primarily a biographical character sketch. Does not make
a close analysis of the work in all its many kinds. Nor is
it ever very profitable to explain in detail what a poet is
writing about, since what he says can be said only in the
way that he says it. One can but point out his general
methods and note the tendencies of his moods. With his
tragic sense we find nearly always an ironic touch which
makes it not only moving but always interesting.

522 _____, Henry Seidel Canby, and William Rose Benét, eds.
Twentieth-Century Poetry. Cambridge, Mass.: Houghton,
Mifflin, 1929. Robinson, pp. 316-326. Prints a generous
selection from Robinson, including mostly well-known items.
Also, not so well-known, is "The Valley of the Shadow,"
from the volume The Three Taverns. Poems are preceded
with a brief introductory comment: "His idiom is strictly
his own.... He can pack the gist of long narrative, with
many implications, into a sonnet. He is a wizard craftsman
and a technician unsparing in self-criticism. Three times
he has won the Pulitzer Prize for poetry.

523 DU BOIS, Arthur E. "The Cosmic Humanist." Mark Twain
Quarterly, 2 (Spring, 1938), 11-13, 24. The cosmic humorist is a kind of ultimate role for the comedian to play. Few
have known enough.... It is a strange brotherhood in
which Robinson is found. Aware of inevitable disparities
between the permanent and the changing, the fated and the

willed, the apparent and the real, Robinson laughed cos-
mically. He saw continuously that to a humorist like Jonson
a Shakespeare must be fairly incomprehensible fiction.  In
other words, he laughed at the laugh-watchers, even himself.  Anticipating his own fate at the hands of critics, he
protested on his own behalf in "Nimmo" against the sensational misrepresentations of biographers.  Laughing even
with God and finding serenity, Robinson was the cosmic
humorist.

524  DUDLEY, Dorothy.  "Wires and Cross-Wires."  Poetry, 24
(May, 1924), 96-103.  Review of Roman Bartholow.  This
book has the cast of something it took a long time to make,
but it is hard to understand, and the reader is not likely
to grasp the logic or reason of its being the first time
through.  Roman Bartholow uses incident as framework for
a deliberate design of thought in as many dimensions.  The
poem is a cypher of human wires and cross-wires; a journey through thickets, without seeming to lose the way, to
the fringes of speculation.  The key might be this:  Nature
has ways, not reasons.  Knowledge knows no rules.  Life
at ease with the gross, the sentimental, the counterfeit,
seems content just to live.

525  DUFFY, Sister Mary Mauritius.  "Study of Some Phases of the
Poetry of Edwin Arlington Robinson."  State University of
Iowa, 1932.  M.A. thesis.

526  DUNBAR, Olivia Howard (Mrs. Ridgely Torrence).  A House
in Chicago.  Chicago:  University of Chicago Press, 1947.
Robinson, pp. 107-120 et passim.  A biography of Mrs.
William Vaughn Moody, the patroness of the arts.  After
the death of her husband she opened her house and heart
to poets, artists, sculptors, and musicians from every corner
of the earth....  Robinson did not visit Mrs. Moody in Chicago, but they did write letters, and a very warm friendship ensued.  Robinson promised to send something for the
magazine Poetry, but such contributions were rare.  One
of Mrs. Moody's last letters was to Robinson, in which she
commended his poem Tristram, hoping to read it in the near
future.

527  DUNCAN, Joseph E.  The Revival of Metaphysical Poetry:  The
History of a Style, 1800 to the Present.  Minneapolis:  University of Minnesota Press, 1959.  Robinson, passim.  Does
not feature Robinson who was not a metaphysical poet.

528  DUNN, N. E.  "Wreck and Yesterday:  The Meaning of Failure
in Lancelot."  Colby Library Quarterly, 9 (September, 1971),
349-356.  By dramatizing the causes of failure in the medieval ideal society of Arthur's Round Table, the poet intended

to reveal some of the reasons for failure in the modern
ideal: twentieth-century American democracy.... Time
bears one fruit, and that is change. The change time
brings to Arthur's kingdom is destruction, "a thing of
wreck and yesterday." Whether the change and the fall
of the old order is for the better is not the question. As
a realist, Robinson knew that even at their best the ideals
of man are flawed in their implementation and "we are not
all safe/ Until we are all dead." In the story of the wreck
of yesterday, however, he has shown the necessities of
today.

529    _____. "Riddling Leaves: Robinson's 'Luke Havergal.'"
       Colby Library Quarterly, 10 (March, 1973), 17-25. This
       is one of Robinson's earliest poems in the Symbolist mode,
       and as such it may not "mean" anything. The purpose of
       a Symbolist poem is essentially to create mood, music, and
       mystic feeling, as though by means of a disembodied voice.
       If there is, however, meaning, it must surely revolve
       around the leaf imagery, since this is the most insistent
       and organized pattern of the poem. This article explores
       the possibility that Robinson's poem is his version of Aeneas
       and the Sibyl of Vergil. Perhaps it would not do to insist
       too heavily on this interpretation, but it does seem plaus-
       ible.

530    DUPEE, Fred W. "The 'Long Animal': Review of Selected
       Letters." Nation, 150 (March 30, 1940), 427-428. Book
       has been compiled in a modest spirit and yet covers a wide
       expanse, from 1890 to a few days before his death in 1935.
       The letters reveal some of the shyness and loneliness that
       were the great specters of Robinson's personal life. In one
       letter Robinson writes: "my chief mission appears to be
       that of a very long animal who barks and snarls when he
       means to make all sorts of good-natured and affectionate
       noises."

531    DURLING, Dwight L. "A Critical Account of the Work of
       Robinson in the Light of Its Position in American Thought
       and American Literary History." Ph.D. diss., Queen's
       College (of New York City), 1949.

532    DWORSKY, Bess Raisel. "Attitudes of Edwin Arlington Robin-
       son and Certain Similar Ideas Expressed in His Poetry and
       the Poetry of Robert Browning." University of Minnesota
       (Minneapolis), M.A. thesis, 1932.

533    DYKES, Mattie M. "'Trying to Spell God': A Study of Edwin
       Arlington Robinson." Northwest Missouri State Teachers
       College Studies, 13 (June, 1949), 85-124. Long well-
       documented study of Robinson. The article begins with an

overview commentary on the poet's life and work. The
main purpose of the article, however, is built around the
passage in which Robinson said the world was a kind of
kindergarten in which bewildered infants are trying to
spell God with the wrong blocks. The young poet recognized his relationship to the bewildered children:  he must
help them find the right blocks. "To show how the poet
struggled to spell God for himself, how he tried to help
individuals in his art, and finally how he tried to help his
own nation learn to spell God is the purpose of this paper."

534  EBY, Cecil D., Jr.  "Edwin Arlington Robinson on Higher
Education."  Colby Library Quarterly, 5 (September,
1960), 163-164.  Article is based largely on an unpublished
letter of Robinson to Waitman Barbe, in April 1920.  This
letter was not known to Hermann Hagedorn in his biography
of Robinson.  The point of this letter is Robinson's expression that American colleges do not produce poets and novel-
ists.  "I believe in colleges," Robinson says, "but I doubt
if they have much to do with the genesis of literature, except in indirect ways."

535  ELAN, Geoffrey.  "Appreciation of Edwin Arlington Robinson."
Yankee (Dublin, N.H.), 34 (February, 1970), 175.  Review
of collection edited by Richard Cary.

536  ELDREDGE, Frances.  "A Study of the Poet as Agnostic with
Reference to Matthew Arnold, Conrad Aiken, Robinson
Jeffers, T. S. Eliot, and Edwin Arlington Robinson."
Tufts College, 1934.  M.A. thesis.

537  ELIAS, Robert H.  "Edwin Arlington Robinson."  American Literature, 27 (November, 1955), 437-438.  Review of biography by Edwin S. Fussell.  It is this author's intention
and achievement to show where Robinson began--what
literary traditions he apprehended, assimilated, and
contributed to.  His method is to investigate the nature of
Robinson's reading, evinced in poetic allusions and in direct
epistolary references, and to note passages, mainly in the
early poetry, in which Robinson is using or echoing the
work of some other writers....  The value of such a demonstration is insight into Robinson's orientation into the larger
historical perspective of poetry.  It is at this point that
Fussell leaves the reader unsatisfied:  he does not go into
an analysis of the significance of Robinson's literary influences.

538  ELLIS, Milton.  "Review-Comment on Two Books about Robinson."  New England Quarterly, 10 (Autumn, 1937), 806-807.
These two works--Next Door to a Poet by Rollo W. Brown;
and A Bibliography of Edwin Arlington Robinson by Charles

Beecher Hogan--are both significant additions to the slowly
growing body of critical literature dealing with the most important American poet, probably, since Whitman. The bibliography is substantial, workmanlike, and rather handsome,
written more for collectors than scholars. Most of the work
consists of primary source listings, and one section prints
five hitherto uncollected poems and ten pieces of prose by
Robinson.... In his short work Rollo Brown sketches as
much of Robinson's habits of work, his personal traits, his
active though quiet humor, his embarrassments and worries,
his whimsically tolerant foibles and prejudices, and infre-
quent glimpses into the personal history of his earlier and
harder years. Brown came to know Robinson when he lived
in a neighboring cabin at the MacDowell Colony.

539    _____. "Edwin Arlington Robinson and His Manuscripts."
New England Quarterly, 17 (June, 1944), 323-324. Review
of study by Esther Willard Bates. The little monograph,
attractively printed, is an interesting addition to the Colby
Monograph series; and cumulative footnotes call the reader's
attention to the fact that such items are now "in the Colby
Library." Miss Bates was Robinson's chief copyist, a position requiring unusual care in the deciphering of the poet's
difficult handwriting.

540    EMERSON, Dorothy. "Edwin Arlington Robinson: Looking
Back on Our First Contemporary Poet." Scholastic, 26
(October 12, 1935), 9-10.

541    EVANS, David Allan. "An Earned Tribute to a Fine Poet."
Minneapolis Tribune, April 12, 1970. P. 10-E. Review of
collection edited by Ellsworth Barnard.

542    EVANS, Nancy. "Edwin Arlington Robinson." Bookman, 75
(November, 1932), 675-681. Article is based upon conversations with Robinson, and consists mainly of a review of
Robinson's life and running comment on his work. The
essay is informal and friendly, but manages to avoid excessive sentiment and succeeds in creating a creditable portrait of the poet. The author thinks Robinson belies his
reputation of being aloof and unfriendly. She had gone to
talk with a poet, and found that she was talking to a man.

543    EWERS, Patricia O'Donnell. "Merlin, Lancelot, and Tristram:
Edwin Arlington Robinson's Arthurian Poems on Man's Dilemma." Loyola University (Chicago), 1966. Ph.D. diss.

544    FAIN, John Tyree and Thomas Daniel Young, eds. The Literary Correspondence of Donald Davidson and Allen Tate.
Athens: University of Georgia Press, 1974. Robinson, pp.
68 and 138. Robinson is referred to in a letter of May 21,

1925 from Allen to Donald, in which he says: "I was damn
sorry Ransom didn't get that prize; he was the only one
who actually deserved it. But the Committee could be safe
in giving it to Robinson and didn't have to exercise the
cortex in order to pick him out." Robinson won the Pulitzer Prize in 1925 for The Man Who Died Twice.

545  FAIRCHILD, Hoxie Neale. Religious Trends in English Poetry,
Vol. 5, 1880-1920: Gods of a Changing Poetry. New York:
Columbia University Press, 1962. "Realists," pp. 222-253;
pp. 238-243, Robinson. Fading from Robinson's mind,
Christianity leaves a faint afterglow of what admirers of
his wisdom like to call "idealism." It is not always easy to
distinguish between the glory-of-the-imperfect doctrine and
the decadent doctrine of salvation through damnation; but
although Robinson is tinged by the latter he is predominant-
ly loyal to the former. His strugglers have retained their
spiritual integrity against fearful odds; through the darkness of despair and shame they follow the inextinguishable
gleam. They are entitled to say, as Robinson says in his
poem "Credo," "I cannot find my way."

546  FARRAR, John. "The Literary Spotlight: Edwin Arlington
Robinson." Bookman, 56 (January, 1923), 565-569. Reprinted in The Literary Spotlight. New York: George H.
Doran, 1924. Pp. 116-124. With a caricature by William
Gropper. Principally a character sketch. The one obscure
thing about Robinson is Robinson himself, his personality,
in other words. He has never seated himself in the middle
of the market place and permitted the curious public to
stroll about him. He has his own circle of friends and he
is a welcome adjunct to their gatherings, although he much
prefers to sit and listen rather than talk. The outward
manifestation of Robinson's life may be divided into two
phases, and from them the visible aspects of the poet may
be constructed. The phase under caption A has its locale
in New York; under B is centered the pleasant greenery of
the MacDowell Colony....

547  _____. "Review of Roman Bartholow." Bookman, 57
(June, 1923), 450-451. For me it is a veritable House of
Mirrors, a Crystal Maze in which I can only grasp vainly at
the slightest reflected, distorted, inverted image of Robinson's actual thought. Perhaps it is the poet's contribution
to psychoanalysis. At any rate you will find it fascinating
in all its pristine murkiness.

548  _____. "Review of Tristram." Bookman, 65 (June, 1927),
465-466. In this work we find a Robinson freed of manner-
ism, a mature poet writing a poem which is, for beauty, for
technique, for passion, for dramatic skill, the equal at least

of any great narrative poem in the English language....
Not abandoning his absorption with the psychological moods
of men and women, Robinson has accompanied them with the
pound of physical passion and the rhythm of natural beauty.
Moreover the whole poem impresses as strikingly original.
It will never remind the reader of Tennyson, and only in
its stark beauty of Homer. It reminds the reader of Robinson at his very best.

549 FAUSSET, Hugh I'A. "Poets and Poetry: Roman Bartholow,
A Tragic Complex." Spectator, 131 (November 17, 1923),
759-760. Robinson's blank verse is lucid and satisfying,
finely modulated, too, in the minor key. In spite of psychological complexity, there is no problematic writing; his
vision is as tenacious as it is finely focused.

550 FICKE, Arthur Davison. "Cool, Intelligent Astringence: Review of Selected Letters." New York Herald Tribune Books,
February 25, 1940. P. 6. Ridgely Torrence, principal
editor of the letters, has performed his task with a simplicity and severity of taste that would have pleased Robinson.
Neither the editor nor his author seem to regard literature
as an "unlocking of the heart" in any such sense as is admired by readers of True Confessions. The book offers no
thrills, but is a pleasant companion for thoughtful half-
hours. It gives the privilege of being alone with a whimsical, serious, and very noble gentleman.

551 FIGUEIRA, Gastón. "Poetas y Prosistas Americanos: I.
Edwin Arlington Robinson, II. Thomas Wolfe." Revista
Iberoamericana (Iowa City, Iowa), 11 (October, 1946),
329-332.

552 FINCH, John. "Review of Selected Letters." New England
Quarterly, 13 (December, 1940), 733-735. By the nature
of the letters themselves, it is a man rather than a poet
who emerges with clearness from them. There are occasional explicit discussions of individual poems, but they tell
us little that the poems do not say more succinctly. Instead of poetic insight the letters offer us portraiture....
This is not to say that the author of the early letters is
not recognizably the author of the poetry. he is a withdrawn New Englander, "never much of a light in company,"
born into a world which is "at best a diabolically practical
place."

553 FIRKINS, O. W. "Review of Captain Craig." Nation, 100
(May 20, 1915), 562-563. Commentary on Robinson's poem
contained in article touching on some ten other volumes.
Robinson has two grave faults: a talkativeness, even glib-
ness, and a frequent baldness--or even meanness--of rhythm

and diction which is probably in his case half negligence
and half insurgency. What he can do and what is well
worth doing is to sketch one class of realities vividly and
to give clear lyrical embodiment to certain rare shades of
universal feeling.

554 _____. "Review of The Man Against the Sky." Nation, 103
(August 17, 1916), 150-151. Comments contained in article
dealing with several other recent publications of poetry.
In this volume the narrative ability of the poet sleeps. It
contains dramatic monologues which are sometimes excellent.
His verse sets out to be homespun; it seems ready at any
moment to become humdrum and jogtrot, and it ends by
snatching the reader up and making off with him to Fairy-
land. He sometimes hazards a rawness, often a pomposity;
but his verse sports blithely in the exhilaration of these
perils.

555 _____. "Review of Avon's Harvest." Weekly Review, 5
(July 9, 1921), 38-40.

556 FISH, R. S. "The Tempering of Faith in Edwin Arlington
Robinson's 'The Man Against the Sky.'" Colby Library
Quarterly, 9 (March, 1972), 456-468. Thinks this poem is
a key work in the study of Robinson, and proceeds to show
as much. Perhaps the chief problem is in the poem's per-
sona--the poem does embody a philosophy similar to that
found in other Robinson poems, but the speaker is not
Robinson, but a dramatized persona speaking within a
dramatic situation. The poem is primarily dramatic rather
than didactic in nature. The speaker is a man of faith,
and the poem is a test of his faith, the development and
resolution of his struggle. Within the situation of the hill-
top as fiery trial, the "I" addresses himself in an attempt
to strengthen his faith.

557 FISHER, John Hurt. "Edwin Arlington Robinson and the
Arthurian Legend." Studies in Language and Literature,
edited by Brahmer et al. (1966), pp. 117-131. Discusses
Merlin, Lancelot, and Tristram. Whatever his original impulse may have been, in his development of the Arthurian
material he concentrated on the personal conflicts of the
individual characters. These conflicts between love and
duty, human and divine love, and domestic love and destructive passion, Robinson found as true for the twentieth
century as for the twelfth.... Another way of looking at
the poems is from the vantage point of medieval chivalric
tradition. Robinson's three poems emphasize three aspects
of the chivalric dilemma: conflict of love and duty; conflict
of earthly and divine love; and the conflicting nature of
love itself.

558  FITZELL, Lincoln. "The Sword and the Dragon." South Atlantic Quarterly, 50 (April, 1951), 214-232. Includes comments on "Luke Havergall." Long article in which a number
of authors are discussed around the theme of "the Dragon
of the North," defined as "a power of evil, guardian of
hoards, the greedy withholder of good things from men;
and the slaying of the dragon is the crowning achievement
of heroes." Among authors discussed are James Joyce,
Yeats, Hart Crane, etc. Only a small body of contemporary
poetry has anything to do with tragedy. The poetry of
Robinson comes closer to scrutiny of individual disaster than
does that of most modern poets. The poem "Luke Havergal," illustrates the theme that death cannot be conquered,
or the conquest of death be decisively attempted through
the idle and sorrowful riddling of a mystery. Only through
abiding faith in the immortality of love can death be set at
a distance and understood as trial or interruption.

559  FLANAGAN, John T. "Robinson: Centenary Essays." South
Atlantic Quarterly, 70 (Winter, 1971), 129-130. Review of
collection edited by Ellsworth Barnard. Despite some over-
lapping in treatment and especially in quotation, the essays
focus on diverse themes and range from Robinson's early
environment and training to his mature philosophy and poetic craft. Most of the essays are eulogistic, but one must
conclude reluctantly that they do not establish Robinson as
a first rate poet nor do they leave the reader with a compelling urge to read widely in the chronicles of Tilbury
Town and Camelot.

560  FLETCHER, John Gould. "Some Contemporary American Poets:
Edwin Arlington Robinson." Chapbook, 2 (May, 1920), 1-5.
Regards Robinson as the greatest of modern American poets,
both in his use of language and in sheer intellectual abil-
ities. Thinks The Man Against the Sky is the greatest work,
and Merlin the most inferior.

561  _____. "Mr. Robinson's Poems." Nation and Athenaeum, 30
(November 19, 1921), 307-308. Reprinted in Living Age
(see below).

562  _____. "Mr. Robinson Abroad." Living Age, 311 (December
17, 1921), 744. In a letter to the editor, Fletcher gives
four reasons for regarding Robinson as a great poet: The
poem "The Gift of God" (ironic and tender study of mother-
hood); "Cassandra" (a most penetrating analysis of American
failings); "Ben Jonson Entertains ..." (the most complete
and comprehensive picture of Shakespeare by an English or
American poet); and "The Man Against the Sky" (a plea for
faith, impressive, austere, and ennobling). Cannot think of
anyone else who has accomplished quite so much.

563 _____. "Edwin Arlington Robinson." Spectator (London),
130 (February 10, 1923), 216. Review of Collected Poems.
Comments principally on the differences between Robinson
and Whitman in their innovative subject matter and prosaic
diction. He is most like the novelist James. Robinson's
chief value is in his ability to sustain intellectual analysis.

564 _____. "Portrait of Edwin Arlington Robinson." North
American Review, 244 (August, 1937), 24-26. Consists of
a 65 line poem which describes and characterizes Robinson.
The details are vivid and specific: "the fine forehead, just
above the eyes"; "a face like a fine-chiselled mask"; "eyes
like a hurt dog's"; etc. In conclusion he is described as
"mournfully patient, waiting, hoping," that after all his
years of groping there might be reward. His reward perhaps will be no more than that "for which few men might
thank him, but most would soon forget."

565 FLINT, F. Cudworth. "A Review of Matthias at the Door."
Symposium, 3 (April, 1932), 237-248. Once more he has
written a long narrative poem, with the same introspective
and baffled characters, the same chill and somber background, the same attempt to wrest a hope from Time and
Fate, the same low-voiced melody that we are familiar with.
Thinks the work suffers from three deficiencies: Robinson's
imagination is too nihilistic, his interests are too specialized,
and finally Robinson is too hesitant, by which is meant that
this poet will not write about anything he does not know,
he will not express his faith before he has found it.

566 FOSTER, Isabel. "More from Mr. Robinson: Nicodemus."
Christian Science Monitor, October 1, 1932. P. 6. What
Robinson has said well before, he says again and says it
with a surety and ease that make what sometimes was a difficult feat, halting, involved, and only half articulate, an
accomplishment of all but impossible penetration into the
depths of the human heart.

567 _____. "A New Edwin Arlington Robinson: Talifer."
Christian Science Monitor, September 30, 1933. P. 9.
The surprise which Robinson has in store for his readers
will cause wide comment and delight. It is a happy ending
to a novel in verse which is nowhere particularly gloomy.
Robinson, preoccupied with somber undertones and inner
conflicts from the beginning, is not so in this work. It is
undoubtedly the most cheerful and optimistic of his longer
poems. For its contemporary simplicity and its high dramatic value within the limits of normal life, it should prove the
most read and enjoyed of any of Robinson's poems since
Tristram--which was none of these things and yet was tre-
mendously popular.

568 _____. "Robinsonian Avernus: Amaranth." Christian Science Monitor, September 26, 1934. P. 14. The poem, despite its grim power of literary expression and its penetration into the hearts and thoughts of those doubters who hug their proud dreams to them, is not likely to bring Robinson a host of new friends as did Tristram in 1928. It explores a dark wood, but finds few gleams of moonlight, few night-blooming flowers, few nutritious fruits. He has returned with his lifelong curiosity and sympathy to the struggles and strange victories of the apparently defeated.

569 _____. "Mr. Robinson's King Jasper." Christian Science Monitor, December 31, 1935. P. 12. The language in which Robinson realizes his profound thoughts with felicity is not so difficult nor so mannered as once it was. The grief is less bitter and more patient. The glints of humor which have brightened every poem, no matter how dark the theme, still shine.

570 _____. "Robinson, Poet of America." Christian Science Monitor, May 26, 1937. P. 10. Comments on the latest edition of Collected Poems, which is called the life-work of a great poet and his reflection of almost half a century of American literature and thought. No one would deny that his contribution is typical of America or more exactly, of New England. For those who have once learned his rhythm, vocabulary and difficult style, such a collected work as this giant will be invaluable.

571 FOY, John Vail. "Character and Structures in Edwin Arlington Robinson's Major Narratives." Ph.D. diss., Cornell, 1961. DA, 22 (1961), 1996. Traces the history of Robinson's interest in the long blank-verse narrative poem as the major form for his investigation of the enigma of human character. From the beginning he had preferred dramatic as opposed to lyric presentation. He attempted to adapt some already existing plots of the Arthurian legend and then returned to inventing his own characters and plots. At times he overburdened his narratives with inconsistent or unrelated symbols and allusions, excessive personification, and occasionally, even incorrect syntax. Near the end of his career, his narratives become easier to understand. He reduced the number of symbols and allusions, carefully related those he used, and relieved his characters' discourse of extended and difficult syntax. In the concluding allegories the plot structure and characterization are clearer without sacrifice of depth or complexity.

572 _____. "Robinson's Impulse for Narrative." Colby Library Quarterly, 8 (March, 1969), 238-249. Reprinted in Cary, ed. (1969), pp. 253-262. Robinson's single-minded devotion

to a career as poet is so obvious that frequently his work
in two major experiments is overlooked: the prose short
story, or sketch, as Robinson called it and the play. After
1916 his poetry was principally the extended blank-verse
narrative, his chief concern with the dramatic and the
enigma of human character. It is interesting to speculate
as to the course of his career had his sketches and plays
been remotely successful.... His failures, however, indicate the problem that Robinson had to overcome as he developed a narrative structure and technique of characterization to complement his indirect and allusive style of poetic
expression.

573 FRANCHERE, Hoyt Catlin. "Comparative Analysis of the Tristram of Masefield and Robinson with Historical Background."
State University of Iowa, 1931. M.A. thesis.

574 _____. Edwin Arlington Robinson. New York: Twayne,
1968. United States Authors Series, No. 137. Consists of
161 pages with a preface and chronology. The six chapters
follow a chronological order: 1. My Father Was to Me a
Mighty Stranger; 2. The Gold I Miss for Dreaming; 3.
Wine and Wormwood: The Robinson Myth; 4. Of Lost Im-
perial Music; 5. Darkness over Camelot; 6. Bugs and
Emperors. Notes and references, select bibliography, and
index. The author says in his preface: "I have not attempted to restore the poet's reputation. He never really
lost it. I have tried to discover his associations, the books
he read, the letters he wrote, the works he failed to do or
succeeded in doing. What shaped and influenced his mind."

575 FRANKENBERG, Lloyd. Pleasure Dome: On Reading Modern
Poetry. Boston: Houghton, Mifflin, 1949. Robinson passim.

576- FREE, William J. "Edwin Arlington Robinson's Use of Emer-
77 son." American Literature, 38 (March, 1966), 69-84.
Robinson's admiration for Emerson cannot be overlooked by
anyone seeking to understand the pattern of ideas in his
poetry. But no one has been able to point with certainty
to specific Emersonian ideas in specific Robinson poems.
Article is devoted to showing how the Emersonian idea of
Compensation can be demonstrated in several of Robinson's
poems. Robinson knew and was deeply moved by Emerson's
essay "Compensation." In a sense, Robinson's use of Emerson's doctrine of compensation was a search that faltered,
if not failed. Robinson was too much a man of his time for
certainties. Endurance, compassion, and a dogged faith in
the reality of the spirit were in the long run more meaningful to him than the too-symmetrical patterns of Emerson's
law.

578 _____. "The Strategy of 'Flammonde,'" in Barnard, ed.
(1969), pp. 15-30. Notes that "Flammonde" is the first
poem in The Man Against the Sky and the Collected Poems.
Has been argued that Robinson valued the poem, but few have
said why. Some readers ignore the adverse criticisms of the
poem. It is not sentimental in its total effect and cannot
be easily dismissed. Robinson's strategy of language, character, and viewpoint in this poem illuminates one aspect of
the problem which he faced in finding a suitable language
in which to express his vision of life.... Robinson's poetic
problem was to transform the abstract ideas and sentimental,
cliché-ridden metaphors of his day into poetry. In a sense
he was trying to restore life to a worn-out language without
abandoning that language.

579 FRENCH, Joseph Lewis. "A Poet in the Subway." New York
World Magazine, May 1904. P. 10.

580 _____. "The Younger Poets of New England." New England Magazine, 33 (December, 1905) 424-428.

581 _____. "An Interregnum of Genius: Matthias at the Door."
Commonweal, 15 (February 10, 1932), 412.

582 FRENCH, Robert. "On Teaching 'Richard Cory.'" English
Record, 24 (Fall, 1973), 11-13. Describes the event of his
first teaching "Richard Cory," the utter disaster which the
students made of it, and his own "wrong reasons" for even
wanting to teach it. Students learn most from poetry when
they do not know what to think. Confer approval upon a
poem, and students will shut off their own feelings and rely
on the conditioned response. In the future this teacher
learned not to approach any poem as a "classic."

583 FROST, Robert. "Foreword" to Robinson's King Jasper.
New York: Macmillan, 1935. Reprinted in Murphy, ed.
(1970), pp. 33-39. The style is the man. Rather say the
style is the way the man takes himself; and to be at all
charming or even bearable, the way is almost rigidly pre-
scribed. If it is with outer humor, it must be with inner
seriousness. Neither one alone without the other under it
will do. Robinson was thinking as much in many of his
poems.... Robinson has gone to his place in American literature and left his human place among us vacant. We
mourn, but with the qualification that, after all, his life
was a revel in the felicities of language. So sad and at
the same time so happy in achievement. Not for me to
search his sadness to its source. And there is solid satisfaction in a sadness that is not just a fishing for ministra-
tion and consolation.

584  FRYXELL, Lucy Dickinson.  "Edwin Arlington Robinson as
     Dramatist and Dramatic Poet."  Ph.D. diss., Kentucky Uni-
     versity, 1955.  DA, 20 (1960), 4110-4111.  This study un-
     dertakes to show the extent of Robinson's interest in the
     theater and in playwriting, to analyze his published plays,
     and to demonstrate the influence which his experience had
     upon his later long narrative poems....  All his adult life
     Robinson was interested in plays and in the theater; his
     letters reveal his appreciation of the dramas, as well as his
     critical judgment.  Robinson's two published plays reveal
     that he did master certain of the techniques of stagecraft;
     but sometimes he is oversubtle and goes to the other ex-
     treme of making his theme too obvious.  The plays have
     faults, but they also have something to say about Robin-
     son's methods in the long narrative poems.

585  FUSSELL, Edwin S.  "The Early Poetry of Edwin Arlington
     Robinson."  Ph.D. diss., Harvard, 1949.

586  _____.  "An Unpublished Poem by Edwin Arlington Robinson."
     American Literature, 22 (January, 1951), 487-488.  Refer-
     ence is to a short poem "Broadway," in Robinson materials
     at Harvard.  It has never been published, or mentioned in
     Robinson scholarship or bibliography.  One more rejected
     poem will hardly alter Robinson's stature; moreover this
     poem suggests nothing new about Robinson's career or qual-
     ity.  That he had long engaged in attempting to write a
     modern poem of the American city is well known; and the
     syntactical complexity, formal balance, and style of wit in
     this poem can be observed in a score of poems more per-
     fectly realized.

587  _____.  "'For a Dead Lady.'"  Explicator, 9 (March, 1951),
     item 33.  Comments principally on one line:  "The laugh
     that love could not forgive," and thinks perhaps too much
     has been made of its complexity.  It can be read quite sim-
     ply if one bears in mind Robinson's accuracy in realizing
     and obliquity in presenting the complexity of emotional ex-
     perience.  The reference here is probably to that slight as-
     pect of possessiveness, coupled with the desire always to
     be taken seriously, which forms a part of any strong emo-
     tional attachment.  The context of the line limits the pos-
     sibility that any kind of depreciation is intended, for it oc-
     curs in a stanza in which the charm, grace, and elegance
     of the subject are being developed.

588  _____.  "Robinson to Moody:  Ten Unpublished Letters."
     American Literature, 23 (May, 1951), 173-187.  Though
     Robinson and Moody had been at Harvard at the same time,
     their friendship dates from the winter of 1899, when they
     apparently talked about poetry in New York.  Summer found

Moody back in Chicago, at a time when Robinson, about to
return to New York, wrote the first of ten letters. They
are published here for the first time. The last letter is
dated October 13, 1908. Both poets knew that Robinson's
poetry would ultimately have to be reckoned with, and that
they would then compete for critical honors among the poets
of their generation. Both poets were aware that they were
writing into a new age and certain that poetry was to take
a changed course.

589 _____. "A Note on Edwin Arlington Robinson's 'Credo.'"
Modern Language Notes, 66 (June, 1951), 398-400. Many
obscurities in Robinson can be cleared up by reference to
information outside the poem. Such a poem is "Credo."
The transition from the octave to the sestet is of particular
pertinence, for in this transition is the crux of Robinson's
philosophy. Robinson's "transcendental optimism" was always dependent upon a sturdy confrontation of tragedy and
evil; he phrased this aspect of his philosophy in a number
of ways, but never more cogently than when he wrote, "I
still stick to my thesis that the world is a Hell of a Place,
and that it should be one if it means anything."

590 _____. "The Americanism of Edwin Arlington Robinson."
Claremont Quarterly, 1 (January, 1952), 9-12. Answers
some poorly-grounded charges that Robinson did not pay
proper respect to the concept of "America." As a matter
of fact Robinson's philosophy and poetry is far from bur-
dened with any form of "isms," and certain it is ridiculous
to discuss Robinson, who died in 1935, in light of any of
the 1950's communistic propaganda.

591 _____. "Robinson's Poetry." Kenyon Review, 14 (Autumn,
1952), 694-697. Review of biography by Ellworth Barnard.
This work talks directly and copiously about Robinson as a
poet. The criticism is sensitive, judicious, and thorough;
it ought to persuade some of the critics that this poetry
merits more attention than it has had lately, and it may
remedy some of the loss involved in sending a poet to the
archives before he has been fully and thoughtfully read.
The general reader who is interested in modern poetry but
does not know Robinson well may occasionally feel lost, although Barnard does a good job of showing how all this detail connects with his clear and coherent account of the whole
poetry.

592 _____. Edwin Arlington Robinson: The Literary Background
of a Traditional Poet. Berkeley & Los Angeles: University
of California Press, 1954. Pp. 171-186, "One Kind of Traditional Poet," reprinted in Murphy, ed. (1970), pp. 95-109.

Some of Robinson's early poetry was conventional in every
possible way. But in those poems in which he had truly
discovered his talent, what was the nature of his diver-
gence? Most important, perhaps, was his refusal to admit
that nature, and not man, was the proper study of mankind.
His skepticism on this point marked the end of one of the
strongest conventions of romantic poetry. If man was to be
the subject, the dormant dramatic instincts would return to
English poetry. Robinson brought them back in 1896. Wit,
generally suppressed in English poetry for more than a century, returned in Robinson's poetry, together with irony
and a sterner intellectual discipline. Ridding his verse of
the stilted romantic diction, he turned to a conversational
and argumentative manner ... and provided poetry that had
power and resiliency. Consists of 210 pages with notes and
index. In 7 chapters, mostly dealing with Influences: 1.
Introduction: Plan and Method; 2. The American Past;
3. The Literature of England; 4. European Naturalism;
5. The Classical Influence; 6. The English Bible; 7. One
Kind of Traditional Poet. Chapters 2 and 3 are major chapters. These are presented in chronological order. Conclusion demonstrates how Robinson's creative talent was sharp-
ened and developed by his acquaintance with great writing.

593 GANNETT, Lewis. "Books and Things." New York Herald
Tribune, October 5, 1938. P. 15. Includes commentary on
Hagedorn's biography of Robinson.

594 GARDINER, Harold C., ed. American Classics Reconsidered:
A Christian Appraisal. New York: Scribner's, 1958.
Robinson passim. Robinson not discussed individually; is
referred to in several articles.

595 GARVIN, Harry R. "Poems Pickled in Anthological Brine."
College English Association Critic, 20 (October, 1958), 1 &
4. Refers to "Richard Cory." Sometimes the immediate success of a fine poem, "Richard Cory" for example, keeps it
from being read properly. Readers exhaust the aesthetic
possibilities of merely good poems; but a poem that is greatly
good or even finely good is inexhaustible; and a failure in
sensitiveness towards such a poem lies with the reader.
Famous poems force their reputations and accepted meanings
upon an unsure and unwary teacher.

596 _____. "Comprehensive Criticism: A Humanistic Discipline."
Bucknell Review, 10 (May, 1962), 305-327. Long, well-
written article about criticism. Begins with a review of
several schools of criticism, and shows how each in turn
became dated, served its time, and passed into the "history
of criticism." Garvin argues for a "comprehensive" criticism,
one that is open to any possibility that may assist in

establishing the meaning of a work of art. His remarks are
applicable to all of the arts, but his interests are primarily
literary. Takes Robinson's "Richard Cory," a poem he never
had much use for, and shows how it takes on more and more
meaning in ratio to the amount of critical openness it receives.

597  GENTHE, Charles V. "Edwin Arlington Robinson's 'Annandale'
     Poems." Colby Library Quarterly, 7 (March, 1967), 392-
     398. The three "Annandale" poems were published as "The
     Book of Annandale" (1902), "How Annandale Went Out"
     (1910), and "Annandale Again" (1929). The three poems
     should be read in a narrative rather than a chronological
     order, with the 1910 poem, the death of Annandale, coming
     last. The trilogy is a dark tale of a love triangle, murder
     and revenge, and should be read against Robinson's influ-
     ence from Molière and from allusions within the Bible. These
     poems fit the general Robinson pattern, and are too carefully
     contrived for the characters and story to be merely a matter
     of coincidence.

598  GIERASCH, Walter. "Luke Havergal." Explicator, 3 (October,
     1944), item 8. Abridged in The Case for Poetry, edited by
     F. L. Gwynn et al. (1954), p. 297. Feels that much of the
     poem is inexplicable, however some basic points are discern-
     ible. There are three persons involved in the situation:
     the mysterious speaker, Luke, and the loved one. The
     problem is that the speaker's advice is dark and full of un-
     certainty and doubt. Later it becomes more positive and
     clear. Luke must learn from God's slaying himself, there
     is no perfection by itself alone, that all is relative, with
     pleasure amounting to less than half of life. Luke is blinded
     because he expects absolute, rather than relative love.

599  GOHDES, Clarence, ed. Essays on American Literature in Hon-
     or of Jay B. Hubbell. Durham: Duke University Press,
     1967. "Edwin Arlington Robinson in Perspective," by Floyd
     Stovall, pp. 241-258. See Stovall.

600  GORHAM, Robert David. "E. A. Robinson--New Study by
     Emery Neff." New York Times Book Review, October 24,
     1948. Pp. 14, 16.

601  GORLIER, Claudio. "Edwin Arlington Robinson e Robert Frost."
     Paragone (Florence), 12 (February, 1966), 126-132. In
     Italian.

602  GORMAN, Herbert S. "Edwin Arlington Robinson and a Talk
     With Him." New York Sun Books and Book World, January
     4, 1920.

603  _____. "Review of Lancelot." The Evening Post Book Review
     (New York), April 17, 1920. P. 5.

604 _____. "Review of Lancelot." New Republic, 23 (July 28,
         1920), 259-260. Robinson can say more in two lines than
         most poets can say in several verses. His vision is somber;
         it is marked by an uncompromising consistency in the han-
         dling of eternal values.

605 _____. "Authentic Poetry: A Review of The Three Tav-
         erns." Freeman, 2 (November 3, 1920), 186-187. Here is
         a great virtue that belongs peculiarly to Robinson among
         American poets. His work is always packed with thought.
         The Three Taverns is a big book and it grows with each
         reading. It is the work of lonely hours, of unfailing medi-
         tation, and of authentic genius, if such a thing may be ad-
         mitted to exist in these troublous times.

606 _____. "Edwin Arlington Robinson, Edgar Lee Masters:
         Poets of Today." New York Times, January 16, 1921. P.
         18. Review of The Three Taverns. This work is a finished
         product. It is a book such as only a master, touched with
         the authentic fire of genius, could make possible. Within
         its 120 pages is crystallized the best of modern American
         poetry. No European could find better introduction to
         American achievement in letters than through the poems that
         are contained in The Three Taverns.

607 _____. "Destiny's Hooded Face: Avon's Harvest." New
         York Evening Post, April 2, 1921.

608 _____. "Review of Avon's Harvest." Literary Review, April
         2, 1921. P. 6. A particularly Robinsonian poem, with all
         those niceties of spiritual analysis that form so large a part
         of the poet's virtues. Robinson is now, in his complete
         maturity, absolutely sure of his instrument and undeniably
         the most finished and consistently inspired poet in America.

609 _____. "Edwin Arlington Robinson's poetry: A Review of
         Collected Poems." New York Times, October 30, 1921.
         P. 6. Assembles poems from eight volumes with some poems
         not previously published. He has perfected an individual
         utterance, a particular originality, for he has not relied on
         new and bizarre verse forms, but worked in those old and
         conservative meters that it is now the fashion to treat flip-
         pantly. Yet he has so tightened and poured into those old
         forms a substance so unmistakably his own that they take
         on a new color and melody.

610 _____. "Review of Collected Poems." New Republic, 29
         (February 8, 1922), 311-313. It offers in its nearly 600
         pages the best of modern American poetry, a wealth of unique
         and individual matter that will slowly and surely penetrate
         the consciousness of the American poetry-reading public.

611 _____. A Procession of Masks. New York: B. J. Brimmer,
1923. Robinson, pp. 15-39. Consists of five sections,
which repeat some of the material in earlier reviews of
Robinson's work. Part I discusses the poet's entrance into
the "uncrowded stage" of American letters with The Torrent... (1896); Part II analyzes the Tilbury figures with special emphasis on "the man against the Sky." Part III deals
with the dramatic monologs, of which "The Three Taverns"
is a brilliant example; Part IV undertakes to assess Lancelot and Merlin, and Part V concludes with brief remarks on
Avon's Harvest and Roman Bartholow.

612 _____. "A Crop of Spring Verse: The Man Who Died
Twice." Bookman, 59 (June, 1924), 467-468. Here is undoubtedly the best of Robinson's narratives of modern life,
a more inspired revelation than Roman Bartholow and a subject more pregnant with objective color.

613 _____. "Edwin Arlington Robinson and Some Others: Dionysus in Doubt." Bookman, 61 (July, 1925), 595-596.
This poem will grieve some of the Robinson readers and
delight others. The two major poems are disconcerting ac-
cusations directed at an over-legislated land where the
privilege of independent living has become a mean dependency of an organized Drive for Salvation.

614 _____. "Review of Tristram." New York Evening Post Literary Review, May 7, 1927. This poem has a fine passionate
clarity and an unfaltering command of form. Robinson has
delivered himself in Tristram of the best long poem in American letters. At the same time he has rehandled and rear-
ranged the story of Tristram and Isolt so admirably that his
version immediately supersedes all other variants of the
legend.

615 _____. "Review of The Letters of Thomas S. Perry," edited
by Edwin Arlington Robinson. Century, 119 (Autumn, 1929),
155-156. Although it is but a selection there does emerge
a full-length figure from this volume, selected and with an
introduction by Robinson. A very great bookman, not so
much a writer himself as an appreciator and amateur critic,
appears in this correspondence which is very entertaining
both for what it has to say about contemporary events and
for its betrayal of the late Mr. Perry's personality. Robinson's introduction is a triumph of tact and appreciation. His
disciples will want this volume whether or not they are interested in Thomas Sergeant Perry.

616 GORMAN, Jean Wright, and Herbert S. Gorman, eds. The
Peterborough Anthology. New York: Theatre Arts Inc.,
1923. Robinson, pp. 20-29.

627 _____, and Marya Zaturenska. A History of American Poetry, 1900-1940. New York: Harcourt, Brace, 1946. "La
Comédie Humaine of Edwin Arlington Robinson," pp. 107-
132. From 1904 onward to the day of his death in 1935
Robinson' poetry has been subject to extraordinary and
erratic bursts of praise; and the praise has always been
followed by longer periods of critical silence and indifference.... Reviews Robinson's career in terms of his publications and concludes that the poet had his share of attention and acknowledgment. At his death, it might have
been said that he was "a man who had neither been ener-
vated by applause, nor intimidated by censure or indifference."

628 _____. "A Poet's Honest Self-Appraisal: Review of Untriangulated Stars ...." New York Times Book Review, February 8, 1948. P. 1, 24. The time is ripe for further
disclosures of Robinson's imagination and wit, and if in
editing this volume Mr. Sutcliffe has not taken the first
step toward revealing Robinson as he should be known, he
has taken a second step of considerable length. His only
step backward has been that awkward (and one wishes one
could forget it) title, Untriangulated Stars.

629 _____. "Out of One Century He Spoke to Another." New
York Times Book Review, February 10, 1952. Review of
biography by Ellsworth Barnard.

630 GRIFFIN, Glenn. "Time Deals Kindly with the Poet." Atlanta
Journal & Constitution, March 29, 1970. P. 16-D. Review
of Centenary Essays (1969) edited by Ellsworth Barnard.

631 GRIFFIN, Lloyd W. "Where the Light Falls: A Review." Library Journal, 90 (April 1, 1965), 1706. Work by Chard
Powers Smith.

632 GRIFFITH, B. W. "A Note on Robinson's Use of Turannos."
Concerning Poetry, 4 (Spring, 1971), 39.

633 GRIGSON, Geoffrey. The Contrary View: Glimpses of Fudge
and Gold. First published, 1905. Reprinted Totowa, N.J.:
Rowman & Littlefield, 1974. "Poems in Early Plain English:
Edwin Arlington Robinson," pp. 108-111. Here is one good
(American) poet who has suffered, certainly in England,
from a pair of unblest causes. Not many English readers
know much more of Robinson than his excellent yet not so
characteristic "Miniver Cheevy." Life in his poems is
haunted by nothingness, by no explanation, and there is
no consolation. For the men and women, in their separate
poems, who inhabit his Tilbury Town, living is a cage, even
in comfort, under the rule of uncertainty or illusion, or

might have been, or disillusion. A poetry dismal in effect.
Rather one which pricks the reader out of his complacency,
disturbs him, and then lays a rhythmical benediction, if not
absolution, on his disturbance.

634  GRIMM, Clyde L. "Robinson's 'For a Dead Lady': An Exer-
     cise in Evaluation." Colby Library Quarterly, 7 (Decem-
     ber, 1967), 535-547. Reprinted in Cary, ed. (1969), pp.
     243-252. Robinson, more than some other significant poets,
     has suffered a deficiency in criticism that "evaluates."
     Take "For a Dead Lady" as example: it is frequently
     anthologized and is one of Robinson's most highly regarded
     poems. But little has been said as to why it is highly re-
     garded. This article analyzes the poem in terms of its
     structure, imagery, appropriate diction, and a more than
     mechanical or arbitrary use of form. Conclusion is that
     "For a Dead Lady," is indeed a valuable poem.

635  GRIMSHAW, James. "Robinson's 'Lost Anchors.'" Explicator,
     30 (November, 1971), item 36. Does not accept the usual
     nautical interpretation of Robinson's poem, but sees the
     Anchors as representing the tenets of Judeo-Christian
     Faith. They are lost in that Robinson seems to be reflect-
     ing the religious skepticism which permeated the end of the
     century, and the beginning of the twentieth century. That
     skepticism resulted partially from the scientific revolution
     of the period, partially from a major world war, and par-
     tially from the increased pulse of Society.... Most images
     of the poem are analogous to basic Christian symbols, the
     fish, the fisherman-sailor, the Virgin Mary, etc.

636  GRISCOM, Isobel. "Moon's Other Side: Review of Selected
     Letters." Chattanooga Daily Times, April 7, 1940. P. 5.

637  GROSS, Harvey. Sound and Form in Modern Poetry: A Study
     in Prosody from Thomas Hardy to Robert Lowell. Ann Ar-
     bor: University of Michigan Press, 1964. "Modern Poetry
     in the Metrical Tradition," pp. 42-78; Robinson, pp. 63-67.
     In selected examples of Robinson's loosened blank verse,
     metrical analysis shows how the lilt of New England speech
     gets into the versification. Those who do not like this kind
     of verse may mutter about low words creeping in dull lines;
     others will declare that the monosyllabic word has been a
     traditional source of power in English blank verse.

638  GUITERMAN, Arthur. "The Bloomin' Lyre: The Man Who
     Died Twice." Outlook, 136 (April 16, 1924), 649. The
     poem, although it contains fine passages, is unfortunate
     in its resemblance to the average street parade; it is late
     in getting started, and is far too long in passing a given
     point.

639 _____. "Parnassus and Thereabout: Dionysus in Doubt."
    Outlook, 140 (May 20, 1925), 112-113. The title poem is
    based upon a presumed conversation with Dionysus, Bac-
    chus, and is designed to protest the Eighteenth Amend-
    ment, which was a limitation on the freedom of the indi-
    vidual to work out his own salvation or damnation. There
    are also a dozen well-wrought sonnets and two other long-
    er poems in which nothing happens, but states of mind are
    illuminated by indirect lighting in the fine Robinsonian
    manner.

640 _____. "Poet's Housekeeping." Saturday Review of Liter-
    ature, 2 (July 3, 1926), 903. Is a poetic tribute to Robin-
    son, consisting of 12 lines of rhymed verse. In the proc-
    ess of describing Robinson, the writer says: "He tells us
    with ever increasing stress/That man and his world are a
    sorry mess;/He's as gay as a whippoorwill...." Also com-
    ments on Robinson's reputation for "growing austerity."

641 _____. "Epitaph on a Poet." Mark Twain Quarterly, 2
    (Spring, 1938), 12. Verse on Robinson. Four-line poem:
    "He lived to sing, to all the world unknown/Save for his
    singing, like a secret bird;/We only knew our hermit
    thrush had flown/Because no more that golden song was
    heard."

642 GUTHRIE, William Norman. "Devil's Advocate." Churchman
    (New York), 153 (May 15, 1939), 5. Review of Hagedorn's
    biography.

643 GWYNN, Frederick L., Ralph W. Condee, and Arthur O. Lew-
    is, eds. The Case for Poetry. Englewood Cliffs, N.J.:
    Prentice-Hall, 1954. Prints abridged version of article on
    "Luke Havergal," by Walter Gierasch, p. 297. Is discussed
    under Gierasch.

644 HAAS, Richard. "Oral Interpretation as Discovery Through
    Persona." Oral English, 1 (1972), 13-14.

645 HAGEDORN, Hermann. "The Peterborough Colony: A Work-
    shop, with a Wonderland Thrown in, for Creative Workers
    in the Seven Arts." Outlook, 129 (January 12, 1921),
    686-688. Is an introduction to and description of the Mac-
    Dowell Colony which was established by the widow of Edward
    MacDowell at Peterborough, New Hampshire. Like MacDowell
    himself, this has become one of the most serious, inspired,
    and sophisticated art colonies in the United States. The
    poet Robinson spent at least a dozen summers here, and
    in his poem "Monadnock Through the Trees" has commem-
    orated the majesty of the forests for all time into American
    literature.

646-  HAGEDORN, Hermann.  Edwin Arlington Robinson Memorial.
47    Gardiner, Maine:  privately printed, 1936.  pamphlet, 36
      pages.

648   _____.  Edwin Arlington Robinson:  A Biography.  New
      York:  Macmillan, 1938.  402 pp.  Consists of 25 chapters
      with titles, in chronological order.  Is not primarily criti-
      cal, but comments on all works.  Is based on two main
      sources, Robinson's letters and the recollections of his
      friends supplemented by some printed material, and the
      author's personal memories of a 25-year friendship.  The
      Robinson who emerges from this work is not the whole
      Robinson; he is only the Robinson whom the author, with
      the evidence at his disposal, has been able to discern, or
      comprehend.  Others, no doubt, will see deeper and farth-
      er.  Meanwhile, here is a portrait and a record for those
      who loved the man or cherish the poetry.

649   _____.  "From the Official Biographer."  Mark Twain Quar-
      terly, 2 (Spring, 1938), 16.  Remarks that he has known
      Robinson for over twenty-five years, but did not really get
      to know him until he started working on the biography.
      If he had known formerly what he knows now, he would
      have been a wiser and kinder friend.  Robinson was not
      only a great poet; he was a great soul.

650   HALL, Edward B.  "Review of The Glory of the Nightingales."
      Boston Transcript, 6 (October 18, 1930), 3.  This is not
      to be classed in the first order of Robinson's work.  It is
      charged with a certain heavy atmosphere of deadly futility.
      There are striking passages in the poem, but fewer than
      one is accustomed to expect from the pen of Robinson.
      Yet this is not to suggest that it will not well repay read-
      ing.  Everything of Robinson's is worth reading.

651   HALL, Harold E.  "Literary Enthusiasms of a Colby Alumnus."
      Colby Mercury, 7 (January, 1941), 15-16.  Is a brief recol-
      lection of his early enthusiasm for Thomas Hardy and com-
      mentary to the effect that he still regards Hardy as one of
      the world's greatest novelists, and doubts that any other
      novelist will ever make such a deep and lasting impression
      upon him.  Recalls also his first meeting with E. A. Robin-
      son, at a concert at which Hall was usher.  Robinson is
      referred to as "America's greatest poet," and it gives this
      writer the greatest pleasure to see Thomas Hardy and Rob-
      inson come together under the housing of the Colby College
      Library.

652   HALL, James Norman.  The Friends (Verse).  Muscatine, Iowa:
      Prairie Press, 1939.  34 pp.

653 _____. "Reading and Meditating: Edwin Arlington Robinson's Poems." (Verse). Atlantic Monthly, 174 (September,
1944), 59-60. Is a tribute in free verse to Robinson's
poetry which he characterizes as autumnal, if not wintry.
The first lines are perhaps the most revealing: "He rarely
saw, on any day, on all his lonely way,/A brighter sky
than gray./Autumn he loved and knew,/But not its gold
and blue."

654 HALPERIN, Maurice. Le Roman de Tristan et Iseut dans la
Littérature Anglo-Américaine au XIXe et au XXe Siècles.
Paris: Jouve & Cie, 1931. 146 pp. "La vérité psycho-
logique," pp. 107-119.

655 HAMMOND, Josephine. "The Man Against the Sky: Edwin
Arlington Robinson." Personalist, 10 (July, 1929), 178-
184. Article is a general appraisal and tribute to Robinson
as the most distinctive figure in American poetry today.
Sometimes he is charged with dryness, narrowness of
range, and excessive melancholy. However, the face and
figure of America have been richly celebrated in our recent
poetic renascence; Robinson, more potently than any other
of our singers, is reminding her that she has a spiritual
significance to fight for. His work falls in line with our
best critical tradition.

656 HANSEN, Harry. "Review of Cavender's House." New York
World, April 23, 1929. P. 15.

657 HARCOURT, John B. "Edwin Arlington Robinson: A Biography by Emery Neff." American Quarterly, 3 (Spring,
1951), 81-87. Review of Neff's book included in comments
on five other recently published volumes. In the main
Neff has written a sound, old-fashioned biography--the
kind that believes that a fact is after all a fact and to be
treasured on that account. Most of what there is to be
known of Robinson's life is here despite Neff's lack of
psychological insight or aesthetic interpretation. There
are no hypotheses, no flights of speculation; this is safe
scholarship, guaranteed, within its limitations, to weather
well. Neff has an impressive background in the history of
American and European poetry, and is able to place Robinson carefully and skillfully within the larger patterns of
the poetic tradition.

658 HARDON, R. V. "The President's Poetical Protégé." Boston
Evening Transcript, October 31, 1905. P. 12.

659 HARKEY, Joseph H. "Mr. Flood's Two Moons." Mark Twain
Journal, 15 (Summer, 1971), 20-21. It is generally assumed
that Mr. Flood is something of a drunk, but there is actually

no evidence for this. It would seem that old Eben is not
using his loneliness as an excuse to get drunk. When one
encounters the "two moons listening" the inclination is to
think at once that Eben is tipsy and experiencing double
vision. Perhaps not. The two moons could be the present
one--a harvest moon--and a harvest moon of the past con-
jured up by him. One main theme is Mr. Flood's attempt
to create the illusion of the past, and this interpretation
seems not far-fetched.

660  HAROLD, Jessie. "A Study of the Women Characters in the
     Poetry of Edwin Arlington Robinson." University of Kan-
     sas, 1933. M.A. thesis.

661  HART, James D. Oxford Companion to American Literature.
     New York: Oxford University Press, 1965, 4th edition.
     Robinson, pp. 718-719. Biographical sketch with titles
     and dates of his works. Each work is characterized with
     a general statement, and the sketch concludes with: "As
     an heir of the New England traditions of Puritanism and
     Transcendentalism, with their emphasis upon the individual,
     Robinson has been termed a sober Transcendentalist who
     deals primarily with the ethical conflicts within the indi-
     vidual, and measures the value of the isolated person by
     his truth to himself. He frequently employs the objective
     form of dramatic monologue, and confines his experimenta-
     tion to the use of common speech rhythms, not new stanzaic
     forms."

662  HART, Sylvia, and Estelle Paige. "Robinson's 'For a Dead
     Lady.'" Explicator, 10 (May, 1952), item 51. Comments
     on the troublesome line, "The laugh that love could not
     forgive," which has been taken as Robinson's love for his
     mother. If we suppose that the love was hers and not his,
     everything falls into place, and the line means that occa-
     sionally the lady, in spite of herself, was moved to laughter
     at her family. At such times her own love for them would
     not let her forgive herself.

663  HEFFERMAN, Thomas Carroll. "Edwin Arlington Robinson:
     A Critical Estimate of His Poetry." Boston College, 1929.
     M.A. thesis.

664  HENDERSON, L. J. "Edwin Arlington Robinson (1869-1935)."
     Proceedings of the American Academy of Arts and Sciences,
     70 (March, 1936), 570-573. Article is an obituary and re-
     view of Robinson's life. Quotes lengthy passage from Rob-
     inson's article, "The First Seven Years," (Colophon, De-
     cember 1930). Expresses view that the best understanding
     of Robinson will be gained by studying his origin in Gard-
     iner, Maine. One of Robinson's chief contributions is the

discovery of his own poetic diction and idiom, the unmistakable mark of his work throughout his life. Long un-
recognized by the public, the critics and other poets, it
seems to belong to the second decade of the present century, and thus became one of the most important factors
in the development of recent American poetry.

665 HENDERSON, W. B. "Edwin Arlington Robinson," Introduction, with selections. Warner Library, Vol. 20.

666 HEPBURN, James G. "Edwin Arlington Robinson's System of
Opposites." PMLA, 80 (June, 1965), 266-274. Reprinted
in Cary, ed. (1969), pp. 210-224. The phrase "system
of opposites" appears in a Robinson letter of 1894, and
does not occur elsewhere in the published writings. What
Robinson meant by this phrase and the varying extent to
which the term can be properly applied to some of his early poems are the subjects of this article. Robinson's general indifference to poetic theory makes it difficult to come
by any documented account of the system, yet it is possible
to shed some light on the matter. In sum, Robinson associates his poetry opposites with objectivity and realism;
he sees such poetry to be divorced from his own voice and
vision; and he seems generally to regard it as the lesser
work.

667 HERRON, Ima Honaker. The Small Town in American Literature. Durham: Duke University Press, 1939. Reprinted
New York: Pageant Books, 1959. Robinson, pp. 130-136.
Reviews some of the most prominent Tilbury Town persons,
and comments on the volumes in which they first appeared.
In these Robinson has added a new approach to the interpretation of American townspeople. Avoiding treatment of
the spectacular and the sensational, he has developed a
psychological type of village drama in concentrated narrative, dramatic monologue, and dialogue. Though he denies
none of his New England legacy, Robinson has employed
his materials with a literary independence vitalized by the
modern spirit. His is an uncompromising presentation of
the repressed folk of his native towns and countryside
where the wind "is always north-north-east."

668 HERTZ, Robert N. "Two Voices of the American Village:
Robinson and Masters." Minnesota Review, 2 (Spring,
1962), 345-358. The average reader would come away with
the impression that never in the history of one place is
there a more grotesque assemblage of the freakish, the
deluded, the unhappy, and the insignificant than in Tilbury
Town and Spoon River. Whatever their enduring value in
the universal scheme of life, such men appear to be social
and moral derelicts, without purpose and worldly attainments.

Robinson, however, is interested in the disparity between
outward aspect and secret spiritual reality. Robinson's
characters, then, are on the periphery of things, although
there are many other characters in Tilbury Town whom
Robinson does not write about.

669  HICKEY, Jerrold. "A Bagpipe in a Madhouse." Sunday Globe
     (Boston), 195 (June 22, 1969), 37-B. Review of biography
     by Louis O. Coxe.

670  HICKS, Granville. "Review of Collected Poems." Springfield
     Republican, February 12, 1928. P. 7 ff. This volume is
     an excellent opportunity for an evaluation of the work of
     this poet. For more than thirty years, Robinson's poems
     have been appearing with some regularity, and his work
     in this new edition, makes a most substantial showing.

671  _____. "The Talents of Mr. Robinson." Nation, 131 (Oc-
     tober 8, 1930), 382. Review of The Glory of the Night-
     ingales, and Introduction to E.A.R. by Charles Cestré.
     That Robinson has weaknesses, The Glory of the Night-
     ingales once more makes clear. There are times when his
     methods become mannerisms and his psychological analyses
     move along, in the worst Jamesian manner, by their own
     momentum. His perceptions, it is obvious, function only
     within a limited area of experience, and his imagination is
     subtle rather than intense. He has known, however, how
     to make excellent use of the talents with which he is en-
     dowed, and the method he has evolved for his longer poems
     is close to perfection. For passages of exposition his blank
     verse lapses into an unobtrusive flow that has all the use-
     ful flexibility of prose, but it can rise, when the occasion
     requires, to an elevation richly poetic. Cestré's book makes
     a clear argument that Robinson's work is of a piece and
     that through his work, there has been no breakdown of
     intellect and imagination such as occurs with unpleasant
     frequency in American artists. By discussing all of the
     longer poems and many of the shorter ones, Cestré does
     give the reader a fair idea of the scope and the more ob-
     vious qualities of Robinson's work; but though the book
     may be of some assistance to the beginner, it has little to
     say to the advanced student.

672  _____. The Great Tradition. New York: Macmillan, 1933.
     "Two Roads," pp. 207-256; Robinson pp. 242-245. Robin-
     son's world is an abstraction. He is primarily interested
     in problems of personality, especially in the problem of
     success and failure. To see this problem he isolates his
     characters from many of the complexities of modern life.
     The men and women stand at a certain distance from the
     routine difficulties of daily existence. Only such kinds of

experience as are apparently unaffected by changes in
politics and economics, developments in science and tech-
nology, and fashions in art and morality, exist for his
poetry. Much of his poetry has enriched American literature, but much in his long narratives is tedious and trivial. His poems are precisely planned and firmly molded,
but some of it has no significance for the Age in which it
was written.

673 _____. "Poet of the Recent Past." Saturday Review, 48
(April 10, 1965), 31-32. Review of Where the Light Falls,
by Chard Powers Smith. Begins with a brief review of
Robinson's career, "miserably slow in winning recognition,"
but fairly well-assured after publication of The Man Against
the Sky in 1916. Robinson was never popular with the
Marxist school of criticism (those who demand to see the
social significance of an author), nor was he congenial to
the school of New Critics. Even so he has not been totally
neglected. This latest work by Chard Powers Smith "might
be regarded as a sort of rescue operation." It is in a way
three books: a personal memoir; an analysis of Robinson's
life in relation to his work; and an interpretation of his
attitudes towards the great problems of existence.... Smith
has done well by his old friend and master. He has not
only made good use of his own recollections, but has done
a careful job of research. This is the best book on Robinson we have thus far.

674 HILL, Archibald Anderson. "New Light on Some Literary
Lives." Virginia Quarterly Review, 16 (Summer, 1940),
454-455. Article is a review of three recent biographical
works on Joyce, Hardy, and the Selected Letters of Edwin
Arlington Robinson. The Robinson work is much slighter
than the two huge biographies, but is of quiet and mildly
acid charm. Almost from the first letter Robinson begins
to emerge, sometimes as much in his reticences as in his
revelations. These letters were never written with the
thought of publication, but revealing the man perhaps better than any outside biographer ever can. The book is
intended as a supplement to the biography of Hermann
Hagedorn, and so avoids any extended account of the
events or situations out of which the letters grew.

675 HILL, Dora May. "A Study of the Treatment of Some Arthurian Material by Tennyson and Robinson." Chicago, University of Chicago, 1927, M.A. thesis.

676 HILL, Robert W. "More Light on a Shadowy Figure: A. H.
Louis, the Original of Edwin Arlington Robinson's 'Captain
Craig.'" Bulletin of the New York Public Library, 60 (Au-
gust, 1956), 373-377. The material dealt with in this article

was found in a pile of scrapbooks turned over to the library by a lady who knew Francis G. Howard (a New York
landscape architect and designer). The hodge-podge did
not seem worth a great deal until it was discovered that it
contained three items in the handwriting of Alfred H. Louis, a colorful, intriguing figure of real importance in American literary history. It is generally accepted that Louis
was the pattern for the central character in Robinson's
poem "Captain Craig." The items discovered are a sonnet
and two letters in Louis' handwriting.

677  HILLYER, Robert. "E. A. Robinson and His 'Tristram.'"
     New Adelphi, 2 (Summer, 1928), 90-94.

678  _____. "Review of Collected Poems." New England Quar-
     terly, 3 (January, 1930), 148-151. The publication of this
     second collection is a convenience to the general reader
     and something of a challenge to criticism. This poet dur-
     ing his lifetime is enjoying a classical eminence which few
     living have known, for already he is more praised than
     read, and with the reviewers he is one to measure by in
     those vague dimensions which reviewers use. He is by all
     odds the most impressive figure on our literary horizon,
     not only because of his success in the shorter works, but
     also because of his great failures in the longer works.

679  _____. "Review of Amaranth." New England Quarterly,
     8 (March, 1935), 113-114. This new poem, an allegory,
     is one of his finest works. It has several levels of signifi-
     cance, linked by the main theme of the disillusionment which
     art metes out to its minor disciples.... The poem also re-
     flects that dark night of the soul which even the great art-
     ist passes through when he doubts his powers. There are
     hints of the futility of all human endeavors when Amaranth,
     the unfading flower looks upon them with his unconquer-
     able eyes. And we find a steady argument for form and
     seriousness in art; a quiet onslaught, also, against the
     precious school of criticism which maintains that poetry
     need not mean anything.

680  _____. "Edwin Arlington Robinson." Harvard Alumni Bul-
     letin, 37 (May 24, 1935), 992-994.

681  _____. In Pursuit of Poetry. New York: McGraw-Hill,
     1960. Robinson, pp. 82-87 et passim. Modern blank verse
     is best exemplified in the works of Robinson and Frost.
     For some reason today Robinson is largely ignored and al-
     most forgotten. His greatest poem, Amaranth, partly sat-
     irical and partly philosophical, was passed over even at the
     time of its publication, and received scant justice at the
     hands of the reviewers. It is a study of misfit characters,

all of them in the wrong profession or self-deceived that
they are artists.  It is a dark poem, but shot through
with the best of Robinson's wry wit.  The opening scene
is in a shadowy Bohemian tavern that has the atmosphere
of a nightmare.  Here he introduces his various characters,
one after the other, all the misfits of the modern world.

682  HINDEN, Michael C.  "Edwin Arlington Robinson and the The-
     atre of Destiny."  Colby Library Quarterly, 8 (December,
     1969), 463-471.  Article explores a similarity and possible
     influence of Robinson's play Van Zorn and T. S. Eliot's
     The Cocktail Party....  Admittedly Robinson's two plays
     were not very successful, and it would be imprudent to
     proclaim that they are significant landmarks in the develop-
     ment of American drama.  On the other hand, neither are
     these plays wholly deserving of the oblivion to which they
     have been relegated.  If for no other reason, Van Zorn
     extends a claim upon our interest for those respects in
     which it so clearly anticipates Eliot's later dramaturgy.

683  HIRSCH, David H.  "'The Man Against the Sky' and the Prob-
     lem of Faith," in Barnard, ed. (1969), pp. 31-42.  "The
     Man Against the Sky" is one of those poems about which
     controversy--both philosophical and aesthetic--persists
     without any apparent hope of resolution.  Some critics find
     the poem a failure, though they continue to find it interest-
     ing as E. A. Robinson's fullest statement of his beliefs on
     ultimate questions.  Others cannot agree on just what the
     ultimate beliefs stated in the poem are.  It is not clear, or
     at least it has not been agreed upon, whether Robinson in-
     tends the poem as an affirmation or as a statement of de-
     spair.  Aims at reading the poem "poetically" with attention
     given to poetic conventions.  Examines fire imagery and
     allusions to dispel any reservations about "loose structure"
     of the poem.

684  HOGAN, Charles Beecher.  A Bibliography of Edwin Arlington
     Robinson.  New Haven:  Yale University Press, 1936.  Re-
     printed Folcroft, Penn.:  Folcroft Press, 1971.  221 pages.

685  _____.  "A Poet at the Phonic Shrine."  Colophon, 3 (Sum-
     mer, 1938), 359-363.

686  _____.  "Edwin Arlington Robinson:  New Bibliographic
     Notes."  Papers of the Bibliographic Society of America,
     35 (Spring, 1941), 115-144.  This article, written four
     years after the Robinson bibliography, includes items that
     escaped the author originally.  In his introduction Hogan
     says:  "This information I have divided into three sections.
     In the first I give the bibliography of new items consisting
     in whole or in part of work by Robinson.  In the second

are given additions and corrections to the first three parts
of my bibliography, and in the third section are listed
books and articles dealing with Robinson that have been
discovered or written subsequent to the publication of my
bibliography."

687  HOLMAN, Catherine Elizabeth. "Edwin Arlington Robinson's
Struggle Against Puritanism." Norman: University of
Oklahoma, 1925 M.A. thesis.

688  HOLMES, John Haynes. "The Latest Robinson: A Review of
Amaranth." Unity (Chicago), 114 (October 29, 1934), 95-
96.

689  _____. "Review of King Jasper." Virginia Quarterly Review, 12 (April, 1936), 288-295. Remarks on Robinson are
a part of article "Five American Poets." In this latest and
last book, Robinson returns to the theme of dissolution,
and writes a symbolic story of the crumbling of an entire
industrial order. Robinson with the eyes of a man who
knew he would not live long, looked at the contemporary
world and saw nothing to rejoice in. Only that persistent
hope which he had otherwise and often expressed let him
end this poem by saying that, at any rate, life must and
will go on; but there is nothing left at the end except life.

690  _____. "Review of Selected Letters." Boston Transcript,
May 9, 1940. P. 2. The book within certain limitations
makes excellent reading, and is valuable for anyone concerned with the artist's life in this country. To the reader without background, perhaps the more unfortunate aspects would obtrude; to the reader already well-prepared
in Robinson's life and in the history of modern American
poetry, it will be extremely interesting, and not wholly
satisfying. As a prelude to larger books to come, this
selection of letters is arresting and revealing.

691  HOPPER, V. Foster. "Robinson and Frost." Saturday Review
of Literature, 13 (November 2, 1935), 9. Letter to the
Editor, in which Hopper objects to the critic who said
Robinson took for his motto "STOP, LOOK, LISTEN," as
in the railroad crossing. Frost might have done this, but
Robinson would say "LOOK OUT FOR THE ENGINE." External or adventitious peculiarities interested him not at all.
His was the search for motivation, for the hidden springs
to human action. His study was the engine which hauled
its human load over a roadbed considerably more hazardous
and toward a terminal even more uncertain.

692  HOWARD, Leon. Literature and the American Tradition. New
York: Doubleday, 1960. Robinson, pp. 236-238. In many

of his early poems Robinson showed a mastery of disciplined verse forms and an epigrammatic wit which makes him
one of the most quotable of modern American poets, but
his novelist's interest in people was also accompanied by
a tendency toward verbosity which led him into a kind of
colloquial verse narrative that was effective and sometimes
magnificent.

693 HOWE, Irving. "Tribute to an American Poet." Harper's
     Magazine, 240 (June, 1970), 103-108. By Robinson's time
     Puritanism was no longer a coherent religious force. It
     had become a collective memory of moral rigor, an ingrained
     and hardened way of life surviving beyond its original mo-
     ment of strength. Yet to writers like Hawthorne and Rob-
     inson, the New England tradition left a rich inheritance.
     The assumption that human existence, caught in a constant
     struggle between good and evil, is inherently dramatic.
     Also related is the habit of intensive scrutiny into human
     motives. These are the principal characteristics of Robin-
     son.

694 _____. "A Grave and Solitary Voice: An Appreciation of
     Edwin Arlington Robinson," in The Critical Point on Liter-
     ature and Culture. New York: Horizon Press, 1973. Pp.
     96-108. Notes that Robinson's centennial came and went with
     very little notice. Was angry at first, but then realized
     that it did not matter what we said about our great writers.
     Praise is for living authors. Writers like Robinson survive
     in their work, appreciated by readers who aren't afraid to
     be left alone with an old book.... Robinson lived mainly
     within himself. Among his obsessive subjects are solitude
     and failure, both drawn from his immediate experience and
     treated with a richness of complication that is unequalled
     in American poetry. Robinson will never please the crowds,
     neither the large ones panting for platitude, nor the small
     ones supposing paradox an escape from platitude.

695 HOWES, Victor. "Poet of Loner, Loser, Anti-hero, Outsider."
     Christian Science Monitor, 61 (March 15, 1969), 9. Review
     of biography by Louis O. Coxe. Robinson is a major Amer-
     ican poet in partial eclipse. The reasons for this eclipse
     are many, and they are referred to again and again in
     the pages of Coxe's new book: Robinson is out of fashion,
     neither he nor his characters are of this age, out of step
     with this age of heroes, etc. Mr. Coxe's book is useful,
     not as an introduction to Robinson, but as a persuasive
     argument for us to read him. We get just enough of
     Robinson's biography to focus our understanding on the
     poems.

696 HUBBELL, Jay B. and John O. Beaty. An Introduction to

Poetry. New York: Macmillan, 1923. Reprinted, 1936. "Edwin Arlington Robinson," pp. 210-211 et passim. The contrast between Masefield and his greatest rival sonneteer, the American poet, Robinson, is the contrast between the Shakespearian and the Italian sonnet. Masefield shows fire; Robinson, restraint. Masefield is exuberant; Robinson, subtle. "Firelight" and "Souvenir" illustrate Robinson's mature manner.

697    _____. Who Are the Major American Writers? Chapel Hill: University of North Carolina Press, 1972. Contains many references to Robinson, but does not discuss. Robinson listed in several charts as an important American poet. Is named in chapter on literary prizes, critical, polls, etc. Robinson won Pulitzer award three times, 1921, 1924, and 1927.

698   HUDSON, Hoyt H. "Edwin Arlington Robinson." Literary Digest, 107 (October 25, 1930), 24.

699    _____. "Robinson and Praed." Poetry, 61 (February, 1943), 612-620. Article is a carefully worked out comparison of the English poet Winthrop Mackworth Praed (1802-1839), with Robinson. The comparison is based on several similarities: their handling of the character sketch, some basic attitudes; similarities in cadence, tone, and temper. Article also explores the avenues by which Robinson may have become familiar with Praed, and the improvements which the American poet made on his sources, if indeed they were sources.

700   HUGHES, Dorothy. "Arthurian Material in American Literature." University of Nebraska, 1935. M.A. thesis.

701   HUGHES, Robert Norris. "Poetic Technique in the Verse of Millay, Robinson Jeffers, and E. A. Robinson." M.A. thesis, Ohio State University, 1932.

702   HUMPHRY, James, III. The Library of Edwin Arlington Robinson: A Descriptive Catalogue. Waterville, Maine: Colby College Press, 1950. Monograph No. 19, 52 pages. Begins with a brief Preface followed by a listing of the books in Robinson's library, now in the Colby College Library. In the Preface Humphry says: "He grew up with books, and every careful reader of his poems must have been struck by the evidence they present as to the large part that books played in his life and thought.... At Harvard the reading continued, and in literary discussion Robinson blossomed. Unlike Coleridge, who left a pencil trail through every book he handled, Robinson read without marking his books. Very few of the more than three hundred in this collection have any marginal comments, or even underlinings."

703  HUTCHINSON, Percy A. "This 'Unransomed Juvenile Miscalled Democracy': Dionysus in Doubt." New York Times (Book Review Section), March 29, 1925. Reprinted in Current Review, edited by L. W. Smith. New York: Henry Holt, 1926. Pp. 308-314. Robinson has many short-comings. His is not a prophetic voice; and the greater part of his work lacks what Pater called so happily "mystic perfume." But there is ever a finely repressed anguish of thought. And if he permits no lustre to his lines, no accessory beauties, his style is not open to the accusation of hardness."

704  _____. "American Poetry at Its Best: Tristram, a Narrative of Great Power." New York Times, May 8, 1927. P. 27. It is not too much to say that Robinson's Tristram may be placed first among all modern versions of the ancient tale. For those who have despaired of American poetry, here is cause for change of heart.

705  _____. "Tragedy of Cavender's House." New York Times, April 21, 1929. As the narrative progresses the woman becomes more and more the inexorable voice of Cavender's conscience. It is a subtle, powerful objectification of the inner voice that Robinson has created and developed in the poem. It is a work of starkly tragic import, done with an austerity of manner possible only to a truly great poet.

706  _____. "Robinson Returns to Modern Life: The Glory of the Nightingales." New York Times, September 14, 1930. The poem is a literary achievement the magnitude of which must grow with renewed reading. Psychological analysis of a peculiarly penetrating and accurate sort, philosophic profundity, and a dramatic human episode--only Robinson can so weave such things together that one exclaims that he has achieved, or nearly achieved, the ultimate in his elected genre. The work is not a repetition of the gorgeous panoply of Tristram, but it is not without an austere perfection of its own.

707  _____. "Robinson's Dramatic Poem: Matthias at the Door." New York Times, October 4, 1931. This work seems to be the crowning achievement of what the poet has been striving to do and has not before so completely accomplished. Within its lines is everything that is the poet Robinson. Whether it be all in all, what one would like for a poet's crowning work, does not matter. Robinson clearly has sought to be an ethical teacher as well as a poet. In the present work he superlatively attains that combined purpose.

708  _____. "Robinson's New Collection: Nicodemus." New York Times, October 2, 1932. P. 2. Robinson is truly a great

poet, perhaps the foremost poet of the present day, for the
reason that he thinks deeply and judges sagaciously, forc-
ing his words to their white heat under the intensity of his
imagination. His followers will not be disappointed in the
poems in the Nicodemus volume.

709 _____. "Robinson's New Narrative: Talifer." New York
Times, October 1, 1933. Talifer is an idyll, more Tenny-
sonian than Robinsonian, a concoction including many beauties, but the whole failing to impress one as does this poet's
strongest and most beautiful works.

710 _____. "Edwin Arlington Robinson's Dramatization of Dream:
Amaranth." New York Times, September 30, 1934. Not the
fires of emotion but the white fires of intellect animate this
poem. It is the peculiar genius of this man that he can so
inject his own poetic intensity into a fabrication that his
lines, taut as drawn wires, tingle and vibrate as if to a
more emotional theme.

711 _____. "The Poetry of E. A. Robinson." New York Times,
April 21, 1935. Pp. 2, 11.

712 _____. "Robinson's Satire and Symbolism: King Jasper."
New York Times, November 10, 1935. P. 5. This work is
as intricate and as devious in thought as anything Robinson
has ever written. It is at once a poem beautiful and ex-
coriating. If this is Robinson's swan song, and apparently
it is, it strikes a resonant chord. The poem is at once
both blinding in intensity and fiercely illuminating.

713 _____. "Review of Selected Letters." New York Times,
February 25, 1940. P. 5. Those well acquainted with
Robinson's genius who would like to become more intimately
acquainted with this personality will not only read, but also
reread these letters. Others knowing nothing of Robinson
will find here revealed a great American.

714 _____. "A Revealing Biography: Robinson by Hagedorn."
New York Times Book Review, October 16, 1938. P. 5.

715 INGALLS, Mildred Dodge. "Metaphysical Aspects of American
Poetry." Tufts College, 1933. M.A. thesis.

716 ISAACS, Edith J. R. "Edwin Arlington Robinson, A Descriptive List of the Lewis M. Isaacs Collection of Robinsoniana."
Bulletin of the New York Public Library, 52 (May, 1948),
211-233. Article is a listing of this material which has been
given to the New York Public Library, with a brief introductory note. The material is called the Lewis M. Isaacs
Collection because he owned it and it was his most treasured

personal possession; however, the collection was largely
made by the poet himself, who knew exactly what he wanted
in it and why. This perhaps gives it a peculiar distinction.
The listing is in several parts: Manuscript Material (letters
to and by Robinson), Poems by Robinson, Prose and Fragments by Robinson, Printed Items (Works by Robinson,
Works about Robinson).

717 ISAACS, Lewis M. "Edwin Arlington Robinson Speaks of Music." New England Quarterly, 22 (December 1947 or 1949),
499-510. Without any pretense to technical knowledge of the
art, Robinson was peculiarly responsive to the appeal of music, both intuitively and intellectually. The fountain of his
poetry and the well of his musical memory were close together, and can be illustrated by the number of references
to music, from his earliest to his latest poems, including
the musical-poetic achievement in "The Man Who Died
Twice." Even Sidney Lanier did not match Robinson's
felicity in this field, although he was a professional musician as well as a poet.

718 ISLEY, Elise Dort. "The Sources of the Imagery in the Poetry
of Edwin Arlington Robinson." Ph.D. diss., University of
Arkansas, 1967. DA, 28 (1967), 1436A. In this study the
interest is centered on the sources from which the imagery
has been derived. The principal areas of this study are
(1) the Bible, Greek literature and mythology, and from
unusual stories drawn from various languages; (2) every-
day living, domestic surroundings, the house itself and its
furnishings, routines; (3) music, including the instruments
of music, and the ones who make music; and (4) the world
of the outdoors, nature, animals, plants, the atmosphere
and the heavens. Concludes with the deduction that almost
all of the images come from the early environment and early
events of the poet's life.

719 JACOBS, Willis D. "Edwin Arlington Robinson's 'Mr. Flood's
Party.'" College English, 12 (November, 1950), 110. Article is an objection to the comment made by Brooks, Purser,
and Warren in their anthology An Approach to Literature.
They ask the question, "Why is Eben Flood a drunkard?"
but the fact is that Eben is not a drunkard. Robinson says
specifically that Eben drinks but seldom. In addition there
are at least four indirect but forceful indications that dis-
prove the slander of drunkenness. Actually the poem is
the usual but always sad theme of transience and death,
the loneliness of old age without friendship and understanding. He is defeated by longevity alone and not by frailty
of character.

720 JANE, Mary C. "Journey to Head Tide." Christian Science

Monitor, February 25, 1950. P. 10. Tells the story of a
visit to Head Tide, Maine, during a Christmas vacation in
Newcastle, Maine. Head Tide was remembered as the birth-
place of Edwin Arlington Robinson, a little village consisting
of some five or six white houses and a big general store,
with a bridge over the river leading to the church and
schoolhouse on the hill.... After a long visit around the
village, it was time to go, the afternoon light was beginning
to fade. But we had made a journey of love and found it
better than our dreams.

721 JARRELL, Randall. Poetry and the Age. New York: Knopf,
1953. Reprinted in paperback, 1955. Robinson, passim.
Not significantly treated.

722 _____. "Fifty Years of American Poetry." Prairie Schooner,
37 (Spring, 1963), 45-52. When you read Robinson's poems,
you are conscious of a mind looking seriously at a world with
people in it and expressing itself primarily in terms of these
human beings it has observed and created. Robinson's
steady human sympathy is accompanied by a steady hatred
of the inhuman world that people have made for themselves,
the world of business and greed and hypocritical morality.
He is far better when he is reserved and prosaic than when
he is poetic; his poetic rhetoric is embarrassingly threadbare
and commonplace, as when he writes about his own lost belief.... Robinson wrote a great deal of poetry and only a
few good poems; and yet there is a somber distinction and
honesty about him--he is a poet you respect.

723 _____. The Third Book of Criticism. New York: Farrar,
Straus, & Giroux, 1969. Reprints "Fifty Years of American
Poetry," pp. 295-333.

724 JENCKES, Edward N. "A Poet's Letters: Review of Selected
Letters." Springfield Daily Republican, February 24, 1940.
P. 6.

725 JENKINS, Ralph E. "Robinson's 'Lost Anchors.'" Explicator,
23 (April, 1965), item 64. Reviews other explications of
Robinson's poem, and feels that these studies have failed
because the authors did not see the simplest interpretation
of the poem. The old sailor had lost his anchor when he
left home and went to sea. The analogy is as old as time
immemorial: ships have sunk and legends have grown up
around them, just as sons have always left home to go to
sea. The final line is an ironic comment on the sailor's
failure, and emphasizes that the sialor, like so many of
Robinson's other characters, ends his life as an interesting
failure.

726  JOE, Wanne J.  "A Brief Discussion of Edwin Arlington Robin-
       son Based on His Life and Poetry."  English Language and
       Literature (Seoul, Korea), 14 (1963), 18-39.  In English.
       Good over-all survey of Robinson's life and poetry.  Article
       is well-documented, but with mostly standard works on
       Robinson.  Although it does not make too much new con-
       tribution to Robinson scholarship, it is valuable for its cov-
       erage, and summary qualities.  Some emphasis is placed on
       Robinson as a poet of his age, and the poet's war on tradi-
       tional Puritanism.  The late nineteenth century, troubled
       with evils of society, notwithstanding its splendid achieve-
       ments, demanded an explanation for the paradoxical state
       of affairs which naive transcendentalists were no longer
       capable of apprehending.

727  JOHNSON, Edgar.  "Edwin Robinson Sonnets."  New York Eve-
       ning Post, December 1, 1928.  P. 8.

728  JOHNSON, Merle.  American First Editions.  New York: R. R.
       Bowker, 1932.  Robinson, pp. 304-307.  Includes reprint of
       Latham, Harold S. (1923).  Lists first editions of works by
       Robinson with few items about Robinson.

729  JOHNSON, Oakley.  "Man, Woman, and Poetry:  Cavender's
       House."  Book League Monthly, 2 (July, 1929), 183-184.

730  JOHNSON, W. H., Jr.  "Two Aspects of the Poetry of Edwin
       Arlington Robinson."  Vanderbilt University (Nashville),
       1926, M.A. thesis.

731  JOHNSTON, Laura C.  "Influences on Edwin Arlington Robinson."
       Fordham University, 1931, M.A. thesis.

732  JONES, E. B. C.  "Review of The Man Who Died Twice."  Na-
       tion and Athenaeum, 35 (May 24, 1924), supplement, p. 248.
       If this were a first book, it might be regarded as promis-
       ing, but it is a twelfth, and very depressing.  The theme,
       treated with extreme directness by Robert Frost or with
       some music and some imagination by Conrad Aiken, might
       have passed; but here, related in lines alternately grandi-
       ose and pedestrian, it seems a poor, flat, unconvincing little
       story.  There is a great deal of mud stirred up; but the
       puddle remains shallow.

733  JONES, Howard Mumford.  "Poetry and Time."  Virginia Quar-
       terly Review, 7 (January, 1931), 138-143.  Article skims
       over 15 volumes of recently published poetry and includes
       comment on Robinson's The Glory of the Nightingales.  This
       work has the technical dexterity, the subtleties of insight,
       the revelation of past drama by soliloquy which we have
       come to associate with this great poet.  Once more we view

the broken and defeated of the earth, once more we learn
that apparent success and apparent failure are not fundamental gain or loss.... As of old, a large part of the
strength of the poem is found in the sententiae of a
Shakespearian wisdom which stud the poem as aside or observation. It is these sudden large views of life and men
which the minor poets never achieve.

734        . "Imagination Does But Seem." Virginia Quarterly
Review, 8 (January, 1932), 143-150. Review of seven volumes of poetry including Robinson's Matthias at the Door.
The theme of this work is nothing new, and the execution
seems a bit inferior. In the beginning Matthias is a successful man of the world, but by the end he has lost everything, material and spiritual, and is contemplating suicide.
The book is almost wholly without decoration and adorn-
ment, and seems to be cast in the wrong form. It might
make a novel; it does not make a good poem.

735 JONES, Llewellyn. "E. A. Robinson's Fine 'Lancelot.'" Chicago Evening Post, May 21, 1920. P. 9.

736        . "Edwin Arlington Robinson." American Review, 1
(March-April, 1923), 180-189. Is a rather general review
of Robinson's life and works which focuses, if anything on
the Arthurian poems, which brought him the greatest recognition and fame. The most constant interest throughout
Robinson's work, however, is personality and character.
In sonnets or in other poems he presents them directly and
succinctly. There is no obscurity in these poems and no
moralizing, and they are among the best things he has done.

737        . First Impressions: Essays on Poetry, Criticism and
Prosody. New York: Knopf, 1925. Robinson, pp. 13-36.
In most of Robinson's poetry his complex and subtle style
is appropriately used for studies of complex and recondite
human situations. This explains, of course, the slow growth
of his popularity, the legend of his obscurity, and the
rather grudging praise of English critics.... Every admirer
of Robinson should read the play "Van Zorn," for it reveals
the poet to be aloof and rather stern, as having a warmly
human touch and a very considerable humor. This comedy
verges so nearly upon the tragic but has a delicious humor
and a very real depth of insight into character.

738        . "Levitation by Bootstrap: Review of Amaranth."
The Midwest (Chicago), 1 (November, 1934), pp. 1, 7.
Agrees with a good many critics in that "this poem doesn't
quite work." It is too much allegory to be good psychological analysis, and too much analysis to be good allegory.
The poem is heavy going, the deep intellectual thought con-
veyed through images of fantasy and dream.

739  JONES, Richard Foster. "Nationalism and Imagism in Modern
      American Poetry." Washington University Studies (St.
      Louis, Mo.), 11 (October, 1923), 97-130. Robinson not
      significantly discussed. Article is based on the premise
      that a new movement in poetry was shaping itself at that
      time, a desire for liberty to abandon a poetic tradition, a
      desire for liberty to abandon a poetic tradition, a desire
      to leave traveled roads and to discover untrodden paths in
      a new country. The two schools of poetry may be desig-
      nated the nationalistic and the imagistic. it is with the first
      group that we most readily identify E. A. Robinson, etc.
      These poets very rigidly restrict poetry to contemporary
      life but permit great freedom in the treatment of a subject.

740  JOYNER, Nancy Carol. "Edwin Arlington Robinson's View of
      Poetry: A Study of His Theory and His Technique in the
      Late Narratives." Ph.D. diss., University of North Caro-
      lina (Chapel Hill), 1966. DA, 27 (1967), 2531A-2532A.
      There is considerable difference between Robinson's early
      and late poetry, although recent scholarhsip has suggested
      that his habits of writing were established in his earliest
      work. This dissertation, presented in four chapters, is a
      study of his theories about poetry, especially as they apply
      to the late narratives. The first chapter deals with remarks
      he made about the nature of poetry and his career; the sec-
      ond chapter deals with the effect of this criticism on his
      poetry after 1921; the third is a study of the techniques
      of the long narratives; and the final chapter approaches the
      poems from the point of view of theme.

741  _____. "Robinson's Pamela and Sandburg's Agatha." Amer-
      ican Literature, 40 (January, 1969), 548-549. Early ver-
      sions of Robinson's poem used the name Agatha. Later he
      discovered that Sandburg had used Agatha in a somewhat
      similar connection. Robinson expressed regret at having
      to make the revision, saying "I hated to do it, for somehow
      Agatha was the girl." The Sandburg poem is almost certain-
      ly "Plaster," which appeared in 1920. The similarity of the
      two poems is immediately apparent, but the differences in
      style and structure are worlds apart.

742  _____. "An Unpublished Version of 'Mr. Flood's Party.'"
      English Language Notes, 7 (September, 1969), 55-57. Short
      article based upon a manuscript version of the poem, up-
      dated, but probably of earlier origin than the version in
      Collected Poems, the one that is commonly reprinted. Most
      changes in the poem do not amount to much, but in this
      case the entire last stanza radically changes the meaning of
      the poem. In the manuscript version the poem ends with
      condescension and even mockery with ironic surprise. In
      the familiar version the poem ends with a tone of nostalgia

and sympathy and a note of admiration for Mr. Flood's stoic
endurance.

743 _____. "Edwin Arlington Robinson's Concessions to the
Critics." Research Studies at Washington State University,
40 (March, 1972), 48-53. It is usually taken for granted,
based upon very little evidence, that Robinson cared nothing
for literary fads, public taste, or current critical thinking.
There is good reason to believe that Robinson was very
sensitive to what critics said about him, so much so as to
suggest that his dependence upon critical acceptance was a
determining factor in shaping his career.... It was not until he was well-established that he turned to writing the
long narrative poems, which were never too well received,
except for Tristram, Lancelot, and Merlin. The critics always responded more favorably toward the shorter poems,
and he seems to have given them what they wanted.

744 _____. "Robinson's Poets." Colby Library Quarterly, 9
(March, 1972), 441-455. Robinson always had very little
to say about poets and the writing of poetry, so his comments in letters and interviews have become the primary
source for discovering his critical attitudes. The eight
poets that Robinson wrote about have little in common, and
his attitude toward the writers vary: Verlaine, Shakespeare, Crabbe, Hood, Arnold, Poe, Emerson, and Whitman.... Robinson makes extensive use of poets and poetry
as subject matter. While he employs an impressive variety
of approaches, the ideas about the role of the poet and the
nature of poetry remain within rather narrow limits. Of
primary importance to Robinson is the poet's ability to communicate truth to his audience. A poet is able to do this
only insofar as he has an "inner fire," an attribute that
he cannot choose for himself.

745 _____. Edwin Arlington Robinson: A Reference Guide.
Boston: Hall, 1978. Excellent, two hundred page listing
of secondary source material. The work begins with a brief
"Selected Articles about Robinson, 1894-1915," but concen-
trates on publications from 1916 to 1976. The format of the
book is difficult to deal with, listed chronologically in terms
of book length works and shorter works. An extensive Index helps greatly, but does not make easy the finding of
items desired. The Index is not primarily of subject matter,
but of authors and titles.

746 _____. "Whatever Happened to Tristram?" Colby Library
Quarterly, 16 (June, 1980), 118-122. Begins with brief review of publication history of Tristram, easily the most
popular and best-seller of Robinson's works. After Robinson's death, however, his reputation declined, and while

high regard for some of the shorter poems has been recovered, Tristram has not fared so well. Nevertheless, there
has been considerable scholarship on the poem. The purpose of this article is to survey this scholarship: source
studies, comparisons, and analysis of the poem itself.
Tristram has lasted, but it clearly deserves more attention
than it has received.

747  KAHN, Sy.  "Kenneth Fearing and the Twentieth Century
     Blues," in The Thirties: Fiction, Poetry, Drama, edited by
     Warren French. Deland, Fla.: Everett/Edwards, 1969.
     Pp. 133-140, Robinson passim. Commenting effectively on
     an era and society through ironic portraiture of general
     types is characteristic of the best poems of E. A. Robin-
     son.... Fearing shares with Robinson the technique of
     using portraiture as a way of rendering a double irony:
     the poem's and the poet's. Robinson, however, succeeds
     by giving more intimate details of feature, gesture and
     dress of the subjects, and in rendering them in more formal
     and traditional diction, line length, rhyme scheme and struc-
     ture.... Robinson's characters are at once more particular-
     ized and more mythic than Fearing's whose figures are closer
     to the free and easy line of the impressionistic or surrealistic
     cartoon.

748  KAPLAN, Estelle. "Philosophy in the Poetry of Edwin Arlington
     Robinson." Ph.D. diss. (in Philosophy), Columbia Uni-
     versity, 1940. Published as Philosophy in the Poetry of
     Edwin Arlington Robinson. New York: Columbia University
     Press, 1940. 162 pp. with Bibliography and Index. The
     work is in two parts: "The Sources of Robinson's Ideal-
     ism," and "Philosophical Analyses," which consists of four
     thematic divisions. Using Robinson's occasional figures,
     we may characterize each of the four groups of poems in
     terms of his symbols for the tragic forces: first shadows,
     then castles, then houses, then chimneys. The shadows
     are the objects of his doctrine of "light"; the castles are
     the dark stage-settings for romantic passion and for Chris-
     tendom and the Grail; the house (of marriage) all have their
     dark "doors," which open usually into the "night"; the
     chimneys are the evils of power by which economic material-
     ism defeats itself. However, regardless of period the theme
     of tragedy remains, and the problem of self-knowledge, with
     its transcendence of darkness, is forever present.

749  KART, Laurence. "Richard Cory: Artist Without an Art."
     Colby Library Quarterly, 11 (June, 1975), 160-161. Reply
     to Kavka article listed below. If this reading of the poem
     is placed alongside the pattern of Robinson's career, then
     Richard Cory can be seen as an artist without an art, or an
     artist whose practice lacked certain qualities that might have

sustained him.... That Cory is something of an artist is
clear from the beginning. His art is flawed because he
is its sole product, and his art allows no room for the audience to transmit value back to him. His lavish aesthetic
is only on himself, and is unable to appreciate the effect
that elegantly surfaced self has on other human beings.

750  KAVKA, Jerome. "Richard Cory's Suicide: A Psychoanalytic
     View." Colby Library Quarterly, 11 (June, 1975), 150-159.
     Article is by a psychoanalyst, and is written largely to re-
     ply to other critics who have interpreted Richard Cory in
     one way or another. This writer suggests that the power
     of Robinson's poem lies in its implications of the personal
     and social limitations of the narcissistic personality. What
     is important about Cory is the absence of true relationships
     with other humans. He was unable to socialize with others
     as separate and independent beings. A suicidal crisis
     brought about because of a relative weakness of the ego vis-
     à-vis the overly strong system of ideals--a condition known
     as depression, would have drawn forth a kind of sympathy
     from the onlooker on the basis of an identification with a
     kindred soul. The shock effect is a diagnostic clue to the
     exquisitely narcissistic nature of the suicide.

751  KEARNEY, Clytie Hazel. "Edwin Arlington Robinson." New
     York: Columbia University, 1918, M.A. thesis.

752  KELLY, Blanche Marie. "Review of Cavender's House." Chris-
     tian World, 130 (January, 1930), 500.

753  KENNER, Hugh. "Glow-Worms and Antimacassars." Poetry,
     92 (May, 1958), 121-126. Review of seven volumes, liter-
     ary criticism, biography, etc. Comments include mention
     of Edwin S. Fussell's biography Edwin Arlington Robinson.
     In this work Fussell is not tenaciously reconstructing a life,
     nor is he writing criticism, or history; he is making a book.
     He does this by surveying Robinson's reading in and use
     of the American Past, the Literature of England, European
     Naturalism, Classical Literature, and the English Bible....
     The question of how much Robinson may be read without
     fatigue and why, does not arise, although it is possible to
     conclude that the reason is that Robinson's adaptation to the
     twentieth-century was not radical enough.

754  KENNY, Herbert A. "Silent Approval." The Sunday Globe
     (Boston), 194 (September 8, 1968), 46-A. Review of Let-
     ters to Edith Brower.

755  KENYON, Bernice. "Review of Matthias at the Door." Outlook
     and Independent, 159 (October 28, 1931), 282-283. This is
     a dark fable, which Robinson might have made more

understandable had he chosen to unravel a little the metrical complexity of his statements, and to speak out, now and
then at least, in a manner clear and plain.  But he does
not choose, and many of us are left in the dark, and still
wishing for a return of the old Robinson, whose work was
less complex, but far more moving and alive.

756  KILMER, Alfred Joyce.  "A Classic Poet."  New York Times
     Book Review, September 8, 1912.  P. 487.

757  _____.  "Edwin Arlington Robinson Defines Poetry."  New
     York Times Book Review, April 9, 1916.  P. 12.

758  _____.  Literature in the Making By Some of Its Makers.
     New York:  Harper & Brothers, 1917.  "A New Definition
     of Poetry:  Edwin Arlington Robinson," pp. 265-273.  Is
     presented in the form of a conversation with Robinson,
     who responds to certain questions put by the narrator.
     For the most part the answers are evasive:  are modern
     poets better or worse than in the past?  Robinson does not
     know, and of course thinks it is a matter of definition.
     As to his own poetry, he is equally ambiguous, and will
     not commit himself to any real opinion.  It all depends on
     Time, he concludes, and understands that the question is
     a difficult one.

759  KING, Carlyle.  "Edwin Arlington Robinson."  Canadian Forum,
     32 (August, 1952), 119.  Review of biography by Ellsworth
     Barnard.

760  KING, Ronald W. P.  "Philosophy of Light:  An Essay on the
     Poetry of Edwin Arlington Robinson."  New York, Univer-
     sity of Rochester, 1927.  M.A. thesis.

761  KIRBY, Thomas Austin and William John Olive, eds.  Essays
     in Honor of Esmond Linworth Marilla.  Baton Rouge:
     Louisiana State University Press, 1970.  "Lorraine and the
     Sirens:  Courtesans in Two Poems by E. A. Robinson," by
     Ronald Moran.  Pp. 312-319.  Discussed under Moran.

762  KLOTZ, Marvin.  "Robinson's 'The Tree in Pamela's Garden.'"
     Explicator, 20 (January, 1963), item 42.  This sonnet de-
     scribes a particularly interesting addition to his gallery of
     "grotesque" characters.  The poem may be divided into
     four sections which alternately reveal truth and deceit, un-
     derstanding and misunderstanding, while, at the same time,
     they describe a morbid and warped personality.  Concludes
     that Pamela has deceived her neighbors who regard her as
     pitiable, whereas in truth she is mad, regarding herself as
     the embodiment of the Daphne-Eve figure, destructively
     frigid.

763  KNICKERBOCKER, Frances Wentworth. "Faith in the Pieces:
     Review of Selected Letters." Sewanee Review, 49 (January-
     March, 1941), 125-126. Those who care for the poetry of
     Robinson will welcome these letters which tell what manner
     of man wrote "Richard Cory" and Tristram. In Robinson's
     letters to his intimate friends, we penetrate the mask of
     super-New-England reserve to the free play of his sym-
     pathies, the warmth of his affection. The quality of the
     man behind the poetry is his utter integrity, the single-
     minded devotion to his art that never wavered, throughout
     the long years of poverty and neglect. His scorn of notor-
     ity and outward success runs through his life and his work;
     some of his most characteristic poems depict the frustrated,
     the seeming failures and the seeming successes.

764  KNIGHT, Grant C. American Literature and Culture. New
     York: Ray Long & Richard R. Smith, 1932. Robinson,
     pp. 463-467. It is too early to give a final judgment on
     Robinson, who gives no indication of a radical departure
     from the technique or the mood of his earlier writing.
     Tragedy hangs heavy over a majority of the people he
     characterizes in short poems. Robinson is a psychologist,
     being lured by the Spectacle of human failure and defeat.
     Honors have been heaped upon Robinson. Critics agree
     that his blank verse and his sonnets are among the finest
     in our literature.

765  _____. The Strenuous Age in American Literature. Chapel
     Hill: University of North Carolina Press, 1954. Robinson
     pp. 74-75, 209-210. In 1910 Edwin Arlington Robinson,
     sad with the knowledge that he had failed to win either
     critical or popular approval and with the memory of priva-
     tions caused by poverty, felt already outdistanced and old.
     But this feeling that he was a Watcher by the Way strength-
     ened his forbearance for the odd gifted persons character-
     ized in his Town Down the River of that year--persons who
     had also stumbled or halted on the journey to self-fulfillment,
     men and women who were sometimes wastrels, sometimes sin-
     ners, sometimes aliens in a materialistic civilization, but who
     were wise in their assertion of individuality, in their refusal
     to reduce the angles of personality so as to fit into a high
     place.... Though some reviewers still complained about ob-
     scurity, this was the first of Robinson's books to receive
     anything like approving notices, a fact to be attributed not
     so much to the championship of Roosevelt and other influ-
     ential friends as to the sensing that here was genuinely
     original poetry.

766  KNIGHT, Martha Peace. "The Poetry of Edwin Arlington Rob-
     inson." Cornell University, 1930. M.A. thesis.

767 KNOWLES, Frederic Lawrence. "The Poetry of Edwin Arlington Robinson." National, 17 (March, 1903), 798-799.

768 KOHN, Marjorie R. "Review of Robinson's Letters to Edith
Brower." Library Journal, No. 3788 (October 15, 1968),
93. An excellent introduction, copious footnotes and ap-
pendixes, forward the picture of a lonely talented man
and an intelligent creative woman. The letters are a welcome addition to collections of American poetry and criticism.

769 KOSTER, Richard Bradley. "To Be Poet Is More Than to
Write Verse." Christian Register, 117 (October 20, 1938),
606. Review of Hagedorn's biography.

770 KRAMER, Aaron. The Prophetic Tradition in American Poetry,
1835-1900. Rutherford: Fairleigh Dickinson University
Press, 1968. Robinson, pp. 322-324. His few war references are oblique. His most questioning, unsettling war
poem is "Captain Craig," written in 1899. Here he emphasizes spiritual warfare as his theme. The indiscreetly blared
funeral music celebrating the old man's victory over a harsh
life contrasts with the brass band for a soldier "who fought
one fight and in that fight fell dead." Not until "Cassandra," in 1914, does Robinson drop his reticence; in this
poem he forces his country to hear its own voice.

771 KRESENSKY, Raymond. "A Poetic Melo-drama: The Glory of
the Nightingales." Christian Century, 47 (December 24,
1930), 1595.

772 KREYMBORG, Alfred. Our Singing Strength: An Outline of
American Poetry, 1620-1930. New York: Coward-McCann,
1929. "The Wise Music of Robinson," pp. 297-315. Robinson is one of the principal characters in his own work.
His favorite character is the man who fails while seeking
the highest light. He is constantly absorbed in these failures, and through them, the failure of even the best of beings to survive the outlines of time. His art is salutary in
its austere devotion to intangible truth and its downright
acceptance of the defeat of the noblest of characters. But
the defeat is also a triumph and the Robinsonian character
a small hero groping through time and eternity.

773 _____, ed. An Anthology of American Poetry: Lyric Amer-
ica, 1630-1930. New York: Tudor Publishing Co., 1930.
Prints six poems by Edwin Arlington Robinson, pp. 255-265.
Prints "Flammonde," "The Poor Relation," "Veteran Sirens,"
"The Gift of God," "Eros Turannos," and "Mr. Flood's
Party," without biographical or critical introduction. Most
of these are familiar items by the poet, excepting perhaps

"The Poor Relation," but are nonetheless among Robinson's
most excellent short poems.

774  KUNITZ, Stanley J.  Living Authors: A Book of Biographies.
     New York: H. W. Wilson, 1931. Robinson, pp. 344-346.
     Biographical sketch with slight comment on the published
     works. Concludes with a list of works and their dates.
     Robinson is called a kindly fatalist and agnostic, who has
     thought and written much of men who have failed, the sort
     of men he knew in the days of his poverty about 1896. He
     shows the world of tragedy in the individual's futile strug-
     gles against a fate too powerful for him.

775  _____, and Howard Haycraft, eds.  Twentieth Century Au-
     thors: A Biographical Dictionary of Modern Literature.
     New York: H. W. Wilson, 1940. Robinson, pp. 1185-1186.
     See also First Supplement, 1955. P. 834. Repeats some
     of material in above item, although it updates the Robinson
     biography, with the poet's death in 1935. In conclusion it
     is said, "Robinson's least permanent poems are perhaps his
     long mediaeval narratives, and his most permanent are the
     shorter sketches of personalities, with their bare Yankee
     speech, their wry humor and implicit tragedy." Quotes
     several critics and their opinions of Robinson, which in
     these instances are mostly negative.

776  LANDINI, Richard.  "Metaphor and Imagery in Edwin Arlington
     Robinson's 'Credo.'"  Colby Library Quarterly, 8 (March,
     1968), 20-22. This poem is an artfully structured sonnet
     dealing with the question of ultimate purpose and meaning
     in life. The narrator advances to the very edge of despair,
     but despite his sense of lost direction, says he "knows" and
     "feels" the coming glory of the Light. The poem is con-
     structed around "journey" metaphor and imagery, and are
     so presented as revealing the narrator's sensibility that
     when he makes his final resolution of faith, it seems logi-
     cally acceptable, perhaps even inevitable.

777  LARSSON, Raymond.  "Review of Amaranth."  Commonweal, 21
     (January 18, 1935), 349. Among Robinson's poems this is
     a minor one. Composed, one supposes, in a genuine desire
     to illumine the darkness of these times, it shows Robinson
     not yet assured of his illumination. If it were Robinson's
     purpose to write "a philosophical" poem, sure there is suf-
     ficiently reason to apprehend his meaning and purpose, that
     it is only a quasi-fatalistic justification of the self.

778  LATCHEM, Dorothy Margaret.  "Character Portrayed in the
     Works of Edwin Arlington Robinson." State University of
     Iowa, 1934. M.A. thesis.

779 LATHAM, G. W. "Robinson at Harvard." Mark Twain Quarterly, 2 (Spring, 1938), 19-20. Recalls that he met Robinson a month or so after he entered Harvard as a "Special
Student." They soon discovered that they had much in
common, and saw a great deal of each other during the
next two years.... Robinson's tastes and ambitions were
already clearly defined, he knew exactly what he wanted.
He would know everything about literature, and he would
express himself in poetry. He had written considerable
verse before coming to Harvard, and soon his work began
to appear in the Advocate.... Robinson was very fond too
of music and drama, but his greatest delight was prolonged
conversations on every subject, even political.

780 LATHAM, Harold S. "American First Editions: Edwin Arlington Robinson. Publishers' Weekly, 103 (March 17, 1923),
945. Number 25 in the series. Lists thirteen first editions
of Robinson's poems. List is reprinted in Johnson, Merle
(1932).

781 _____. My Life In Publishing. With an introduction by
Sterling North. New York: E. P. Dutton, 1965. Robinson,
pp. 42-47. Reviews Robinson's publishing career, which
started slowly enough, but over the years gradually in-
creased until 1927, when he published Tristram. This was
the zenith of his career although afterward his works sold
well enough, but never anything like the Tristram, which
also won for Robinson the Pulitzer Prize in that year. It
was to Latham that Robinson finally delivered the manuscript
of King Jasper, after he became ill and hospitalized. As a
matter of fact Robinson died within a few hours after he
made the gesture of handing over his last work, his work
complete. Robinson never questioned the importance of his
work or its ultimate place in American literature. He saw
no reason for false modesty.

782 LATTA, Ruth E. "The Poetry of Edwin Arlington Robinson."
New York: University of Rochester, 1927. M.A. thesis.

783 LEARY, Lewis. "Edwin Arlington Robinson: A Biography by
Emery Neff." South Atlantic Quarterly, 48 (October, 1949),
617-618. Neff finds Robinson impressive and important,
the greatest intellectual force in our poetry, bringing to it
new powers of irony and wit.... He follows Robinson's
career with economical care, dwelling on experiences which
influenced his literary development. He comments on individual poems, but with great understanding of Robinson's
personal and aesthetic problems. As critical biography, it
is more fair than some recent studies. This book is per-
suasive and may lead others to a careful rereading of Robinson's verse.

784 _____. Articles on American Literature, 1900-1950. Durham: Duke University Press, 1954. Robinson, pp. 258-
263. Consists of some 150 items of biography, criticism,
notes, etc., published during the last half-century.

785 _____. Articles on American Literature, 1950-1967. Durham: Duke University Press, 1970 Robinson, pp. 467-
470. Consists of some 50 items of criticism, biography,
notes, etc., published during this period.

786 _____, and John Auchard. American Literature: A Study
and Research Guide. New York: St. Martin's Press,
1976. Robinson, passim. Robinson does not receive major
treatment, but the book is a valuable guide for students
as an introduction to criticism: types and schools, genres,
bibliographical guides, etc.

787 _____, and John Auchard. Articles on American Literature,
1968-1975. Durham: Duke University Press, 1979. Robinson, pp. 443-445. Consists of some 50 items of criticism,
biography, notes, etc., published during this period.

788 LECHLITNER, Ruth N. "The Arthurian Story Retold by Edwin Arlington Robinson." State University of Iowa (Iowa
City), 1926. M.A. thesis.

789 _____. "A Page About Poets: Amaranth." New Republic,
80 (October 17, 1934), 282. To read this poem is a painful
experience, when one remembers the true flame that burned
once in his short dramatic lyrics. Not even his occasional
flare of sardonic wit can survive the odor of decay that
smolders up from the ghoulish symbolism of his poem, the
scene of which is a spiritual purgatory of delusion and mis-
direction. The compulsion that called forth the writing of
this poem, doesn't keep it from being a most pathetic revelation of the bitter--yet heroic--self-doubt in the mind of
a poet who once struck genuine fire, knows that he did, and
fears that he never will again.

790 LEDOUX, Louis V. "A Discussion of the Exact Value of Robinson's Poetry." New York Times Review of Books, September 29, 1912. P. 533.

791 _____. "In Memoriam: Edwin Arlington Robinson." Saturday Review of Literature, 11 (April 13, 1935), 621. Reprinted in Mark Twain Quarterly, 2 (Spring, 1938), 10.
In this brief moment only the friend can be remembered;
the gentleman of quiet humor, of subtle intuitions; the man
who could be trusted to be loyal and who in all the give
and take of life never failed in that kindness of judgment
which though it was in essence an expression of his own

marked personality, yet was based on an intuitive and
sympathetic understanding of all that is most pathetically
human ... the possibility of good in what seems evil. In
nearly thirty years one cannot recall an instance in which
Robinson's attitude was anything but kindly.

792 _____. "Psychologist of New England." Saturday Review
of Literature, 12 (October 19, 1935), 3-4, 16-18. Is a
general discussion and appraisal of Robinson's work, written not too long after the poet's death. Critic does not
presume to an ultimate ranking of Robinson's work, but
thinks he stands clearly above the rank and file of those
who write. He was a man of powerful intellect and penetrating insight, and he was a master of technique, particularly the technique of blank verse. Ledoux was a literary
executor of Robinson, and one of his closest friends.

793 _____. "Edwin Arlington Robinson," in Dictionary of American
Biography. New York: Scribner's 1944. Vol. 21, pp.
632-634. Supplement, No. 1. Biographical sketch with little critical commentary. In conclusion, however, he is said
to stand clearly above most of those who write. He was a
man of powerful intellect and penetrating insight, master of
form and technique.

794 _____. "Collection of Letters in Library of Congress."
Quarterly Journal of the Library of Congress, 7 (November,
1949), 9-13. Also listed under Adams, Léonie, ed.

795 LE GALLIENNE, Richard. "Three American Poets." Forum,
45 (January, 1911), 88-90 Robinson has passed the period
of "sturm und drang." He has gone through the mill and
his book is occupied almost exclusively with men who have
gone through the mill too. Sad, cynical, good-hearted men,
comrades in the misfortunes of existence, with whom he has
been accustomed to foregather at Calverly's. He is a poet
of steel and grit, but he has been influenced by Browning
and Housman, and this has resulted in somewhat too string-
ent and tight-packed a style, in too many dark sayings and
drastic abbreviations of his meaning.

796 _____. "Mr. Robinson's Novel in Blank Verse: Roman
Bartholow." International Book Review, 1 (May, 1923),
23-24. The defect of the poem from a psychological point
of view is that in the case of the psychological hero we
get no clear idea of what was originally the matter with his
soul, the nature of the salvation brought ot it by Penn-
Raven, or of its final value. As to the form of the poem,
it cannot be said to justify the novel in blank verse as one
adapted to psychological purposes. Too much of it is neither
a novel nor a poem.

797 LENHART, Charmenz S. Musical Influence on American Poetry.
    Athens: University of Georgia Press, 1956. Robinson,
    passim. Does not feature Robinson; see Chapter IV for gen-
    eral background to the subject.

798 LENSING, George. "Robinson and Stevens: Some Tangential
    Bearings." Southern Review, 3 (Spring, 1967), 505–513.
    To what extent Robinson may have influenced this greatest
    of living and of American poets, one cannot say, but in
    at least three of the Octaves, one phase of Stevens' later
    work is certainly foreshadowed. In the ensuing decades
    Robinson and Stevens were to stand together as two major
    American poets relying upon traditional metrical form, par-
    ticularly blank verse. Dramatically opposed in personality
    and even poetic aim, Robinson and Stevens shared a common
    New England environment.... More generally, both sought
    a replacement for conventional theology, a harmony between
    the inner world of imagination and the outer world of reality.
    With their contemporary Robert Frost, each went on to re-
    claim the thematic hold of New England darkness in his work.

799 LEOFF, Eve. Review Notes and Study Guide to Twentieth Cen-
    tury British and American Poets. New York: Monarch
    Press, 1964. Robinson, pp. 39–41. Standard, superficial
    analysis of well-known poems, "Richard Cory," "Miniver
    Cheevy," "Bewick Finzer," "The Unforgiven," and "The
    Mill."

800 LEVENSON, J. C. "Robinson's Modernity." Virginia Quarterly
    Review, 44 (August, 1968), 590–610. Reprinted in Barnard,
    ed. (1969), 157–174, and in Murphy, ed. (1970), pp. 164–
    181. The traditional and the timeless in his work do not
    mean that he is a poet for the ages only. Looking to tradi-
    tion is his cultural habit and generalization is his character-
    istic mode of speech, but he is also a full-fledged citizen of
    the twentieth-century. When he defines the present in rela-
    tion to the past, he is trying to fix a particular present.
    And when he generalizes most broadly, he still is giving ex-
    pression to a particular historical moment.... Doubt is cer-
    tain, disbelief plausible, despair sympathetic, and hope ob-
    scure. These are the first principles of Robinson's imagina-
    tive world. That they have also been primary facts of
    twentieth-century life accounts, from one point of view, for
    the continuing modernity of his work.

801 LEWIS, B. Roland. Creative Poetry. California: Stanford
    University Press, 1931. Robinson, p. 60. Does not discuss
    Robinson, but does quote him as having said: "Poetry is a
    language that tells us, though a more or less emotional re-
    action, something that cannot be said. All poetry, great or
    small, does this. And it seems to me that poetry has two

outstanding characteristics. One is that it is, after all, in-
definable. The other is that it is eventually unmistakable."
This is quoted in the chapter "Theme of a Poem," and is
notable since Robinson so seldom said anything about the
nature of poetry.

802  LEWIS, J. S.  "A Note on Robinson's 'Forestalling.'"  American
     Notes and Queries, 5 (March, 1967), 106. The term is al-
     most unknown in this sense today, from photoengraving,
     equivalent to the modern term "to dodge," to reduce the in-
     tensity of by selectively shading. This meaning fits the
     context of Robinson's poem perfectly. In any modern mean-
     ing of the word the poem would be practically void, an al-
     most complete sacrifice of sense to sound. The scrupulous
     and fastidious poet Robinson was not guilty of such flimsi-
     ness of technique, elsewhere or in this poem.

803  LEWISOHN, Ludwig.  The Story of American Literature.  New
     York: Harper's, 1932. Robinson, pp. 553-560. First pub-
     lished as Expression in America (1932). Robinson has cre-
     ated a style of writing in blank verse that is far more con-
     tinuously interesting as style, as verse, than that of his
     lyrical measures. Hence even the later poems of contempo-
     rary manners and psychology continually attract the student
     and lover of poetry despite their cold intricacies and blood-
     less ingenuities. This, however, is not their fatal defect;
     it is the simultaneous absence of any fusing ardor. This
     poet has not inner heat enough. The poems are cold. This
     has nothing to do with the subject or method. Lucretius is
     an intellectual poet, too. But out of his empty universe he
     wrings the eternal cry....

804  LIE, Ulf.  "The Speaker Personae in Edwin Arlington Robinson's
     Early Dramatic Poetry."  American Norvegica, 4 (1973),
     193-210.

805  LIPPINCOTT, Lillian.  A Bibliography of the Writings and Criti-
     cisms of Edwin Arlington Robinson.  Boston: F. W. Faxon,
     1937. 85 pages, divided into 7 sections: writings of and
     critical writings about, with biographical articles.

806  LOGGINS, Vernon.  I Hear America.  New York: Crowell,
     1937. "Questioning Despair: Edwin Arlington Robinson,"
     33-70. It has been said that Robinson was greatly influ-
     enced by Freud. He was psychoanalytical a long time before
     he heard of Freud. His method of portraying a bewildered
     infant was to get at the source of the bewilderment. He
     probed for the satanic sort of kink which makes a man what
     he is. He is not interested in determining the cause of the
     kink, nor in offering suggestions for straightening it. He
     merely wanted to identify the kink and build a portrait about
     it.

807 _____. "Hagedorn's Biography of Poet Robinson is Ready."
Lewiston Journal & Illustrated Magazine, October 8, 1938.
P. 9.

808 LORD, Alice Frost. "Gardiner Associations of Poet Recalled
by Present Resident." Lewiston Journal & Illustrated Magazine, March 30, 1940. (Lewiston, Maine), P. 8.

809 _____. "Gardiner Woman Cherishes Letters from Poet Robinson." Lewiston Journal & Illustrated Magazine, April 13,
1940. P. 8.

810 LOVETT, Robert Morss. "The Castle of Doubt." New Republic, 97 (November 30, 1938), 107-108. Review of biography
by Hagedorn. With a scarcity of external matter, Hagedorn
has reverted to a type of biography which originated with
Izaak Walton and became classic with Boswell--that of portraiture. He has accomplished a complete feat of evocation.
By diligent search he has supplemented his personal knowledge with the recollections of others.... Hagedorn has re-
constructed a mental experience which was as rich as the
physical was limited. And he has drawn upon Robinson's
poetry with great skill to clinch the total effect of a human
being struggling against the oppression of an unintelligible
and intolerable world, with something of the baffled, tortured mysticism of a character by Dostoevsky.

811 LOWDEN, Samuel Marion. Understanding Great Poems. Harris-
burg, Pa.: Handy Books Corp., 1927. 340 pages. Robinson's poem "The Gift of God," pp. 265-273. Prints the poem
in its entirety, and then sets up several divisions on which
the poem may be studied: "Background," "Aim for Analysis,"
"Outline for Analysis," "Interpretation," "Style," "The Author," and "Teaching Points." The chapter concludes with
a dozen quotations from other poems by Robinson. Contrary
to most lyrics Robinson's poems, while eloquent and metrical,
are more or less objective, slightly tinged with irony; however, human sympathy and understanding prevail in most of
them and many have been built on personal experiences of
the author. Robinson is a student of character and mental
reaction. He does not blame or praise; he merely records.

812 LOWE, Robert Liddell. "Two Letters of Edwin Arlington Robinson: A Note on His Early Critical Reception." New England Quarterly, 27 (June, 1954), 257-261. The two letters
which follow were written to William Allan Neilson, then a
young instructor of English at Harvard University, and later
the president of Smith College. They require only a brief
introductory comment. Robinson expresses his regret at not
seeing Neilson when Neilson had called upon him, once in
Boston and later in New York. The formality of the salutations

shows that the two men, who were born in the same year,
were not close friends; Robinson usually addressed his male
correspondents whom he knew well by their last names.
The letters imply that Robinson found in Neilson an early
supporter, and that Neilson was alert to the best in contemporary poetry.

813 _____. "Edwin Arlington Robinson to Harriet Monroe: Some
Unpublished Letters." Modern Philology, 60 (August, 1962),
31-40. Article consists of one letter from Miss Monroe to
Robinson and twelve from Robinson to Monroe; also one
letter to a Mrs. Tietjens, sometime editor of Poetry. Robinson was to appear in the magazine only four times. His letters were to sketch lightly his association with the magazine,
which in part is his friendship with Miss Monroe. At first
Miss Monroe did not recognize Robinson's significance. Later
she admitted that in his ascetic style and realistic approach
was the beginning of a movement that led poetic art away
from Victorian tradition and practice.

814 _____. "A Letter of Edwin Arlington Robinson to James Barstow." New England Quarterly, 37 (September, 1964), 390-
392. In August, 1899, Robinson wrote a letter of biographical interest to James Barstow, who was at the time the literary editor of the Kansas City Star. The letter is important because it is the only complete one from Robinson to
Barstow, and because it illuminates Robinson's ambitions and
personality. Also the letter shows the effort Barstow made
to gain recognition for the little-known poet.

815 LOWELL, Amy. "Review of Van Zorn." Boston Herald, October, 1914.

816 _____. "Review of The Man Against the Sky." New Republic, 7 (May, 1916), 96-97. Dynamic with experience and
knowledge of life.... His poems do not invigorate; they
mellow and subdue. But in our material day, the spirituality
of Robinson's work is tonic and uplifting. The title poem
is remarkable, but hardly so original or so interesting as
some of the other poems.... The cryptic expression of many
of these poems can hardly be considered as other than a
flaw. Robinson prunes every tendency to luxuriance from
his style, aiming at the starkness of absolute truth.

817 _____. Tendencies in Modern American Poetry. New York:
Macmillan, 1917. Reprinted Boston: Houghton, Mifflin,
1921. Robinson, pp. 3-75. Reviews poems published by
Robinson as of that date. It is idle to ask if the greatest
poetry can be built upon such negative lines. Certainly,
no one will ever go to Mr. Robinson's books to make a gay
mood more gay, to fill himself with the zest and sparkle of

life. These things Mr. Robinson has not to give. His
poems do not invigorate; they mellow and subdue. But in
our material day, the spirituality of his work is tonic and
uplifting.... Robinson is a painstaking poet, a poet of
many revisions. He prunes every tendency to luxuriance
from his style. He aims at the starkness of absolute truth,
and granted that what he sees be the truth, he usually attains it. This poetry is "cribbed, cabin'd, and confined"
to a remarkable degree, but it is undeniably, magnificently
noble.

818 _____. A Critical Fable. Boston: Houghton, Mifflin, 1922.
      Is written in the manner of James Russell Lowell's "Fable for
      Critics" (1848). Of Robinson she says (pp. 26-29): To
      speak of seclusion is to think of a man/Who is built on a
      totally otherwise plan./I mean.../Edwin Arlington Robinson,
      excellent poet,/And excellent person, but vague as a wood/
      Gazed into at dusk.... For a man of his stamp,/So con-
      scious of people, it seems odd to scamp/Experience and con-
      tact, to live in a hollow....

819 _____. "A Bird's Eye View of Edwin Arlington Robinson."
      Dial, 72 (February, 1922), 130-142. Reprinted in Poetry
      and Poets, by Amy Lowell. Boston: Houghton, Mifflin,
      1930. Also reprinted in A Dial Miscellany, ed. William Was-
      serstrom (1963), pp. 75-87. Robinson's is not a wide or in-
      clusive art, it is narrow and deep. He has almost no early
      failures to look back upon with regret. His later work shows
      no marked advance over his earlier, even in the matter of
      technique. He gained his full stature remarkably young,
      and we can scarcely expect any increase of cubits to come.

820 _____. "A Tribute to Edwin Arlington Robinson on His
      50th Birthday." New York Times, December 24, 1922.

821 LUCAS, John. "The Poetry of Edwin Arlington Robinson."
      Renaissance and Modern Studies (University of Nottingham),
      13 (1969), 132-147. His position has never been more se-
      cure, but an important consideration is that he deserves to
      be kept alive in his best works. Admittedly Robinson wrote
      too much; he wrote too many long narratives out of too little
      material. His plays are dull, at times his style is prosy,
      his regard for the trivial is often trivial. Yet all his faults
      do not harm the virtues. The reader is advised to accept
      his vices from the outset, pointing to the pages that can be
      skipped, and finding that there still remains a sizeable body
      of work that anyone who cares about poetry should want to
      read and re-read.

822 LUCCOCK, Halford Edward. Contemporary American Literature
      and Religion. Chicago: Willett, Clark & Co., 1934. Robinson,

p. 139 et passim.  In considering the work of Edwin Arlington Robinson as "disillusioned" or marked by a sense of
futility, it should be remembered that the varied qualities
of so great a poet cannot be expressed by any one label.
Again and again there is a desperate sort of resignation to
a fatalism which drives mortals through the course of a life
which they do not understand and from the decrees of which
they cannot escape.  The utmost good which they seem to be
able to expect is the possible escape from the delusion of
false hopes.  In Robinson there is a note of skepticism which
is reverential and even deeply religious in quality.  It is
not the complacent dogmatism of denial; it is rather groping,
wonder; at times, hope.  There is stoic and resigned agnosticism in his volume Children of the Night.

823  LUDWIG, Richard M., ed.  Aspects of American Poetry:  Essays Presented to Howard Mumford Jones.  Columbus:  Ohio
State University Press, 1962.  Robinson, passim.  Not treated
significantly.

824  _____.  "Supplement to Thomas H. Johnson's Bibliography."
Literary History of the United States, edited by Spiller,
et al.  New York:  Macmillan, revised edition, 1962.  Robinson, pp. 705-708.

825  LUHAN, Mabel Dodge.  Movers and Shakers:  Volume Three of
Intimate Memories.  New York:  Harcourt, Brace, 1936.
Robinson, pp. 127-139.  Recalls her first meeting with Robinson, saying:  "At that first meeting, then, E. A. and I,
in a reciprocal flicker of the utmost brevity, met, exchanged
a certain essential knowledge of each other, realized each
other, and for so long as we lasted, I knew, would be
cronies, pals, comrades, friends, affinities, or whatever;
too much en rapport to be lovers, too sympathetic, perhaps,
to be lovers, if ever in this mortal universe he should take
a lover, that man whose whole emotional drama had been carried on with the Bottle."  Later Mrs. Luhan's recollections
are based on a number of letters which she received from
Robinson, the subject of which was consistently poetry.

826  MacAFEE, Helen.  "The Dark Hill of the Muses:  Review of
Cavender's House."  Yale Review, 18 (June, 1929), 813-814.
Here as elsewhere his revelation has a stark, intense vitality, unrelieved by ornamentation or picturesqueness of any
kind.  The work is essentially dramatic tragedy, which could
almost be put in the strict form of drama.

827  McCLURE, John.  "Review of Collected Poems."  Double Dealer,
3-4 (April, 1922), 217-219.  Thinks Robinson "is the second
large identity in American verse," the first, of course being
Whitman.  This large volume makes clear that in Robinson we

have a serious and capable, challenging and admirable artist
in words, of major, if not of majestic proportions. He has
contributed to the literature of English an idiom that is
definitely new. He has produced rare poems in the startling
intellectual patterns that are satisfying and delightful. Not
all the poems in this collection are good, or that the best
ones are uniformly good. His philosophy should not concern
the reader in evaluating his poetry: His themes are old and
universal, and interest us as art only when they are beautiful or pleasing.

828  McCORMICK, Virginia Taylor. "Review of Collected Poems."
     Norfolk Ledger-Dispatch, March 18, 1922.

829  McCULLOCH, Warren Sturgis. One Word After Another. Chi-
     cago: Chicago Literary Club, 1945. Tribute to Robinson,
     read before the club March 12, 1945. 28 pp.

830  McDONALD, G. D. "Edwin Arlington Robinson." Library Jour-
     nal, 77 (February 15, 1952), 358. Review of biography by
     Ellsworth Barnard. The form and content of Robinson's
     poetry, without biographical addenda, is treated to detailed,
     critical study. The author considers poetics, barriers to
     understanding, words and music, organic form, characters,
     virtues and values, showing how, when, and why these ap-
     pear in Robinson's work. Many poems come under close
     scrutiny in more than one chapter, and almost all of those
     most difficult to interpret are eventually elucidated.... This
     is a full-sized work, clear and simple in exposition, but most
     appropriate for the special student of Robinson.

831  MacDOWELL, Mrs. Edward. "Robinson at the MacDowell Colony."
     Mark Twain Quarterly, 2 (Spring, 1938), 16. In this per-
     sonal recollection, Mrs. MacDowell says: "It is one of the
     great joys of my life that we had an opportunity of giving
     Robinson something he could not have found save at the
     MacDowell Colony.... Twenty-four years before he died,
     someone suggested his coming to us. He rejected the invita-
     tion totally, but he did come, and was with us twenty-four
     summers. The outstanding quality of the man was his great
     simplicity, to which one might add quality of mercy--his com-
     passion for man and his possible weakness--rather than judg-
     ment."

832  McFARLAND, Ronald E. "Robinson's 'Luke Havergal.'" Colby
     Library Quarterly, 10 (June, 1974), 365-372. Reviews some
     of the numerous interpretations which have been made of
     this poem, admitting that many of them are rather persuasive.
     McFarland, however, believes that Luke Havergal may be
     identified with the protagonist of Dante's Divine Comedy and
     offers convincing suggestions that Robinson's entire poem may

be viewed as a journey of penitence, with the "she" of the
poem corresponding to Dante's Beatrice.  Many of the images
and nearly all of the tone are consistent with Dante's "Inferno."  We do not know if Luke Havergal makes his journey,
but at least we see him at the beginning of the decision to
go forward.

833 _____.  "Some Observations on Carew's 'Song' and Robinson's
'For a Dead Lady.'"  Markham Review, 10 (Fall, Winter,
1980-1981), 29-32.  Makes a careful textual comparison of
the two poems.  Of particular interest is the subtle but persistent note of dissolution and death which pervades both
poems.  The summer is over, winter is at hand; it is the
dead of night, and the stars are falling.  Robinson's poem
has a subtlety alien to Carew's, and prefers the tones of
understatement.  Both are poems of ideas, not celebration
of personalities.  They offer an opportunity for comparison
and contrast in technique and theme that may lead to the
enhancement of each.

834 McGREGOR, Elisabeth Johnson.  "The Poet's Bible:  Biblical
Elements in the Poetry of Emily Dickinson, Stephen Crane,
Edwin Arlington Robinson, and Robert Frost."  Ph.D. diss.,
Brown University, 1978.  DA, 39 (1979), 6133A.  This is a
study of each writer's adaptation of biblical language and
content to his or her own poetic use, and similarities among
the four in attitude, technique, and religious and cultural
situation are suggested....  Robinson and Frost read a Bible
already tamed for them by liberal Protestantism and the
"higher criticism."  They still quarrelled with the Bible,
but the most pressing need was to salvage something of the
spiritual values and tradition it represented.  Robinson both
retold its stories and tried to use its language to support
and define his own confused religious hopes.

835 MacKAYE, Percy W.  "Through the Dark," in Poems and Plays,
2 vols.  New York:  Macmillan, 1916.  Vol. 1, p. 124.  Is
an eighteen line poem, "To 'E. A.' with Cake and Candles,"
written on Robinson's birthday, December 23, 1914.  The
imagery of the poem is reminiscent of the dark stairs leading
to Robinson's upper floor room, the darkness of the place
in general, offset by the light of Robinson's kind face, and
the light of his friendship.

836 _____.  "'E. A.'--A Milestone for America."  North American
Review, 211 (January, 1920), 121-127.  Is a tribute to Robinson on his 50th birthday, and thinks it is more than a
milestone for his individual progress:  "E. A." himself is a
milestone for America.  Other American poets may have a
longer record of sporadic achievement; none other has his
distinctive continuity.  Others have produced more abundance

of good and bad; none other has reached his excelling ratio
of good.... Robinson is an American of reality, a leader
who has guided, a lover of his fellows, a maker of viewless
images.

837 _____. "In Memoriam Twenty Years After: October, 1910
     to October, 1920: A Sonnet to Edwin Arlington Robinson."
     Harvard Graduates' Magazine, 39 (December, 1930), 140.
     Had first appeared in Boston Evening Transcript, October
     18, 1930. Sec. 1, p. 9.

838 MacKILLOP, I. D. "Robinson's Accomplishment." Essays in
     Criticism, 21 (July, 1971), 297-308. Article is a discussion
     of three books by or about Robinson: Selected Poems (ed.
     Zabel), Selected Early Poems and Letters (ed. Davis), and
     A Collection of Critical Essays (ed. Murphy). All of these
     books have been recently published. Thinks it is unfair to
     compare the two selections of poems, since they have differ-
     ent purposes. The Selected Early Poems is carefully anno-
     tated and well-introduced. Some of the essays in Murphy's
     collection are hard to get through, primarily because the
     authors are too busy arguing the pointless question of Rob-
     inson's place in Twentieth-Century poetry.... Even so,
     all three volumes are interesting additions to the Robinson
     shelf.

839 MacLEISH, Archibald. "On Re-reading Robinson." Colby Li-
     brary Quarterly, 8 (March, 1969), 217-219. Reprinted in
     Cary, ed. (1969), pp. 3-5. Brief, informal comments from
     another poet's point of view. What strikes the reader of
     Robinson now is not so much the shape or sound or even
     substance of what is being said as the manner of the say-
     ing.... What is new is the speaker. He developed in his
     work a Voice in the sense in which Villon had a Voice which
     gave humanness a different timbre, etc. He did not speak
     for the American idea. He speaks for us in our aborted
     time as no one else, even among the very great, quite does.
     We do not hope or despair, and neither does Robinson.

840 MacVEAGH, Lincoln. "Edwin Arlington Robinson." New Repub-
     lic, 2 (April 10, 1915), 267-268. Is a general appraisal of
     Robinson with specific comment on certain poems here and
     there. In conclusion one may say Robinson prefers the sud-
     den, unconscious gestures, finished almost as soon as be-
     gun, which reveal character in a flash. His genius is punc-
     tual and intense. There is no exposition of contemporary
     thought, though the minds he portrays are contemporary,
     no controversy, no didacticism. He reveals; he does not
     criticize. And his revelation, at the same time that it is
     complete, is so indirect and oblique that we may say he
     really never expresses himself, but rather symbolizes himself.

841  MACY, John. "The New Age of American Poetry." Current
     History, 35 (January, 1932), 554-555.

842  MALOF, Joseph Fetler. "The Engaging Mask: Isolation in the
     Early Poems of Edwin Arlington Robinson." Ph.D. diss.,
     University of California (Los Angeles), 1962.

843  MANHEIMER, Joan. "Edwin Arlington Robinson's 'Eros Turan-
     nos': Narrative Reconsidered." Literary Review, 20 (1978),
     253-269. Writer views this poem by Robinson as typical of
     his verse as a whole, with special reference to those narra-
     tives which seem to offer the completeness of story and then
     retracts the offer. In this and in other poems the stories
     revealed to us by Robinson's speakers are concerned with
     the act of telling a story. "Eros ..." is ostensibly about
     passion's power to wreck the boundaries of self, but it turns
     out to be a poem about the nature of such boundaries ...
     the poem questions our passion for seeking patterns to de-
     scribe and be done with experience. Robinson reminds us
     that such closure is, at best, illusory.

844  MANLY, John Matthews, Edith Rickert, and Fred B. Millett.
     Contemporary American Literature. New York: Harcourt,
     Brace, 1922. Robinson, pp. 130-132. Revised edition,
     1929, "Poets of New England: Robinson and Frost," pp.
     47-48. Brief biographical note followed by section called
     "Suggestions for Reading." here are listed ten ideas or
     questions that would be worthwhile for students (high school
     or college) to explore in a study of Robinson. Article con-
     cludes with a list of Robinson's works, and a few books and
     articles about Robinson.

845  MARCUS, Mordecai. "Edwin Arlington Robinson's 'Flammonde':
     Towards Some Essential Clarifications." Markham Review,
     3 (1972), 77-80. For the poem to be among Robinson's best
     works, and also one of the best according to Robinson, it
     is surprising to find so little useful explanation of the whole
     poem. Reviews some of the critical comments on the poem,
     including Robinson who said "Flammonde is the man who sees
     but cannot do for himself." The argument is strong that
     Flammonde is some form of Christ-like figure, although not
     the figure of resurrected Christianity. This is a failed
     Christ, perhaps even something of a Satan, but who never-
     theless was able to bring about good in the lives of numer-
     ous people.

846  MARK TWAIN QUARTERLY, 2 (Spring, 1938), 24 pages. Spe-
     cial issue on Robinson. Each article listed in alphabetical
     sequence under author. The following items are included:
     "E. A. Robinson: 1869-1935," by Cyril Clements, editor,
     pp. 1-2. "The Big Bed," by John Cowper Powys, p. 2.

"Edwin Arlington Robinson ... Maker of Myth," by Charles
Cestré, pp. 3-8, 24. "Robinson as I Saw Him," by Richard
Burton, p. 9. "In Memoriam: Written in 1935," by Louis
V. Ledoux, p. 10. "Perfect Artistic Integrity," by William
Rose Benét, p. 10. "An Appreciation," by John G. Nei-
hardt, p. 10. "The Cosmic Humorist," by Arthur E. Du-
Bois, pp. 11-13, 24. "A Letter ..." by Rollo Walter Brown,
pp. 14, 24. "Robinson's Interest in Music," by Mabel Dan-
iels, pp. 15, 24. "Robinson at the MacDowell Colony," by
Mrs. Edward MacDowell, p. 16. "An Appreciation," by C.
T. Copeland, p. 16. "Dean of American Poets Pays Tribute,"
by Edwin Markham, p. 17. "Robinson Collection at Gardiner,
Maine," by Cyril Clemens, p. 18. "Robinson at Harvard,"
by G. W. Latham, pp. 19-20. "A Friend of Young Poets,"
by John Hall Wheelock, p. 20. "An Appreciation," by Christopher Morley, p. 20. "The Last Look," a poem by Mark
Van Doren, p. 21. "Epitaph on a Poet," by Arthur Guiterman, p. 21.

847  MARKHAM, Edwin. "Robinson, My Hand to You." New York
     American, February 13, 1909. P. 13.

848  _____. "Dean of American Poets Pays Tribute." Mark Twain
     Quarterly, 2 (Spring, 1938), 17. Reprints a quatrain which
     Robinson wrote for Markham's "Birthday at Eighty." In addi-
     tion Markham says: "No one can take his place. Let all
     lovers of great poetry carry the memory of Robinson in their
     hearts ... I had the happiness to call him friend."

849  MARR, Carl W. "The Torrent and the Night Before." (poem).
     Colby Library Quarterly, 7 (December, 1967), 511. Poem
     consisting of 24 lines blank verse, written in 1921. Theme
     is created around the idea of individuality and unity: "Each
     life in its immortal cloak repines/Until the blended whole
     makes song divine,/The strong and weak together, all as
     one,/So noble is the purpose of the line/That we are broth-
     ers till the course is done."

850  MARTIN, Jay. Harvests of Change: American Literature,
     1865-1914. Englewood Cliffs, N.J.: Prentice-Hall, 1967.
     Robinson, pp. 152-159. The idealism he achieved--he called
     it a kind of optimistic desperation--was hard won and would
     consequently be kept cautiously hidden in the poems tracing
     the problem and character of personal and collective failure.
     He faced as his central problem the resolution of solitude,
     the problem particularly of the artist, but actually of any
     individual, to find meaning in the sterile societal dead-end
     of a now fruitless tradition. Exploring personal alienation
     and social failure, he achieved success; setting forth the
     actuality of despair, he secured hope; dramatizing the reign
     of the anti-hero, he defined and made relevant a hero for
     the modern world.

851     _____. "A Crisis of Achievement: Robinson's Late Narratives," in Barnard, ed. (1969), pp. 130–156. This crisis is defined as that which occurs in the lives of American writers, especially poets, in whose career artistic achievement precedes popular acceptance by a number of years. This happened to Robinson. None of Robinson's late narratives are obscure. They deal with few characters in simplified settings and use transparent symbolism in an all-out effort to focus on the experience important to one personality, and thus to make the whole poem a crystalline symbol of the manifestation of personality. What vagueness they possess is used with precision to suggest the complexity of relations which make that experience, and may make it meaningful.

MARY CATHERINE, Sister. See Sister Mary Catherine.

852 MASON, Daniel Gregory. "Edwin Arlington Robinson: A Group of Letters." Yale Review, 25 (June, 1936), 860–864. Consists of five letters which Robinson wrote to Mason in 1899, 1900, and 1908. In the first four letters the subject was Thoreau, Emerson, Emily Bronte, William Vaughn Moody--all authors which Robinson was reading at the time. The last letter shows Robinson's reaction to the routine clerical work in the Customs Service as a result of President Roosevelt's interest in the poet. Roosevelt had reviewed The Children of the Night in 1905.

853     _____. "Early Letters of Edwin Arlington Robinson: First Series." Virginia Quarterly Review, 13 (Winter, 1937), 52–69. Consists of 17 or so letters bearing the dates 1899 and 1900. Content of these letters is varied: books Robinson had been reading, poetry he had been working on, what he had been thinking. Letters are particularly devoid of any comment on what the poet had been "doing" the truth being that he always did very little, talked very little, visited very little. He expressed very few hopes that his work would ever amount to anything, but did not seem particularly upset over his ill fate.

854     _____. "Letters of Edwin Arlington Robinson to Daniel Gregory Mason: Second Series." Virginia Quarterly Review, 13 (Spring, 1937), 223–240. Another 14 letters bearing the dats 1900, 1901, 1904, 1915, and finally in May, 1934, the last letter Mason had from Robinson, who died April 6, 1935. Again the content is varied: work Robinson had finished including "Captain Craig" which was hard to get published; further comment on William Vaughn Moody; the death of a good friend Philip Henry Savage; comment on his perpetual poverty, etc.

855 _____. Music in My Time, and Other Reminiscences. New
York: Macmillan, 1938. Robinson, pp. 121-134 et passim.
Comments on Robinson included in a number of letters which
the two friends exchanged, comments which also include remarks and appraisals of William Vaughn Moody. Best comment contained in Mason's journal of February, 1901, the
year which marked for Robinson and Mason "the lowest,
most hopeless, and most monotonous period of his long
struggle with poverty and obscurity." By that time Robinson was living in a hall-bedroom, at the back of the fourth
floor of a rooming house in West Twenty-third Street. One
had to grope up ill-lighted flights to reach his eyrie. This
was the period during which Robinson was trying without
much success to place Captain Craig for publication.

856 MASON, Madeline. "A Friend Tells the Story of a Man Born
to be a Poet." The Sun (New York), October 31, 1938.
P. 26. Review of Hagedorn's biography.

857 MASTERS, Edgar Lee. "The Poetry Revival of 1914." American Mercury, 26 (July, 1932), 272-280. Long discussion
involving numerous poets who lived from early American literature to 1914 or later. Robinson is included in the discussion. Robinson grew out of the last decade of the last
century. His metaphysical portraits, done with minutiae,
are elaborations of poems like "Luke Havergal" and the like.
His Arthurian experiments, are examples for which the claim
is made that they are better than Tennyson's. He has an
individual cast, and does not fit easily into any school or
movement. What his future will be anyone may speculate
for himself.

858 MATHER, Frank Jewett, Jr. "E. A. Robinson: Poet." Saturday Review of Literature, 6 (January 11, 1930), 629-631.
Review of Collected Poems. It is no easy task to bring to
book the great, the almost legendary distinction of Edwin
Arlington Robinson. Everywhere one meets anomalies which
strain the customary useful critical categories. Robinson
can sing superbly, but by and large he is not a singing
poet. This cuts him off from that generation of melodious,
if generally feeble songsters with which he grew up.... He
is one of the greatest stylists of our age, but you cannot
represent him by touchstone lines. He has held on the technical side, to traditional plastic forms at a moment when his
not much younger colleagues were seeking new forms as
delinquescent as the stream of consciousness itself.

859 MATTFIELD, M. S. "Edwin Arlington Robinson's 'The Sheaves.'"
CEA Critic, 31 (November, 1968), 10. Adopts the method of
examining poems written before and after a specific poem
which may be troublesome in determining its meaning. Such a

poem is "The Sheaves," in some respects atypical and inferior to much of the better-known earlier work.  Nevertheless it repays a consideration both of Robinson's metrics
and his attitudes.  Technically, "The Sheaves" is an interesting little poem, though not entirely successful.  Perhaps
what is lacking is the gleam of irony, even of bitter humor
in despair.  The "mighty meaning" is never made clear to
the reader--as it was never made clear to Robinson--and the
poem communicates little more than a gentle melancholy.  The
hopefulness of the green wheat and the richness of the harvest lead only to a bare field, with no hint that there lies
beyond anything more than the cosmic chill of an endless
winter.

860  MATTHIESSEN, F. O.  "Yeats and Four American Poets:  Review of Talifer."  Yale Review, 23 (March, 1934), 611-617.
This poem deals with the material with which Robinson has
made his most distinguished achievement, with the dramatic
portrayal of characters against a New England background.
As Robinson has handled it, there is no fully wrought texture of psychological notations; the development of the characters seems bare and manipulated.  The root of the difficulties may be that these characters are living in our immediate present, and Robinson is not capable of seeing such
characters against a definite social background.

861    _____.  "Society and Solitude in Poetry:  Review of King
Jasper."  Yale Review, 25 (March, 1936), 602-607.  Robinson's most enduring work, the earlier dramatic monologues,
voice the loneliness of the individual, of the isolated man
seen against a darkening sky from which the last aftershine
of transcendentalism is fading away.  In King Jasper Robinson made the effort to come to grips with contemporary society, to present the story of an industrialist whose domain
is crumbling under him.  The partial failure of the poem
may be attributable to the fact that the long solitude of
Robinson's grief for the lot of individual man--disqualified
him for the full handling of a social problem, and caused
his treatment, despite the energy of its thoughtful verse,
to fall into allegory that is at once both bare and obscure.

862    _____.  "Review of Edwin Arlington Robinson by Hermann
Hagedorn."  American Literature, 12 (January, 1941), 509-
512.  Reprinted in The Responsibility of the Critic, essays
and reviews by F. O. Matthiessen, selected and edited by
John Rackliffe.  New York: Oxford University Press, 1952.
Pp. 100-103.  Hagedorn has the advantage of twenty-five
years of close acquaintance with the poet.  He was also in
touch with the small circle of Robinson's other friends.  He
has thus preserved much that would have otherwise been
lost.  This biography makes no effort at criticism, yet from

it we can gather the materials that are essential to an understanding of Robinson's poetic career.

863  MAYNARD, Theodore. <u>Our Best Poets: English and American</u>.
New York: Henry Holt, 1922. "Edwin Arlington Robinson:
A Humorist Who Cannot Laugh," pp. 153-168. Article is an
overall review of Robinson's work (as of that date); the author does not praise Robinson to be on the safe side, but
because he really deserves it. Quite accurately Maynard
predicts that whatever is said at this time, will be unsaid
and said again, and again. In conclusion, the gift of greatness was withheld from Robinson. Something prevents him
from being either simple, sensuous or passionate. The difficulty may be his somber temperament, but something has
been left out of Robinson's genius. If he had been able to
abandon himself he might have become not merely the greatest poet of America (he has become that) but one of the
half-dozen of the world's greatest poets.

864  _____. "Edwin Arlington Robinson." <u>Catholic World</u>, 115
(June, 1922), 371-381. Article is largely incorporated into
material in above item. Conclusion is the same, that true
greatness was not Robinson's, because he could not abandon
himself. Had he been able to do so, he would have become
one of the greatest poets of America and one of the world's
greatest poets.

865  _____. <u>Preface to Poetry</u>. New York: Century, 1933.
Robinson, pp. 50-51 et passim. Prints "Mr. Flood's Party"
in chapter on "The Poet's Audience." "It is about an old
man, and as in the ordinary course of nature you will become an old man, it is not without point in your case....
To conclude my case about the universality of poetic experience, I will say that only when we by an effort of the
mind extract only the intellectual concept bare of emotion,
do we quite escape from poetry. The square on the hypot-
enuse of a right-angled triangle is equal to the sum of the
squares on the other two sides--that is empty of poetry."

866  _____. "Edwin Arlington Robinson." <u>Catholic World</u>, 141
(June, 1935), 266-275. Refers to other articles about Robinson, and says that any present concern is with the man.
Any references to his poetry are incidental. On the other
hand, this is not merely an obituary, stuffed with facts and
dates. It is an analysis of his life in relation to his poetry.
Robinson never gave of himself freely to friends or the public. His work depended on his life, but--looking back upon
him as I knew him--his life appears to be even greater than
his work.

867  _____. <u>The World I Saw</u>. Milwaukee: Bruce Publishing Co.,

1938. Robinson, pp. 232-338. Robinson is recalled in the chapter "The MacDowell Colony," where Maynard and Robinson met and became friends. Maynard says: "To me the MacDowell Colony will always connote Robinson, not merely because it was there that my friendship with him began, but because all the work of his later years was produced here, after he reached middle age. It was only in those prolific summers that he became poetically alive. Upon returning to New York he practically went into hibernation."

868 _____. "Review of Selected Letters." Catholic World, 151 (May, 1940), 248-249. The group of letters offered here, edited by Ridgely Torrence, are perhaps better than any attempt to present Robinson's correspondence in two or three huge volumes. Here is a taste of Robinson's quality as a human being, and as wit, friend, and critic. Taciturn as this man was in company, in solitude he could sometimes commit to paper what he would not say. Yet he did not unlock his heart, and there are no "confessions." But neither did he in his poetry, he was not that kind of poet.

869 _____. "Review of Untriangulated Stars." Catholic World, 168 (October, 1948), 87. Though it is less important than the letters edited by Ridgely Torrence and does no more than confirm what the Hagedorn biography relates of the poet's 'twenties, it is nevertheless good to have. In these letters we find a Robinson who was a good deal more expansive than he permitted himself to be in later life. It is also a Robinson strangely worried in conscience because he wished to be a poet instead of earning money like every other respectable Maine man.

870 MAZZARO, Jerome, ed. Modern American Poetry: Essays in Criticism. New York: David McKay, 1970. "Edwin Arlington Robinson and the Integration of Self," by H. R. Wolf, pp. 40-59. Discussed under Wolf.

871 MENCKEN, H. L. "Review of The Man Against the Sky." Smart Set, 51 (February, 1917), 398.

872 MERTON, John Kenneth. "A World His Own." Commonweal, 26 (May 14, 1937), 79-80. Review of Collected Poems. Apart from every other consideration, the publishers give us vast bulk for our money.... One of the most extraordinary things about Robinson was that roughly about five-sixths of his work was written in middle age, and that the older he grew the more prolific he became. Toward the end there are signs of weariness. He drove himself faster and faster because he had so much to say and knew that he had very little time in which to say it. There was, however, no appreciable falling off, and in the whole huge

volume, there is not a single poem that is not distinguished.
It stands as the most impressive poetic achievement of America.

873 MICHAUD, Régis.  Panorama de la Littérature Américaine Con-
temporaire.  Paris: Kra, 1926.  275 pp.  Robinson, pp.
184-186.

874 MILES, Josephine.  "Robinson and the Years Ahead," pp. 130-
140.  Poetry and Change.  Berkeley: University of California Press, 1974.  Writers on Robinson have agreed that his
first books revealed the method and manner of his maturity,
and that his background and environment all kept him to
"the seasons and the sunset as before." He was no explorer
or revolutionary.  He saw each man trying to cope with his
own demon, and each child "trying to spell God with the
wrong blocks." So he saw experience and expectation often
at odds, and so his characteristic early vocabulary gives us
the heart of his poetry with its blend of sense and sensibility.

875 _____.  "Robinson's Inner Fire," in Murphy, ed. (1970), pp.
110-116.  Original publication in a volume of otherwise reprints.  What have the Gleam, the Vision, and the Word to
do with dry, plain, and unpoetic understatement?  How does
Robinson reconcile objects of nature with concepts of desire,
Tennyson's atmospheres with Browning's interior psycholo-
gizing, rich sense with metaphysical thought, so that he
seems at once archaic and modern, reminiscent and inventive?
His major vocabulary suggests one answer:  that his chief
material is romantic natural beauty, but that his treatment
of it is skeptical and unhappy, in a metaphysics of shame,
lonely, and sick.  Such a tone preserves him his modernity
through a moonlit world.

876 MILLER, John H.  "The Structure of Edwin Arlington Robinson's
The Torrent and the Night Before." Colby Library Quarterly,
10 (June, 1974), 347-364.  In most of his books Robinson arranged the short poems roughly according to form--sonnets,
octaves, ballades, quatrains, etc.--rather than theme.  However, in his first book, he arranged them by theme, in
groups of two, four, six.  This ordering of poems by theme
is important for several reasons:  we may gain new insight
into poems which have been difficult; we can get some idea
of what Robinson thought his major themes were; and the
entire book may be seen as a unity.

877 MILLER, Michael G.  "Miniver Grows Lean." Colby Library
Quarterly, 12 (September, 1976), 149-150.  Article advances
the notion that Miniver's physical state may not be wholly
psychosomatic, but that he may be suffering from tuberculosis

or "consumption" as it was commonly known. Certainly
Robinson was familiar with the disease, and the symptoms
manifested by Miniver Cheevy are very accurate. His
physical state is used to parallel and emphasize his spiritual
wasting away. To make Miniver a literal consumptive is a
brilliant re-inforcement of his mental state as he drifts irre-
versibly toward spiritual degeneration and death.

878 MILLER, Perry. "The New England Conscience." American
Scholar, 28 (Winter, 1958-1959), 149-158. Is a long philosophical discussion of what Miller calls "the New England
Conscience," which he describes as the "habit of obeying
with slavish fidelity the inner promptings of rectitude," a
tradition which goes back to the Puritans.... Edwin Arlington Robinson rang many changes on and within the paradox,
and summed it up in a sonnet called "New England." Here
"the wind is always north-north-east," "children learn to
walk on frozen toes," and to envy those who elsewhere
shamelessly enjoy a lyric feast.

879 MILLETT, Fred B. Reading Poetry. New York: Harper &
Brothers, 1950. "Flammonde," p. 64, 145-148. Prints poem
in its entirety, with study questions in Chapter on characterization. In a brief commentary the poem is called "bare
of figures, although a few metaphors are used effectively."
This portrait of a personality has meaning beyond its literal
significance because it is made up of symbols which stand
for a type of person and experience that has occurred in
the nature of things.

880 _____. Contemporary American Authors. New York: Harcourt, Brace, 1940. Robinson, pp. 548-554. Consists of
brief biographical statement followed by several pages of
Bibliography. Items consisting largely of "Studies and
Articles," but contains listing of Robinson poems which
have been set to music. See also work by Manly, Rickert
and Millet (1928), containing much the same material.

881 MIMS, Edwin. The Christ of the Poets. Nashville: Abington-
Cokesbury Press, 1948. "Contemporary Poets: Edwin Arlington Robinson," pp. 222-224. Of no other contemporary
American poet can it be said that religion was a major interest.... It is a striking fact that America, which has
been identified with popular and even fundamental religion,
has had few poets who have given expression to religious
faith. It is a fact that there is no material in the major
writers of the earlier period bearing upon our survey. In
the poetry of Emerson, Whitman, and Poe one would never
know that Jesus had lived. When we consider contemporary
poets, we have to say that the same statement may be made.
It is only here and there that one finds a poem of the best

quality which relates in any way to Jesus.... One explanation of the melancholy and even pessimism of Robinson is
that he found so little faith.

882  MIMS, Puryear. "Robinson and the Arthurian Legend." Vanderbilt (Nashville), 1928. M.A. thesis.

883  MINOT, John Clair. "Maine's Contribution to Literature."
Maine Library Bulletin (Augusta), 9 (January, 1920), 58-59.

884  MITCHELL, George. "Robinson's Sonnets." Ph.D. diss., Tem-
ple University (Philadelphia), 1949.

885  MITCHELL, Stewart. "Review of The Three Taverns." Dial
(Chicago), 70 (May, 1921), 569-571. Book is not likely to
be very popular, nor is Robinson likely to care. A poem
in blank-verse on the subject of Saint Paul's advent to Rome
is almost incredible in these days of peep-show poetry....
What is commonly called a vital objection might be offered
against the work of Mr. Robinson: austere and conventional
--many poets have been so--his failure is his neglect to express the spirit of his time. But a glib certainty as to that
spirit has cost more than one poet dear these last seven
hundred years.

886  MONROE, Harriet. "A Pioneer." Poetry, 8 (April, 1916), 46-
48. Review of The Man Against the Sky. Regards this latest volume as among the best that Robinson has done. Comments on several poems specifically, in which characters are
drawn against the background of tragedy and disillusionment,
demonstrating certain odd and unexpected tricks by which
fate keeps a relentless control over human lives. Only in
the final poem does the poet seem to reflect about life in his
own person, putting a bitter question to his soul.... And
he finds no more quieting answer to the question that a dim
perception of something "too permanent for dreams."

887  _____. "Mr. Robinson in Camelot." Poetry, 10 (July, 1917),
211-213. Review of Merlin. The characters in this poem do
not show very disquieting signs of life at the touch of Robinson's blank-verse wand, although they indulge freely in
long discursive monologues and dialogues. It is too late to
touch them without magic, even though the poet's purpose
is not mainly with their familiar drama but with his philosophy
of life. One would have thought Robinson immune from the
fascination of old tales; now that he has had a light case of
the fever perhaps he will be.

888  _____. "Mr. Robinson's Jubilee." Poetry, 15 (February,
1920), 265-267. Is a tribute to Robinson on his fiftieth
birthday. Comments briefly on some of his poems and what

some of the critics have said about him.  He led the modern
procession for his countrymen; wilful and self-advised, he
struck his own path, and found that he had blazed a trail
for others.  And now, as they pass on, he turns to the
legend-encrusted past and dreams of Guinevere.  May he
live several decades more and crowd them with poems as
good as "Miniver Cheevy," "Richard Cory," or the "Man
from Stratford."

889    _____.  "Review of The Three Taverns and Avon's Harvest."
Poetry, 18 (August, 1921), 273-276.  Both books are mainly
in this poet's most characteristic vein, mainly studies of his
gnarled and weather-beaten neighbors; of incomplete, un-
rounded characters in tragically ill-fitting human relationships.  Perhaps Avon's Harvest is the most distinguished.
It weaves a formidable tragedy out of meagre materials--a
college antagonism, a blow, a long worm-eating revenge, and
all the more powerful because of the poet's restraint....
The Three Taverns is mostly dramatic narratives, which interest intellectually, but bring little emotional thrill.  They
are searching essays in character analysis, but they leave
one cold.  It is in Mr. Robinson's meditative poems that one
tastes most keenly the sharp and bitter savor of his high
aloof philosophy.

890    _____.  "Comment:  Edwin Arlington Robinson."  Poetry, 25
(January, 1925), 206-217.  Reviews her long friendship with
Robinson, from their first meeting about 1905 in the early
days when Robinson had few readers until the present when
he has a dedicated coterie of followers.  If one reads the
Collected Poems in chronological order one notes a gradual
and sure development....  If Robinson had been deflected
from his purpose by the lack of response to his first two
books, we should have had the imprint of an exceptional
mind in a few memorable poems, but we should hardly have
suspected the new poet's range and power.  Robinson stands
today, as in his more obscure yesterdays, adequate, uncompromising, a big man, a thorough and keen-visioned artist.
He led the modern procession; wilful and self-advised, he
struck his own path, and found that he had blazed a trail
for others.

891    _____, and Alice Corbin Henderson, eds.  The New Poetry:
An Anthology of Twentieth-Century Verse in English.  New
York:  Macmillan, 1925.  Robinson, pp. 419-431.  Prints
some twelve familiar poems without comment.  Among those
printed are:  "The Master," "John Gorham," "Richard Cory,"
"Cassandra," "Demos," "Miniver Cheevy," "Eros Turannos,"
"Mr. Flood's Party," etc.

892    _____.  Poets and Their Art.  New York:  Macmillan, 1926.

Robinson, pp. 1-11.  If the psychology of failure, or of
that uncertain middle ground between spiritual success and
failure, is Robinson's recurrent motive, it may be interesting to study his attitude and his methods in presenting that
motive in art.  It is heroic, not ignoble, struggle that en-
gages him, or if not heroic, at least the struggle of highly
strung sensitive souls to fulfill their manifest destiny; ending either in acceptance of compromise, or in tragic spiritual revolt that induces some kind of dark eclipse.  The
form is usually narrative, with the poet as the narrator,
under some assumption of friendship or at least neighborliness; but in the longer poems we have, as a rule, monologue and dialogue, the characters unfolding their perplexities.

893      _____.  "On Foreign Ground."  Poetry, 31 (December,
1927), 160-167.  Review of Tristram.  There is a glamour
about these old tales which wins the public.  The combination of this rusty-rich love-legend with modern psychological
insight in character analysis is enough to account for the
public favor which has pushed this book to a record sale,
far exceeding any of the poet's earlier volumes.  And of
course the poem has enough beauty and shapeliness to reward the most exacting readers.  It is perhaps a finer work
than Merlin or Lancelot, but even so Robinson does not seem
as much at ease with these subjects as, say, Matthew Arnold
and other 19th-Century poets.

894      _____.  "Review of Matthias at the Door."  Poetry, 39 (January, 1932), 212-217.  His people are a bit theoretic and
shadowy.  Intellectualized and defiant, they do not quite
obey his call.  But if we admit what no one, probably, would
deny, that Robinson can not stand in such glorious company
(as Marlowe, Shakespeare, Homer, etc.) we must yet grant
him a proud place among the masters of irony.  And of all
his narratives which record the bitter conflict between God
and the seven devils for possession of the human soul, only
"The Man Who Died Twice" may rank with this latest book
in clarity and sympathy.

895      _____.  "Robinson as Man and Poet."  Poetry, 46 (June,
1935), 150-157.  Reprinted in Cary, ed. (1969), pp. 38-42.
As one surveys his symmetrically rounded life in its com-
pleteness, it becomes impossible to grieve for him--the elegy
should be a song of triumph.  In youth he had outlined an
austere and difficult pattern to live by, and with rare precision he had devoted his later years to filling in the design
with strong lines and ardent delicate colors.  His work was
done.  Bad health had begun to undermine his strength and
threaten his creative power.  Against all odds this poet kept
the faith.  His fame is now ours to cherish, his life ours to
admire.

896  MONTEIRO, George. "Addenda to Hogan's Robinson." Papers
     of the Bibliographic Society of America, 65 (October-
     December, 1971), 414. Is a correction to Hogan's bibliogra-
     phy, which does not indicate that a poem in The Torrent
     and the Night Before, the sonnet "God's Garden" had been
     previously printed at least twice.

897  _____. "'The President and the Poet': Robinson, Roosevelt,
     and The Touchstone." Colby Library Quarterly, 10 (March,
     1974), 512-514. Article contains a short introduction, and
     an article printed in The Touchstone, a short-lived periodi-
     cal of five issues in Chicago, January 1906. This article,
     which is an imaginary conversation between Robinson and
     President Roosevelt on the subject of Robinson's appointment
     to a government position, has not been reprinted before nor
     included in any Robinson bibliography.

898  _____. "Addenda to the Bibliographies of Robinson (et al.)."
     Papers of the Bibliographic Society of America, 69 (April-
     June, 1975), 272-275. Robinson occupies a very small por-
     tion of this article, item no. 10, which adds a review of
     Cavender's House by Winfield Townley Scott (Brown Library
     Quarterly, Vol. I, 1929, pp. 16-17), to the bibliographies
     of Hogan and White.

899  _____. "Addenda to Hogan and White: Edwin Arlington
     Robinson." Papers of the Bibliographic Society of America,
     72 (October-December, 1978), 246-247. Adds six items to
     the Bibliography of Hogan & White, Biographical and Critical
     Material Dealing with Robinson. These items are in foreign
     languages, and are translations into other languages. There
     is one exception, a book by Carlin T. Kindelien (1956) which
     includes a discussion of Robinson.

900  MOODY, William Vaughn. Letters to Harriet, edited with Intro-
     duction and Conclusion by Percy MacKaye. Boston: Hough-
     ton, Mifflin, 1935. Robinson, passim. Robinson re-
     ferred to many times, but not too significantly. Moody and
     Robinson exchanged several letters, but they did not know
     each other, and what is more important they did not under-
     stand each other. At Moody's untimely death, Robinson wrote:
     "Thank God he lived to do his work--or enough of it to place
     him among the immortals." He went on to say, "I hope that
     I may see you again sometime and perhaps make you under-
     stand more clearly how fully I realize that you, and the world,
     have lost...."

901  MOON, Elmer Samuel. "Organic Form in the Shorter Poems of
     Edwin Arlington Robinson." Ph.D. diss., University of
     Michigan, 1956. DA, 17 (1957), 145. The purpose of this
     study is to bring a knowledge of Robinson's beliefs and

temperament to bear upon the style of his poetry in order
to show the significance that his style acquires from its organic relationship to those beliefs and feelings. Robinson's
beliefs center upon a pattern of the growth of the mind
which is typically transcendental, and which he felt that all
men and women followed in whole or in part. His transcendentalism led him to value truth as the end of poetry, rather
than beauty.

902   MOON, Lois Burton. "Review of Tristram." Lyric West, 7
      (November, 1927), 57-59.

903   MOORE, Marianne. "Review of The Man Who Died Twice."
      Dial, 77 (August, 1924), 168-170. In a day of much shal-
      lowness, muddy technique, and self-defended mystery, one
      is grateful for this highly developed obedience to a sensibil-
      ity which is a matter not only of the nerves, but of the
      whole man.... Robinson's work is completely self-vindicating
      in its sensitive, self-corroborating, rhetorically measured,
      elegant articulateness.

904   MOORE, Virginia. "Review of Dionysus in Doubt." Atlantic
      Monthly, 135 (June, 1925), 8. When George Meredith, a
      decade or more ago, challenged the literary world with his
      cry for "Brain! More Brain!" Robinson was the tardy and
      triumphant answer to the Muses. A scorn for the mentally
      inexpensive--a scorn which burns hotter and whiter in his
      latest book, is the salient quality of his meticulous art.
      Linked with superb craftsmanship and a nipping irony, it
      produces a first-water poet who, while reminiscent of
      Browning at his subtlest, remains inimitably himself.

905   MORAN, Ronald Wesson, Jr. "Avon's Harvest Re-examined."
      Colby Library Quarterly, 6 (June, 1963), 247-254. This
      work has been interpreted as a ghost story, as a chronicle
      of hate-inspired vengeance, and as the record of the deter-
      ioration of a man's mind. Whatever the poet's intention,
      the poem presents the mind of a man tortured by the re-
      membrance of a hasty act executed in a youthful passion.
      The dynamics of Avon's Harvest rest upon Avon's profound
      sense of guilt, on his inability to reconcile diverse elements
      within himself, and on the suspense generated by the am-
      biguous nature of the ghost.

906   _____. "With Firm Address: A Critical Study of Twenty-
      Six Shorter Poems of Edwin Arlington Robinson." Ph.D.
      diss., Louisiana State University, 1966. DA, 27 (1966),
      1378A. This study is an analysis and an appraisal of the
      most significant shorter poems of Robinson. The first chap-
      ter begins with a review of periodical and book-length treat-
      ments of Robinson. The next three chapters are individual

discussions of the twenty-six poems in something of chronological order.  In the final chapter the consistencies of subject matter, themes, and techniques that are recognizable in
the poems.  This final chapter also provides an index to the
Robinson method in his most successful shorter poems.

907 _____. "Meaning and Value in 'Luke Havergal.'" Colby Library Quarterly, 7 (March, 1967), 385-392.  Begins with
the observation that "Luke Havergal" is the most widely
explicated and perhaps the least understood of Robinson's
short poems.  Robinson's remarks on the poem, "a piece of
deliberate degeneration," and "my comfortable abstraction"
are misleading in the Robinson manner of understatement.
This article presents a reading of the poem as the experience of a man contemplating death, whether he finally does
kill himself is not needed, because the subject is the argument of pro and con on suicide.  The average reader cannot
identify with Luke, but the poem is an excellent one for il-
lustrating that the reader does not have to agree in order
to judge the poem as valuable.

908 _____. "'The Octaves' of Edwin Arlington Robinson." Colby
Library Quarterly, 8 (September, 1969), 363-370.  Reprinted
in Cary, ed. (1969), pp. 315-321.  Robinson remarked that
he had written forty octaves, but if he did, only twenty-
eight are extant.  These poems are usually excluded from
discussions of his poetry, but they should not be because
they provide statements in which Robinson is the persona:
his beliefs on the function of poetry, the presence of God,
the state of the age, the condition of man, and his basis
of Idealism for a life-style.  Robinson wrote the Octaves
when he was twenty-six and seven, and they provide us,
as no other single body of work, with insights that are personal.

909 _____. "Lorraine and the Sirens:  Courtesans in Two Poems
by E. A. Robinson," in Essays in Essays in Honor of Es-
mond Linworth Marilla, ed. Thomas Austin Kirby and William
John Olive.  Baton Rouge:  Louisiana State University
Press, 1970.  Pp. 312-319.  It is certainly true that many
of Robinson's people live outside or on the fringe of acceptable society.  They have serious problems, and they need
both understanding and compassion.  His men are most familiar, but he has written many poems in which women figure
chiefly.  The two poems here, "The Growth of Lorraine,"
and "Veteran Sirens," share problems of a sexual nature.
There is no doubt that Lorraine is a prostitute and evidence
both external and internal pointing to the Sirens as prostitutes.

910 MORLEY, Christopher.  "An Appreciation." Mark Twain

Quarterly, 2 (Spring, 1938), 20. Admits to having never
met Robinson, although he had several opportunities to do
so, and deliberately refrained. Morley admired Robinson's
work, but felt that he already was sufficiently annoyed and
bothered by people who admired him and kept him from his
work. Thinks there are very few people who have sufficient
respect for the arts not to interfere with the artist.

911  MORRILL, Paul H. "Psychological Aspects in the Poetry of
     Edwin Arlington Robinson." Ph.D. diss., Northwestern
     University, 1956. DA, 17 (1957), 363-364. To explore and
     define the concept of "psychological poet" the poems and
     letters of the poet and criticisms of the poetry were exam-
     ined. Fifty-three short or medium length poems and eleven
     longer narrative poems were analyzed. Using current psy-
     chological theories of interpersonal relations, the themes
     of the poet were outlined and discussed under the following
     sections: characters involved in love or affection; self-
     evaluation or self-assertion, success-failure themes; a crea-
     tive place in society; pathological delusions or obsessions;
     and characters of an archetypal nature.

912  _____. "'The World Is ... a Kind of Spiritual Kindergarten.'"
     Colby Library Quarterly, 4 (Winter, 1969), 435-448. Re-
     printed in Cary, ed. (1969), pp. 346-356. It is generally
     agreed that Robinson's "subject" was first and foremost peo-
     ple. This interest has resulted in his being labeled a psy-
     chological poet, referring to his analytical style. Others be-
     lieve that it was his content, his studies of failures, mistaken
     idealists, and unsure lovers which earned him the title "psy-
     chological poet." This article reviews his content and meth-
     ods in the total context of his work, with emphasis upon the
     psychological, not upon categories or philosophy. The argu-
     ment is built upon the quotation given in the title of the
     article.

913  MORRIS, Celia B. "The Makaris of Camelot." Ph.D. diss.,
     City University of New York, 1968. DA, 29 (1968), 1516A-
     1517A. This is a study of the three most substantial works
     in English that share as common material the Arthurian leg-
     ends: Malory's La Mort d'Arthur, Tennyson's Idylls of the
     King, and Robinson's Lancelot and Merlin. These three are
     works separated by time and place, yet all of them are by
     poets of great stature. There has been a great deal of criti-
     cism devoted to Malory and Tennyson, but very little to
     Robinson. The works are very different from one another,
     and many of their differences have historical implications.
     What each poet does with the material is determined by more
     than their own peculiar artistic talents.

914  _____. "Robinson's Camelot: Renunciation as Drama."

Colby Library Quarterly, 9 (March, 1972), 468-481. To
have any success with the Arthurian material Robinson had
to radically change its emphasis. Robinson is not a poet of
action, and never really tells a story. Most critics say that
the Arthurian material appealed to Robinson because it is
about the end of a world, and this is partially true. However, there are two other important contributions: the
material did provide a story, a sequence of events, characters, and a set of relationships; also the material is not
mainly about the end of a world, it is about that world and
the adventures of the people who rule it.

915 _____. "Edwin Arlington Robinson and 'The Golden Horoscope of Imperfection.'" Colby Library Quarterly, 11 (June,
1975), 88-97. With faith neither in salvation nor the prospect
of eternity, Robinson shared the Puritan assumption that the
essence of a man lay in his struggle with his demons, and
that nothing else really mattered. And somewhere he developed a compassion so profound that no other American
poet approaches it. He presents characters (as in Merlin
and Lancelot) in relation to each other, and shows that human worth and dignity lie in grappling with guilt and loss.
Integrity means fully accepting one's "golden horoscope of
imperfection" by recognizing the way deep needs can make
one hurt others and cripple oneself.

916 MORRIS, Charles R. "Robinson's 'Richard Cory.'" Explicator,
23 (1965), item 52. Agrees with other comments that Richard
Cory is a king, but judging from the terms of the poem
(pavement, sole to crown, schooled, etc.) he is an English
king. Nearly all of the diction of the poem is British, not
American. Furthermore, Amy Lowell has described Gardiner,
Maine, as the most "English atmosphere in America."
Richard Cory is perhaps one of those arch-Tories of the
American Revolution, an aristocratic English gentleman liv-
ing in a modern democratic society. His character and sui-
cide may be patterned on that of Frank Avery, of Gardiner,
Maine.

917 MORRIS, Lloyd R. The Poetry of Edwin Arlington Robinson:
An Essay in Appreciation, with Bibliography by W. Van R.
Whitall. New York: George H. Doran, 1923. Reprinted
New York: Haskell House; Freeport: Books for Libraries
Press; and New York: Kennikat Press, 1969. Consists of
116 pages in six chapters: "Men," "History," "Legend,"
"Plays," "Ideas," and "Postscript." Bibliography consists
of primary sources only.

918 _____. "Mr. Robinson's Progress: Review of Roman Bartholow." Freeman, 7 (April 18, 1923), 140-141. It is both a
dramatic narrative of unusual emotional power and a reading

of life distinguished by the intellectual subtlety and high
seriousness that qualify the mood of the poet's mind.  Into
it have gone the vision and insight, the striking command
of expression and the spiritual integrity, which constitute
Robinson's contribution to our poetry.

919 _____. "Review of Tristram." Nation, 124 (May 25, 1927),
586.  It may be said not only that Tristram is the finest of
Mr. Robinson's narrative poems, but that it is among the
very few fine modern narrative poems in English.  It occupies a special position, and takes its place as the most complete and most characteristic expression of his genius.

920 _____. "The Rare Genius of Edwin Arlington Robinson."
World Review, 5 (December 12, 1927), 182-183.

921 MORRISON, Theodore.  "Two Harvard Poets." Harvard Alumni
Bulletin, 26 (May 29, 1924), 983-985.

922 _____. "Review of The Glory of the Nightingales." Atlantic
Monthly, 146 (December, 1930), 28.  The story is based on
a tragic triangle of two men and one woman, and is ultimately
the tale of thwarted vengeance, coming as it does when one
of the friends is at the point of death, and vengeance is
pointless.  The woman dies, and at the end the two men regard each other with pity and blame.  On this human note
the poem ends.

923 _____. "Review of Nicodemus." Bookman, 75 (November,
1932), 750-751.  This volume contains no poem likely to rank
with Robinson's most famous pieces.  It contains a number
of highly representative performances, characteristic in theme
and treatment.  The themes of four of these ten poems are
biblical, and three have their settings in the West Indies.
Robinson finds his poems among people and situations; he
is interested in the spiritual aspects of his themes; he frequently finds the dramatic monologue or lyric a natural vehicle.

924 _____. "Modern Poets: Amaranth." Atlantic Monthly, 155
(March, 1935), 10, 12.  Sees this poem as different from
anything Robinson has recently undertaken.  The theme of
failed genius is made interesting by the use of irony, the
highly imaginative quality of the poem, and the really acid
humor.

925 MOSELEY, Richard Samuel, III.  "Narrative Form in the Long
Poems of Edwin Arlington Robinson." Ph.D. diss., Cincinnati University, 1967.  DA, 28 (1968), 3193A.  This
study presents a set of formalistic analyses of the long narratives, aiming to describe and evaluate the poems according

to their narrative ends and means.  The twelve major narratives of Robinson's last twenty years, however, are generally disparaged by critics of Robinson's poems, primarily
because of the critics' tendency to judge these long works
by criteria derived from the excellence of his earlier, shorter poems....  The traditional emphases on such elements as
character, conflict, choice, and change are important to
Robinson's art, and his effects grow out of the resolution
of these elements according to carefully prepared expecta-
tions and probabilities.

926  MOTT, Sara L.  "The Happy Ending as a Controlling Comic
     Element in the Poetic Philosophy of Edwin Arlington Robinson."
     Ph.D. diss., University of South Carolina, 1965.  DA, 26
     (1966), 6047.  Robinson's poetry is dominated by darkness
     and despair, in a world of failures and causes of despair.
     Being a realist, he could not deny the presence of this
     world; being an idealist, he perceived and developed an
     alternate point of view that goes beyond the fixed boundaries
     of the present situation.  For Robinson, this cosmic quality
     is essentially a belief that temporal misfortune can be en-
     dured because a happy ending is assured or because the
     faith in a happy ending is a sustaining force.

927  MOULT, Thomas.  "The Poetry of Edwin Arlington Robinson:
     Collected Poems."  London Bookman, 63 (January, 1923),
     206-207.

928  MULLIGAN, Louise Griffith.  "Mythology and Autobiography in
     Edwin Arlington Robinson's Tristram."  Ph.D. diss., Uni-
     versity of Mass., 1975.  DA, 36 (1976), 6102A.  Tristram,
     whose theme had its origin in the Middle Ages, may be read
     in relation to Robinson's own reputed life-long love for his
     sister-in-law, Emma, particularly when one is aware of the
     omissions and additions that he makes to the old legend.
     A familiarity with the original tale and with particular events
     in Robinson's life is necessary if one is to understand how
     close the relationship is.  An examination of the triangle
     theme in poem after poem reveals that it seems to have be-
     come an obsession with the author, and corresponds with
     certain important events in Robinson's life.  An examination
     of Robinson's life and the events in Tristram leads to a feel-
     ing that some of the critics knew or at least suspected the
     existence of the romance in the poet's life, although they
     were careful not to say so definitely.

929  MUNSON, Gorham B.  "Edwin Arlington Robinson."  Saturday
     Review of Literature, 3 (May 21, 1927), 839-840.  Tristram
     represents Robinson at his highest level, and yet it does not
     remove our query:  Has the poet added somewhat to his skill,
     to his depth and scope of interpretation, to his power as a

singer of man? The answer might be brief. There is a re-
finement of what he has sung before, but no development
of it.

930          . Destinations:  A Canvass of American Literature
     Since 1900.  New York:  J. H. Sears, 1928.  "Between
     Autumn and Winter in New England Poetry:  A Descriptive
     Note on Edwin Arlington Robinson," pp. 57-66.  "I wonder
     if, in actuality, he is the best of contemporary American
     poets.  Such a poet is difficult to estimate exactly while he
     is alive.  His virtues have some of the weight of traditions
     which in an age of transition are either rejected or acclaimed
     too whole-heartedly for justice.  It may be that he has
     chiseled out a recess in some order of genuine poetry, but
     which order?"  Comments on several poems to the purpose
     of trying to establish the alleged supremacy of Robinson
     among living American poets.  Tristram does not give a
     clear answer.  It is a consummation of Robinson's talents
     that renews our admiration on several scores but equally
     renews all our former doubts of his magnitude.

931  MURPHY, Francis, ed.  Edwin Arlington Robinson:  A Collec-
     tion of Critical Essays.  Englewood Cliffs, N.J.:  Prentice-
     Hall, 1970.  Twentieth Century Views Series, 186 pages of
     reprinted material, with one original essay by Josephine
     Miles.  Contents:  each item is listed in regular alphabetical
     sequence.  "Introduction" by Francis Murphy, pp. 1-7.
     "A Cool Master," by Yvor Winters, pp. 8-15.  "Three Re-
     views," by Conrad Aiken, pp. 15-28.  "Robinson in Amer-
     ica," by Morton D. Zabel, pp. 29-32.  "Introduction to King
     Jasper," by Robert Frost, pp. 33-39.  "The Shorter Poems,"
     by Yvor Winters, pp. 40-59.  "E. A. Robinson:  The Lost
     Tradition," by Louis O. Coxe, pp. 60-76.  "Edwin Arlington
     Robinson:  The Man Truths," by James Dickey, pp. 77-94.
     "One Kind of Traditional Poet," by Edwin S. Fussell, pp.
     95-109.  "Robinson's Inner Fire," by Josephine Miles, pp.
     110-116.  "The 'New' Poetry:  Robinson and Frost," by
     Warner Berthoff, pp. 117-127.  "The Alienated Self," by
     W. R. Robinson, pp. 128-147.  "E. A. Robinson:  The Cos-
     mic Chill," by Hyatt H. Waggoner, pp. 148-163.  "Robinson's
     Modernity," by J. C. Levenson, pp. 164-181.

932  MURRAY, Philip.  "Reviews of Current Books and Publications."
     Poetry, 120 (July, 1972), 231-235.  Among other volumes,
     comment is made on the reprint edition of Yvor Winter's
     biography of Edwin Arlington Robinson, first published in
     1946.  Winters is the ideal critic for Robinson.  He under-
     stands his subject thoroughly and, especially in his analysis
     of the shorter poems, illuminates Robinson perfectly....  It
     is only in the chapter on "the other long poems" that the
     book gets tedious.  The many plot summaries of long poems

is heavy going, and should not occupy forty pages. But over all, he is right about Robinson's best work.

933 NADIG, Henry Davis. "I'd Rather Read Poetry: Review of Nicodemus." New Canaan Advertiser, October 27, 1932. P. 9.

934 NEFF, Emery. "The Intimate Robinson." Nation, 165 (November 8, 1947), 506-507. Review of Untriangulated Stars. Robinson's early maturity has been largely undocumented until now. In this volume we have abundant information which is the first major collection of Robinson's early letters. These 158 letters to Harry de Forest Smith have been fortunate in their editor. Written for his friend's eyes only, sometimes with injunctions that they be burned, they are a faithful, often week-by-week report of the state of Robinson's mind and heart from the bewildered years between high school and college through a period of growth and frustration until Theodore Roosevelt directed national attention to his neglected verse.

935 _____. Edwin Arlington Robinson. New York: William Sloane Associates, 1948. American Men of Letters Series. Reprinted New York: Russell & Russell, 1968. Consists of 283 pages with index. In eight chapters: "Father and Sons"; "New Forms and Faces"; "Oh for a Poet"; "The Pauper"; "The Town Down the River"; "The Man Against the Sky"; "Afterglow"; "I shall have more to say when I am dead." Robinson's verse is rooted firmly in our soil and character. Its themes are almost wholly American, and its humor is unmistakably New England. But its American quality is not of the flamboyant sort attractive to European seekers and exploiters of novelty. His fresh and original observation of life flows into traditional verse forms, and his idiomatic language shuns slang and the merely picturesque.

936 NEIHARDT, John G. "An Appreciation." Mark Twain Quarterly, 2 (Spring, 1938), 10. Remembers that he met Robinson in the winter of 1907 when he was living in Washington Square. At the time Robinson had a rather small but enthusiastic following.... Testimonials could have helped him then, but now his fame has outgrown the need.

937 NELSON, John Herbert and Oscar Cargill, eds. Contemporary Trends: American Literature Since 1900. New York: Macmillan, 1949. Robinson, pp. 668-720. Reprints a variety of poems, mostly well known, without comment or critical introduction.

938 NETHERCOTT, A. H. "'Ways that Make Us Ponder While We Praise.'" Voices, 12 (December-January, 1932-1933), 42-47. Review of Nicodemus.

939  NEWELL, Emily (Mrs. Blair). "For Those Who Love Poetry."
     Good Housekeeping, 85 (December, 1927), 208-209. Dis-
     cussed under Blair, Emily Newell.

940  NICHOLL, Louis Townsend. "The New Poetry: The Glory of
     the Nightingales." Outlook and Independent, 156 (Septem-
     ber 24, 1930), 145-146. Hate and revenge loom like smoke
     over Robinson's latest poem, and then the smoke drifts off
     and we are left blinking at what, supposedly, is light....
     The book is overlaid with nightmare quality; evil itself rises
     up like genii out of the bottle and dominates the scene into
     unreality. It all seems squarely set in Hell. The monotone
     of metre of the mercilessly leveling blank verse, seems to
     become the rhythm of that nether place. A newspaper clip-
     ping could have told the tale with more succinctness, a
     stage drama with less terrific accumulation and monotony;
     nobody but Robinson could have piled up the terrible weari-
     ness and horror of vengeance and disgrace as he has done.

941  _____. "The New Poetry: Matthias at the Door." Outlook
     and Independent, 159 (October 28, 1931), 282. This long,
     abstruse and darkly imaginative tale has more real poetry
     than can be found in The Glory of the Nightingales, but it
     is not the sharp and vital poetry that appeared in Tristram.
     This brutal and uncompromising story is called a "study of
     the underworld of emotions in the lives of four people, each
     of whom meets defeat in a different way." The poem is hard
     to understand, and many readers are left in the dark, wish-
     ing for a return of the old Robinson, whose work was less
     complex, but far more moving and alive.

942  NICKERSON, Paul S. "Review of Collected Poems." English
     Journal, 11 (December, 1922), 657-659. Here is the work
     of over thirty years, previously published in eight separate
     volumes, now assembled in a distinctive collection the con-
     sistently high excellence of which is most impressive....
     To come into the presence of Robinson's poetry is like com-
     ing into the presence of old mountains. It is impressive,
     solemn, often majestic, sometimes almost inscrutable. It has
     the elemental quality of great cliffs clear against the sky.
     The climb to the summit of its significance is at times a dif-
     ficult one, but once we are there, the view is worth all the
     effort it has cost--and more.

943  NILON, Charles H. Bibliography of Bibliographies of American
     Literature, in one vol. New York: Bowker, 1970. Robin-
     son, pp. 235-237. Consists of some 25 items in alphabetical
     order of works which either contain bibliographies or are
     totally of bibliography. Emphasis is on works listing mainly
     primary sources.

944 NITCHIE, Elizabeth. "Philosophy in the Poetry of Edwin Ar-
    lington Robinson." Modern Language Notes, 56 (April,
    1941), 317-318. Review of Estelle Kaplan's study. Miss
    Kaplan distinguishes four stages in Robinson's intellectual
    growth, marked by four chief themes: the tragedy of light,
    the tragedy of love in conflict with duty, the tragedy of
    marriage, and the tragedy of power.... Greater clarity and
    ease, however, in organization and in style would be desir-
    able in a book of this kind. Also she is more successful in
    analyzing philosophical thought than human emotion. She
    does not always penetrate to the feelings and motives of
    the characters or recognize and appreciate a dramatic situ-
    ation.

945 NIVISON, David S. "Does It Matter How Annandale Went Out?"
    Colby Library Quarterly, 5 (December, 1960), 170-185. Re-
    printed in Cary, ed. (1969), pp. 178-190. In a sense, it
    does not matter how Annandale went out. What matters is
    the kind of question Robinson put to the event. Here in
    life he was confronted with the problem which is presented
    in poem after poem, of a human enigma in which we must
    learn to accept that we must remain in ignorance and doubt.
    The physician is not telling us what happened--he is saying
    what Robinson conjectures he might have said could we ask
    him. For no one knows how Annandale went out, really.
    Except, perhaps, Annandale himself.

946 NORRIS, William A. "The Laboratory of a Poet's Soul: Roman
    Bartholow." Boston Transcript, 8 (April 21, 1923), 5.
    Robinson has that rarest of accomplishments or gifts, a per-
    fect identification of style with subject matter. His peculiar
    idiom grows out of his philosophy; his circuitousness and
    his veracity are one; there are no pitfalls behind the thorny
    hedge that he presents to the world. Jump that, and he is
    yours, and you will wonder that you ever saw any barrier
    at all.

947 _____. "The Dark Wood: Review of The Man Who Died
    Twice." New Republic, 41 (January 21, 1925), 238-239.
    We have long been aware that Robinson walked at the edge
    of a dark wood.... Now he has been swallowed utterly.
    The actual story is left practically untold. It is the spirit-
    ual story that is recounted in full detail. We have sense-
    contact with trees and people, with stars and insects, but
    never with such abstractions as heaven or hell, God or
    eternity. Hence Robinson's spiritual psychology is a study
    of a mind grappling with mental concepts. It never gets
    beyond the lobs of the human brain. It has no windows
    opening upon the world of common experience.

948 NORTH, Jessica Nelson. "A Classic of Indirection: Review of

Cavender's House." Poetry, 34 (July, 1929), 233-236.
Robinson has no imitators, so unless you tire of Robinson
you cannot tire of Robinsonian poetry. We have all gone
astray after color and form, and one poet alone has resisted
the warm appeal of the senses to spend his life putting down
the elusive intricacies of the mind. In this poem this technique is more than apparent. At the end we have a fairly
clear image of what the hero and heroine are like, and of
the central purpose of the book. But it would have been
far more effective if Robinson could have been less elaborate, less devious, less inclined to play with his conceptions,
letting them almost escape and then snatching them back.

949 NOTOPOULOS, James A. "Sophocles and Captain Craig." New
England Quarterly, 17 (March, 1944), 109. Article is based
on a conversation the author had with Harry de Forest Smith
in 1942. Smith and Robinson were boyhood friends, and in
this conversation Professor Smith recalls the origin of the
lines in "Captain Craig" which are a rendering from one of
the choral odes in Antigone. Smith and Robinson expressed
their love for Sophocles, and Smith made a prose translation
of Antigone which Robinson used as the basis for one in
verse form. The Robinson translation was later destroyed,
but the lines in "Captain Craig" are a memorable fragment.

950 NYREN, Dorothy Curley, et al., eds. A Library of Literary
Criticism: Modern American Literature. New York: Frederick Ungar, 1960. Robinson, pp. 404-407. 4th edition,
1969. Robinson, Vol. 3, pp. 79-86. Reprints excerpts from
23 critics.

951 O'CONNOR, William Van. Sense and Sensibility in Modern Poetry. Chicago: University of Chicago Press, 1948. Robinson, pp. 200-201. Robinson employs an abstract diction because the idiom he inherited was from the nineteenth century.
The integrity of Robinson's characters, despite their weaknesses and isolation, is a part of the moral fiber that was in
Robinson himself. However shabby their way of life or however frustrated some of his characters are, they maintain a
margin of dignity and self-respect. It is with the margin itself that Robinson was preoccupied. He was able in the face
of a great deal of evidence to the contrary to justify something very close to a tragic vision.

952 OLIVER, Egbert S. "Robinson's Dark-Hill-to-Climb Image."
Literary Criterion (Mysore, India), 3 (Summer, 1959), 36-52.
Reprinted in Studies in American Literature: Whitman,
Emerson, Melville, and Others. New Delhi: Eurasia Publishing House, 1965. Pp. 139-154. In "Captain Craig" the motivating imagery is struggling or climbing upward toward light
and truth. The image appears in a variety of contexts.

The imagery is sustained and goes far toward achieving ful-
filment in the study of the old man who has been cast aside
by life's measure of success.... Thus early in his career
Robinson was struggling and climbing toward the image of
life which found such conclusive expression in "Flammonde"
and "The Man Against the Sky." He achieved mastery of
this central image around which he built some of his most
poignantly memorable poems twenty years after his first
poems appeared. Robinson's gallery of studies in human
destiny is one of the most challenging and magnificent which
any modern writer has given to the reading world. In his
own quiet way he climbed his own darkening hill, but for-
tunately on the way he conversed with us of the men and
women of Tilbury Town--men and women of every Town;
and he gave excellent poetic expression to the depth of
character which he encountered on his mountain journey.

953   O'NEILL, George. "Poetry from Four Men: Review of Son-
      nets." Outlook and Independent, 151 (January 16, 1929),
      3, 110, 111, 114, 120. This book affords that richness
      which sonnet lovers search with their own intensity more
      abundantly than one dares expect in these sterile times.
      It is a book which old readers of Robinson will be glad to
      have, and one which should address new readers. The
      poems are arranged with diversity, avoiding the monotony
      of placing poems of related themes one after the other.
      Each poem stands by itself, unwebbed by the echoes of
      the preceding work.

954   OSBORN, Edward Bolland. "An American Master-Poet." The
      Morning Post (London), November 3, 1922. P. 6. Review
      of Collected Poems.

955   _____. "America's Chief Poet." The Morning Post (London),
      April 8, 1935. P. 6. Notice of Robinson's death and obitu-
      ary.

956   OWNBEY, E. Sydnor. "'Mr. Flood's Party' lines 17-24." Ex-
      plicator, 8 (April, 1950), item 47. Is an answer to Profes-
      sor Randall Stewart's observation that the reference to Ro-
      land is incongruous in a New England setting. A close
      study of the allusion reveals more resemblances. Moreover,
      it may be argued that whatever incongruity, it is studied,
      sought deliberately by the poet for a special effect. The
      effectiveness of the simile lies in its ambivalence, its com-
      bination of humorous incongruity and more serious relevance.
      A poorer poet would have emphasized only the pathos of
      Mr. Flood's plight, and the result would have been senti-
      mentality. Robinson, through the play of his wit, has fused
      the pathetic and the comic in that rich complexity so fre-
      quently characteristic of the best poetry.

957  PARISH, John E. "The Rehabilitation of Eben Flood." Eng-
     lish Journal, 55 (September, 1966), 696-699.  The unwar-
     ranted assumption that the people of Tilbury Town have
     sternly ostracized Eben Flood because of something in his
     past, is largely because of a misunderstanding of the "par-
     ty" itself, as a drunken orgy.  There is no evidence to
     support this theory.  Old Eben Flood has simply outlived
     his time, there is nobody left to greet him, and he is stunned
     to realize that since his last visit to the hill the last of his
     friends has died.  Robinson makes clear that there is no
     estrangement between the old man and his contemporaries.
     His language to himself is very civil, not unlike that he
     might have used to someone in the town.

958  PARLETT, Mathilde M. "Robinson's 'Luke Havergal.'" Explica-
     tor, 3 (June, 1945), item 57.  Believes that "Luke ..." is
     not a love poem, but another of Robinson's many portraits
     of "varieties of religious experience."  The poet's own grop-
     ings towards religious faith are well known, and his great
     knowledge of the Bible is well-documented.  The woman who
     may call to Luke is Truth, who has been studying the reli-
     gions of the East.  Failing to find there the answers to his
     questions, he remembers the arguments of a friend, now
     dead, who, though himself repelled by dogmatic institutional
     Christianity, had found assurance in the example and teach-
     ings of Christ.  In memory, the friend speaks "out of a
     grave." and affirms that if you have faith in the fundamen-
     tal teachings, you will find Truth and a satisfying individual
     religion.

959  PATTEE, Fred Lewis. The New American Literature: 1830-
     1930, A Survey. New York:  Century, 1930.  "The New
     England Poets," pp. 293-298.  Recognition came late.  His
     high tide did not come until nearly a quarter of a century
     after his first volume--in 1921 it was, after the publication
     of his collected poems, a volume awarded the Pulitzer prize
     and formally pronounced by the American Authors' League
     "the book of the most enduring value of the year."  Among
     the discerning few, the poetry-minded, he is already
     crowned as the leading poet of his time....  Never, how-
     ever, will he be the poet of the people.  His lyrics lack the
     singing quality that most readers demand; they lack emotion.
     He has written too much.  His long poems are full of vast
     desert areas that can be described by no other word than
     dull.  His sentences oft-times are interminable, one hundred
     and fifty words in one of them.  His vocabulary is for the
     few; his meanings are often more difficult to find than are
     Browning's.

960  PAYNE, Leonidas Warren, Jr. "The First Edition of Edwin Ar-
     lington Robinson's 'The Peterborough Idea.'" University

of Texas Studies in English, 19 (1939), 219-231.  Article is
a bibliographical and textual study of an essay which Robinson wrote and published in September 1916 in the North
American Review.  By then Robinson had spent several
summers at the MacDowell colony near Peterborough, New
Hampshire, and he wanted to do what he could for the en-
largement and future support of the colony.  Payne's article is a listing of the several bibliographic references to
Robinson's essay, followed by a comparison of the text of
the original publication with that of the Peterborough Idea,
Pamphlet which does not bear a date but is probably of 1917.
This publication, with numerous corrections, is regarded as
the first edition.

961  PAYNE, William Morton.  "Review of Captain Craig."  Dial, 34
(January 1, 1903), 18-19.  Several years ago Robinson
brought out a slender volume of poetry, and those lucky
enough to get the volume felt that the voice was at least
distinctively individual, and took pleasure in an utterance
that seemed to scorn rhetorical trickery, and came arrayed
in the strength of sincerity and truth.  Now we have a new
volume, and the impression made by his earlier collection is
intensified.  He has a philosophy of life, not clearly formulated in all respects, but traceable in its main outlines, and
clearly held with the deepest conviction.  The character of
Captain Craig is the chief vehicle of Robinson's theory of
life.  Craig displays shrewdness in getting at the heart of
life's problems, and zeal in his warfare on insincerity and
hypocrisy.

962  _____.  "Review of The Town Down the River."  Dial, 50
(March 1, 1911), 164-165.  He is a reticent poet, but a few
of his words will outweigh the fluent utterance of the more
voluble.  He is a parsimonious poet, but when he gives us
dole of his riches, we know that the coin is no counterfeit.
Robinson's attitude toward life in its conventional manifesta-
tions is bitter or contemptuous, his expression almost acrid,
and yet his vision is transfigured with gleams of idealism.
The City of God may be as yet unbuilded, but somewhere--
possibly in this land of ours--its foundations are being laid.

963  PEARCE, Roy Harvey.  The Continuity of American Poetry.
Princeton:  Princeton University Press, 1961.  Robinson,
pp. 256-269.  Robinson invented his own variations on the
nineteenth-century basic style and made it into an instrument for poetic fictions in which protagonists and circumstances so interpenetrate as to result in that marvelous complex of self-discovery and self-deceit which characterize the
sort of understanding available to his modern men....  His
poems at their best are anecdotal, tending toward the tale
and thus toward the novelistic.  Poems expound life in its

"intenser phases." The intensity is great to the degree
that the phases, the slices of life, are narrow and con-
strained, quickly exhausted of their potentiality for freedom
and joy.

964 PEARSON, Edmund Lester. "Review of The Three Taverns."
Review, 3 (September 29, 1920), 269.

965 PELL, Edward. "Character in Verse: A Review of Selected
Poems." The New Leader, 49 (January 17, 1966), 29-30.

966 PELTIER, Florence. "Edwin Arlington Robinson, Himself."
Mark Twain Quarterly (Webster Groves, Missouri), 1 (Summer, 1937), 6, 11-14. Article is an informal sketch based
upon the author's personal acquaintance of and letters from
Robinson, covering a long period of time from 1903 until
1931. Robinson was far from being a fluent talker, and on
occasions when he was a house-guest, he usually kept to
himself and wrote. Sometimes, however, he actually conversed, and what he then said remained as fixed in memory
as did his poetry.... The letters included in this article
were written from Peterborough, N.H., where Robinson
spent a good many of his summers.

967 PERRINE, Laurence D. "'Veteran Sirens.'" Explicator, 6
(November, 1947), item 13. Article replies to Yvor Winters
misinterpretation of the poem. The poem deals with middle-
aged or elderly spinsters who refuse to accept either their
age or their spinsterhood gracefully, but continue to invoke
rouge, lipstick, nail paint, hair dye, bright clothes, and
artificial gaiety in an effort to simulate youth and attract
men. This is not a poem of old prostitutes who must continue as best they are able at their trade.... Robinson's
creed of forgiveness through understanding is expressed
in sympathy for the failures of whom he writes and charity
for their delusions. His charity is least, however, for the
spirit of commercialism, and there is no evidence that he had
any sympathy for commercialized love.

968 _____. "Edwin Arlington Robinson and Arthurian Legend."
Ph.D. diss., Yale University, 1948.

969 _____. "Robinson's Tristram." Explicator, 6 (May, 1948),
item 44. Comments on Sections IX and X, just before and
after the death of the lovers. Thinks that the imagery of
the ship, which has been substituted by Robinson for the
rose-tree and vine which spring from the lovers' graves.
The ship, putting out to sea as it is, symbolizes the passing
of the souls of the lovers into the "transcendent whole"--or
that it symbolizes that their love is not dead, but has merely
passed to another sphere.... Robinson's poetic faith was

compounded of transcendentalism and agnosticism. He felt
that a Creative Will was discernible in the universe, which
gave life meaning and purpose and made it something more
than "a riot of cells and chemistry."

970 _____. "Tristram, cont." Explicator, 7 (March, 1949),
item 33. Refutes idea that Isolt was stabbed to death; Tristram was killed by Andred. In other uses of the legend
Tristram met his death in various ways, but without exception Isolt died, almost simultaneously, of the shock and of
her love. For Robinson this was a genuine and transcendent love, and he had no reason to reject the tradition of
Isolt's death for love. As realist and psychologist, Robinson
does reject its suddenness: it really occurs over a period
of two or more years. When Tristram is killed, she is already dying, and no incident has been more carefully prepared for in the last five pages of dialogue between the two
lovers.

971 _____. "Robinson's 'Eros Turannos.'" Explicator, 8 (December, 1949), item 20. In Greek literature passionate love
was conceived of as a "tragic madness" which plunged "otherwise sane people into crime and disgrace." Robinson's
poem exhibits this tyrannical driving power of the God of
God in a New England setting. Here the results are marriage, disillusion, and repression. The poem is evenly divided between the madness and the tragedy. The first three
stanzas show Love blinding and trapping its victim; the last
three, after marriage, exhibit the tragic results. The central unifying figure of the poem is the personfiication of
Love as a tyrant who blinds, maddens, and whips. Structure is further given by the repeated images of trees and
leaves, waves and ocean, which serve both as setting and
symbol.

972 _____. "A Reading of 'Miniver Cheevy.'" Colby Library
Quarterly, 6 (June, 1962), 65-74. The main features of the
poem are immediately apparent. Here is the portrait of a
misfit, a failure. Unable to adjust himself to the present
and meet the problems of reality, he escapes this reality in
two ways: dreaming of the romantic past, and by drinking.
The past seems romantic to him because it is not of the
present. Miniver is the kind of person who is always longing "for the good old days," and who thinks the present
cheap and commonplace, unromantic and unexciting.

973 _____. "Contemporary Reference of Robinson's Arthurian
Poems." Twentieth Century Literature, 8 (July, 1962), 74-
82. Article is a long well-documented essay on the Arthurian poems. When Robinson published these poems, critics
reacted in two directions. Some saw them as a retreat into

the romantic past; others found them just the opposite, a
treatment of the contemporary world.  No point-to-point
explication of this latter concept has been made, but the
purpose of this article is to determine as precisely as possible how far this statement may be considered true.  In
evaluating this point of view we must not overlook Robinson's
warning not to carry "too far" any reading of political symbolism into the poems.  The poems, however, do portray
worlds that are crumbling, and the world of the poet, when
these poems were written, was on the brink of crumbling.

974 _____.  "Tennyson and Robinson:  Legalistic Moralism vs.
Situation Ethics."  Colby Library Quarterly, 8 (December,
1969), 416-433.  Robinson was fully aware that he was directly challenging Tennyson.  He too was attempting a
large-scale work which would invest old legend with modern
moral significance.  Like Tennyson he was concerned with
the relationship between private and political morality; like
Tennyson he saw in the fall of Camelot the passing of one
social order and the beginning of a new.  Robinson's morality,
however, is in almost direct contradiction to Tennyson's.
Where Tennyson's is a rigid moral conventionalism, in which
judgments are made by a legalistic application of rules, Robinson's is a complex morality, in which judgments are based
on a consideration of all aspects of a unique situation.  As
opposed to the morality of rules, Robinson's is what has
since become known as Situation Ethics.  The difference is
most apparent in the two poets' treatment of sexual relationships.

975 _____.  "Robinson's 'The Tree in Pamela's Garden.'"  Explicator, 30 (October, 1971), item 18.  Unlike most inter-
pretations of this poem, this critic does not see Pamela either
as a pathetic spinster or as a morbid and warped personality.  He thinks that Pamela has had, or is having a secret
love affair....  The poem is not without ambiguity, but
Pamela's smile at the end is partially a smile of satisfaction
at the success of her deception.  This interpretation removes all difficulties, and in addition is the only one which
allows the poem to exploit fully the tree of knowledge allusion.

976 _____.  "The Sources of Robinson's Merlin."  American Literature, 44 (May, 1972), 313-321.  Malory is the chief
source for the political sections of Merlin--for those parts
that concern the story of Camelot; but for the love relationships of Camelot, Robinson's chief source is a much earlier
one:  the twelfth-century French prose romance generally
known as the vulgate Merlin.  Malory, and also Tennyson,
exert some influence, but the basic conception and the coloring are drawn from the French romance.  There is no reason

to suppose that Robinson had read this work. It is a huge
tome, not readily available, written in Old French. Robinson found the story summarized in a book by S. Humphreys
Gurteen called The Arthurian Epic (1895), borrowed from
his friend Louis Ledoux.

977 _____. "The Sources of Robinson's Arthurian Poems and
His Opinions of Other Testaments." Colby Library Quarterly,
10 (June, 1974), 336-346. Begins by remarking the two
other recent studies of this subject have appeared, but this
article will complete, not duplicate. Article is arranged into
compact sections, each one dealing with a source and indicating what Robinson thought of it. These references are:
Malory, The vulgate Merlin, Tennyson, Joseph Bédier's Le
Roman de Tristan et Iseult (a composite version of the medieval Tristram romance), Richard Wagner, Algernon Charles
Swinburne, Matthew Arnold, Richard Hovey, John Masefield,
James Russell Lowell, Hermann Hagedorn's long narrative
poem, The Great Maze, dealing with the return of Agamemnon
from Troy and his murder by his wife's lover, and Gawain
and the Green Knight.

978 PERRY, Bliss. "Poets Celebrate Edwin Arlington Robinson's
Birthday." (50th). New York Times Book Review, December 21, 1919. P. 1.

979 _____. With preface. Ed. Charles Cestré. Selected Poems
of Edwin Arlington Robinson. New York: Macmillan, 1931.
It has been easy to choose the poems printed here, and the
range is rather extensive. Arrangement is mostly by chronology, in sections. The sonnets are printed together.
There are judicious selections from some of the longer poems.

980 PERRY, Thomas Sergeant. Selections from the Letters of
Thomas Sergeant Perry, edited with introduction by Edwin
Arlington Robinson. New York: Macmillan, 1929. Consists
of 255 pages selected from many hundreds. In the introduction Robinson says: "he was a great reader, a great
friend, and a great gentleman. Whether or not he might
have been a great writer is more than one can say, for he
never took the trouble to find out." Comments at length on
Perry's reading, and sketches his biography. He was born
in 1845 and died in 1928. He graduated from Harvard in
1866 and then studied abroad. He was editor of the North
American Review, instructor in English at Harvard, and
professor of English in a Japanese University. He was the
author of several books, many articles, and numerous translations.

981 PETTIT, Henry. "Robinson's 'The Whip.'" Explicator, 1 (April, 1943), item 50. Notes how many explanations of this

short poem there have been.  This comment thinks it is a
triangle poem in which  one of the lovers, having outstripped
the other, is speculating on the death of the latter when he
is suddenly shocked at the dawning suspicion that he himself as the survivor may have won a pyrrhic victory--meant
to imply that a lover's conquest is inevitably an enslavement.
According to this interpretation, the implications of the poem
closely parallel those of Keats' "La Belle Dame sans Merci."

982  PHELPS, William Lyon.  "Edwin Arlington Robinson."  Bookman,
     47 (July, 1918), 551-552.  Reprinted in The Advance of
     English Poetry in the Twentieth Century.  New York:
     Dodd, Mead, 1919.  Pp. 209-212.  Robinson is not only one
     of our best known American poets, but is a leader and rec-
     ognized as such.  Many write verses today because the
     climate is so favorable.  But if Mr. Robinson is not a
     germinal writer, he is at all events a precursor of the mod-
     ern advance.  The year 1896 was not opportune for a ven-
     ture in verse, but the Gardiner poet has never cared to be
     in the rearward of a fashion.  The two poems that he pro-
     duced that year he has since surpassed, but they clearly
     demonstrated his right to live and to be heard.

983  _____.  "As I Like It."  Scribner's Magazine, 89 (January,
     1931), 95.  Comments on The Glory of the Nightingales, say-
     ing it does not have the universal appeal of his Tristram.
     But it is a noble and austere poem, with that smouldering
     flame so characteristic of its author's dignified reserve.
     It is not for all markets, but it will not disappoint those
     who rejoice that its author is an American.

984  _____.  Autobiography with Letters.  New York:  Oxford
     University Press, 1939.  "Tribute to Edwin Arlington Rob-
     inson," pp. 693-698.  Reprinted from New York Herald
     Tribune, November 13, 1936.  Pp. 14-15.  Recalls the event
     of Robinson's first publication, 1896, and does not remember
     if he read the book or not.  The next year he received
     Children of the Night, of which he read every word.  He
     finally met Robinson in 1922, after which they corresponded.
     When Robinson began to publish his poetry in the late nine-
     ties, the times were not favorable; but the true poet should
     have genius for the inopportune.  These two early volumes
     were doomed to speedy and complete oblivion, but about fif-
     teen years later, in the revival of poetry in America, Robin-
     son came into his own; and he deserved his fame, both for
     the excellence of his work and because he was one of the
     leaders in this renaissance.

985  _____.  "Edwin Arlington Robinson," in American Academy of
     Arts and Letters, 1905-1941.  New York:  The Academy
     Press, 1942.  Pp. 323-328.  When Robinson began to publish

his poetry in the late nineties, the times were not favorable;
but the true poet should have genius for the inopportune.
These two early volumes attracted very little attention; and
apparently they were doomed to speedy and complete obliv-
ion, the inescapable fate of ninety-nine out of every hundred books. But about fifteen years later, in the revival
of poetry in America, Robinson came into his own; and he
deserved his fame, both for the excellence of his work and
because he was one of the leaders of the renaissance. In
1927 he produced his masterpiece, Tristram. It is not only
his best poem, it is the best poetic version of that immortal
story that has ever appeared in English. It glows with
passion and is radiant with beauty.

986  PHILIPS, David E.  "Robinson's Letters to Edith Brower:  A
     Review."  Down East, 15 (November, 1968), 66.

987  _____.  "Appreciation of Edwin Arlington Robinson:  A Re-
     view."  Down East (Camden, Maine), 16 (April, 1970), 88.
     Review of collection edited by Richard Cary.

988  PIERCE, Frederick E.  "Review of Tristram."  Yale Review,
     17 (October, 1927), 176-178.  What was best and deepest
     in the romantic attitude has been preserved, the sense of
     life's transitoriness, the sense that we are breaking bubbles
     on changing seas of time and being.  What was best in mod-
     ern realism has been preserved too:  the clean-cut analysis
     of human nature; the realization that ancient characters did
     not seem dimly romantically "ancient" to themselves; the
     realization that the seeming villain of a piece is often a de-
     generate rather than a devil.  The verse flows on within
     narrow limits, perhaps, but with unerring judgment and un-
     failing beauty.  Such poetry does not belong to any age or
     movement.  It is part of the lasting heritage of the race.

989  PIPKIN, E. Edith.  "The Arthur of Edwin Arlington Robinson."
     English Journal, 19 (March, 1930), 183-195.  Reprinted in
     Cary, ed. (1969), pp. 6-16.  The Arthurian conception of
     the average reader is still largely Tennysonian.  It was this
     reading public that Robinson came to when he decided to
     rekindle the Arthurian legend.  It was soon recognized that
     he was not at all like Tennyson, but that he gave a highly
     individual view of the situation at Camelot.  Not only are the
     poems dramatic, they are tragic, depending on some fatal
     weakness of the characters themselves.  His Arthurian fig-
     ures are no mere puppets, they are men and women, highly
     individualized and yet universal.  His Arthur is introspective,
     emotionally disturbed; his nerves are worn raw by vague
     fears and suspicions.

990  PISANTO, Tommaso.  "La Poesia di Edwin Arlington Robinson

tra Ottocento e Novecento." <u>Ansonia</u> (Siena, Italy), 19 (1964), 32-35.

991 _____. "Robinson e la poesia Americana." <u>Nuova Antologia</u> (Rome, Italy), 524 (1975), 239-244.

992 POLICARDI, Silvio. <u>Breve Storia della Letteratura Americana.</u> Milan: Istituto Edioriale Cisalpino, 1951. Robinson, pp. 218-219.

993 PORTE, Joel. "Lancelot 'Rode on Alone.'" <u>Christian Science Monitor</u>, 57 (July 8, 1965), 7. Review of <u>Where the Light Falls</u>, by Chard Powers Smith. This biography is by no means entirely devoted to proving that Robinson led a life of pure allegory. Smith resents a vivid and sympathetic portrait of Robinson, in his folly as well as in his wisdom. One of the most entertaining aspects of Robinson exhibited in the book is the poet's humor, which, if it is often dry and bitter, is frequently also playful and gay.... And yet finally, it is as a paradigm of courage and achievement in the face of great adversity that Smith finds the value and meaning of Robinson's lonely life. As Robinson said of Lancelot, so we might say of Robinson: "... always in the darkness he rode on,/Alone: and in the darkness came the Light."

POWER, Sister Mary James. See Sister Mary James Power.

994 POWYS, John Cowper. "The Big Bed." <u>Mark Twain Quarterly</u>, 2 (Spring, 1938), 2. Is a personal recollection of meeting Robinson, about 1905, in New York. Powys went with Robinson "to his attic," which was entirely occupied by his bed and filled by his bed, for the attic was very small. When asked why he lived with nothing but a bed, Robinson replied that he was "a faithful servant of Apollo."

995 PRESTON, John Hyde. "Three American Poets." <u>Virginia Quarterly Review</u>, 3 (July, 1927), 450-462. Contains comments on Robinson's <u>Tristram</u>, of which Preston says he has conflicting emotions. He does not see any reason for rewriting the old legend, any more than he sees a reason for re-writing <u>Hamlet</u>. It seems curious that the one poet who has drawn such vivid characters should fail in this new poem to delineate, with two exceptions, anything resembling very closely a human being. Robinson is utterly unable to describe great passion, or even the effects of passion.... To those who say that Robinson has written himself out, this latest effort is doomed to add volume and assurance.

996 _____. "Poetry, Giants, and Lollypops." <u>Virginia Quarterly Review</u>, 5 (April, 1929), 307-320. Is a long review of a

"shelf of books more or less representative of the poetry of 1928." The accumulative effort is not exciting. Among this vast array of books, "mostly depressing," is the collection of Robinson's Sonnets. All the eighty-nine are mostly things that we know fairly well by this time. Few men have been able to handle character and situation so gracefully in this restricted form: Robinson has given the sonnet new life; or rather, he has made an old (and noble) vessel hold water again.

997 PRITCHARD, William H. "Edwin Arlington Robinson: The Prince of Heartaches." American Scholar, 48 (1978-1979), 89-100. Reprinted in Pritchard, Lives of the Modern Poets. New York: Oxford University Press, 1980. Pp. 83-107. Article is a re-appraisal of Robinson, "whose stock does not stand very high at present and is not likely to rise." Although the long poems are often blamed for putting readers off, it is not evident that the shorter poems fare much better. Article continues with general commentary on some of Robinson's works and also on some of the works written about him. Conclusion points up that the life and challenge of Robinson's poetry lies in its way of saying rather than in the truth or relevance or wisdom of the idea communicated. Yet Robinson's voice is often a dead one, so discussion of the poems is all the more likely to take place with only cursory attention paid to those particular sequences.

998 PULSIFER, Harold Trowbridge. "Books and Book Folks: Review of Selected Letters." Portland Press-Herald, March 23, 1940. P. 5.

999 PYE, John William. Edwin Arlington Robinson: A Biographical-Bibliographical Study. Hartford, Conn.: Watkinson Library of Trinity College Press, 1970. 48 pages.

1000 QUINN, Arthur Hobson, ed. The Literature of the American People. New York: Appleton-Century-Crofts, 1951. Robinson, pp. 819-822. His work as a whole represents a gradual fading out of values derived from a previous epoch. From the beginning he was aware that the world in his time was less and less concerned with individual fulfillment, and that the transcendental confidence in man's inexhaustible resources was not justified in the lives of his contemporaries.... Though too shrewd to delude himself with romantic hopes, he could not discard altogether the attitudes of the past. He set himself with whimsical resignation to reflect upon the anomalies and distortions characteristic of a time of transition. Though he lived and wrote in loneliness, he was as far from being self-absorbed as any man can be. With all his power as a master of vibrant language

he exposed, denounced, and riddled with irony the idols
of a materialistic age and people.  At a time when this nation was in danger of sinking into the recklessness and
corruption of an easy prosperity, it is something to remember that this man achieved the grandeur of an essential
martyrdom for his faith in the inescapable need of life in
the spirit and in truth.

1001 QUINN, Sister M. B.  "Edwin Arlington Robinson:  Vision and
      Voice."  America, 74 (May 15, 1948), 141-143.

1002 _____.  The Metamorphic Tradition in Modern Poetry.  New
      Brunswick, N.J.:  Rutgers University Press, 1955.  Robin-
      son, passim.  Not treated in detail.  Treats Pound, Stevens,
      Williams, Eliot, Hart Crane, Jarrell, and Yeats.  Book con-
      tains no index.

1003 QUIRK, Charles J.  "Edwin Arlington Robinson."  Thought,
      23 (December, 1948), 729-730.  Review of biography by
      Yvor Winters.  Winters attempts, and quite successfully,
      to give an account of Robinson's poetic growth, together
      with a careful and scholarly scrutiny of the poet's most
      important poems.  When read along side of a copy of his
      poems, the work will yield a lucid and solid understanding
      and appreciation of Robinson as a man and as a poet.  Some
      may be surprised to learn that Winters considers Robinson's
      most successful efforts among his shorter poems and those
      of medium length.  The enormously popular (with readers
      and critics) Tristram he ranks among Robinson's inferior
      achievements.

1004 RAMOS, José Antonio.  Panorama de la Literatura Norteameri-
      cana (1600-1935).  Mexico: Ediciones Botas, 1935.  Robin-
      son, pp. 173-175.  In Spanish.

1005 RANCK, Edwin Carty.  "Edwin Arlington Robinson Defines and
      Illustrates Poetry."  The New York Herald Magazine and
      Books, January 2, 1921.  P. 10.

1006 _____.  "Blank Verse Tale of Hate and Fear."  The New
      York Herald Magazine and Books, June 5, 1921.  P. 12.
      Review of Avon's Harvest.

1007 _____.  "A Poet Rewrites a Tragedy of Love:  Tristram."
      Boston Transcript, 6 (May 7, 1927), 4.  This work is mov-
      ingly dramatic and poignantly beautiful.  Not only is it a
      long love poem of outstanding beauty in American poetry,
      it is about the only one to come forth.  Edna Millay's work
      "The King's Henchman" is far inferior to this as a work of
      art.  In nobility of conception, execution and sustained
      beauty of phrasing, Tristram towers head and shoulders
      above Millay's work.

1008 _____. "Within the Walls of Cavender's House." Ibid., 6
        (April 27, 1929), 2. Judged by any standard this is a
        remarkable achievement. If it were the work of a new poet,
        it would be hailed as a masterpiece. Its story is told with
        the clear-cut distinction that is to be found in all of Robin-
        son's work.

1009 _____. "Four People Caught in the Meshes of Fate:
        Matthias at the Door." Ibid., 6 (October 3, 1931), 8.
        Robinson has done it again! It is unquestionably the fin-
        est long poem he has written since Tristram. It glows with
        a rich vitality and has beauty of phrasing, shrewd and
        telling characterization, keen insight into life, and a prodi-
        gality of arresting lines that tempt one constantly to quota-
        tion. There is no poet writing in English today who can
        say so much in one line as Robinson.

1010 _____. "Nicodemus and Other Robinsonian Poetry." Ibid.,
        6 (October 1, 1932), 2. This is a fascinating book because
        it reveals a great poet writing in moods of pity, irony,
        humor, and stark tragedy. If you admire the work of
        Robinson, you will find in this new collection all the quali-
        ties that have appealed to you. The magic and glamour
        are still there. Nicodemus adds new and memorable por-
        traits to Robinson's ever-lengthening gallery of permanent
        picture.

1011 _____. "Edwin Arlington Robinson as Poet Humorist:
        Talifer." Ibid., 5 (September 30, 1933), 1. In no long
        poem since "Captain Craig" has Robinson revealed the
        subtly humorous workings of his mind. Here is the author
        of Tristram taking his sabbatical year in the land of comedy
        and enjoying his jaunt hugely. The reader will enjoy it as
        much as Robinson seems to have enjoyed writing it.

1012 _____. "An American Poet in a Nightmare Land: Amar-
        anth." Ibid., 3 (September 26, 1934), 2. This is the
        most original theme that Robinson has selected as subject
        matter for a long poem, and he has treated it with an au-
        thority that compels attention. In the hands of a lesser
        poet this subject might have degenerated to vacuity, but
        in Robinson's poem there is a dignity, a beauty of phras-
        ing and a compassion for human suffering that elevates
        it to the zone of great art. It is an epic of frustration.

1013 _____. "Last Work and a Great One: King Jasper." Ibid.,
        3 (November 27, 1935), 2. This is a great poem, written
        in the great manner that was uniquely Robinson's. It is
        full of drama, shrewd character drawing and subtle beauty,
        and the poet never permits his symbolism to hold up the
        action of the story.

1014 RANDALL, David A. <u>Dukedom Large Enough</u>. New York:
     Random House, 1969. Robinson, 230-234. Is most attracted
     to the Arthurian poems, with which he was "literally en-
     chanted." Recalls his first meeting with Robinson, and
     they became good friends, or at least "as good as he would
     allow a youthful idolator to become, being pleased somewhat
     by my ability to recite much of his poetry from memory--
     which I can still do." Article continues with an evaluation
     of Frost and Robinson, in which Randall says he was utter-
     ly wrong as to Frost's recognition. He continued his pas-
     sion for collecting books, but somewhere along the way, he
     knew that Frost would outstrip Robinson in the recognition
     game.

1015 RANSOM, John Crowe. "Review of <u>King Jasper</u>." <u>Southern</u>
     <u>Review</u>, 1 (Winter, 1936), 612-614. Remarks on the Intro-
     duction by Robert Frost written in good prose suitable to
     the work for which it is written. Of the poem it may be
     said that it is "another narrative poem by E. A. R." These
     later narrative poems were distinctly his, each new one
     showing that he was not fooling. But as he grew old and
     fabulous the poetic phrensy had abated, and he declined
     into this gentle melancholy, this riddling dialogue and moral
     earnestness.... The melody is pleasant, the tone is au-
     tumn-grey and very consistent. The emotional grip of the
     scene is probably not transferred to the reader unless he
     is an esoteric Robinsonian, and knows how to shut his
     eyes and let the words grow big in his thoughts.

1016 _____. "On a New England Lyre." <u>New York Times Book</u>
     <u>Review</u>, January 19, 1947. See also February 16, 1947.
     Review of biography by Yvor Winters.

1017 _____. <u>American Poetry at Mid-Century</u>. Washington: Li-
     brary of Congress Press, 1958. Robinson, pp. 1-14, "New
     Poets and Old Muses." Article deals extensively with
     Robinson's poem "Eros Turannos." The language of the
     poem is sharply stylized. It is intended for an accomplished
     reader, using Latinate words to make a mighty rhetorical
     clang, and altogether it is in the diction of the universities.
     Yet it is assimilated successfully to a stanza made of the
     folk line.

1018 _____. <u>Selected Essays of John Crowe Random</u>, edited with
     an introduction by Thomas Daniel Young and John Hindle.
     Baton Rouge: Louisiana State University Press, 1984.
     "New Poets and Old Muses," pp. 306-321. Essay is re-
     printed from Ransom's <u>American Poetry at Mid-Century</u>
     (1958), pp. 1-14.

1019 RAVEN, A. A. "'Luke Havergal.'" <u>Explicator</u>, 3 (December,

1944), item 24. This critic sees Luke as a bereaved lover, but he is not contemplating death or suicide. In fact, he is clinging to life in order to preserve its vivid memory of his love. By his too vivid memory he has been blinded to the way that he should go. In other words the way to preserve love is to submit oneself to the future, to have faith. This may well be the meaning of the poem, but the meaning is far less important than the atmosphere of anguish, longing, and pity.... The atmosphere results from the sounds of the lines and from the imagery, which is highly suggestive rather than explicit.

1020　READ, Arthur M. "Robinson's 'The Man Against the Sky.'" Explicator, 26 (February, 1968), item 49. Article comments on the line, "The sun rises and the sun goes down," which obviously alludes to Ecclesiastes. Thinks it may also relate to lines 9-11 of Donne's poem "Good Friday, 1613, Riding Westward." In the Biblical reference the device of a constantly setting and rising sun, a trapped sun, is used to represent the futility of man's existence. In Donne's poem the rider ponders his dilemma as man, riding westward into a sunset he can never reach.

1021　REDMAN, Ben Ray. "Review of Roman Bartholow." New York Herald Tribune Books, October 14, 1923. P. 34. There is nothing in this poem which surpasses what Robinson has done before; but neither is he "running to seed" as one reviewer has noted.

1022　_____. "Satiric Tracts in Verse: Review of Dionysus in Doubt." Ibid., September 6, 1925. P. 4. This volume is the work of a poet presumed to be the greatest of present-day American poets. Yet this work has little to recommend it. It has a beginning, a middle, and an end, and in the middle section there is much that will delight the lover of Robinson's highly individual art.

1023　_____. Edwin Arlington Robinson. New York: Robert M. McBride, 1926. Modern American Writers Series. Consists of 96 pages, without Index or other addenda. In the Introduction Redman says: "it seems to me that there are, even among Robinson's contemporaries, American men and women who have soared as high on lyric wings as he has soared, poets who have dipped for brief moments into a well of human understanding as deep as his, poets who have written lines as beautiful as any he has written; but who among them has produced so large a body of poetry that is so excellent as his? And which of his predecessors, who can match bulk against bulk, can match sustained quality against sustained quality?... His poetry is the product of a thoughtful, enveloping, deeply penetrating mind, that

must at times achieve expression in unfamiliar terms and
patterns, because it has traveled much alone. He is above
all a biographer of souls, who is bound to humanity by the
dual bond of sympathy and humor."

1024 _____. "White Fire and Red: A Review of Tristram."
New York Herald Tribune Books, 4 (May 8, 1927), pp. 3-4.
Comments on several changes in the legend which Robinson
made in his version, showing that the changes serve this
modern composition well. Review also repeats the general
evaluation that this could be the best poem written by an
American.

1025 _____. "Old Wine in New Bottles: A Review of Sonnets."
New York Herald Tribune Books, 5 (December 9, 1928),
p. 23. The sonnet is well molded for this poet's genius,
and he has turned to it for many of his most memorable
utterances. Robinson's most characteristic sonnets are the
portrait-biographies, in which every other line is an epi-
gram and the whole composition hard, round, bright, and
self-sufficient.

1026 _____. "Review of Cavender's House." Ibid., 6 (September 8, 1929), p. 10. The chill wind which blows through
Cavender's House is somewhat disappointing after the white
fire and red fire of Tristram. It is an ingenious conception, but there is less poetry in this work than we have a
right to expect from a great poet.

1027 _____. "The Way Fate Works: The Glory of the Nightingales." Ibid., 7 (September 21, 1930), p. 5. Robinson
has said all these things before, and has said them better.
The diction never becomes magically effective, as it does in
many hundreds of lines scattered through Robinson's work.
It is all a little cold and dry and labored, and as such must
rank among the minor productions of a poet who has amply
proved his greatness.

1028 _____. "New Poems by Edwin Arlington Robinson: Nicodemus." Ibid., 9 (September 25, 1932), p. 2. This new
book must be accepted as a quantitative rather than a
qualitative addiction, and its component poems will in all
likelihood slip unobtrusively into the packed company of
Robinson's works, without any one of them lifting its head
above its neighbors, or sinking noticeably below the average
level.... The technical range of the artist remains unalt-
ered, unexpanded, and he has discovered no hitherto un-
tapped poetic power over himself.... We are following the
middle flight of a poet who, at other times, has soared.

1029 REED, Edward Bliss. "Recent American Verse: A Review of

The Man Against the Sky." Yale Review, 6 (January,
1917), 417-422. There is more packed away within its few
pages than the most receptive reader will discover in volumes of our modern rhapsodists. Robinson's poem offers
no concessions to prevailing tendencies and tastes. It is
austere in its restraint; it is surcharged with thought; it
has no appeal through melody or color; and yet it is one
of the most significant books of the year because of its art
and its force.

1030 _____. "Review of Merlin." Yale Review, 6 (July, 1917),
859-864. Of all our modern writers, Robinson most resembles Meredith, never in his technique or in his choice of
subjects, but in the solidity of his work and in the sense
of intellectual force. Much of our contemporary verse is
painfully thin; here the foundations are dug deep.... Each
volume deepens the conviction that he is our foremost
American poet.

1031 _____. "Review of Lancelot." Yale Review, 10 (October,
1920), 205-206. Robinson's Lancelot is a finer achievement
than his Merlin. Splendidly imagined and unerringly wrought,
this book reaffirms the conviction that Robinson is today
the most significant figure in American verse. The two
books are written in different keys though both have the
same repression, the same power of revealing in a phrase
a landscape or a mood. It is not in technique that Lancelot surpasses Merlin but in its greater variety of characters
and the conflicts of stronger passions.

1032 _____. "Review of Dionysus in Doubt." Yale Review, 15
(July, 1926), 808-813. Readers of Robinson will not be
disappointed in this latest volume, for it is in his best
manner and has the familiar qualities of thought and style
that make his work unique in American letters. He is our
most intellectual poet and yet his pages are never arid;
and that is because he goes at once to the heart of the
matter, to the mind, to the soul, and because he is so
thoroughly interested in human personality and experience.

1033 REEDY, William Marion. "Review of Merlin." Reedy's Mirror,
26 (July 13, 1917), 454.

1034 REEVES, Paschal. "Robinson's Letters to Edith Brower: A
Review." Georgia Review, 24 (Summer, 1970), 238-239. In
Miss Brower, a gifted spinster twenty-one years his senior,
the usually reticent poet found a trusted and admiring con-
fidante. Although he insisted that she destroy his letters,
she preserved 189 of them. These letters are ably edited
with a cogent introduction, and are amply annotated. A
list of his books and a comprehensive index complete the

volume. While this volume will appeal mainly to specialists, it will also be of interest to the general reader for its valuable insight into the life and times of the dedicated artist who became the major poet of his generation.

1035 REICHERT, Rabbi Victor E. "Mishandled Heritage: A Review of Amaranth." The American Israelite (Cincinnati), 81 (December 27, 1934), 4.

1036 REIDY, Marcella. "A Comparative Study of the Tristram Story of the Old English Legend as it is Told in Modern Poetry by Matthew Arnold, Algernon Charles Swinburne, and Edwin Arlington Robinson." University of New Mexico, 1929, M.A. thesis.

1037 REILLY, J. J. "Review of Collected Poems." Springfield Republican, May 28, 1922. P. 7a.

1038 REIN, D. M. "The Appeal of 'Richard Cory.'" CEA Critic, 26 (November, 1963), 6. This is one of the most popular American poems of the present century. Because of its appeal and its brevity it has often been read aloud to students, and the last line--which reports a suicide--always provokes a hysterical laugh. This is interesting, and the answer is found in what students think of Cory before the last line. For the most part sympathetic, they said the ending made them feel good, more satisfied with their own situations. Some students felt envy, but felt no satisfaction from another's misfortune. Some students do not like the poem, will have no part of it, and think that anyone who does "displays his subconscious dislike or jealousy of the rich and well-mannered."

1039 RHOADES, Nell Snyder. "The Metrics, Imagery, and Philosophy of Edwin Arlington Robinson as Shown in His Non-Blank Verse Poetry." M.A. thesis, New Mexico University, 1932.

1040 RIBNER, Irving, and Harry Morris. Poetry: A Critical and Historical Introduction. Chicago: Scott-Foresman, 1962. p. 417. Robinson's poem "For a Dead Lady," is commented upon in the possibility of influence, one way or the other, between Thomas Hardy's "After the Last Breath" and the Robinson work. Ultimately the theory is dismissed, perhaps prematurely.

1041 RICHARDS, Bertrand F. "'No There Is Not a Dawn.'" Colby Library Quarterly, 9 (September, 1971), 367-374. Title refers to the article which does not succeed, or attempts, in clearing up all the troublesome lines of the poem, no dawn in understanding the work. However, a careful

reading of the poem, with particular attention to the quality of the imagery, in the nouns and the verbs of the
poem, will result in a rewarding experience, although it
may not clear up all the confusions.

1042   RICHARDS, Laura Elizabeth Howe. Stepping Westward. New
       York: D. Appleton, 1931. Robinson, pp. 377-383. Author
       is the daughter of Julia Ward Howe, who wrote "The Battle
       Hymn of the Republic." This book is an autobiographical
       narrative, the second part of which takes place in Gardi-
       ner, Maine, where Mrs. Richards moved with her family
       in 1876. In the chapter on Robinson, who later became
       the most illustrious resident of Gardiner, Mrs. Richards
       recounts Robinson's first book, The Torrent and the Night
       Before, the copy the poet sent her, and later becoming
       close friends with the shy reclusive boy. In conclusion
       she says: "We have seen the reserved, silent boy grow
       into the foremost poet of our country. We have seen a cult
       formed; we have seen him, in the hands and his young and
       ardent admirers, grow into a tradition, while he is yet in
       the fullness of vigor, with, I hope, much good work still
       ahead of him."

1043   _____. "Recollections of 'E. A.' as a Boy in Gardiner."
       New York Herald Tribune Books, May 12, 1935. P. 10.

1044   _____. "Edwin Arlington Robinson." Ibid., June 2, 1935.
       P. 20.

1045   _____. Edwin Arlington Robinson. Cambridge, Mass.:
       Harvard University Press, 1936. Reprinted New York:
       Russell & Russell, 1967. 61 pages. Deals with the early
       years of the poet, childhood, high-school days, transition,
       and departure. In conclusion Mrs. Richards says: "We
       never wholly lost him, nor need we lose him now. He took
       the town and the countryside with him. Open his volumes
       almost where you will (except in the Arthurian romances),
       you find somewhere the singing pine-tree, the whispering
       water, the rugged, grave, kindly folk. Yes, my Friend,
       ours imperishably for all time. And so good-bye!"

1046   _____. "Edwin Arlington Robinson." Horn Book Magazine,
       12 (January-February, 1936), 52-53.

1047   _____. "A Book and Its Author." Yankee (Dublin), 2
       (June, 1936), 26-29.

1048   RITCHEY, John. "'Dear Friends, Reproach Me Not....' A
       Review of Selected Letters." Christian Science Monitor,
       March 30, 1940. P. 11. Robinson was much the same in
       his letters as he was in his poems. The subject is always

the thing, interwoven with an aura of nostalgia about the
words. In his letters, as in his poetry, he is inclined to
ruminate. His honesty with himself would not permit him
to be other than honest with his friends. He would have
no commerce with compromise. In that, he was fortunate,
since he became a part of the sudden popular passion of
his times for "culture," understandable or not. No serious
critic can have any doubt of Robinson's place in poetry,
but it is unlikely that he will be the "popular" poet again.
He was not a great letter writer, and his book serves
merely as a confirmation of the poems. The man is in his
poetry, and that was, after all, where he wanted to be.

1049  RITTENHOUSE, Jessie Belle. "Memories of Madison Cawein."
      Bookman, 56 (November, 1922), 305-312. Cawein, the
      American poet, knew a great many other poets of the late
      nineteenth and early twentieth century scene. His mod-
      esty about his own work was equalled only by his enthusi-
      asm for that of his fellow poets.... One of his favorite
      stories was that of Robinson's reaction to President Roose-
      velt's review of The Children of the Night: "I shall never
      live it down," feeling that this sudden flash of recognition
      would be harmful in the end.

1050  _____. "Poetry of New England," in Braithwaite, ed.
      (1926), pp. 12-16.

1051  _____. My House of Life: An Autobiography. Boston:
      Houghton, Mifflin, 1934. Robinson, pp. 211-212. Repeats
      some of the remarks of the 1922 article (entry 1049).
      Robinson was at this time (about 1905) working in the
      Custom House, a position to which he had been appointed
      by President Roosevelt after the latter's article which ap-
      peared in The Outlook. At a distance of so many years,
      this author finds it amusing to imagine that anything could
      have "stayed the tide of Robinson's genius."

1052  _____. "Edwin Arlington Robinson." Rollins College Bul-
      letin (Winter Park, Fla.), 36 (June, 1941), 5-10. Selected
      faculty papers.

1053  ROBBINS, Howard Chandler. "The Classicism of Edwin Ar-
      lington Robinson." Congregational Quarterly, 14 (April,
      1936), 166-171. Classic is, of course, the obvious term
      by which to characterize the more important poems of Rob-
      inson. They are classic in their timelessness. Many of
      them might have been written in any age, or in any cir-
      cumstances, dealing as they do with what is primary and
      universal in human experience, love in its whole gamut of
      hope and fear, possession and frustration; the fear of old
      age, the pathos of loneliness, the majesty of death....

Robinson's poems are also classic in the serenity of their
art, in their reserve, their restraint, their symmetry,
their proportion. Such religion as finds expression in his
poems appears to be founded upon stoic models, and not
upon the Christian ideals. It is modern classicism at its
best; deep though somewhat detached and impersonal in
human experience; trust in the essential reasonableness of
the universe; grave decorum, and self-restraint befitting
one who is conscious that the world is governed by very
ancient laws; piercing insight into human motivation; sympathy with the unquenchable hope of man, and realization
of the greatness of his destiny.

1054  ROBINSON, Edwin Arlington (born December 22, 1869, died
April 6, 1935). The following items, listed in chronological
order, are not meant to be a complete bibliography, but
are included here merely for the convenience of the reader.

The Torrent and the Night Before. Cambridge, Mass.:
   privately printed, 1896.
The Children of the Night: A Book of Poems. Boston:
   Richard G. Badger, 1897.
Captain Craig. Boston: Houghton Mifflin, 1902. Revised
   and reprinted, 1915.
The Town Down the River: A Book of Poems. New York:
   Scribner's, 1910. Dedicated to Theodore Roosevelt.
Van Zorn: A Comedy in Three Acts. New York: Macmil-
   lan, 1914.
The Porcupine: A Drama in Three Acts. New York:
   Macmillan, 1915.
Collected Poems. New York: Macmillan, 1915. Consists
   of The Children of the Night (1890-1897) and Captain
   Craig (1902).
The Man Against the Sky: A Book of Poems. New York:
   Macmillan, 1916.
"The Peterborough Idea." North American Review, 204
   (September, 1916), 448-454. Privately printed as a
   pamphlet, 1917.
Merlin: A Poem. New York: Macmillan, 1917.
Lancelot: A Poem. New York: Thomas Selzer, 1920.
The Three Taverns: A Book of Poems. New York: Mac-
   millan, 1920.
Avon's Harvest. New York: Macmillan, 1921.
Collected Poems. New York: Macmillan, 1921. Awarded
   Pulitzer prize for poetry.
Collected Poems, with an introduction by John Drinkwater.
   London: Sidgwick & Jackson, 1922.
Roman Bartholow. New York: Macmillan, 1923.
The Man Who Died Twice. New York: Macmillan, 1924.
   Awarded Pulitzer prize for poetry.
Dionysus in Doubt: A Book of Poems. New York: Mac-
   millan, 1925.

Tristram. New York: Macmillan, 1927.
Collected Poems. New York: Macmillan, 1927.
Sonnets, 1889-1927. New York: Macmillan, 1928.
Selections from the Letters of Thomas Sergeant Perry,
     edited by E. A. Robinson. New York: Macmillan, 1929.
     See Perry.
Cavender's House. New York: Macmillan, 1929. Dedi-
     cated to William Vaughn Moody.
The Glory of the Nightingales. New York: Macmillan,
     1930.
"The First Seven Years." The Colophon, December, 1930.
     Pp. 71-78. Reprinted in Breaking into Print, edited by
     Elmer Adler. New York: Simon & Schuster, 1937. Pp.
     163-170.
Matthias at the Door. New York: Macmillan, 1931. Dedi-
     cated to Ridgely Torrence.
Edwin Arlington Robinson Poems, selected, with a preface,
     by Bliss Perry. New York: Macmillan, 1931.
Nicodemus. New York: Macmillan, 1932.
Talifer. New York: Macmillan, 1933.
Amaranth. New York: Macmillan, 1934.
King Jasper: A Poem, with introduction by Robert Frost.
     New York: Macmillan, 1935.
E. A. R.: A Collection of His Works from the Library of
     H. Bacon Collamore. Hartford, Conn.: Hawthorne
     House, 1936.
Collected Poems. New York: Macmillan, 1937. Completed
     and edited with additional poems. First published in
     1921.
"Robinson to Robinson." Poetry: A Magazine of Verse,
     54 (May, 1939), 92-100.
Tilbury Town, Selected Poems of Edwin Arlington Robinson,
     introduction and notes by Lawrance Thompson. New
     York: Macmillan, 1953.
Selected Early Poems and Letters of E. A. Robinson, edited
     by Charles T. Davis. New York: Holt, Rinehart, and
     Winston, 1960.
Selected Poems of Edwin Arlington Robinson, edited by
     Morton D. Zabel. Introduction by James Dickey. New
     York: Macmillan, 1965.

1055 ROBINSON, Henry Morton. "Review of Collected Poems."
     Commonweal, 11 (November 13, 1929), 60-62. Regards this
     collected edition as an epitaph. But Robinson is far from
     poetical interment. Had he written nothing after the young
     period, he would have been ranked as the most considerable
     American poet, but more kept coming. The mass and carry
     of his poetic energy seems to be still unimpaired. He seems
     to be rounding into a lusty second harvest, from which he
     will glean many a collection before the epitaph-chiselers get
     him.... These thousand pages point to a single dramatic

problem, the problem which has always gripped tragic writers: man cannot escape the Fate which has been dealt out to him in his character.

1056 _____. "Review of The Glory of the Nightingales." Commonweal, 13 (November 12, 1930), 53. By now it is fairly easy to predict with fair certainty what Robinson's poem is going to deal with; this is no exception. This book cleaves true to the general tradition of Robinson's poetry by contributing two important portraits to the gallery of men who failed.... In manipulating these tragic protagonists against the background of dark destiny, Robinson is always the portrayer of deep psychological flaws, the analyst of men's spiritual futilities.

1057 ROBINSON, William Ronald. "Edwin Arlington Robinson: The Poetry of the Act." Ph.D. diss., Ohio State, 1962. DA, 24 (1963), 303-304. Book published with same title, Cleveland: Western Reserve University Press, 1967. Chapter from book, "The Alienated Self," pp. 75-95, reprinted in Murphy, ed. (1970), pp. 128-147. Individual man is the moral center of Robinson's poetry. He begins with a 19th Century interest in character and carries over its corresponding ideal of the whole or complete person. We know all too well that the 20th Century is the age of alienation, and alienated man is found with ease and in abundance in Robinson's poetry. Though segregation and disintegration are there, especially in the early and middle poems, but also as the starting point for the later ones, they are not final but remediable conditions. Robinson's treatment of his characters, particularly the course of events he puts them through, is his most specific means for displaying the achievement and meaning of integration.

1058 _____. "Edwin Arlington Robinson's Yankee Conscience." Colby Library Quarterly, 8 (September, 1969), 371-385. Reprinted in Cary , ed. (1969), pp. 322-334. Thinks the fact that Robinson was a New Englander must be heavily underscored. Not only did New England constitute the primordial physical environment for his human life and poetic career, but it also impressed itself upon his being, as in the normal course of events it naturally would, as an ineluctable spiritual presence and moral force. He acknowledged the degree to which his native region occupied his imagination in "New England," a sonnet first published in 1923.... Robinson's commitment to life provides the prevailing drive or aspiration of his imagination from the beginning of his career but traditional attitudes he inherited initially blocked his acting upon it to create poems of life.

1059 ROMING, Edna Davis. "Tilbury Town and Camelot." <u>Univer-</u>
     <u>sity of Colorado Studies</u>, 19 (June, 1932), 303-326. Re-
     printed in Cary, ed. (1969), pp. 17-37. Article touches
     on a number of Robinson poems in a long detailed compari-
     son of the so-called village poetry with that of Arthur's
     court. A poet speaks in our own tongue, with all the
     gradations of contemporary conditions in our social life--
     and we have Tilbury Town; he speaks again in the same
     language and we have Camelot. There are delusions and
     delusions, hopes and fears, wrongs, frustrations, joy,
     tragedies--boys and girls, old men and women, all trying
     to find "the lost imperial music," the Holy Grail.

1060 ROOSEVELT, Kermit. "An Appreciation of the Poetry of Ed-
     win Arlington Robinson." <u>Scribner's Magazine</u>, 66 (De-
     cember, 1919), 763-764. As shown in his poetry, Robinson's
     philosophy of life is basiclaly vigorous and sound; there
     are the inevitable tragedy and sorrow, the periods of
     depression which come in greater or less degree.... There
     is ultimate justification of existence; there is no snuffing
     out; the torch is to be handed on, responsibility does not
     end there. We must not only justify existence to others,
     but first and last to ourselves.

1061 ROOSEVELT, Theodore. "Review of <u>The Children of the</u>
     <u>Night</u>." (1905 edition) <u>Outlook</u>, 80 (August 12, 1905),
     913-914. Reprinted in Vol. 14, Memorial Edition. New
     York: Scribner's, 1924. Pp. 360-364. There is an un-
     doubted touch of genius in the poems collected in this vol-
     ume, and a curious simplicity and good faith, all of which
     qualities differentiate them sharply from ordinary collections
     of this kind. There is in them just a little of the light
     that never was on land or sea, and in such light the sub-
     jects described often have nebulous destinies. But it is
     not always necessary in order to enjoy a poem that one
     should be able to translate it into terms of mathematical
     accuracy. A good many poems are not easily understood,
     but they may be liked nonetheless.

1062 ROOT, E. Merrill. "The Decline of Edwin Arlington Robinson:
     Amaranth." <u>Christian Century</u>, 51 (December 5, 1934),
     1554. American critics are bell-wethers; the American pub-
     lic, sheep; probably, therefore, this latest book by Robin-
     son will win a Pulitzer prize. The verdict of eternity,
     however, is: "Thumbs Down!" The poem is long, repeti-
     tious, dull; one is lost in endless talk "about it and about,"
     and comes out the same door wherein he went. There is
     no communication of reality, purging us with pity and ter-
     ror.

1063 _____. "Prince of Castaways." <u>The Christian Century</u>, 55

(November 2, 1938), 1337. Review of Hagedorn's biography. This informative, sympathetic, finely written life of Robinson--lacking only plangence and bite--leaves one a heretic and infidel, but understanding better the pity of the fifty-below-zero night where Robinson lived.... Robinson was an etcher in black and white. His scope and power were minor, his mood was a fine pity, edged into ironic restraint; his poetic excellence the music of a sad small wind blowing through dark pines. The attempted epics, speaking the crash and glitter of ending ages, are imitation tapestry and passionless "passion." The long, later psychological nightmares, fashioned of fog-wreaths, will dissolve in the sun.

1064 _____. "Review of Selected Letters." Christian Century, 57 (March 6, 1940), 316. This book of letters underlines the fact that Robinson was a talented mediocrity. His prose is a lucid, grave etching; superior in clarity and wit to much of his poetry, yet fundamentally the same cold austere nihilism. One has only to compare his letters with those of Keats, "innumerable of stains and splendid dyes," or with the noble spirituality of the letters of Sidney Lanier, to see where they belong. They are dry faggots, containing scanty store of sun.

1065 ROSENBERG, Harold. "Judgment and Passion." Poetry, 41 (December, 1932), 158-161. Review of Nicodemus. In the title poem and others Robinson turns to Biblical situations, but the difference in material creates no substantial disparity in Robinson's meditative analyses. The reason that subject matter is not determinative is that his characters converse in terms of the most generalized and ultimate judgments. No matter what the scene--historical or local domestic--Robinson's protagonists shake their heads in meaning-laden dialogues which occur always on the same depth level.

1066 ROSENTHALL, M. L. The Modern Poets: A Critical Introduction. New York: Oxford University Press, 1960. "Rival Idioms, The Great Generations: Robinson and Frost," pp. 104-112. Robinson early determined not to evade "the racked and shrieking hideousness of Truth" but to seek "the sure strength" with which it endows those who do not fear it. Still, truth to him seems necessarily marked by "hideousness"; it is an evil to be endured with high-spirited grace and, if possible, sub-ordinated by an almost secret asceticism. Behind much of Robinson's work, in both its more successful and its less successful aspects, lies a deeply American obsession with the theme of failure; failure of a career, failure of a social class or a society, failure of a needed meaning to sustain itself--and finally, the inevitable failure of life to resist death's encroachment.

1067  ROTH, Georges. "Edwin Arlington Robinson." Larousse Men-
      suel Illustré (Paris), 10 (February, 1936), 339-340.

1068  ROTH, Samuel. "Edwin Arlington Robinson." Bookman, 50
      (January, 1920), 507-511. Is an appreciative summary of
      Robinson's publications up to 1917: Children of the Night,
      Captain Craig, The Town Down the River, and The Man
      Against the Sky. Of Merlin, which had just been pub-
      lished it is too early to say much, and its value will be
      better understood when the sequel Lancelot is issued. Of
      these works the critic thinks best of The Man Against the
      Sky, saying that with this work Robinson brings into Eng-
      lish poetry a poetic personality strongly suggestive of the
      prophet of the ancient world.

1069  _____. "Robinson--Bridges--Noyes, 1920: The Three Tav-
      erns." Bookman, 52 (December, 1920), 361-362. The
      Man Against the Sky indicated very clearly the place of the
      poet, it was very high--how high we had not the standards
      by which to measure. The Three Taverns brings us much
      nearer to him, closer within the embrace of his sympathies,
      and by the same law, lifts him much farther above us.

1070  _____. "A Bookshop Night's Adventure." Bookman, 58
      (October, 1923), 140-146. Article is built around a story
      about a beautiful woman who came into the bookshop and
      wanted to buy "The Works" of Max Beerbohm. This the
      bookseller didn't have, but the owner proceeded to intro-
      duce the woman to E. A. Robinson's poetry. To begin
      with he read poem after poem to her, to which she replied
      that Robinson was not very musical; the owner continued
      by telling her that Robinson frequently visited the shop,
      how he sat by himself, and how he was the greatest poet
      of the modern world. At the end the woman departed,
      promising to read Robinson.

1071  ROURKE, Constance. "Mr. Robinson's 'Lancelot.'" Freeman,
      2 (October 27, 1920), 164. It has no pictorial exuberance.
      Scarcely a line could be quoted for self-sufficient imagery.
      For the rest, the beauty of the poem is a low-keyed, in-
      tense but quiet beauty of cadence and rhythm. Its matter
      speaks with restraint and with completion. Its power lies
      in the immanence of its people and their struggle with their
      fate.

1072  _____. American Humor. New York: Harcourt, Brace,
      1931. Robinson, pp. 271-274. He used American traditions
      with freedom and fullness. He has chosen types recurrent
      throughout American comedy, ne'er-do-wells, liars, the
      quirky, the large-hearted and lost, spend-thrifts of time
      and money and love. He is master of that unobtrusive irony

that has belonged to the Yankee. Burlesque appears in
his use of rolling measures for mock romance. Under-
stated comedy lies beneath many of his shorter poems.

1073  RUSH, N. Orwin. "Our Latest Robinson Accession." Colby
      Mercury, 7 (January, 1941), 14-15. The accession is a
      poem, a sonnet, which Robinson called "For a Book by
      Thomas Hardy." The poem first appeared in November,
      1895, in a New York magazine, The Critic. The next year
      Robinson included this poem in his volume The Torrent and
      the Night Before and sent Thomas Hardy a copy of the
      book. Now Colby College has received the copy of The
      Critic which contains Robinson's poem.

1074  _____. "Some Recent Acquisitions." Colby Library Quar-
      terly, 1 (January, 1943), 12-13. Among letters and manu-
      scripts recently acquired by the college library, special
      mention must be made of several holograph letters of Edwin
      Arlington Robinson, given by Mrs. Laura E. Richards.

1075  RYAN, Kathryn White. "The Grim Nostalgic Passion: The
      Man Who Died Twice." Voices, 3 (May-June, 1924), 89-91.

1076  SABEN, Mowry. "Obituary Notice for E. A. Robinson." The
      Argonaut, (San Francisco), 113 (April 12, 1935), 4-5.

1077  _____. "Robinson's Final Poem: King Jasper." The Argo-
      naut, 114 (January 10, 1936), 4.

1078  _____. "Edwin Arlington Robinson: A Review of Selected
      Letters." The Argonaut, 119 (March 29, 1940), 21-22.

1079  _____. "Memories of Edwin Arlington Robinson." Colby
      Mercury, 7 (January, 1941), 13-14. Robinson was, in a
      sense, all things to all men. He kept most of the friends
      he made in separate compartments, and many of his friends
      did not know the others existed. Robinson was a true
      poet, but as a philosopher one could not take him very
      seriously. "There's something in it," he would say to any
      idea that he had not previously heard. He was never too
      careful to pursue the matter of what was in it.

1080  St. ARMAND, Barton L. "The Power of Sympathy in the
      Poetry of Robinson and Frost: The 'Inside' vs. the 'Out-
      side' Narrative." American Quarterly, 19 (1967), 564-574.
      Is a detailed analysis of the similarities and differences in
      these two New England poets, although at first glance they
      may appear to have much underlying in common. The sim-
      ilarities soon run out when we start to compare Robinson's
      basic technique and literary stance with that of Frost.
      While both poets may have roamed the same woods and fields,

their psychic journeys are miles apart.  The key to these
differences is the "outside" narrative of "the cautious
romantic," Frost--as opposed to the "inside" narrative of
"the sympathetic agnostic," Robinson.

1081  St. CLAIR, George.  "Review of Matthias at the Door."  New
      Mexico Quarterly Review, 2 (February, 1932), 92-93.  This
      story is told in some twenty-five hundred lines of blank
      verse.  Robinson is probably the most original, but also
      the least musical.  He likes run-on lines, he is fond of
      feminine endings, he frequently substitutes one type of
      rhythm for another, and often comes to a full pause within
      the line.  Thus, his verse lacks the smooth even flow of
      such a poet as Shelley, for example.  It is the story of a
      man, apparently successful, who in reality is a failure,
      but stands upon the threshold of a true success, a spirit-
      ual one.  The "Door" symbolizes Death, which Matthias is
      unable to enter because he has not been "born."  Robinson
      is more interested in the soul states of his characters than
      in the external events of their lives, so it is likely that
      one must read the poem at least a second time.  His people
      have a power of, and a delight in, self-analysis, and some-
      times their rather cryptic utterances make the poem obscure
      and difficult.

1082  _____.  "Review of Nicodemus."  Ibid., 2 (November, 1932),
      346-349.  No evidence of decline here, nor in any of the
      other blank verse poems.  The short poems lack the charm
      of the blank verse narratives.  Comments individually on
      the five poems, as to who the characters are and their
      significance.  Perhaps the greatest of these is "Toussaint
      L'Ouverture," the negro slave who has risked death for
      the sake of the slaves.  Here the poet shows his profound
      pity and sympathy for the oppressed and defeated.  A
      great poet sings here!  Critics have compared this Robinson
      to Browning, but in the long run this is a "sorry" pastime.
      Both poets are fine; both deserve a larger audience; both
      have delved deeply into the obscure recesses of the human
      heart and brought up rich treasure.  Is that not enough?

1083  _____.  "Edwin Arlington Robinson and Tilbury Town."
      New Mexico Quarterly Review, 4 (May, 1934), 95-107.
      Article is a fanciful presentation in the form of a trial, the
      setting in a court room situated somewhere out in space.
      Robinson has just died, and is being detained for question-
      ing by the "Recording Spirit."  Robinson is accused of
      painting a false and unsympathetic picture of the village
      in which he passed his childhood.  He is charged with hav-
      ing drawn only harsh, crabbed, and bitter failures, often
      incomprehensible, but just as cold and hard as the rocks
      of his native Maine.  He has failed to see the hidden

kindliness and neighborliness of these no doubt dour souls,
and in his preoccupation with wasted and futile lives, he
has betrayed his high calling as an Apostle of Beauty and
Truth.... Robinson defends himself against these charges,
and calls in certain characters from Tilbury Town who
answer: Reuben Bright, Aaron Stark, Annandale, Richard
Cory, Miniver Cheevy, Mr. Flood, Isaac and Archibald,
and Captain Craig.

1084 _____. "Edwin Arlington Robinson on Time." Ibid., 9
(August, 1939), 150-156. Is an interesting composition
written in blank verse, after the style of Robinson, on a
subject which much occupied the poet. It is based on
thorough research, and although presented in verse form,
is not a trivial piece of writing. The Collected Poems,
1937, containing 1,488 pages and 207 poems, is the basis
for the work, with a total of 44,685 lines. In looking at
this work, the author became aware of certain words that
kept recurring: Peace, Light, Darkness, Fate, Time, etc.
By actual count, the word "Time" and variations on the
term was used a thousand times, and in eighty-eight
poems. Such allusions are most numerous in the narrative
poems, especially in the Arthurian series. In Tristram,
for instance, variations of the word occur 170 times.

1085 SALPETER, Harry. "Edwin Arlington Robinson, Poet." New
York World, May 15, 1927.

1086 SAMPLEY, Arthur M. "Quiet Voices, Unquiet Times." Midwest Quarterly, 3 (Spring, 1963), 247-256. Is not principally about Robinson, but Robinson is included in the
twenty or so poets (British and American) considered to
be the major writers of the first half of the twentieth century. Sampley gives his view of a major poet: one who
achieves an organic structure that has independent life;
one who creates a considerable body of work; one who makes
a statement of significance about life. The great poet of
our day must have the tragic sense. He must see man
broken on the wheel of his own being, but his work must
achieve the catharsis of pity and fear which illuminates and
gives meaning to tragedy.... He plunges beyond empty
platitudes and moral clichés into the tragic struggle which
in each age and in each environment takes place within the
soul of man. The great poet of today must, like Dante
and Milton, create and transcend his own inferno.

1087 _____. "The Power or the Glory: The Dilemma of Edwin
Arlington Robinson." Colby Library Quarterly, 9 (September, 1971), 357-366. Discusses a number of the longer
poems in terms of the demands of society on the individual
and the desire of man to fulfill his own happiness. It is a

question with which man has grappled since he began to
record his thoughts. Robinson did not solve it. His attitude changed along the way from Captain Craig to Amaranth, but he never quite lost his respect for the lonely
man groping out his own way. He seemed gradually inclined to place his hope on society and the individual.

1088  SANBORN, John Newell. "Juxtaposition as Structure in 'The
      Man Against the Sky.'" Colby Library Quarterly, 10 (De-
      cember, 1974), 486-494. Begins with a good background
      discussion of the device of structural juxtaposition, the
      balancing of opposites, one major theme opposed to its
      opposite. The usual composition has a beginning, middle,
      and end, but the other method is also effective, although
      not used too often. Read as composed of two juxtaposed,
      contrapuntal parts, each a standard vision of man's exist-
      ence--faith and despair--this poem is, as Robinson claimed,
      a hopeful poem rather than a despairing one. The poem
      consists of two parts which play against each other ...
      Robinson confronts each starkly, and in the result the
      reader may find his own answer.

1089  SANBORN, Robert Alden. "Review of Merlin." Poetry Jour-
      nal, (June, 1917), 104-109.

1090  SAPIR, Edward. "Poems of Experience: A Review of Collected
      Poems." Freeman, 5 (April 19, 1922), 141-142. Robinson
      is the one American poet who compels, rather than invites,
      consideration. We may like or dislike him, but his accents
      are too authentic, his aloofness too certain, to give our
      spirits the choice whether to attend or not.

1091  _____. "The Tragic Chuckle: Dionysus in Doubt." Voices,
      5 (November, 1925), 64-65.

1092  SATTERFIELD, Leon James. "Major Categories of Irony in the
      Poetry of Edwin Arlington Robinson." Ph.D. diss., Univer-
      sity of Nebraska, 1969. DA, 30 (1970), 3022A. Although
      it is agreed that irony is one of the basic characteristics
      of Robinson's poetry, no full-length study has been devoted
      to the subject. This dissertation is an effort to fill the gap
      by systematically examining in detail the four major cate-
      gories of irony found in the poetry of the 1500-page Col-
      lected Poems. The study begins with a review of definitions
      of irony, traditional and new, and establishes the four ma-
      jor categories--all deriving from a tension between the ap-
      parent and real: (1) verbal irony; (2) ironic coloration
      achieved through allusions, names, titles; (3) dramatic
      irony; (4) double-imagery irony, the result of two conflict-
      ing views presented simultaneously.

1093 _____. "Robinson's 'Leonora.'" Explicator, 39 (Spring, 1981), Pp. 7-9. Robinson was never very sympathetic with the moral certitude he depicts in his citizens of Tilbury Town, as in the poem "Leonora." The poem begins with a burial, that of Leonora, a prostitute who has morally outraged the town for some years. The line "Darker nights for Leonora than to-night shall ever be" is troublesome. It has been said that it means Leonora will suffer an eternity of punishment in the fires of hell. It probably means that the townsmen see her death as a blessing which will keep Leonora from a life of sin and shame. This is monstrously presumptous and sanctimonious, but both adjectives consistently characterize Robinson's conventional Tilburnians.

1094 _____. "Robinson's 'An Evangelist's Wife.'" Explicator, 41 (Spring, 1983), Pp. 36-37. Thinks an interpretation of this poem hinges on an allusion in II Samuel 6: 20-23, in which Michal, the wife of David, accuses him of debauchery and lust. In Robinson's poem the wife denies that she is jealous of any particular woman or that she is jealous of God himself. She finds him monstrously hypocritical and self-righteous, and is about to depart his bed and board.

1095 SAUL, George Brandon. "Selected Poems: A Review." College English, 27 (March, 1966), 517. A fairer selection from Robinson, or a more sensitively perceptive and memorably phrased introduction than James Dickey's would be hard to conceive of. With such competent selections and analyses, even the most serious student of Robinson has all he needs for guidance. Would that every worthy poet could anticipate similarly intelligent posthumous handling in a volume equal to this in beauty of format and letterpress.

1096 SCHELLING, Felix E. Appraisements and Asperities as to Some Contemporary Writers. Philadelphia: Lippincott, 1922. "An Old Myth Revitalized: Lancelot," pp. 91-95. The thing about myth is that it is never outworn; but told and retold is adaptable to all time. Take this old story of Lancelot, told once more so beautifully, so directly, so novelly, by this American poet. It is of imperishable material and will ever be new. Robinson's work is a comparatively brief narrative, or perhaps a semi-dramatic poem. Most of the story is unfolded in dialogue of direct and limpid diction, and the thought is deep but not subtle.

1097 SCHMITT, Howard George (of Buffalo). "Some Robinson Letters in My Collection." Colby Library Quarterly, 1 (January, 1943), 8-12. The letters referred to are four items which have come into possession of the author, and somehow were not included in the collection at Harvard. Two

of the letters are addressed to a boyhood friend, Arthur
R. Gledhill, dated 1930. Robinson comments on the old
"Cooper's Virgil" which had meant so much to him, and
wonders if his friend still has his copy. The other two
letters are addressed to Edwin Markham (1924) and to Miss
Esther W. Bates (1933), his typist.

1098 _____, ed. Letters of E. A. R. to Howard George Schmitt,
ed. Carl J. Weber. Waterville: Colby College Press, 1943.

1099 SCHOLNICK, Robert J. "The Shadowed Years: Mrs. Richards, Mr. Stedman, and Robinson." Colby Library Quarterly, 9 (December, 1972), 510-531. Article is constructed
around five unpublished letters from Mrs. Laura Richards
to Edmund Clarence Stedman, New York poet, critic, anth-
ologist, and stockbroker. These letters are in the Stedman
Collection at Columbia University, and although they touch
on numerous subjects, the central subject is Robinson.
These letters are dated 1898, 1899, one about ten years
earlier, 1900, and one from Laura Stedman (Edmund's
granddaughter, when he could not write) to Laura Richards. These letters are printed here for the first time,
and are accompanied by detailed discussions of matters related in the letters.

1100 SCHONEMANN, Friedrich. "Edwin Arlington Robinson." Lit-
eratur und Sprache, 35 (May, 1933), 446-448. In German.

1101 SCHRIFTGIESSER, Karl. "An American Poet Speaks His Mind."
Boston Evening Transcript, 5 (November 4, 1933), 1.

1102 SCHWAB, Arnold T. "The Robinson Connection: New Jeffers
Letters." Robinson Jeffers Newsletter, 57 (November,
1980), 26-35. The two poets were on friendly, but slight,
acquaintance. Their correspondence was very brief, and
is now in the Jeffers papers at the University of Texas.
The two poets never met, but they had a friend in common,
who was something of a letter writer. This person was
Craven Langstroth Betts. Though Betts' letters have dis-
appeared, fourteen letters to Betts--four from Jeffers and
ten from Una--have survived. They are printed here for
the first time.

1103 SCHWARTZ, Jacob. 1100 Obscure Points. London: Ulysses
Bookshop, 1931. Bibliography of 25 English and 21 Amer-
ican authors. Robinson, p. 83. Lists some two dozen
Robinson items, although the list is far from complete.

1104 SCOLLARD, Clinton. "Review of Captain Craig." The Critic,
42 (March, 1903), 232.

1105  SCOTT, Winfield Townley.  "Edwin Arlington Robinson."
      Brown Literary Quarterly, 2 (November, 1929), 13-18.
      Article is an overview of Robinson, beginning with The
      Children of the Night and concluding Tristram which ap-
      peared in 1927.  He has not wavered.  It has been worth-
      while to the world that he has so steadily kept his course.
      By so doing he has produced a large quantity of poetry,
      the volume of which is matched by its excellence.  At the
      present time he has numerous honors and prizes to his
      credit; he has recently attained rewards long delayed; he
      has only recently completed the Arthurian cycle which
      seems to be his finest work.  He is assuming international
      proportions.  In Camelot, perhaps more than any other
      place, there were those who tried hardest to see a Light
      --who came nearest to spelling "God" with the right blocks.
      That they failed fits them precisely into this poet's gallery.

1106  _____.  "Elegy for Robinson: A Poem."  New York:  Bach-
      rach Press, 1936.  16-page pamphlet, unpaginated.  In con-
      clusion Scott says the face hardened to stone (when Robin-
      son died), and "There was no voice at all; then gradually/
      The room filled with voices.  They were all one./They were
      all like light.  They kept speaking on./They were music and
      light together."

1107  _____.  "The Unaccredited Profession."  Poetry, 50 (June,
      1937), 150-154.  Includes comment on four books about or
      by Robinson; by Laura Richards, Rollo Brown, Collected
      Poems by Robinson, and Charles Hogan.  The first two
      books are personal recollections, the fourth is a bibliogra-
      phy.  The Collected Poems, running to perhaps 45,000
      lines, needs more discretion.  Repetition, verbosity, and a
      restraint at times over-stylized are to be found in abun-
      dance....  Even if disagreements over the value of Robin-
      son's work are at last settled at a lower estimate, we may
      be sure that his career must still remain in its integrity
      a profound and unforgettable example.

1108  _____.  "Robinson to Robinson."  Poetry, 54 (May, 1939),
      92-100.  Also listed under Robinson.  Article is a review-
      commentary of Hermann Hagedorn's biography of Robinson.
      The first half of the book is a study of the Robinson fam-
      ily, their illnesses, their eccentricities, their deaths.  The
      remainder of the story is told in terms of the friendships
      which Robinson made.  In the preface Hagedorn says this
      "is not the whole Robinson; he is only the Robinson whom
      the author, with the evidence at his disposal, has been
      able to discern, or to comprehend."  On the whole the book
      is competent, perhaps not brilliant, yet within the limits
      Hagedorn has set is a necessary contribution as the first
      "official biography."

1109        . "Review of Selected Letters." The Providence Sun-
      day Journal, February 25, 1940. Part 6, p. 6.

1110        . "Robinson in Focus." Poetry, 65 (January, 1945),
      209-214. Is a review of Edwin Arlington Robinson and His
      Manuscripts by Esther Willard Bates. Miss Bates is in a
      unique position to write this particular book for she was
      Robinson's typist. It was she who took that microscopic,
      difficult penmanship into copy for his final revision and
      for the printers. She was his first reader. What Miss
      Bates has to say of the manuscripts themselves is naturally
      of special interest. She rarely saw the first draft, but
      says there were not generally too many revisions, mostly
      cuttings of lines. It is astonishing how much this book
      suggests, how crammed it is with the perceptive phrase,
      the vivid recollection, so that the man and his work are
      brought close and clear.

1111        . "Great and Austere Poet." Poetry, 70 (March,
      1947), 94-98. Review of Edwin Arlington Robinson by Yvor
      Winters, for whom the reviewer has little else but praise.
      He brings to the criticism of Robinson a usually more pene-
      trating understanding than that of his predecessors; and
      although he is more stringent in his judgment, his admira-
      tion of Robinson's best achievements is no less than the
      most fervid.... The book is well planned, the poems are
      discussed according to their length, with Winters showing
      a preference for the method by which ideas are bodied
      forth from particulars, and the clarity of language and
      poetic structure.

1112        . "Perspectives on a Poet." Saturday Review, 35
      (March 15, 1952), 13. Review of biography by Ellsworth
      Barnard. There is much to Mr. Barnard's credit. The
      thoroughness is real in every sense. He knows all his
      sources, and he has used them. He has examined the
      concern with inward experience rather than with outward
      actions, with psychic rather than with physical conflict
      which characterizes Robinson's poetry early and late....
      He has altogether performed a labor of love, flawed, as
      such labors often are; but when the definitive perspective
      on Robinson is attained, this book should be far from the
      least of those that patiently, honorably helped.

1113        . "Traditional Poet." Saturday Review, 37 (Novem-
      ber 20, 1954), 39. Review of biography by Edwin S. Fus-
      sell. His purpose is an attempt to determine what can be
      learned about Robinson by knowing where he started. He
      thinks Robinson the only major American poet of his gen-
      eration. Mr. Fussell insists that we can neither fully un-
      derstand nor assess Robinson's great contribution to

American poetry unless we clearly know both what he ap-
propriated and what he rejected.... This book has been
written with such scholarly particularity without fussiness
that the only disappointment is that the author did not do
more.

1114 _____. "To See Robinson." New Mexico Quarterly Review,
26 (Summer, 1956), 161-178. Reprinted in Exiles and
Fabrications. Garden City: Doubleday, 1961. Pp. 154-
170. Includes discussion of "The Man Against the Sky."
Recalls the summer of 1929 when he drove to Peterborough
"to see Robinson." Even then Robinson was well-known,
and easily the most eminent poet in America. Article is a
recollection of their friendship from that day forward, in-
terspersed with letters from Robinson to Scott. Conclusion
comes with the last time Scott saw Robinson, in January
1935, not too long before the poet's death.... A number
of poems are referred to, but commentary on them is not
significant. The author is an admirer of Robinson's, and
his remarks are fully laudatory.

1115 _____. Exiles and Fabrications. Garden City: Doubleday,
1961. Robinson, pp. 154-170. Reprints article listed above.

1116 _____. "Who Was the Poet's Guinevere?" New York Times
Book Review, 70 (September 5, 1965), 4. Review of Where
the Light Falls, by Chard Powers Smith.

1117 SESSIONS, Ina Beth. A Study of the Dramatic Monologue in
American and Continental Literature. San Antonio: Adams
Printing Company, 1933. 197 pages. Robinson pp. 108-
116. A cursory reading would acclaim Robinson as para-
doxical, because Browning has exerted so great an influence on him that he seems rather un-American. He is
particularly good in character delineation, and nowhere
any better than in some of his dramatic monologues like
"Ben Jonson Entertains ..." and "The Three Taverns."
Robinson wrote difficult poetry. His technique is almost
unapproachable. he never sacrifices straight-forward
speech for display. He is epigrammatic, poetic, and
esthetic in his methods. For the most part, however, his
monologues lack dramatic situations and clearly defined
audiences.

1118 SHEPARD, Odell. "Review of Merlin: Versified Henry James."
Dial, 63 (October 11, 1917), 339-341. The subject is new
to him, but his method and manner are unchanged. Subject and method do not harmonize. Here are unmodern
characters being treated as simple, conventional, naive.
The result in less skillful hands would have been burlesque.
Robinson resembles his own Merlin who has much to say

about a great many things, but is not very specific in saying any of them.

1119 _____. "Review of The Glory of the Nightingales." Bookman, 74 (September, 1931), 97-98. To have done as quickly as possible with complaints, one must say first of all
that this work contains no glory and no song.... The
story is depressing rather than impressive. We see love
and friendship ruined, honor sullied, even hatred made
futile, and a firm intent to commit murder foiled by mock-
ing chance. It may be that Robinson intended this strange
and forbidding narrative as a prophecy of years coming on
into which neither he nor any other sensible man would care
to live. But the poem is not altogether a prophecy; in
some respects it is painfully like a description of what we
now see about us.

1120 _____. "Recent Verse: Matthias at the Door." Yale Review, 21 (March, 1932), 590-591. Another long blank-
verse poem, perhaps not in quite the first flight of Robinson's works, but better than some. It is a story of defeat, faced this time from four different angles and by four
persons sharply delineated. The poem is subtle in thought,
often obscure in expression, replete with ironic innuendo
and understatement. There is no suggestion of song or of
ecstasy anywhere in it; the mood is monotonous and
weary.... Yet the poem works out to a conclusion of
tragedy, rather than of mere despair, which lifts it to a
high level.

1121 _____. "Poetry in a Time of Doubt: Review of Nicodemus."
Yale Review, 22 (March, 1933), 592-595. Article consists
of comment on seven recent volumes of poetry, of which the
reviewer says there is very little "demanding close attention." In his present collection of monologues, Robinson
continues the strong, thoughtful work we have learned to
expect from him. There is some slight gain in clarity here,
but he still makes his verses out of his inhibitions, singing like a man who would far rather be silent. Most of the
poems in this book the reader has to make for himself, feeling all the while that Mr. Robinson could do it much better
if he would only be more communicative, and if his understatements did not so frequently amount to zero.

1122 _____. "Edwin Arlington Robinson: A Biography." Key
Reporter, 4 (Winter, 1939), 7. Review of Hagedorn's
biography.

1123 SHERMAN, Dean. "Robinson's 'The Battle After War.'" Explicator, 27 (April, 1969), item 64. Remarks that because
of its complexity the poem has been largely ignored. It

appears certain that Robinson is equating light with Reason and Intelligence, and darkness with Chaos and Death.
The poem makes use of several classical allusions, suggestive of Hesiod and Plato. The image of struggle is created
by the use of such words as "thrust" and "groping," and
by the title "Battle After War." When the poem was first
published it was "After the War." This single alteration
of the text underlines the importance of the struggle or
battle, which must be won before the persona of the poem
can enter the light.

1124  SHERMAN, F. D. "Recent Poetry: A Review of Captain
      Craig." Book Buyer, 25 (December, 1902), 429.

1125  SHINN, Thelma J. "The Art of a Verse Novelist: Approach-
      ing Robinson's Late Narrative Through James' The Art of
      the Novel." Colby Library Quarterly, 12 (1976), 91-100.
      It has become commonplace to recognize the influence of
      Henry James on Robinson, and even to compare their life
      styles. These similarities become more apparent when we
      examine Robinson's late narratives in light of the principles
      set forth by James in The Art of the Novel. In subject
      matter, characterization, and style Robinson's poems
      achieve the intentions of the novelist as clearly as the
      novels upon which these prefaces were based. This ap-
      proach also clarifies any departure Robinson made in the
      basic nature of poetry.

1126  SHIPLEY, Joseph T. "Review of Collected Poems." Guardian,
      1 (February, 1925), 148-149.

1127  _____. "Review of Dionysus in Doubt." Guardian, 1 (Oc-
      tober, 1926), 452-456. Also printed in New York Evening
      Post Literary Review, April 4, 1925. P. 5. In the son-
      nets of this volume Robinson is at his best, and--in com-
      pression, in psychological suggestion and in difficulty of
      comprehension--most like Browning. Where the poet, mas-
      tering the psychologist, turns from man's anguished soul
      to more contemplative moods, he wins an austere beauty.

1128  SIEGRIST, Mary. "A Poet Satirizes the Age of Prohibition:
      Review of Dionysus in Doubt." International Book Review,
      3 (August, 1925), 386, 389. The sonnets of this volume
      are a group of fine lyric quality. Always there are the
      careful, workmanlike lines, full of delicate, subtle traceries
      of thought; always the rich, delicately etched perspective
      with its deep philosophic implication. It is the deep,
      rugged quality of the poet, the large native nobility, the
      broad-based humanity with its sure insights and awareness
      that give peculiar pointedness and power to this volume.

1129  SINCLAIR, May. "Three American Poets of Today." <u>Atlantic</u>
      <u>Monthly</u>, 98 (September, 1906), 325-335. Also in <u>Fort-</u>
      <u>nightly Review</u>, 86 (September 1, 1906), 429-434. The
      three American poets are William Vaughn Moody, Ridgely
      Torrence, and Edwin Arlington Robinson. At that time
      Moody had accomplished most, and in many ways promised
      to be the best of them to come.... Robinson is a poet of
      another world and another spirit. His poems fall into three
      groups: lyrics, character sketches, and psychological
      dramas. In some of his shorter poems he has pressed al-
      lusiveness and simplicity to the verge of vagueness. In
      his longer poems he is frequently analytically diffuse. In
      all he has rendered human thought and human emotion with
      a force and delicacy which proves him a master of form.

1130  _____. "A Novelist and a Poet Visit Spoon River." <u>Inter-</u>
      <u>national Book Review</u>, 3 (December, 1924), 32-33.

1131  SINCLAIR, Upton. <u>Money Writes!</u> New York: Albert &
      Charles Boni, 1927. "Choose Your Poet," pp. 152-155.
      Does not think too highly of Robinson, and in his commen-
      tary on <u>Tristram</u>, Sinclair says he doubts that he will fin-
      ish it, the long involved paragraphs in verse are too in-
      volved, too repetitious, and generally labyrinthine. Thinks
      the greatest American poetry is that which deals with every-
      day realities of the America we live in, and dealing with
      them from a point of view which embraces the future as
      well as the past, and is free and creative in the highest
      sense of those words.

1132  SISTER Mary Catherine. "The Psychology of Robinson."
      <u>Catholic Education Review</u> (Washington, D.C.), 38 (June,
      1940), 354-360. Robinson, with his interest in the soul of
      man, provides ample material for character study, and since
      religion is inevitably bound up with the growth and perfec-
      tion of man's character, his poetry can easily be used either
      in religion classes to give a modern application to the time-
      less doctrines of Christ, or in English classes where his
      psychology might simply be stressed after the Socratic
      method till pupils deduce practical conclusions on life and
      how it should be lived.

1133  SISTER Mary James Power. <u>Poets at Prayer</u>. New York:
      Sheed & Ward, 1938. "Edwin Arlington Robinson: The
      First of the Seekers," pp. 71-82. A member of no church,
      an observer of no ritual, a believer in no creed, Edwin
      Arlington Robinson did not completely ignore religion. He
      formulated his own. Rejecting revealed religion and the
      teaching of a visible church, alone he sought truth. His
      quest refuted any tendency to agnosticism, for he thereby
      denied his inability to know with certainty. It refuted, as

well, any charge of fatalism, for he seems to have acknowledged a higher divinity. That divinity he usually called
God. Into the mouth of some of his characters, he put
the name "fate" but he seldom capitalized it. His search,
therefore places him definitely among those for whom religion means an infinite amount of groping and searching.

1134 SKARD, Sigmund. "Edwin Arlington Robinson: 'Eros Turannos,' A Critical Survey." Americana Norvegica, 61 (1966),
286-330. Magazine edited by Sigmund Skard and Henry
H. Wasser (Philadelphia).

1135 SLETHAUG, G. E. "The King in Robinson's 'Old King Cole.'"
The English Record, 21 (February, 1971), 45-46. Although
Robert Frost said that "Old King Cole" could not be explicated because of Robinson's deliberate ambiguity, some conclusion can be reached by using evidence from King Jasper
and a short poem "The Old King's New Jester." The poem
suggests that Cole may see something that he cannot communicate to his silent listener; that something may well be
a vision of the new age ushered in by his rebel sons, but
one that he cannot participate in, relate to others, or ac-
tively prevent. The widowered King is impotent and power-
less. He can only sigh, smoke his pipe, and bore his listener.

1136 SLOTE, Bernice. "Robinson's 'En Passant.'" Explicator, 15
(February, 1957), item 27. Poem has frequently been "not
understood." The title has a double meaning: "in passing,"
and specifically a move in chess. The sonnet is a drama
in two scenes, and involves three characters. The references to chess are overtones in the poem, but they mirror
the larger play of human movements plotted with friend and
enemy; of human needs and their fulfillment; of human
chances taken, and chances won or lost.... In the framework of an historic game, played with various and subtle
strategies. Robinscn presents his most typical concern:
the problem of human communication and understanding
that must relieve the essential isolation and loneliness of
man.

1137 SMITH, Chard Powers. Pattern and Variation in Poetry. New
York: Scribner's Sons, 1932. Robinson, pp. 316-317 et
passim. It was for America to bring poetry to the earth it
had touched seldom since the death of Shakespeare, and
to clothe it in a vocabulary of observed reality. Whitman
began it, Frost and Robinson simplified and sophisticated
it, using expressions so simple and straight-forward as
to seem at first a new special vocabulary to ears long used
to romantic and moralistic pretense. Following them our
poetry today speaks for the most part the language of common speech.

1138 _____, et al. "Some Personal Tributes to Edwin Arlington Robinson." Saturday Review of Literature, 11 (April 20, 1935), 632 et passim. Letters to the editor by Chard Powers Smith, Leonard Bacon, and Esther Vinson. All of these tributes are written on the death of Robinson which occurred April 7, 1935. Each author recalls pleasant recollections of Robinson, with Leonard Bacon perhaps saying it best: "He was calm and clear and cavalier, noble and strong and tall;/He labored greatly and still and stately has left us beyond recall .../Though the man be dead who might have said what never was said at all."

1139 _____. Where the Light Falls: A Portrait of Edwin Arlington Robinson. New York: Macmillan, 1965. Consists of 412 pages with notes and index. In four parts: "Fragment of God's Humor"; "A Wrecked Empire"; "Thought's Impenetrable Mail"; "What Time Takes Away." The original purpose of this work was to create a memoir of Robinson. This is contained in Parts 1 and 4. The author was still dissatisfied and wrote Parts 2 and 3, which are analysis. Robinson was the first to dramatize common experience at once in the language of common speech and in the standard verse forms.

1140 SMITH, Lewis Worthington, ed. Current Reviews. New York: Holt, 1926. "Dionysus in Doubt," reviewed by Percy Hutchison, pp. 308-314. Reprinted from New York Times Book Review, March 29, 1925. Section 4, pp. 5, 6.

1141 SMITH, Russell. "E. A. Robinson." Washington Post, May 2, 1937. Part III, p. 7.

1142 SNELL, George. "Edwin Arlington Robinson." San Francisco Chronicle, April 13, 1947. P. 20. Comments on biography by Yvor Winters.

1143 SOLOMON, Petre. "Un destin bizarre: Edwin Arlington Robinson." Rominia Literara (Bucharest), 19 (June, 1969), 23.

1144 SOMKIN, Fred. "Tocqueville as a Source for Robinson's 'Man Against the Sky.'" Colby Library Quarterly, 6 (June, 1963), 245-247. Cestré (1930) associated Robinson's theme and imagery with Dante; Robinson never commented on the origin of its setting. So far as the setting may owe anything to a literary source Tocqueville's Democracy in America has a strong relevance which has gone unnoticed. In a chapter the traveler considers the problem of what poetic subject-matter might be available in a land without tradition or class structure. The passage quoted from Tocqueville could be taken for an epitome of Robinson's poem: "Man

springs out of nothing, crosses time, and disappears forever in the bosom of God; he is seen but for a moment,
wandering on the verge of two abysses, and there he is
lost."

1145  SOUTHWORTH, James Granville. Some Modern American Poets.
      New York: Macmillan, 1950. Robinson, pp. 28-41. Among
      the common experiences in which he was interested, failure
      most persistently furnished him with subject matter. The
      failures he particularly enjoyed writing about were those
      which result from excessive idealism rather than from too
      little. They have seen the gleam, but through some para-
      lysis of will, inability to face crass materialism, blemish of
      intelligence, or trick of fate, were unable to transfer their
      idealism to action until it either was--or almost was--too
      late. They may or may not have failed from the world's
      materialistic point of view. Often it is because of their in-
      ability to get an objective view of themselves--in other
      words, because they lacked a sense of humour.

1146  SPEAR, Jeffrey L.  "Robinson, Hardy, and a Literary Source
      of 'Eros Turannos.'" Colby Library Quarterly, 15 (1979),
      58-64. Reviews something of Robinson's opinions of Hardy,
      and what is generally thought to be some of the more ob-
      vious influences of Hardy on Robinson. It would be easy,
      but misleading, to equate the poets merely on the basis of
      their common themes. They do not speak in the same ac-
      cent; they are not even regional poets in the same sense.
      However, it seems that Hardy the poet was more important
      to Robinson than has been generally supposed, and that in
      at least one instance Robinson found in a Hardy lyric the
      germ of one of his best Tilbury Town poems, "Eros Turan-
      nos." The poem by Hardy appeared in 1902 in Poems of
      the Past and Present, under his title "Wives in the Sere"--
      the claw of time, time-in-marriage. Though not well known
      today, the poem was one of the first of Hardy's to be pub-
      lished in the United States, and Robinson most certainly
      knew it.

1147  SPECTOR, Robert D.  "Other Voices, Other Rhythms: Review
      of Selected Poems of Edwin Arlington Robinson." Saturday
      Review 49 (February 19, 1966), 42-44. This reviewer would
      like to see greater critical interest in Robinson. Yet not
      even Morton Zabel's excellent collection and James Dickey's
      Introduction can make fashionable a style and manner that
      in our climate seem like poetry from another planet. Too
      bad, for Robinson's melancholy ironic voice really speaks to
      modern alienation, loneliness, and frustration.

1148  SPEIGHT, Howard Edward Balme.  "To Understand Is to For-
      give." The Christian Leader, n.s. 33 (November 8, 1930),
      1412-1413. Review of The Glory of the Nightingales.

1149 SPENCER, Theodore, and Mark Van Doren. Studies in Meta-
      physical Poetry. New York: Macmillan, 1939. Lists 540
      books and articles for years 1912-1938. Does not include
      Robinson, but is valuable for study of Robinson.

1150 SPENDER, Stephen and Donald Hall, eds. The Concise En-
      cyclopedia of English and American Poets and Poetry.
      New York: Hawthorne Books, 1963. "Edwin Arlington
      Robinson," by E. N. W. Mottram, pp. 275-276. Biograph-
      ical sketch, encompassing a good deal of information in lit-
      tle space. In commenting on the poet's personal outlook,
      it is said: "... his gloom never reached tragic power:
      his reach is a dry irony and a finished lyricism without
      the grandeur of Hardy. His reading in classical and French
      poetry gave him the strength to resist the mediocre literary
      scene and to express the New England provincial inherit-
      ance."

1151 SPILLER, Robert E., et al., eds. Literary History of the
      United States. New York: Macmillan, 1948. "Edwin Ar-
      lington Robinson," Chapter 69, pp. 1157-1170 by Stanley
      T. Williams. Article is discussed under Williams.

1152 _____. The Cycle of American Literature: An Essay in
      Historical Criticism. New York: Macmillan, 1955. Re-
      printed Robinson New American Library, 1957; also re-
      printed New York: Free Press Paperback, 1967. "A
      Problem in Dynamics: Adams, Norris, Robinson," pp.
      184-210. It was in Robinson that the fin de siècle found
      its authentic poetic voice. This dour New Englander
      looked about him in his native Gardiner, Maine, and
      learned to find poetry in the lives of his fellow towns-
      men.... His quiet rebellion gave to American poetry an
      idiom that was in the native grain, and his leadership in
      the new movement was immediately assured. In The Man
      Against the Sky he stated at once his total reading of
      life and with it won his place in American poetry. Each
      man is measured by his own stature against the evening
      sky, but that he has learned to face death as annihilation
      is his strength.

1153 SPIVEY, Herman E. "Edwin Arlington Robinson: A Biography
      by Emery Neff." American Literature, 24 (May, 1952),
      258-261. Neff's book is both biography and critical study,
      half narrative and half expository. The book weaves a new
      web, containing few new threads but making up attractive
      whole cloth. Into the narrative at appropriate places are
      woven brief critical comments on Robinson's major poems
      and in many instances the history of their composition and
      revision; and all is kept within the remarkable scope of
      only 286 pages, including references and indexes.... Two

of the welcome features of the biography are its clarity and brevity.

1154   SPROAT, Robert H. "Edwin Arlington Robinson." _Quarterly Journal of Speech_, 41 (April, 1955), 204. Review of biography by Edwin S. Fussell.

1155   SQUIRE, John Collings, "Traditionalism," in _Contemporary American Authors_, edited by Fred B. Millett et al. New York: Harcourt, Brace, 1940. Pp. 131-132, 135. Reprinted from _London Mercury_, 13 (February, 1926), 401-413. Robinson is discussed along with several other poets who worked with traditional forms, but brought a new dimension to modern poetry. Robinson is undoubtedly the most distinguished practitioner of the traditional forms. Fifteen years before the outburst of the new poetry, Robinson was perfecting his adroit though unobtrusive craftsmanship. Working almost steadily within the old metrical forms, he gradually achieved a style distinctly his own. He avoided the clichés of the Victorian tradition, and came to utilize the colloquial language of a cultivated and complex personality.

1156   SQUIRES, Radcliffe. "Tilbury Town Today," in Barnard, ed. (1969), pp. 175-183. Begins with observation: "I find that in the centennial year of the birth of Edwin Arlington Robinson and 34 years after his death, I see him as a quite different poet from the one I knew in my youth." Much of Robinson's poetry contemplates the problem of how the self might separate itself from a rigid society, yet remain as a tutelary spirit. In the end Robinson's decision would seem to have been that this could best be done by eschewing the dramatic catastrophes--vengeance, martyrdom--and offering instead temperate ironies, cool understatements and a language calculated to heal. This decision, as one looks back now from the present with its poetry of scrimshaw, its poetry of sociology, requires one to say that Robinson chose not to write for any particular time, for "any particular time" likes to have salt in its wounds. Equally, it requires one to say that Robinson wrote for all time, for "all time" wants to be made healthy and to survive.

1157   STAFFORD, William. "There Yet Remains What Fashion Cannot Kill: Review of _Selected Poems of Edwin Arlington Robinson_." _Poetry_, 108 (June, 1966), 187-188. The present book is for current readers. It displays about a hundred of the more immediately effective poems, a rich selection with a helpful bibliography and a suitably complex introduction, inviting readers to take Robinson seriously again. The introduction contains an analysis, along with a re-reading of the poems, which makes evident some grounds for Robinson's exaltation

by critics and for his relative neglect by readers. Mr.
Dickey gives a packed account of Robinson's "irritating
qualities": prolixity, a belaboring of the obvious, unconvincing philosophy, automatic versifying, and so on....
However, Selected Poems will provide a very useful volume
for reminding current readers of the best in this noted
writer.

1158 STAGEBERG, Norman C. and Wallace Anderson. Poetry as
Experience. New York: American Book, 1952. "Richard
Cory," pp. 189-192. Prints the text and discusses the
poem in Chapter on Indirection, of which Irony and Paradox are important devices. Robinson's poem is a good example of irony of situation, ironic to the reader because he
has been led to expect a different outcome. It is also
ironic to the townspeople of the poem. The irony of the
situation is intensified by irony of character because of
the difference between what he appears to be and what he
is. The effectiveness of the whole poem is the result of
the subtle and delicate interplay of ironies, which give it
a concentration and suggestiveness that could never have
been achieved by direct means.

1159 STANFORD, Donald E. "Edwin Arlington Robinson's 'The
Wandering Jew.'" Tulane Studies in English, 23 (1978),
95-108. Reference is to a poem first published in London,
1919, but which has received no critical commentary since,
not even in the better biographies of Robinson or in the
most notable criticism. The poem can best be appreciated
by an awareness of several fields of reference--legendary,
symbolic, psychological, literary, personal, etc.--all operating simultaneously as one reads the poem. Article discusses these fields, and concludes with: "It has a complexity as well as an historical and biographical background
of interest to serious students of Robinson. It is composed
in a style of great firmness and precision--the plain style
at its best--and deserves a rank equal to that of Robinson's
other great 'character sketches.'"

1160 STARR, Harris E., ed. "First Supplement: Dictionary of
American Biography." New York: Scribner's, 1944.
"Edwin Arlington Robinson," Vol. 21, pp. 632-634, by
Louis V. Ledoux.

1161 STARR, Nathan Comfort. King Arthur Today: The Arthurian
Legend in English and American Literature, 1901-1953.
Gainesville, Fla.: University of Florida Press, 1954. Robinson, pp. 21-39. Though Robinson's cool irony and de-
tachment would seem far removed from the picturesque ex-
citement of the Arthurian tales, early in life he was as much
taken with the legend as any young man of vigorous taste

would be.  When he turned to the Arthurian material for
his own works, however, he stamped the story with his
own seal.  He also transformed the men and women of the
medieval tales to modern characters, all gripped by the
certain doom of Arthur's kingdom.... Very seldom before, if ever, has there been in the Arthurian story such
penetrating revelation of character.  His preference for the
commonplace affected his treatment, stripping the narrative
down to its barest essentials.

1162      _____.  "The Transformation of Merlin," in Barnard, ed.
          (1969), pp. 106-119.  Reviews past history of Merlin, and
          shows that in Robinson the sage and enchanter is a strik-
          ing example of the change and development in the Arthur-
          ian legend.  At least three works after Robinson's time
          have greatly increased Merlin's importance, although Robin-
          son seems not to have influenced any of them.... Robin-
          son's concept of the poem Merlin and the world-view which
          it embodied ensured great breadth for the story.  It was
          written during the First World War, a disaster which caused
          Robinson again and again to express apocalyptic premoni-
          tions of doom facing the world.  The tale of Arthur and
          the fall of his kingdom had gripped his imagination since
          boy-hood; now the destruction of Camelot seemed to him
          all too like the decay of 20th-century civilization.... The
          Tragedy is the impending fall of Camelot.  No less moving,
          possibly even more so, is the pathos of Merlin's love for
          Vivian.  It is an old story--Merlin wrenches the heart for
          he has so much more to lose, psychologically, than Lance-
          lot.  To Merlin the experience of love was an unexpectedly
          demanding reversal.  He who had been the prophetic sage,
          no expert in the ways of women, now had to become a
          lover.  Lancelot always had been the servant of Venus.
          Yet the shattering emotional change Merlin undergoes never
          destroys his nobility, or the devotion of Vivian.  They
          act out their loyalties and their disillusionments in a world
          which constantly suggests a dimension greater than Camelot.

1163      _____.  "Edwin Arlington Robinson's Arthurian Heroines:
          Vivian, Guinevere, and the Two Isolts." Philological Quar-
          terly, 56 (1977), 253-258.  Robinson brings an extraordi-
          nary acute perception to the treatment of his heroines in
          Merlin, Lancelot, and Tristram.  They are light years re-
          moved from the ladies of the Middle Ages and the 19th
          century.  They are in fact intelligent women of the 20th
          century who happen to be acting out one of the most en-
          during of English heroic legends.  They represent the suc-
          cessful resolution of a curious paradox.  Characters in love
          stories of surpassing venerability and power, they give
          vitality to the stories by being completely modern, by speak-
          ing in the accents of the twentieth century, and by wrestling

with the vexations and dangers of love in ways that reveal
them as liberated women of great intellectual ability--
ability, alas, which proves incapable of avoiding frustration
or tragic immolation.

1164  STAUFFER, Donald Barlow. A Short History of American Po-
      etry. New York: E. P. Dutton, 1974. Robinson, pp.
      222-228. Robinson was the great American poet of failure.
      The failure basically seems to be a failure of nerve--a rec-
      ognition in himself of his inability to find life's satisfactions
      in the world of physical sensation and his unwillingness to
      take the transcendent leap toward Romantic release and ec-
      stasy. His poems are not failures, but are about failures....
      It is by the short poems that Robinson is remembered to-
      day. His long poems are largely unreadable today. The
      philosophy in these poems is vague and ambiguous; the
      characters have little flesh and blood, the scenes are pas-
      sionless and unreal. Even less readable are the late long
      poems which have a monotony of tone and style that make
      them formidable to approach.

1165  STEDMAN, Edmund Clarence. "An Appreciation." New York
      World Magazine, May 15, 1904. P. 10.

1166  STEPHENS, Alan Archer, Jr. "The Shorter Narrative Poems
      of Edwin Arlington Robinson." Ph.D. diss., University of
      Missouri, 1954.

1167  STERNER, Lewis G. The Sonnet in American Literature.
      Philadelphia: University of Pennsylvania Press, 1930.
      Robinson, pp. 75-77. Originally a doctoral dissertation.
      Is principally an anthology which prints four sonnets by
      Robinson and calls him "a poet who stands high in the list
      of American sonneteers, in spite of some weaknesses which
      are rather obvious even to a casual reader. In theme, his
      sonnets are descriptive or reflective, with but few excep-
      tions.

1168  STEVICK, Robert Davis. "Edwin Arlington Robinson: The
      Principles and the Practice of His Poetry." Ph.D. diss.,
      University of Wisconsin, 1956. DA, 16 (1956), 2463. Writ-
      ing on Robinson at first was largely "appreciation," but
      since 1945 has been primarily "scholarship." Extended an-
      alysis of individual poems is generally absent. This dis-
      sertation approaches the poems through what can be dis-
      covered of his habitual aims in the writing of poetry, and
      examines the effects of these aims on the technique and
      structure of the poems. Some of the areas examined are
      Robinson's dictional qualities, his allusions which are drawn
      from a wide variety of sources, and techniques of character
      depiction.... Poems combining character and abstract

statement embody Robinson's most complex structural method. It succeeded only when each element stood in consummate adjustment with every other.

1169 _____. "Robinson and William James." University of Kansas City Review, 25 (June, 1959), 293-301. Discussion is
based on Robinson's The Man Against the Sky, and some
of the better-known writings of William James. There is
no external evidence to verify this dependence of the poem
on James' writings, but the abundance of parallels between
them, together with the circumstances of the two men suggest that the hypothesis of Jamesian reference for the poem
is important. The purpose in this article is to assess the
aid the Jamesian influence renders for understanding and
appreciating Robinson's poem.

1170 _____. "Formulation of Edwin Arlington Robinson's Principles of Poetry." Colby Library Quarterly, 8 (June,
1969), 295-308. Reprinted in Cary, ed. (1969), pp. 289-
300. Robinson has not been very helpful in this subject,
maintaining that "poetry-makers should stick to their trade
and leave criticism to others." Neither do memoirs, biographies, conversations, interviews, etc. offer little information. The subject must be studied by way of a remark
here, and a remark there. For the most part his principles
were intuitively held and formulated. Everything else
seems derived from the principle that meter and syntax
should be defined with traditional verse form and the devices of ordinary language should be used.

1171 _____. "The Metrical Style of E. A. Robinson," in Barnard,
ed. (1969), pp. 54-67. His verse is traditional in subjects,
versification, symbols, allusions, sources, and formality;
its familiar appearance is deceptively lulling, inviting the
label "traditional" as adequate and final. But that label
does not account for the qualities that distinguish his work
from other traditional poets. Robinson's worth can be re-
liably assessed through a study of his style. He achieved
the quality of his poetry through a complex semantic interplay generated by word choice within a rigid and ordinary
matrix of syntax and meter.... Robinson's poetry was
never violent, conspicuous in color, or sensationally odd.
Robinson himself never called attention to his style or published a rationale of his poetic technique. His worth and
limitations developed through his steady dedication to the
practice of poetry: his eccentricities of style gave rise to
his distinctive good qualities and his worst qualities in
poetry.

1172 STOVALL, Floyd. "The Optimism Behind Robinson's Tragedies."
American Literature, 10 (March, 1938), 1-23. Reprinted

in Cary, ed. 91969), pp. 55-74. Article is long, well-
documented study of Robinson poems which are sometimes
over-simplified and called "pessimistic." The conclusion
points out that Robinson looks beyond the tragedies of
persons and societies and beholds life as an eternal and
creative will evolving through a succession of changing
patterns towards an ideal of perfection. The law of change
requires that old forms shall decay and die in order that
new and higher forms may come into being. Through knowledge man may hope to hasten and direct the process of
evolution.

1173            . American Idealism. Norman: University of Oklahoma Press, 1943. "Robinson and Frost," pp. 167-186.
He gives us pictures of man torn between faith in his essential divinity and knowledge of his substantial animalism.
If he knew more, reason might confirm his wavering faith;
if he knew less, he might be content to dwell in the world
of his illusions. To evade knowledge is despicable; to seek
it, dangerous and sometimes disastrous. The great major-
ity of people find their moral strength unequal to the demands of truth and sink back into their world of illusions,
where they pursue dim phantoms instead of realities and
never truly know themselves. Robinson teaches self-
knowledge, and many of his poems tell the tragic stories
of people who gained self-knowledge, too soon or too late
and came to destruction thereby.

1174            . "Edwin Arlington Robinson in Perspective," in
Essays on American Literature in Honor of Jay B. Hubbell,
edited by Clarence Gohdes. Durham: Duke University
Press, 1967. Pp. 241-258. The history of Robinson the
poet is one of early neglect, increasing critical recognition
during his middle years, a brief period of fame before his
death, and afterwards a rapid decline in popularity accompanied by a more gradual decline in critical esteem. To
understand this history, one should read the poems in the
light of the author's known temperament and the circumstances of his life. In addition, one must take account
of the revolutionary changes in moral and aesthetic values
that occurred during his lifetime and after his death.

1175            . "Edwin Arlington Robinson: A Critical Introduction." American Literature, 41 (May, 1969), 294-295. Review of work by Wallace L. Anderson. It is not a mere
summary of the work of other scholars. There is much
that is new in the account of Robinson's life and associations, especially in the formative years before 1906. Anderson's discussion of the creative thinkers who influenced
the development of Robinson's mind--of Emerson and Swed-
enborg, for example--adds significantly to what earlier

biographers have said. Allowing for the requirements im-
posed by brevity, the author has achieved his purpose.
His criticism is usually well balanced and deserves the
careful attention of the special student as well as the general reader.

1176  STOVER, Frank Brown. "Review of The Glory of the Night-
      ingales." The Wesleyan Cardinal, 6 (November, 1930),
      28-30.

1177  SUBBIAN, C. "Robinson on Verlaine." American Studies Re-
      search Centre Newsletter (Hyderabad, India), 11 (Decem-
      ber, 1967), 52-54. Article is a study of Robinson's sonnet
      "Verlaine," first published in The Children of the Night.
      In this poem Robinson expresses his disdain for the life
      that Verlaine lived, and says, "Let the man go." The only
      thing that will remain is the verse "nothing clings for long
      but laurel to the stricken brow...."

1178  SULLIVAN, Lucy D. "Edwin Arlington Robinson, Disinherited
      Puritan." The Gordon Review (Wenham, Mass.), 6 (1960-
      1961), 11-20. While embodying the spirit of Puritanism,
      Robinson found it necessary to renounce its dogma. Dis-
      illusioning experience was the cause of his decisive dismis-
      sal of orthodox Christianity. After re-reading the Gospel
      of John he said that the popular misinterpretation of Chris-
      tianity made him sick. Some of his satire was vented in
      Captain Craig, later in Cavender's House, The Glory of
      the Nightingales, to name only three. Much of Robinson's
      concern for the hypocrisy and criticism of religion is con-
      tained in letters which he wrote to friends of the period.
      Robinson conducted a life-long search for an adequate sub-
      stitute for the faith his reason could not accept. In num-
      erous poems Robinson observes that by the illumination of
      the Light or the Word, self-diseased men can find and fre-
      quently do find spiritual redemption.

1179  SULLIVAN, Richard. "Edwin Arlington Robinson." Chicago
      Tribune, June 29, 1952. P. 12. Review of biography
      by Ellsworth Barnard.

1180  SUPER, R. H. "For a Dead Lady." Explicator, 3 (June,
      1945), item 60. Explains the line "The breast where roses
      could not live." It is usually said that the line means the
      breast was so lovely that roses faded in comparison. This
      may well be so, but the line could also have been sug-
      gested by the popular proverb: "They say if the flower
      withers she wears she's a flirt." This reading fits better
      with some of the other lines.

1181  _____. "For a Dead Lady." Explicator, 5 (June, 1947),

item 60. Continues discussion on the same poem, respond-
ing to a critic who denies the above interpretation. This
article fills out all of the details of imagery on which one
may call this woman a flirt. A poem must be read for what
it says, not interpreted on the basis of pre-conceived no-
tions. The poem is frequently thought to be about Robinson's mother, but this is doubtful, since the point of view
is that of a mature man and is not marked by childhood
recollections. Calling the woman a "flirt" is objectionable
because the poem clearly says she has children, and is
fond of them, but the two ideas do not seem to exclude
each other.

1182  SUSS, Irving D. "The Plays of Edwin Arlington Robinson."
      Colby Library Quarterly, 8 (September, 1969), 347-363.
      Reprinted in Cary, ed. (1969), pp. 301-314. Thinks it
      is a fact that Robinson turned to plays by his need of
      money and hope for a quick Broadway success which paid
      high profits. His two plays (1914 and 1915) were aimed
      at the commercial theatre, although Robinson must have
      been aware of their theatrical and dramatic inadequacies.
      His dramatic efforts were concentrated in the years 1906
      to 1913. He had "high hopes" of a comedy he was plan-
      ning in 1905, but unless he was referring to one of the
      plays later published, that comedy was not written.
      Whether he finished more than two plays is open to ques-
      tion, but no shred of manuscript has yet been found.

1183  SUTCLIFFE, W. Denham. "Edwin Arlington Robinson: Prod-
      uct of 17th Century Puritanism." Bates College Garnet,
      May, 1935. Pp. 29-32.

1184  _____. "The Original of Robinson's Captain Craig." New
      England Quarterly, 16 (September, 1943), 407-431. Robin-
      son was never satisfied with Captain Craig, was "always
      fiddling with it." It was first published in 1902, later in
      1915, and in 1921. All three versions were different.
      There was a Captain Craig, a living prototype of that ur-
      bane, loquacious hoboscholiast, and there were those who
      called him Waggles and a dead beat. His name was Alfred
      Louis. Where he had come from no one knew.... He was
      a little man, with a benign face almost hidden in the masses
      of his beard. He was ragged, he stank, and he was in his
      pontific way a consummate beggar. But there was more
      than that, and all who knew him realized it.

1185  _____. "Edwin Arlington Robinson and His Manuscripts."
      Colby Library Quarterly, 1 (October, 1944), 131-133.
      Review of work by Esther Willard Bates. Review thinks
      the small book by Bates is indeed a valuable one. She
      was friend and acted somewhat as secretary for Robinson,

"transcribing the spidery precision of his longhand into
the full flare of type." She saw him often, corresponded
with him, and discussed the poems before they had been
submitted to the popular judgment. She relates some memories of that pleasant association, keeping herself graciously in the background while she quotes directly from Robinson's letters and from his casual remarks. There is not
a line of speculation in this book. What she tells she has
seen for herself or has had from his lips. That in itself
makes the book a valuable source of information, and a
more valuable and extensive one than the modest title implies.

1186        , ed. Untriangulated Stars: Letters of Edwin Arling-
        ton Robinson to Harry De Forest Smith, 1890-1905. Cam-
        bridge: Harvard University Press, 1947. "Still through
        the dusk of dead, blank-legended/And unremunerative
        years we search/To get where life begins, and still we
        groan/Because we do not find the living spark/Where no
        spark ever was, and thus we die,/Still searching, like poor
        old astronomers/Who totter off to bed and go to sleep,/To
        dream of untriangulated stars." 350 pages with index and
        notes. Introduction. I. Business be Damned: September
        27, 1890-September 27, 1891, pp. 1-27. II. The Friends
        of My Life: October 6, 1981-June 21, 1893, pp. 27-105.
        III. Town of Banishment: October 1, 1893-November 1,
        1897, pp. 105-291. IV. The Town Down the River: De-
        cember 17, 1897-August 30, 1905, pp. 291-end.

1187        . "The Library of Edwin Arlington Robinson." New
        England Quarterly, 24 (June, 1951), 270-271. Review of
        work by James Humphry. This work says more of Robin-
        son's friendships than about his tastes. The collection is
        small--about 300 volumes. Robinson never seemed much in-
        terested in collecting books. He read a great many books,
        but he apparently did not care to make a great effort to
        own them. This is not, in short, a distinguished library,
        not even the remnant of one. It is valuable chiefly as
        memorabilia, not chiefly as a source for study. But Rob-
        inson was neither a scholar nor a philosopher; he was a
        poet. It is pleasing to know that the survivors among his
        books have been housed in an appropriate place--the Colby
        College Library.

1188        . "An Essay on Robinson's Reading." Kenyon Review,
        17 (Winter, 1955), 136-139. Review of biography by Edwin
        S. Fussell. Robinson worked in many of the larger tradi-
        tions of poetry, but this biography does not choose to ex-
        plore them. The summary chapter would be hard to improve
        upon; his initial statement of purpose is challenging--nearly
        all his attention is on the early work. Good insights occur

throughout.  Yet the book as a whole is disappointing, for
reasons which may be summarized by saying that, beginning with an intent to discover Robinson's relations with
the literary past, the book quickly became a hunt for verbal similarities.  The book may best be described as an
illustrated essay on Robinson's reading.

1189  SWEET, Charles A.  "A Re-Examination of 'Richard Cory.'"
      Colby Library Quarterly, 9 (December, 1972), 579-582.
      Begins with a general review of criticism of the poem, which
      he thinks is in short supply.  It is a most anthologized
      poem, but "one of the least examined."  Of the criticism
      which exists, most of it emphasizes Richard Cory, and very
      little is said about the narrator, who is essentially unreli-
      able and unaware.  Finally the poem is about the failure
      to communicate, the people with Richard Cory, whom they
      see in certain stereotypes of character, and do not under-
      stand at all.  It matters not that Cory pulls the trigger
      at the end; the townspeople have already killed him, ex-
      tinguished the light that glowed in their midst, even while
      they were searching for it....  The poem is an indictment
      of those who study at a distance, who fail to get a feel of
      their subject, and of those who let petty personal emotions
      deprive themselves of human companionship.

1190  SWIFT, Bruce.  "A Biographer of Souls."  The Christian Lead-
      er (Boston), 121 (December 16, 1939), 1194-1195.

1191  TANSELLE, G. Thomas.  "Robinson's 'Dark Hills.'"  CEA
      Critic, 26 (February, 1964), 8-10.  This short poem can
      form the basis of useful discussions in both composition
      and literature classes.  It is useful to illustrate the impor-
      tance of grammatical knowledge, the value of metaphorical
      language, and the essential characteristics of poetry and
      literature in general.  The poem is valuable for these pur-
      poses because it is short and uncomplicated and particularly
      because it is composed of one extended metaphor....  Since
      the substance of the poem emerges through the metaphor,
      the poem furnishes a good example of metaphor as Essential
      Statement.  If one summarizes the poem merely as descrip-
      tion, he is not representing the poem accurately, since the
      war metaphor plays such an important part.

1192  TASKER, J. Dana.  "Review of Cavender's House."  Outlook
      and Independent, 151 (April 24, 1929), 668.  To this work
      Robinson has brought all the characteristic elements of his
      art, and has built with them an excellent narrative poem.

1193  TATE, Allen.  "The Ironic Mr. Robinson:  Review of The
      Glory of the Nightingales."  New York World, October 12,
      1930.  He is probably one of the great poets, and his

intentions, in these long narratives, has an emotional impact of great power, but the intellectual terms of this effect are elusive.  And this testifies to his greatness.  It
is possible that Robinson's service is at once the slyest
and the most implacable piece of irony in the whole record
of a poet steadfastly devoted to the ironic method.

1194 _____.  "Again, O Ye Laurels:  A Review of Talifer."
New Republic, 76 (October 25, 1933), 312-313.  Robinson's
style in this new poem is uniform with the style of its predecessors, neither better nor worse.  It is hard to keep
his poems of recent years distinct; at a distance they lose
outline; blur into one another.  We get, in them all, a
character doomed to defeat, or a character who is a failure
in the eyes of his fellows, but who wins a secret moral
victory.... Robinson's genius is primarily lyrical; he seldom achieves a success in a poem where the idea exceeds
the span of a single emotion.  His narrative verse yields
but a few moments of drama that are swiftly dispersed by
the dry casuistry of the commentary.

1195 _____.  Reactionary Essays on Poetry and Ideas.  New
York:  Scribner's, 1936.  Reprints review of Talifer (1933),
pp. 193-201.

1196 _____.  On the Limits of Poetry:  Selected Essays, 1928-
1948.  New York:  William Morrow, 1948.  Reprints review
of Talifer (1933), pp. 358-364.

1197 _____.  Selected with Preface and Critical Notes.  Sixty
American Poets, 1896-1944.  Washington:  Library of Congress, 1954.  Robinson, pp. 107-113.  Bibliography and
brief comment.

1198 _____.  The Man of Letters in the Modern World:  Selected
Essays, 1928-1955.  New York:  Meridian Books, 1955.
Reprints review of Talifer (1933), pp. 277-282.

1199 _____.  Collected Essays.  Denver:  Swallow Press, 1959.
Robinson, pp. 358-364.  Reprinted in Essays of Four Decades, by Allen Tate.  Chicago:  Swallow, 1968.  Robinson,
pp. 341-347.  Reprints the review of Talifer, first published in New Republic, 76 (October 25, 1933), 312-313.
See above.

1200 TAYLOR, Henry.  "In the Mode of Robinson and Frost:  James
Wright's Early Poetry," in The Pure Clear Word:  Essays
on the Poetry of James Wright, edited by Dave Smith.
Urbana:  University of Illinois Press, 1982.  Pp. 49-64.
Article does not say much about Robinson's poetry.  Early
Wright acknowledged an indebtedness to Robinson, and

some of the things that the master could teach: the careful setting, the question that deepens the mystery by being somewhat baffling in itself, and the significant details
which are sometimes hard to visualize, despite the specific-
ity of the words.... Wright tried "very hard," to work in
the Robinson mode, but even in his early period the achievement was not too great.

1201  TAYLOR, Walter Fuller. A History of American Letters. New
York: American Book Company, 1936. Robinson, pp.
339-347. Of all the twentieth-century American poets,
Edwin Arlington Robinson moved with the most quiet certainty, with the most unassuming poise, among the conflicting forces of a disturbed era. Neither reactionary nor
radical, he successfully fused tradition and originality.
Neither sentimental nor altogether matter of fact, he admirably tempered romance with realism, realism with romance. Because of his balance, sanity, and poise, because of the unquestionable merit of many poems, and
because of the impressive scope of his work, Robinson is
usually regarded as the principal poet of the twentieth-
century America.... He did not concern himself with in-
culcating in his readers any definite body of ideas. He
had few lessons to teach. His interpretation of life is not
a matter of instruction, but of illumination. With emotions
carefully controlled, he critically presented human nature,
in its in its kindliness, its aspirations, its highest fulfillment; and even more in its imperfections, its tangled cross-
purposes, and its tragic defeats.

1202  THAKUR, G. P. "Tilbury Town as Region: A Study of the
Poetry of Edwin Arlington Robinson." Indian Journal of
American Studies (Calcutta), 7 (1976), 54-66. It is generally agreed among critics and interpreters that this fic-
tional town is Gardiner, Maine. Tilbury Town, in the context of Robinson's poetry, more or less represents the in-
tersection of the old New England of the poet's boyhood
that is disappearing, and the symptoms of the new New
England where the poet found himself in an alien world....
But at this very elementary level itself the critical unanim-
ity ends, and further study of this aspect of Robinson's
poetry is full of controversies centering around the origin
of the name and its place in the appreciation of his poetry.
This article takes stock of some of these controversies at
some length. In the last analysis, be it realism or symbolism, verbosity or reticence, the New England prototype is
in fairness to the text, just a landscape of the mind, rather
than a photographic replica of the earth. All the same,
it is as much an expression of regionalism in literature as
any other kind.

1203  THEIS, O. F. "Edwin Arlington Robinson." <u>Forum</u>, 51 (Feb-
      ruary, 1914), 305-312.  Is an essay of deep appreciation
      for the poetry of Robinson which stands out from the vast
      sea of verse that is "merely pathetic or sadly ludicrous"
      because of its ineffectiveness.  Robinson is indifferent to
      the current fashion or mode of poetry....  There is fresh-
      ness and fullness in his art.  His themes are usually sim-
      ple and consist of common, concrete things of life.

1204  THOMPSON, Lawrence, ed.  With introduction and notes.
      <u>Tilbury Town:  Selected Poems of Edwin Arlington Robin-
      son</u>.  New York:  Macmillan, 1953.  Work consists of 144
      pages of poems which have to do with Robinson's "Tilbury
      Town."  These poems, some 65 of them, are arranged in
      thematic groups:  Predicaments, Passions, The Dead, Edge
      of Town, and Against the Sky.  The book contains an ex-
      cellent eight page Introduction, a good section of Notes,
      and an Index listing the poems in the volume.  From the
      Introduction, Thompson says:  "At first glance we are
      aware of the obvious conflicts within or between these
      imagined characters whom Robinson has brought to life in
      or on the edge of Tilbury Town.  A second glance makes
      us feel that most of these characters are represented as
      being in conflict with the prudent and conventional morality
      of Tilbury Town, where the group tends to pass relentless
      judgment on all misfits and failures who find themselves at
      odds with the money-conscious worship of material success.
      A third glance is not necessary to make us realize that
      the poet-as-observer, standing apart from the Tilbury
      Town group, on the one hand, and from the isolated in-
      dividuals, on the other hand, shows an open hostility
      toward the Tilbury Town group and shows sympathetic
      compassion for the misfits, the failures, the disappointed.
      Because any single one of these conflicts would be adequate
      for purposes of poetic and dramatic narrative, we enjoy
      this rich interplay of conflicts as sheer poetic luxury."

1205  THOMPSON, Lola Rivers.  "Edwin Arlington Robinson's Treat-
      ment of Arthurian Legends."  University of Texas (Aus-
      tin), 1931.  M.A. thesis.

1206  THOMPSON, Ralph.  "Books of the Times:  Review of Hage-
      dorn's Biography."  <u>New York Times</u>, October 4, 1938.
      P. 19.

1207  THOMPSON, William Ross.  "Broceliande:  Edwin Arlington
      Robinson's Palace of Art."  <u>New England Quarterly</u>, 43
      (June, 1970), 231-249.  Reviews critical comment and opin-
      ion of <u>Merlin</u> which of the three Arthurian poems has re-
      ceived least in the way of approbation and the most censure.
      The poem has yet to be subjected to an analysis consistent

with what Robinson said was his intent: reason unassisted
by a higher power, namely imagination, is inadequate to
preserve human values. Camelot represents the house that
reason built; Broceliande, a palace of art and the realm
of the imagination. Merlin's is a disciplined knowledge;
Vivian's, an intuitive. In reality they are complementary
entities, and each is diminished by the absence of the other. Merlin's dual role of counselor to Arthur and lover of
Vivian is consistent and integral to Robinson's purpose.

1208 _____. "The Identity of Edwin Arlington Robinson's Amaranth." Bulletin of the Rocky Mountain Modern Language
Association, 35 (1981), 259-269. Few critics have remarked
kindly on the long narrative poems, and Amaranth is no exception. Some of the confusion centers about the identity
of Amaranth, the voice that speaks to all of the characters
(and there are a great many of them) and guided them out
of "the wrong world." The main character, Fargo, had
freed himself from the obsession a decade earlier. Amaranth has variously been called "the genius of Time itself,"
"Time's judgment on men's work," "Robinson's symbol for
reality," "Truth," "courage to face disaster," "light to re-
sign themselves to either life or death," etc. Although
Amaranth cannot be regarded as a personification of reason,
he is the means by which men may "know the peace of reason." He is, in short, an agent--a semidivine figure
charged with making men mindful of their potentiality for
engaging in rational thought and behavior.

1209 THORP, Willard. American Writing in the Twentieth-Century.
Cambridge: Harvard University Press, 1960. Robinson,
pp. 38-42. In the recent revival of interest in Robinson's
work one can see signs that he is coming to be rightly
valued as one of the best of American poets. It was
through an odd combination of circumstances that he failed
to receive wide acclaim in his lifetime. It has often been
said that Robinson's best poems are psychological portraits
of men and women whose lives are failures. His derelicts
and defeated ones possess a fortitude that is peculiarly
Robinsonian. In his own life Robinson experienced defeat
many times, but he met the blows with courage.

1210 TINKER, Chauncey Brewster. The Good Estate of Poetry.
Boston: Little, Brown, 1929. Robinson, pp. 128-129.
Robinson's literary method in Tristram is the traditional
one of making an ancient story real by setting it forth in
terms of its spiritual issues. The passions with which he
deals are too absorbed to permit any prolonged attention
to the background. He has deserted Tilbury Town for
Tintagel, but he is not concerned about the stage setting
of his piece. Who cares much about the scenery? He

disdains obsolete diction, and declines to visit museums in
order to work up a knowledge of ancient costume, armor,
and love philtres.

1211 TITTLE, Walter. "Glimpses of Interesting Americans." Century Magazine, 110 (June, 1925), 189-192. Robinson discussed as part of a longer article. Author is a painter-
artist and remarks are directed largely to a portrait sketch
which he did of Robinson. In conclusion he says: "A
glance at my sketch proved this to be one of the happy
occasions when the sitter recognizes a likeness and fears
its loss if the work continues. Saying that in his opinion
I had got him absolutely, he suggested that I leave the
portrait overnight, offering to return for another sitting
if I then thought it necessary. Remembering disastrous
experiences as the result of too much effort, I agreed, and
the drawing remains as it was." Sketch included in article.

1212 TODRIN, Boris. "Edwin Arlington Robinson." Book Collector's
Journal, 1 (July, 1936), 1, 4.

1213 TORRENCE, Olivia H. D. "The Poet at the Dinner Table."
Colophon, 3 (Winter, 1938), 92-99. Article begins by
printing a two paragraph piece which Robinson, as well as
a dozen others, wrote for Harriet Moody's Cook Book. The
publisher of the cookbook did not favor the inclusion of
this untechnical and purely literary material. But for the
poet's public, this composition is interesting not only for
its subject, but also one of the few available examples of
his prose. Yet food did not occupy a really important
place in his life. He lived most literally and unaffectedly,
the life of the mind. Toward the end of his life he had to
give up even some of his simple eating pleasures.

1214 TORRENCE, Ridgely, ed. With introduction. Selected Letters
of Edwin Arlington Robinson. New York: Macmillan, 1940.
Consists of 190 pages with notes. Letters in this volume
have been chosen from the large body of correspondence
made available. The intention has been to present Robinson the man. Volume is arranged in four parts: Ages 20-
29, "The Start"; 29-36, "Dust and Heat"; 35-57, "Arrival";
and 56-65, "The Garland." Content covers a wide variety
of people to whom Robinson wrote letters.

1215 TRYON, James Libby. Harvard Days with Edwin Arlington
Robinson. Waterville, Maine: privately printed, 1940.
16-page pamphlet of the address dleivered to the Colby
chapter of Phi Beta Kappa, April 16, 1940. Article is a
personal recollection by Tryon of his friend Robinson when
they were both students at Harvard. He has been helped
immensely in remembering Robinson by friends who have

survived, by pictures, by letters, by available works on
Robinson. Tryon knew Robinson best in college, but
through the years found that the poet did not change in
spite of his great honors as a poet.

1216 TUERK, Richard. "Robinson's 'Lost Anchor.'" Explicator,
32 (August, 1974), item 37. Supports other readings of
the poem in which the Christian symbolism is demonstrated.
The poem demands a Biblical context. Several specific references are suggested with passages from the books of
Habakkuk, Job, Hebrews.

1217 TURNER, C. J. M. "The Sonnets of Edwin Arlington Robinson."
Poetry Review (London), 27 (March-April, 1936), 121-127.

1218 TURNER, Steven. "Robinson's 'Richard Cory.'" Explicator,
28 (May, 1970), item 73. Objects to the reading by
Charles R. Morris that Robinson's poem is full of British
usage, and therefore Richard Cory is perhaps the remnant
of royalty in America. This reading maintains that some
of these expressions are American, and serve a far greater
purpose than creating the fallen image of British royalty.
For instance, "on the pavement" in American slang usually
means completely down and out; "from sole to crown," etc.,
are puns and seem to justify themselves.

1219 ULRICH, Dorothy Livingston. "Edwin Arlington Robinson."
Avocations, 2 (June, 1938), 248-253. Published in pamphlet, Hartford: Privately printed, 1940.

1220 UNTERMEYER, Louis. "... And Other Poems." The Chicago
Evening Post (Chicago), March 10, 1916. P. 11. Includes
review of The Man Against the Sky.

1221 _____, ed. The New Era in American Poetry. New York:
Harcourt, Brace, 1919. Robinson, pp. 111-135. Unper-
turbed by the battle over new forms and metrical innovations, he has gone on, like every first-rate artist, making
old forms distinctive and definitely his own. His rhymes
are brought in with a masterly ease, showing what rhyme,
at its best, should be: a natural, musical punctuation.
They flow, like his lines, as smoothly and pointedly as a
sharp conversation.

1222 _____. American Poetry Since 1900. New York: Henry
Holt, 1923. Robinson, pp. 42-66. At first glance Robinson
seems one of the least American of our poets. He uses
the traditional English forms; there are lines when he seems
to be speaking with the accents of Robert Browning in the
rhythms of W. S. Gilbert. But, beneath a superficial indebtedness, no living writer has achieved a more personal

idiom or a more melodious speech--or a more indigenous
one. His ironic studies of character are as incisive as
those of Masters'; his New England backgrounds are as
faithful as those of Frost's. Robinson has other qualities
which may be less national but are no less local. His
shrewd appraisals, his constant questioning instead of
placid acceptance, his reticence that screens a vigorous
analysis--these qualities reveal the spirit of the early
Puritan operating with the technique of the modern psychologist.

1223  _____. "The Spirit of Modern American Poetry." English
        Journal, 13 (February, 1924), 89-99. Long discussion of
        a number of poets, with not much attention to Robinson.
        Reacting against the old fallacy that poetry must have a
        vocabulary of its own, Robinson brings before us, with
        a remarkable gift of epithet, a living gallery of portraits.
        American literature is richer for a score of Robinson fig-
        ures: Richard Cory, Miniver Cheevy, John Gorham, Be-
        wick Finzer, Merlin, etc. But it is not only his characters
        which are so vivid; his characterizations and cadences are
        splendid in their tawny colors.

1224  _____. "Demos at the Bar: Dionysus in Doubt." Saturday
        Review of Literature, 1 (May 9, 1925), 741. If sonnets
        can assume the proportion of dramatic narratives, Robinson's
        have achieved this almost impossible feat. And--though here
        and there the poet allows his turn of cryptic implication to
        seem a too frequently performed trick--if anything is needed
        to disprove the charge that Robinson is allowing his idiom
        to dictate itself, this volume is a complete and cumulative
        answer.

1225  _____. "Seven Against Realism: Review of The Man Who
        Died Twice." Yale Review, 14 (July, 1925), 791-797.
        Seven books of American poetry have nothing in common
        except their stand against realism, and the pronouncement
        of belief in a return to faith. This poem by Robinson is a
        cross between a grotesque narrative and inspired metaphys-
        ics. Curiously, it is one of Robinson's triumphs. Here
        is unfolded, in an involuted, interrupted set of monologues,
        the descent into hell of one who wasted the divine fire in
        profane prodigality and who, at the very moment when the
        drums of death are pounding in his ears, is lifted into
        heaven on sonorous flames.... Robinson takes his time to
        tell the story, but it is one that is worth telling, and the
        divergent territory which he surveys while he wanders from
        his plot is not the least valuable part of the ground cov-
        ered.

1226  _____. "The Essential Robinson: A Review of Cavender's

House." Saturday Review of Literature, 5 (May 11, 1929),
995-996. This poem is a double story, or two stories, one
coiled darkly within the other. Cavender returns to a
house, revisiting the scene of his crime, the murder of his
wife in a nightmare of uncertainty about her faithfulness.
He gradually discloses the futility of his crime in rendering
him ever to learn the truth. Then the second story begins, the wife returning to his memory and they seem to
converse. He will now find the truth, but she is triumph-
ant, and he learns only that it was she for whom he was
starved and exiled.

1227 _____. "Review of Matthias at the Door." Saturday Review
of Literature, 8 (March 12, 1932), 588. This poem exhibits
more tellingly than any of the long blank verse narratives
the author's narrowing limitations and his power, his very
luxuriance, within those limitations. At the outset one of
the characters commits suicide, and it is this death that
tears holes in the surrounding web of silence and lets in
hafts of pitiless truth. Technically, the poem is better
than some of Robinson's long narratives: there is directness of speech, the blank verse has grown sharper and
more musical.

1228 _____. "Wise and Wicked: A Review of Talifer." Saturday
Review of Literature, 10 (October 7, 1933), 161. The story
itself is simpler than most of Robinson's later works. It
revolves around two women and three men, and is a love
story which is finally resolved by a good friend, Dr.
Quick, to the approximate satisfaction of all concerned....
Talifer is the happiest of all Robinson's longer poems, and
it is also the best. It is the easiest to read, less knotty
in dialectic, less gnarled in diction than most of the
lengthier pieces. It marks a return to Robinson's nimbler
manner, his neat astringency, his uncanny skill as dramatist and dissector. It could be managed by no other American than Robinson, and not too often by him.

1229 _____. "Review of Amaranth." American Mercury, 34
(April, 1935), 505-508. Contained in article "Six Poets."
Amaranth is the apotheosis of his preoccupation with the
social and artistic misfits. Here all of his lesser characters
are multiplied and distorted in a limbo which is something
like an allegory and something like a nightmare. The main
character is the embodiment of Truth, and his pitiless gaze
shrivels the last illusion with which the crowd of incompet-
ents can comfort themselves. Unfortunately, for all its
dramatic possibilities, is wholly without drama, has no
sense of direction, and leaves the reader baffled.

1230 _____. "Unfinished Portrait." Saturday Review of Literature,

18 (October 15, 1938), 34. Review of Hagedorn's biography. Since Robinson's death, readers of his poetry have
been awaiting his biography, and here it is. Consisting
of almost four hundred pages, it is detailed, dutiful, and
dull. Granted Robinson was not a particularly colorful
subject and lived almost entirely in his work.... But it
is not the dull detailing nor the unfortunate style which
makes this book so unsatisfactory. It is the lack of vital
substance, the failure to record or reconcile the contradictions of Robinson's moood and character, of fact and
interpretation. In short there is no synthesis, nothing to
indicate Robinson's significance as a poet, as a social force,
as a contemporary influence. Some day a biographer will
explore the depths beneath Robinson's deceptive surfaces,
the intensity, the anxiety, the lonely man obsessed by
failure and in love with death. Unfortunately, this is not
the book.

1231         . From Another World. New York: Harcourt, Brace,
1939. Robinson, pp. 222-227. Work is an autobiography.
Recalls how well he knew Robinson, but does not feel quali-
fied to be his biographer, perhaps he knew Robinson too
long and too well. But he is awaiting someone else who
will reconcile the calculating and incalculable artist; the
puritan, the man of the world, and the man who, in his
intensity and probity, was always somewhat beyond the
world. A biography of Robinson has been published. The
facts are there, but the quiet contradictory spirit escapes.

1232         . "Review of Selected Letters." Saturday Review of
Literature, 21 (March 2, 1940), 7. If there is little style
or quality in the letters, there are plenty of other values.
It is a record of loyal friendships, deeply attached and
sometimes unexpectedly teasing. It discloses, almost in
spite of the author, some of his literary preferences and
prejudices. Apart from Robinson's loyalties and limitations,
these letters add color to the carefully selected facts in
Hagedorn's dutiful biography.

1233         , ed. Modern American Poetry. New York: Harcourt, Brace, & Howe, 1942. Revised and re-issued many
times. 6th edition, 1942. Edwin Arlington Robinson, pp.
135-159. Reprints some thirty shorter, better known poems
with biographical and critical Introduction. In all his books
there is manifest a searching for the light beyond illusion.
But his intuitions are supported by a vigorous intellectual-
ity. Purely as a psychological portrait painter, Robinson
has given American literature an entire gallery of memorable
figures. These portraits reveal Robinson's sensitive power,
especially in his projection of the apparent failures of life.
Much of his poetry may be seen as a protest against that

standardized definition of success which the world so much
worships.

1234 _____, ed. An Anthology of the New England Poets. New
York: Random House, 1948. E. A. Robinson, pp. 519-
534. Prints 15 of the shorter, more familiar poems together
with a brief biographical and critical preface. As a poet
Robinson was essentially a biographer of the spirit and an
analyst of the soul. He groped through the all-pervading
darkness, somehow hopeful of "the coming glory of the light."
His preoccupation with failure and a lifelong fear of poverty, made him the champion of all outcasts and derelicts,
the unhappy misfits unable to maintain themselves in a
world of powerful efficiency. Robinson depicted a limbo
of lost souls battered by ruthless success-at-any-cost.

1235 _____. Makers of the Modern World. New York: Simon
& Schuster, 1955. Robinson, pp. 399-404. Robinson chal-
lenged contemporary values and questioned the current price
of success more caustically than any poet of his day. Early
in life he discovered that he would have to live in a hard
world with a harsh set of imperatives.... In his later
years he grew more tolerant of "company" but he never
lost his distrust of most men and almost all women. At 60
he was lonelier than ever; his last years were full of suffering. At 66 he weakened, and when he was finally
brought to a hospital, he was nearly dead. He died in
April, 1935.

1236 _____. "Edwin Arlington Robinson: A Reappraisal," with
a bibliography and a list of materials in the Edwin Arlington Robinson Exhibit on Display at the Library of Congress, April 15 to July 15, 1963, in Literary Lectures Presented at the Library of Congress. Washington: Library
of Congress Press, 1963. Pp. 527-551.

1237 _____. "Edwin Arlington Robinson: A Remembrance."
Saturday Review, 48 (April 10, 1965), 33-34. A personal
recollection, thirty years after Robinson's death. He was
not an easy man to know. Shy, withdrawn, reticent, re-
mote--these are the adjectives that encrust descriptions of
him. He was the least public of poets; he had no talent
for making himself popular. He never taught, lectured,
never took part in the politics of the "new poetry." His
letters were dull ... he regarded a public platform as no
less than a public execution. His face was like his poetry,
cool, precise, shrewd, pointed with astringent wit. He had
intensity without passion; again and again he achieved elo-
quence, but never ecstasy.

1238 _____. "Simon Simple." Colby Library Quarterly, 8

(December, 1969), 415.  A poem written in the manner of
Robinson, a sonnet portraiture, in which "Simple Simon"
of the nursery jingle is presented as someone "touched with
fire and prophecy."  The composition does get the flavor
of Robinson, along with the wit, irony, and typical indirection.

1239  VAN DOORN, William.  "How It Strikes a Contemporary."
      English Studies, 7 (October, 1926), 129-142.  Robinson
      comments, pp. 135-138.  Nothing uncouth is here, no tricks
      of speech, nor even any tricks of punctuation.  His verse
      has swing, strength and variety.  He has some fancy, but
      far more imagination.  He has mixed with his fellowmen.
      Saints as well as sinners, he knows them and interprets
      them and presents them to our eyes with three dimensions.

1240  VAN DOREN, Carl.  "Tragedy in Camelot: Lancelot."  Nation,
      110 (May 8, 1920), 622-623.  The verse of "Lancelot" is as
      athletic and spare as an Indian runner, though it walks not
      runs.  At the same time he varies his verse in admirable
      accord with situation and character.  Since Browning there
      has been no finer dramatic dialogue in verse than that
      spoken by Lancelot and Guinevere and no apter characteriza-
      tion than the ironical talk of Gawaine.  One must go out of
      verse, to Meredith and Henry James, to find its match.
      Robinson, however, has the advantage of verse.

1241  _____.  "Wisdom and Irony: Review of The Three Taverns."
      Nation, 111 (October 20, 1920), 453-454.  Separate enough
      in themselves, they yet stand with respect to each other
      in a sort of pattern, like the monoliths of a Druid circle.
      What holds them in the pattern is that tone of mingled wis-
      dom and irony, that color of dignity touched with colloquial
      flexibility, that clear, hard, tender blank verse and those
      unforgettable eight-line stanzas and dramatic sonnets which
      go to make up one of the most scrupulous and valuable of
      living poets.

1242  _____.  "In a Style of Steel: Avon's Harvest."  Nation,
      112 (April 20, 1921), 596.  It is a study of a human char-
      acter seen in revealing moments.  What Avon, the protagon-
      ist, has to tell is a record of hate, remorse, and fear,
      against his enemy whom he hated all his life.  Not even the
      death of the enemy can assuage the hate....  It is vain to
      deny that at times Robinson's brevity becomes obscurity.
      There is no royal road to Robinson.  The summit, however,
      is worth the ascent.

1243  _____.  "Greek Dignity and Yankee Ease: Review of Col-
      lected Poems."  Nation, 113 (November 16, 1921), 570-571.
      Reprinted in The Roving Critic.  New York: Knopf, 1923.

Pp. 231-236. A single volume holds without crowding the
verse into which Robinson has distilled his observations
and judgments during thirty studious, pondering, devoted,
elevated years. His absolute loyalty to the ideals of art
and wisdom thus achieved is a thrilling thing.

1244 _____. "The Unpardonable Sin: Review of The Man Who
Died Twice." Century, 108 (August, 1924), 574. In this
work Robinson finds the unpardonable sin to be the sin of
sloth which leads a gifted man to bury his divine talent and
thus insult the Holy Ghost. His talent dies, and later he
dies again, hence "twice." The poem is not "easy reading"
but is well worth reading twice or many times. The parts
are so close-knit as almost to defy quotation. The blank
verse is flexible, varied in pause and cadence.

1245 _____. "Review of Tristram." Century, 114 (June, 1927),
255-256. What business has an American poet of the twentieth century to go back to heathen England and to retell
a story which has been told over and over by many poets
in many languages? The question does not have to be
answered. It is only in the outline of events that Robinson's story is the legendary one. The characters and the
tragedy are universal, not traditional. It is all Robinson,
modern, fresh, without historical posturing and antiquities
of speech.

1246 _____, ed. American Poets, 1630-1930: An Anthology.
Boston: Little, Brown, 1932. Robinson, pp. 358-390.
Devotes more than adequate space to Robinson, consisting
mostly of familiar short poems, and also "The Man Against
the Sky." The brief biographical note names Robinson's
publications with dates. Poems are printed without critical
commentary.

1247 _____. What Is American Literature? New York: William
Morrow & Co., 1935. Robinson, pp. 106-110. This little
book is a definition not a debate. Having concluded what
writers are the American essence, it tries to define each
of them as precisely as possible. Robinson has been a
poet building a world in his own mind and heart. He has
shaped stories and characters hardly less out of his reading than out of his experience. He is a learned poet, but
his learning has neither thinned nor muddied his imagination. His world exists in his own image, in his own idiom.

1248 _____. "The Literary Twenties: Edwin Arlington Robinson."
Harper's Magazine, 173 (July, 1936), 154-156. Comments
on Robinson part of a longer article. Recalls asking Robinson to review a book of poems by Thomas Hardy, and was
refused because he said he was far too busy, and "that

poetry-makers should stick to their trade and leave criticism to the others." That summer he wrote Avon's Harvest,
but in October he sent "Mr. Flood's Party" for publication
in the Nation. By the time Van Doren met Robinson, he
was already within a small circle a very famous man, and
nobody ever refused an invitation to go where he would be.

1249 _____. Three Worlds. New York: Macmillan, 1936. Robinson, pp. 160-162. Recalls meeting Robinson, whom he
valued above all living poets. Van Doren says: "With me,
at least, he did not gossip, did not play with ideas, did
not bring topics up, and did not say things which stuck in
my mind in the very words he had used. He was not slow
in apprehension, but he liked things said plainly to him.
His subtlety was in his poetry." He was always generous
with praise, though he praised in few words.

1250 _____. "Edwin Arlington Robinson," in American and British Literature Since 1890, by Carl and Mark Van Doren.
New York: Century, 1939. Pp. 13-19. He was, in a
sense, another Hawthorne, more learned and more ironical.
His characters have so much of the Yankee in them that
they cannot cry out with the loud voices of most tragic
heroes. They are most eloquent in their silences. They
do not invite the spectators of their fates to feel with them
merely, but to understand them. Robinson does not help
his readers. He demands that the dramas which he represents shall be listened to attentively, without explanation
on his part.... Precision is Robinson's chief quality as a
writer. His words are selected with exactness, his various
meters handled with dexterity. He does not write loosely,
as he does not think loosely, but ponders every observation he makes upon life, every trait of a character, every
image, till he comprehends it completely, and then seeks
for the words which shall, so far as he can judge, most
truthfully communicate his meaning.

1251 _____. The American Novel, 1789-1939. New York: Macmillan, 1940. "Local and Historical," pp. 213-214. Robert
Frost chose verse in which to distill the final essence of
New England. Robinson in a few brief poems created Tilbury Town and endowed it with a more haunting and more
lasting pathos than that of any New England village in prose.

1252 VAN DOREN, Mark. "Review of Roman Bartholow." Nation,
116 (June 13, 1923), 700-701. Contains comment on work
by Lloyd Morris. This is a poem such as no other living
person could have written. Robinson has not equalled it
for intensity and for cut of dialogue, of drama, of description, of mood. The speech, of course, is too sharp and
profound to be true. People never talked like this. But

people have thought like this, and Robinson's people think
aloud--think vernacularly--in marvelous verse.  Thinks
Morris' book is distinguished, but should concentrate more
on Robinson's poetry and less on his philosophy.

1253  _____.  "A Symphony of Sin: Review of The Man Who Died
Twice."  Nation, 118 (April 16, 1924), 445-446.  It is seldom
or never that a good poem can be legitimately considered to
need music for its fuller expression.  This poem is especially complete within itself; it is a symphony of most gorgeous content, and yet it is authentically a poem; the music is unheard.  At the same time, one rather wishes that
a competent composer would attempt something with these
lines and these ideas for its basis.

1254  _____.  "Review of Dionysus in Doubt."  Nation, 120 (April
15, 1925), 428.  The deadly quiet tread of these irregular
rhymes is the tread of a poet whose accomplishment at its
height has always been uncanny.  But the body of the
piece is a sermon by Dionysus on the perils of false democracy, and the rhymes neither fit such a subject nor compel
it to fit them.  It remains a refractory, almost a trivial
subject in the fine hands of one who has never been impressive as a philosophical poet.

1255  _____.  Edwin Arlington Robinson.  Binghamton, N.Y.:
Literary Guild Press, 1927.  90 pages, has no index.  Sees
the life and work of the poet as "all one piece," one who
has devoted himself to his work with absolute consistency.
Also "Tristram" is unsurpassed, pointing out the degree of
felicity attainable by men in this existence which is a battle
between passion and intellect, between chance and purpose,
between destiny and wisdom.  Robinson's respect for the
mind saves him from weak wailing against fate.  This book
is in four parts: "The Man and His Career," "The Shorter
Poems," "The Longer Poems," and "Tristram."

1256  _____.  "Review of Tristram."  Forum, 78 (August, 1927),
312-313.  The details of the poem, or of its beauty, cannot
be indicated in short space.  But tribute can be paid to
the singleness and speed of the action, to the blank verse,
to the frequent flights into authentic rapture.... It is certainly one of the best narrative poems we have; and it is
safe to say the story has never been better told in English
verse.

1257  _____.  "A Series of Studies: Edwin Arlington Robinson."
Book League Monthly, 1 (January, 1929), 271-273.

1258  _____.  "Edwin Arlington Robinson."  Nation, 140 (April 17,
1935), 434.  Written on the occasion of Robinson's death.

Not merely did he refuse to toss us the customary evaluation about his personal self, but the very poetry he gave
us to read in twenty volumes was agnostic in temper, austere in tone. So much intelligence was needed for understanding either the ideas or the art in these volumes, and
Robinson was so content with his poetry that he made no
comment on it.

1259 _____. "The Last Look." (Verse) Mark Twain Quarterly,
2 (Spring, 1938), 21. Twenty-Eight line poem written after hearing someone describe Robinson on his death-bed.
Is a tribute to Robinson, with emphasis largely on the
mysterious quality of the man. In conclusion: "... this
is where he he lay/and where the ceiling said his last word
for him/and where his eyes still wander past us, listening
and feeling...."

1260 _____. "Edwin Arlington Robinson." Colby Library Quarterly, 8 (June, 1969), 279. Brief commentary of praise
for Robinson, who himself was never very mindful of his
own reputation. Yet he was eminent among American poets,
and it was an eminence never called into question. Neither
vanity nor the absence of it proves excellence in a poet.
Robinson's poems continue to stand quite by themselves:
his sonnets, his lyrics, his character pieces--his portraits
of persons--no less than his extended narratives. He was
a master of every form he tried, and that is enough to say
now in his praise.

1261 VAN NORMAN, C. Elta. "Captain Craig." College English,
2 (February, 1941), 462-475. Is a long, exceptionally well
organized article which explores every conceivable facet of
Robinson's poem. In 7 parts with an Introduction, it covers
the original person on whom the poem was based, the critical reception the poem has received, Robinson's philosophy
which is embodied in the poem, and the technique by which
Robinson avoided the pitfall of sentimentality in dealing with
a derelict old man.

1262 VARLEY, H. L. "Review of Untriangulated Stars." Springfield Republican, January 25, 1948. P. 8B. This is an
extremely important collection, for in Smith, Robinson had
an understanding friend and to this friend he told nearly
every intellectually exciting event that he experienced for
these formative years. Thus the book is a record of the
building of Robinson's character and habits, and it is also
the record of the making of a major poetic mind. Both are
fascinating to watch.

1263 VINCENT, Sybil Korff. "Flat Breasted Miracles: Realistic
Treatment of the Woman's Problem in the Poetry of Edwin

Arlington Robinson." Markham Review, 6 (1976), 14-15.
The element which most securely links Robinson with the
late nineteenth century is his recognition of the changing
position of women. There are no polemics regarding wom-
en. He does not preach about what a woman's position
should or should not be. Rather he dramatizes what women
are. he shows them as real human beings, not archetypes
of virgin goddesses or evil temptresses. At their best
they give off an atmosphere of vitality, passion and gen-
erosity. He ponders the relationship between men and
women, not idealized, not tragic: often cruel, indifferent,
misunderstanding and misunderstood. Perhaps one of the
best things Robinson can do is record a domestic squabble,
mundane and far from tragic.

1264 WAGER, Willis. American Literature: A World View. New
York: New York University Press, 1968. Robinson, pp.
186-189. Increasingly in later life Robinson wrote long
narrative poems with strongly psychological emphasis, concentrated on a few intensely conceived characters--almost
Jamesian, as in King Jasper. Most of the poems written
after World War I are set in more or less modern times.
In his hands the blank-verse form achieved such flexibility
and naturalness that one is scarcely conscious of it as a
pattern in itself. Here the late 19th Century concentration
on prose fiction seems rather to have spilled over into the
area of poetry and to have influenced even a conservative
poet like Robinson.

1265 WAGGONER, Hyatt Howe. "Edwin Arlington Robinson and the
Cosmic Chill." New England Quarterly, 13 (March, 1940),
65-84. Reprinted in The Heel of Elohim: Science and Value
in Modern American Poetry. Norman: University of Oklahoma Press, 1950. Pp. 18-40. Reprinted in Cary, ed.
(1969), pp. 91-104. Also reprinted in Murphy, ed. (1970),
pp. 148-163. Robinson's poetry is that of a man whose
mind and heart are at odds. His didactic poems are ordi-
narily his poorest work, and the more ambitious his effort
in this direction the weaker the result.... The failure is
not a "technical" one but the result of a breakdown of
thought and feeling, an impasse of the soul. If passages
are frequently thin and verbose, unconvincing and even
tedious, it is because they are most often on the theme of
ultimate meaning, and on this theme Robinson could only
think and feel by turns.

1266 _____. "Robinson's 'New England.'" Explicator, 10 (March,
1952), item 33. See also Amacher. The whole poem is indeed a "satirical attack" upon those who are characterized
merely as being "elsewhere" and as holding certain opinions
--false on the face of them--about New England. To read

the poem in any other way is to suppose that Robinson had
an absurdly distorted notion of his own region, and what
is even more difficult to suppose, admired or envied wild-
ness, drunkenness and even the pose of drunkenness by
those who were really not drunk at all.

1267 _____. American Poets: From the Puritans to the Present.
Boston: Houghton Mifflin, 1968. "The Idealist in Extremis:
Edwin Arlington Robinson," pp. 262-292. Robinson responded to Hawthorne surely and acutely from the very
beginning, not as a sage but as an artist. His kinship
with the older writer was temperamental, not philosophic,
a shared response of the whole sensibility to experience,
not the satisfaction of a need for belief. The only thing
he missed in his aesthetic response to Hawthorne was the
"light" that Hawthorne wanted to affirm, and sometimes did
affirm.... Robinson found in Hawthorne a great writer who
was a kindred spirit. His preference for traditional meters
and stanzaic forms, his diction, and especially his hesitant,
tentative rhythms, draw him as close perhaps to Hawthorne
as verse can ever come to prose.

1268 WALCUTT, Charles Child. "Edwin Arlington Robinson."
Arizona Quarterly, 9 (Spring, 1953), 84-85. Review of
biography by Ellsworth Barnard. Thinks Barnard has attempted something very unusual, which is to write only and
centrally about Robinson's poetry. This author asks what
the poem is, what does it do? But he is concerned to go
beyond the New Critics' limitation of viewing a poem as a
"corpse" and to grapple unashamedly with its content and,
where necessary, with its social and personal implications....
What finally makes this a readable and illuminating book
about Robinson is not a poetics, but the exploration of
ideas. Perhaps a book that is only about Robinson's poetry
is impossible to write.

1269 _____, and J. Edwin Whitesell, eds. The Explicator Cyclo-
pedia: Vol. I, Modern Poetry. Chicago: Quadrangle
Books, 1966. Robinson, pp. 245-262. Consists of 16 poems
(24 items) reprinted from The Explicator. Each item is also
listed in regular alphabetical sequence. "Amaryllis," by
William C. Childers (February, 1956). "En Passant," by
Bernice Slote (February, 1957). "Eros Turannos," by
Laurence Perrine (December, 1949). "The Field of Glory,"
by Richard Crowder (February, 1950). "For a Dead Lady,"
by R. H. Super (June, 1945). "For a Dead Lady," by
Richard Crowder (December, 1946). "For a Dead Lady,"
by R. H. Super (June, 1947). "For a Dead Lady," by
E. S. Fussell (March, 1951). "For a Dead Lady," by
Sylvia Hart and E. Paige (May, 1952). "Lost Anchors,"
by Celeste T. Wright (June, 1953). "Luke Havergal,"

by Walter Gierasch (October, 1944). "Luke Havergal,"
by A. A. Raven (December, 1944). "Luke Havergal," by
Mathilde M. Parlett (June, 1945). "Luke Havergal," by
Richard Crowder (November, 1948). "Mr. Flood's Party,"
lines 17-24 by E. S. Ownbey (April, 1950). "New England," by H. H. Waggoner (March, 1952). "New England,"
by Richard E. Amacher (March, 1952). "An Old Story,"
by Richard Crowder (December, 1945). "Richard Cory,"
by Charles Burkhart (November, 1960). "The Sheaves,"
by Richard Crowder (March, 1946). "The Tree in Pamela's
Garden," by Marvin Klotz (January, 1962). Tristram,
Sections IX-X, by Laurence Perrine (May, 1948), (March,
1949). "Veteran Sirens," by Laurence Perrine (November,
1947). "The Whip," by Henry Pettit (April, 1943).

1270 WALDO, Fullerton. "The Earlier E. A. R.: Some Memories
of a Poet in the Making." Outlook, 129 (November 30,
1921), 531-532, 534. Article is a description of Robinson
during his visits to Harvard in 1897-1898 and during the
ten obscure years that followed. Author does not claim to
have really known Robinson, but thinks "a random note or
two of reminiscence, might find their place among the mar-
ginalia of an adequate biography." The thing that impressed Waldo most was Robinson's unending effort to attain "the apple of gold in the picture of silver."

1271 WALKER, Helen. "The Wisdom of Merlin: A Review of Collected Poems." Forum, 67 (February, 1922), 179-181.
Robinson poetry lovers are blessed in the thick volume
recently brought out. If these comprise everything Robinson has ever written, they spell an existence of work and
study and intense feeling such as youth, clamoring to live
life to full, may well envy. Here is a poet who writes of
life--and Merlin--and modern men with the wisdom of Merlin
himself.

1272 WALSH, William Thomas. "Review of Dionysus in Doubt."
Commonweal, 2 (May 13-19, 1925), 26. It is a continuing
record of a difficult personality, acclaimed by many poetry
lovers as the most American, if not the most authentic poet
of our days: and it continues the same elusive coiling of
light and darkness, revelation and concealment, hope and
agnosticism that leave some of us in a troubled doubt regarding the reality of its merits when all is said and done....
In this work he is a preacher who has lost his way back to
the pulpit and wandering rather aimlessly in the outer lights
of many cults and isms.

1273 _____. "Some Recollections of Edwin Arlington Robinson."
2 parts. Catholic World, 155 (August and September,
1942), 703-712 and 522-531. Article is based on the author's

recollection of living in the MacDowell Colony during the
summer of 1929. Robinson was then about sixty-one, and
at the height of the fame that had come to him so late.
In conclusion Walsh says: "I still like to think of him as
Nicodemus.... It may be that a fine mixture of myrrh
and aloes was found in Robinson's work, when all was said
and done, and still more in his charitable heart and deepest intention, perhaps never in any words."

1274 WALTON, Eda Lou. "Irony and Pity in Robinson's Newest
Poem: The Glory of the Nightingales." New York Evening Post, September 13, 1930. The whole is told in Robinson's perfect and fluid blank verse, a medium particularly
his own for the telling of such involuted tales, a blank
verse very different from the more traditional and elaborate form the poet made use of in the Arthurian legends.
Such verse is a fine narrative medium and carries one forward, by means of constant semi-circles, wave upon wave,
idea upon idea, floating to the surface.

1275 _____. "Review of Matthias at the Door." Nation, 133
(October 14, 1931), 403-404. It is a story of the relationship of three men and one woman, and mainly a study of
Matthias, whose faith in himself is utterly destroyed and
he comes to understand the significance of lives other than
his own.... Robinson succeeds because he is capable of
selecting incidents which are highly significant and symbolic. The poet allows his characters fine feelings and
symbolic and highly poetic language. The result is an
achievement of high level.

1276 _____. "Robinson's Women: A Review of Talifer." Nation,
137 (October 11, 1933), 415. The two women in this work
are Althea and Karen, the first a domesticated pussy, the
second a neurotic wildcat. Each one is a projection of
some need in a man, and the man--Talifer--marries Karen,
is disillusioned and turns to Althea. All of these characters are a little tiresome, painted in conventional romantic
poses. It contains some fine passages of poetic philosophy,
and is ultimately beautifully written.

1277 _____. "Defeated Aspirations: A Review of Amaranth."
New York Herald Tribune Books, October 7, 1934. P. 21.

1278 _____. "Review of Amaranth." Nation, 139 (October 17,
1934), 457-458. In this work Robinson deals with what for
him seems like a strange problem. The characters are people who have desired beyond themselves and are lost. Each
one of the many characters has heard the voice of Amaranth, but it is not certain just what Amaranth is--he serves
to free these failures from the hell of self-delusion....

This is the most abstract in treatment of any of the long
narratives, the least dramatic, the least projected from the
inner mind. But its theme is compelling.

1279 _____. "Edwin Arlington Robinson's Last Poem: King
Jasper." New York Herald Tribune Books, 12 (November
24, 1935), 4. This is one of Robinson's better long poems.
It has none of the vagueness of Amaranth, and is more
universal in its appeal. Its only flaw is that Robinson
could not perceive just how, out of all this chaos and destruction, life might, practically speaking, go on.

1280 _____. "Robinson's Last Poem: A Review of King Jasper."
Nation, 141 (December 25, 1935), 749-750. Shortened version of review listed above.

1281 _____. "A Poet's Life." Nation, 147 (October 29, 1938),
460. Review of Hagedorn's biography of Robinson. Hagedorn has written this biography with tenderness but with
something of the quality of understatement that was Robinson's own. It is a very moving story about a life in which,
outwardly, nothing dramatic took place, unless quiet renunciation for the sake of a purpose steadily held is dramatic.

1282 WARING, Walter W. "Appreciation of Edwin Arlington Robinson."
Library Journal, 95 (May 1, 1970), 1743-1744. Review of
collection edited by Richard Cary. This collection offers
pieces written between 1930 and 1969 by a wide selection
of scholars. In general, the methods of approach and
topics treated in the essays are selected for the broadest
representation of the poet. This publication provides the
reader with a record of shifting critical response to the
works of Robinson over a period of nearly 40 years.

1283 _____. "Edwin Arlington Robinson: A Collection of Critical
Essays." Library Journal, 95 (July, 1970), 2480. Review
of collection edited by Francis Murphy. Except for article
by Josephine Miles, the material is reprinted. It was, however, selected to provide the reader with the broadest possible spectrum of views on Robinson's poetry, and for the
most part they do just that. Only two essays, by Coxe and
Waggoner, are duplicated in the book edited by Richard
Cary.

1284 WARREN, Austin. The New England Conscience. Ann Arbor:
University of Michigan Press, 1966. Robinson, pp. 182-193.
I have read that Robinson's letters are flat. The remark
has puzzled me. They are flat only in a Yankee kind of
way: matter-of-fact, blunt. In many ways they are the
best introduction to the poetry, which, when it is not too
short and finely sand-papered, is diffuse: kept going by

what Robinson never lacked in his poetry--a rigid syntax
which reviewers variously ascribed to Browning and Henry
James, neither of whom he seems much to have read.... 
To return to pessimism and conscience: Robinson didn't
in the least relish American so-called optimism. He thought
it the part of wisdom to be prepared for the worst; then
any amelioration is relief, a bonus. Life is a pretty difficult place. Who in his right mind, ever said it wasn't?
That isn't pessimism, that is realism. Pessimism is the
tiresome other side of optimism. The good man has no
business with either illusion.

1285 WARWICK, Diana. "In Roman Bartholow." Life, 81 (March 1,
     1923), 20.

1286 WASSERSTROM, William, ed. A Dial Miscellany. Syracuse:
     Syracuse University Press, 1963. "A Bird's Eye View of
     Edwin Arlington Robinson," by Amy Lowell, pp. 75-87.
     See discussion under Lowell, Amy.

1287 WEARING, Thomas. "Edwin Arlington Robinson--New England
     Poet-Philosopher." Colgate-Rochester Divinity School Bul-
     letin, 14 (February, 1942), 162-174.

1288 WEAVER, John D. "Demands of Poetry Ruled Life of Robin-
     son." Kansas City Star, October 4, 1938. P. 28. Review
     of Hagedorn Biography.

1289 _____. "Robinson's Letters to His Friends." Kansas City
     Star, February 24, 1940. P. 14. Review of Selected Let-
     ters.

1290 WEAVER, Raymond M. "Some Currents and Backwaters of
     Contemporary Poetry." Bookman, 51 (June, 1920), 453-460.
     Article includes comments on Robinson's Lancelot. Any
     modern treatment of the Arthur material challenges compari-
     son at once with some of the illustrious names in English
     literature: Tennyson, Swinburne, Arnold, and Morris, to
     mention only the best known. Robinson's Lancelot is no
     misbegotten changeling in this notable company. The an-
     alysis is subtle, unsentimental, and contagiously sympathetic.

1291 WEBER, Carl Jefferson. "Edwin Arlington Robinson and Har-
     dy." Saturday Review of Literature, 11 (April 27, 1935),
     648. Also includes "Two Sonnets." Article also printed in
     Nation, 140 (May 1, 1935), 508. Presented as letter "To
     the Editor." Raises the question of why no one has ever
     taken any notice of Robinson's poem on Thomas Hardy. It
     was printed in November, 1895 in The Critic, but has not
     appeared since then. It is in the form of a sonnet, with
     the title "For a Book by Thomas Hardy."

1292 _____. "The Cottage Lights of Wessex." <u>Colby Mercury</u>,
6 (February, 1936), 64-67. Based on recollection of the
Memorial service which was held in Gardiner, Maine, May
12, 1935, a service attended by admirers from all over
New England. Most of those who spoke at this affair recalled personal details of Robinson's life, his idiosyncracies,
habits, etc. In all of this, the one thing missing was the
thing that makes Robinson interesting--his poetry. Little
is known about the poet's mental development. Uses the
example of Robinson's sonnet, "For a Book by Thomas
Hardy" to illustrate that so little is known of Robinson's
work.

1293 _____. "Library Notes for Edwin Arlington Robinson's
Birthday." <u>Colby Mercury</u>, 6 (November, 1938), 205-213.
Summarizes the materials which Colby College Library has
acquired or has on loan for an exhibition of Robinson materials, the occasion being Robinson's birthday and the appearance of the first full-length biography, written by
Hermann Hagedorn. In this display are rare books, auto-
graph letters, portraits, and sketches of Robinson. A
good deal of the material is on loan from the library of Mr.
Paul Lemperly of Lakewood, Ohio. In addition to these
manuscripts and printed books there are on exhibition a
number of photographs and drawings of the poet known to
most students as the creator of Richard Cory and Miniver
Cheevy.

1294 _____. "The Sound of Cornish Waves Cold Upon Cornish
Rocks." <u>Colby Mercury</u>, 6 (November, 1938), 215-216.
Suggests that there may be a link between Robinson's line
in <u>Tristram</u>, published in 1927, and that of a similar line
in Thomas Hardy's poem <u>The Famous Tragedy of the Queen
of Cornwall</u>, published in 1923. Whether Robinson learned
of Hardy's work on the Tristram story before or after publication is not known. It is possible  that Robinson was
somewhat critical of Hardy's handling of the love story,
and that he set himself to attempt his own improvement of
it.

1295 _____. "A Maine Poet in a Maine College." <u>Colby Alumnus</u>,
30 (November, 1940), 10-12. Remarks briefly on the growing Thomas Hardy collection at Colby College, and the hopes
with which he approaches the work of acquiring an equal,
if not greater, collection of Robinson material. The Robinson collection should be of greater stature, since the poet
is of Maine descent. He hopes to make it "the most distinguished Robinson Collection that can ever be assembled on
earth."

1296 _____. "Three Newly Discovered Articles by Edwin Arlington

Robinson." Colby Mercury, 7 (December, 1941), 69-72.
The three articles were found in the papers and letters to
Edmund Clarence Stedman, recently deposited in the Library
of the Columbia University. The articles were first published in the editorial column of the "Illustrated Supplement"
of the New York Daily Tribune for Sunday, October 7, 1900,
without Robinson's name. This discovery was made possible
by a remark which Robinson made in a letter to Stedman
about this issue of the paper, together with a reference to
"an enclosure." The enclosure is missing, but this critic
believes it consisted of these three short articles, which
are now published for the first time under Robinson's name.

1297 _____. "Additions to Our Robinson Collection." Colby Mercury, 7 (May, 1942), 94-96. Is a listing of items recently
contributed to the library, most of which are not primary
sources by Robinson but rather books and manuscripts relating to Robinson. Two notable examples are an auto-
graphed copy of Rollo Brown's Next Door to a Poet; and a
first edition copy of Children of the Night. Other items
are discussed which do not relate to Robinson.

1298 _____. "A Robinson Wild-Goose Chase." Colby Mercury,
7 (May, 1942), 96. Brief commentary on an item "by Robinson" which Dr. Jacob Blanck thought he had found early
this year. In The Golden Days Puzzler's Directory, published in 1886, there is an entry signed "1812," believed
to be by Robinson. A page by page search of the magazine from which this directory was compiled was made, but
did not turn up a contribution signed "1812" or one from
Gardiner, Maine. In 1886 Robinson would not have been
quite 17 years old. We are left with a mere surmise: that
Robinson may have sent in a puzzle which he signed
"1812."

1299 _____. "Robinson's Prose: A Retraction." Colby Library
Quarterly, 1 (March, 1943), 31-32. Refers to his article
of December, 1941, in which he printed "three short articles" attributed to Robinson. Later, in December, 1942,
Alice M. Williams was able to support a claim that these
articles were not by Robinson. Weber still thinks "they
sound authentic but has no proof to support his theory,"
and therefore retracts the claim.

1300 _____. "Poet and President." New England Quarterly, 16
(December, 1943), 615-626. Roosevelt's discovery of Robinson is generally well known, but events that led up to and
that followed this famous discovery remain known to only a
few. Article consists of letters from the President to Robinson and to Mrs. Martha Baker Dunn, who had written an
essay and published it in the Atlantic Monthly of September,

1902. Roosevelt's last letter to Robinson is dated March 8,
1918. He died in January, 1919. The poet had received
twelve notes and letters from the President, and carefully
kept them all as long as he lived.

1301 _____, ed. Letters of Edwin Arlington Robinson to Howard
George Schmitt. Waterville, Maine: Colby College Library
Press, 1943. Reviewers remarked that the book was attractive, with good notes and Introduction supplied by the
editor. These letters were written during the last six or
seven years of Robinson's life to a young admirer who had
started reading Robinson's poems in high school. There
are more than sixty of these letters, dated January 9,
1929, to January 22, 1935.

1302 _____. "Edwin Arlington Robinson's Translation of Sophocles." New England Quarterly, 17 (December, 1944), 604-
605. Refers to an article which had stated that Robinson's
translation of Sophocles' Antigone had been destroyed by
the poet. It has now been discovered that some of it is
extant in Harry DeForest Smith's manuscript translations.
and other Greek works now in the Colby Library. Throughout the manuscript there are notes in Robinson's handwriting, and fragments of the composition, which may not be
printed because of Robinson's "solemn" request that this
work never be printed.

1303 _____. "The Jubilee of Robinson's Torrents ...." Colby
Library Quarterly, 2 (February, 1947), 1-12. Article cele-
brates the 50th anniversary of Robinson's first book by
giving something of its history, how the poet came to print
it, what he thought of it, etc. Of the 312 copies, a list
of 112 names has been compiled. This list seems a mere
fragment, yet it could be much shorter. At the end of
1897 Robinson had no copy of the book in his hands....
Article also contains a census of known extant copies--only
56, in private hands, college libraries, public libraries.

1304 _____. "A New Poem by Edwin Arlington Robinson." Colby
Library Quarterly, 2 (February, 1947), 12-13. The new
poem is an octave, in which eight-line form Robinson published 27 known examples. It is certain that he wrote one
other which never achieved print. He wrote it out and
sent it to Miss Edith Brower who pasted it in her copy of
The Torrent .... This book with the poem is now in the
Colby College Library and is here printed for the first time.

1305 _____. "Additions to the Census of The Torrent ...."
Colby Library Quarterly, 2 (August, 1947), 52.

1306 _____. "With Admiration and Love." Colby Library Quarterly,

2 (May, 1948), 85-108.  Article begins with a general background of the subject:  books which are given or received
by a person who values the work for its "association,"
rather than any intrinsic value.  Many such books are
known to exist or to have existed.  Article continues with
a list of 100 books in the Colby Library which are valuable
for this reason.  Many of these volumes are associated with
Robinson, books he gave or books he received from friends.

1307          .  "Two More 'Torrents.'"  Colby Library Quarterly,
2 (August, 1948), 122-123.  See also CLQ, 2 (May, 1949),
161-162.

1308          .  "Two Friends of Robinson."  Colby Library Quarterly, 2 (February, 1949), 147-152.  Article is about Mr.
and Mrs. Thomas Sergeant Perry, whom Robinson met at
one of his annual visits to the Colony at Peterborough.
Focus of article is the portrait of Robinson which Perry
created, and the gift of Perry's entire library to Colby
College.  The other gift was that of Mrs. Pulsifer whose
husband had been poetry editor of The Outlook.  This library of poetry was rich in materials about and by Robinson.

1309          .  "'The Growth of Lorraine':  A Manuscript."  Colby
Library Quarterly, 2 (August, 1949), 187.  This note concerns a photostat of a manuscript in the Pierpont Morgan
Library which the librarian has sent to Colby College.
The sonnet "The Growth of Lorraine" was published in 1902
in Captain Craig and all subsequent publications of the
sonnet have been based on this 1902 text.  The manuscript
of Captain Craig and Other Poems is in the Colby College
Library.  The photostat received from Pierpont Morgan Library is apparently of an earlier origin.

1310          .  "Humphry's Catalogue of Robinson's Library."
Colby Library Quarterly, 2 (November, 1950), 271-272.
It is rather commonly accepted that Robinson's poetry has
"a bookish background," that he was a wide and careful
reader, and had a long and accurate memory.  It was not
however, until Humphry published his full-length catalogue of the poet's library, did scholars know just how extensive was the poet's personal collection of the exact nature of it....  Robinson is known to have checked out very
few books from the library--college or public.  Most of the
books that he used, he owned.  His library is now at Colby
College.

1311          .  "Another 'Torrent' Turns Up."  Colby Library Quarterly, 3 (February, 1954), 220.

1312        _____. "What's In a Name? or in a Signature?" Manu-
            scripts, 8 (1956), 185-188. Article is a brief discussion
            of the different ways authors seem to write their signa-
            tures. Some, like Hardy, have a great variety of signa-
            tures, whereas others, like Dickens and Wordsworth never
            vary. Another author whose letters and manuscripts seem-
            ingly exhibit two different hands is Edwin Arlington Robin-
            son. In his Gardiner High School and Harvard College
            days, he wrote a round, easily legible hand. But in the
            twentieth century, his letters recorded an increasingly
            microscopic trend, and by the time he reached the 1920's
            he was writing letters in which there are often words that
            are almost wholly illegible.

1313    WEEKS, Edward A. "Lost: A Wife and a Genius: Review of
            The Man Who Died Twice." Independent, 113 (July 5,
            1924), 20. A powerful psychological drama which tells the
            story of a man's unpardonable sin--the conscious waste of
            his genius. Fernando Nash was a musician who knew from
            boyhood that he had but to wait to hear the music of his
            symphony "blown down by choral horns out of a star."
            But he sold his birthright, sank himself in dissipation for
            twenty years and at forty-five he was beating a bass drum
            for the Salvation Army and waiting for death.

1314    WEEKS, Lewis E., Jr. "Edwin Arlington Robinson's Poetics."
            Twentieth Century Literature, 11 (October, 1966), 131-145.
            Reprinted in Cary, ed. (1969), pp. 225-242. Although
            Robinson was content to write poetry without theorizing
            extensively about it and had a rather low opinion of self-
            criticism and self-interpretation, it is possible to discover
            an interesting and illuminating "poetics" in his letters and
            works. This subject is particularly pertinent in a period
            when rapid change, automation, and nuclear arms bring
            bewilderment, terror, and inspiration all at the same time....
            In view of the present dehumanization apparent in much of
            our culture, it is worthwhile to reexamine the compassionate
            concern of one of America's greatest poets. The question
            of Why does a poet write is of importance to Robinson.

1315        _____. "Maine in the Poetry of Edwin Arlington Robinson."
            Colby Library Quarterly, 8 (June, 1969), 317-334. There
            are a number of Maine influences in Robinson's poetry, al-
            though he is a poet who transcends the regional and reveals
            the universal. His imagery owes much to the sea, streams,
            towns, farms, and forests of Maine; the weather also had
            its impact. Robinson's chief interest was in character, and
            there were a number of recognizable "Maine" types: the
            tall-tale artist, the eccentric individualist, the ne'er-do-
            well, the strong-willed stoic, and the gossip. His themes
            were frequently related to Maine character and times. The

Protestant Ethic in both its positive and negative aspects
played its role.  The theme of decay and dissolution was
probably most prominent and revealed itself in his characters and in the images that pervade much of his poetry.

1316  WEIRICK, Bruce.  From Whitman to Sandburg in American
      Poetry.  New York:  Macmillan, 1924.  "The Contemporary
      Renaissance:  The Note of Futility in New England and New
      York," pp. 184-192.  Robinson offers us a world of art,
      of subtlety, of libraries and books, of curious cultivated
      persons of immaculate clothes and interesting psychology.
      He is a poet of infinite polish, infinite care, and impec-
      cable reserve.  In him we have less nature and more art.
      He has lived for poetry and nothing else, and the result
      is to-day a collected volume of 600 pages.  He has never
      succeeded in impressing himself on the general American
      public.  His fame has been of slow growth, and with the
      few.  The question arises as to how much of a success is
      it; and how much of it is apt to endure?

1317  WELLS, Henry Willis.  New Poets from Old.  New York:  Co-
      lumbia University Press, 1940.  Robinson, pp. 90-97, 316-
      320.  With the high purpose of one who believes equally
      in reason and inspiration, Robinson winnows chaff from
      grain, preserving the emotional and intellectual richness
      of nineteenth-century verse with the poise of spirit repre-
      sentative of humanity at its best, or of the classical world.
      He acquires a richer tragic sense because he avoids senti-
      mental morbidity, and he has a richer affirmative nature
      because he shuns uncritical and mawkish optimism.  In
      Robinson we find the strength and delicacy of the romantic
      tradition without its weakness and effeminacy.  Above all
      he shows an interest in psychological problems.

1318  _____.  The American Way of Poetry.  New York:  Columbia
      University Press, 1943.  Reprinted New York:  Russell
      & Russell, 1965.  "New England Conscience," pp. 89-105.
      Robinson has one foot on the lowest rung of the religious
      ladder, the other foot on the hard ground.  To understand
      Robinson's attitude, we must look at the past.  He holds
      much of the thought and still more of the coloring found
      in the fading glow of 19th-Century New England culture....
      Robinson is the poet of the soul as seen partly with modern
      eyes and partly from the intense self-scrutiny of the tradi-
      tional New England ideal.  He is a natural mystic, a discern-
      ing moralist, an intuitive psychologist, and our last major
      author to write with deep marks of the New England con-
      science.

1319  WELLS, Louise Rucker.  "The Metrics and Imagery of Edwin
      Arlington Robinson as Exhibited in Sixteen of His Blank

Verse Poems." University of New Mexico, 1933. M.A.
thesis.

1320 WESCOTT, Glenway. "A Succession of Poets." Partisan Review, 50 (1983), 392-406. Discusses Moody, Robinson,
and Maxwell Bodenheim. Article written on the occasion
of the 75th anniversary of the MacDowell Colony in Peterborough. Wescott visited MacDowell in 1921 and in 1957,
and this article is based upon his casual acquaintance with
a variety of poets whom he met during this period.... At
the time he did not know anything about Robinson's melancholy life, dedicated to drink much of the time. But there
were shadows of it in his face: a play of expressions
signifying that he was accustomed to hopeless, lethal embarrassments. Robinson was a man of bad luck, famous
but unsuccessful.

1321 WESTBROOK, Perry D. Acres of Flint: Writers of Rural New
England, 1870-1900. Metuchen, N,J.: Scarecrow Press,
1951. Revised edition, 1981. Robinson, pp. 99-101. Remarks compare aspects of Robinson with those of Mary Wil-
kins Freeman, of whom Robinson wrote "I rather admire her
frankness and nerve." Robinson devoted a lifetime of probing the psychological wreckage of Calvinism.... Like many
of the local-color writers of the period, Robinson created
the mythical community of Tilbury Town for his characters
to live in. Most writers did not go so far as Robinson.
There is little of the bucolic or small-town cosiness in
Robinson, built on the enduring Yankee qualities of humor
or self-dependence. Robinson's is a community of solitaries,
loneliness, despair, drunkenness--a portrait that is frequently too pessimistic.

1322 WHEELOCK, John Hall. "A Friend of Young Poets." Mark
Twain Quarterly, 2 (Spring, 1938), 20. Recalls sending
Robinson a copy of his first published book in 1911, and
with characteristic kindness towards young poets, Robinson
responded with a friendly note asking Wheelock to come see
him some evening. At the time Robinson was working on a
new edition of Captain Craig, and later sent Wheelock an
inscribed copy. This book did not do any better than the
earlier ones, and Robinson tried his hand at playwriting.
He soon came back to poetry, winning his first real response with the magnificent "Man Against the Sky."

1323 WHICHER, George F. "A Poet to His Friend: A Review of
Untriangulated Stars." New York Herald Tribune Books,
January 11, 1948. P. 4.

1324 WHIPPLE, Leon. "Scripts for the Summer Solstice: Tristram."
Survey, 58 (July 1, 1927), 390. The old legend has never

been told with more dignity and emotion, nor in lines that
possess such human simplicity and life-likeness.

1325  WHIPPLE, T. K.  Spokesmen: Modern Writers and American
      Life.  New York: D. Appleton, 1928.  Robinson, pp. 45-
      69.  For Robinson human existence consists in suffering
      and ends in defeat.  Always defeat, always failure:  one
      would not have believed there were so many ways to fail.
      There are total failures, partial failures, material failures,
      spiritual failures.  As a rule Robinson regards his failures
      with pity rather than contempt.  He has tended to see hu-
      man life as an inescapable tragedy of frustration, which is
      only made the bleaker because we cannot bring ourselves
      to admit it.  The dark actuality of defeat is always in con-
      trast to the false brightness of human illusions and hopes,
      and is the source of his irony and of his tragic pity.  On
      the other hand there is a mystery of faith and hope in
      Something that prevents the human race from self-
      destruction, some Meaning, some glimmer of Light.

1326  WHITE, Gertrude.  "Robinson's 'Captain Craig': A Reinter-
      pretation."  English Studies (Amsterdam), 47 (December,
      1966), 432-439.  Begins with a brief review of critical com-
      ment on "Captain Craig," reporting that the poem seems
      not to have received adequate treatment.  Much that has
      been said about the poem is untrue or irrelevant.  Article
      is based upon several beliefs:  this poem is different from
      virtually all of Robinson's other poems; it is not and was
      not intended to be a character sketch, nor is it a philo-
      sophical treatise.  This poem is largely psychological and
      subjective, interior rather than exterior.  It is neither the
      Captain nor his philosophy which form the center of the
      poem, but rather the effect that both have upon four young
      men of Tilbury Town.

1327  WHITE, Lee A.  "And What of Nimbo?  After Fifteen Stanzas."
      Detroit News, June 26, 1922.

1328  WHITE, Newman I.  "Review of Collected Poems."  Sewanee
      Review, 30 (July-September, 1922), 365-369.  Whatever
      may be said of other contemporary American poets, it can
      never be said of Robinson that his reputation was a mush-
      room growth.  When Captain Craig was published twenty
      years ago it impressed very few people.  Robinson has ad-
      vanced no new theories of poetry, engaged in no critical
      controversies, and made no effort to impress his personality
      on the public.  His sole contribution is a solid body of po-
      etry, written in conventional verse forms, but using a most
      unconventional and modern language.  He lacks an easy op-
      timism and a defiant pessimism which will restrict his popu-
      larity.  The present volume contains all of Robinson's

published poems except a few of the earlier ones, omitted
by the poet as below his standard.

1329 _____. "Review of The Glory of the Nightingales and Introduction to Edwin Arlington Robinson by Charles Cestré."
South Atlantic Quarterly, 30 (July, 1931), 334-335. The
Cestré book triumphs over the charge of pessimism and
defeatism and shows us a poet who accepts life graciously,
with a stoical decorum, sees its real essence in the inner
rather than the outer struggle, and finds partial solvents
in sympathetic, aloof observation and controlled humor....
Of Robinson's poem this critic says it has just enough action on which to hang a melodrama which takes place mainly
in the mind. There is the usual interest in the intellectual
power of Robinsonian conversation and the suggestive power
of the imagery. It is a poem not unworthy of America's
greatest psychological artist.

1330 WHITE, William. "Edwin Arlington Robinson and A. E. Housman." Colby Library Quarterly, 2 (August, 1947), 42-43.
The names of these two poets have been linked on occasion, but there is not much evidence that Housman cared
greatly for Robinson. Robinson, on the other hand,
thought very highly of A Shropshire Lad, and believed
Housman "had come to stay." In March, 1923, Robinson
wrote to Mrs. Laura Richards praising Houseman, but now
another letter has come to light, in which Robinson turns
down the opportunity of writing an Introduction to Housman's Lad, an edition published by a Mr. Edmund R.
Brown in 1918.

1331 _____. "The Library of Edwin Arlington Robinson." Papers of the Bibliographical Society of America, 45 (Summer,
1951), 185-186. Review of work by James Humphry. This
work cites 308 titles alphabetically by author. The brief
Preface leaves out much that should be explained, and is
more provoking than informative. There is some carelessness in handling material in the preface. Although the book
is full of inadequacies, it does fulfill its compiler's aim to
give students and scholars more complete information about
Robinson's library than has heretofore been available, and
tells us what books, once Robinson's, are now at Colby.

1332 _____. "What Is a Collector's Item: Emily Dickinson, Edwin Arlington Robinson, D. H. Lawrence?" American Book
Collector, 6 (Summer, 1956), 6-8. Is a bibliographical
study and includes Robinson's Tilbury Town: Selected
Poems, edited by Lawrence Thompson (1953). This, of
course, is not a collector's item, although another book,
Collected Poems, quotes from three unpublished letters from
the poet to Mr. George Lathan, Mr. Arthur Gledhill, and

Miss Edith Brower, and this "squeezes" this work into the
category of collectible items.

1333 _____. "A Bibliography of Edwin Arlington Robinson, 1941-
1963." Colby Library Quarterly, 7 (March, 1965), 1-26.
Brief, accurate listing mostly by dates, including the fol-
lowing categories: Part I. Works Separately Published.
Part II. Letters. Part III. Work Originally Published in
Periodicals. Part IV. Biographical and Critical Material:
Books and Periodicals. Part V. Reviews of Individual
Books.

1334 _____. "Where Is Edwin Arlington Robinson?" American
Book Collector, 16 (March, 1966), 7. Remarks on a new
study, The Twenties Poetry and Prose, edited by Langford
and Taylor (1966), which omits completely any mention of
Robinson. Notes several other books which have mentioned
him. Can his reputation have slipped so far that a book
on his most productive decade does not mention the creator
of "Richard Cory," "Miniver Cheevy," and "Luke Havergal"?

1335 _____. "Edwin Arlington Robinson in India." American
Book Collector, 16 (May, 1966), 32. Is a brief review of
Studies in American Literature by Egbert S. Oliver (1965)
published in New Delhi. Although published in India, the
book is in English. There are essays on Emerson, Thoreau, Melville, Whitman, E. E. Cummings, and one piece
of particular interest on Robinson: "Robinson's Dark-Hill-
to-Climb Image," which concludes with the belief that Robinson's gallery of studies in human destiny is one of the
most challenging and magnificent which any modern writer
has given to the reading world.

1335a _____. "Three Literary Giants." American Book Collector,
19 (April-May, 1969), 4. Includes comment on Letters to
Edith Brower. The Robinson book, containing 189 unpublished letters written from 1897 to 1930 to one of his earliest admirers, is by far the most interesting, the most attractive, and the most important of the three under review.
Mr. Richard Cary, of Colby College, where the letters are
now deposited, provides a lucid introduction, enough anno-
tation to make the letters understandable, and includes
Edith Brower's unpublished memoir on Robinson as well as
her 1897 review of The Children of the Night. With Cary's
notes and comments, the volume is almost a biography.
The Maine poet seems to come alive, not always lively and
more often sad and unhappy than gay, frequently filled with
self-doubt.

1336 _____. "A Bibliography of Edwin Arlington Robinson,

1964-1969." Colby Library Quarterly, 8 (December, 1969),
448-462. Brief, accurate listing mostly by dates, including
the following categories: Part I. Works Separately Published. Part II. Letters. Part III. Work Published in
Periodicals. Part IV. Biographical and Critical Material.
1. Books. 2. Periodicals. 3. Reviews of Individual
Books.

1337 _____. "Remember Edwin Arlington Robinson?" Literary
Sketches, 10 (September, 1970), 8-9.

1338 _____. Edwin Arlington Robinson: A Supplementary Bibliography. Kent, Ohio: Kent State University Press, 1971.
Serif series; supplement to Hogan, 1936.

1339 _____. "Robinson in Leary's Articles ... 1950-1967."
Colby Library Quarterly, 9 (September, 1971), 374-375.
Surveys the latest work by Leary with the idea of observing which writers are the most popular: Faulkner with 837
articles clearly leads the pack; Robinson with only 76 articles is a fairly good showing for a poet whom many feel is
undeservedly neglected.... Leary makes no attempt to be
exhaustive. In fact he has inadvertently omitted 25 or 30
articles, and there are some printing errors.

1340 WHITING, B. J. "Gawain: His Reputation, His Courtesy and
His Appearance in Chaucer's Squire's Tale." Medieval
Studies, 9 (1947), 189-234. Robinson, pp. 212-214 et
passim. Article covers a wide range of discussion, and
Robinson's character therefore occupies relatively little
space. Whiting finds Robinson's portrayal somewhat inconsistent from poem to poem in the Arthurian trilogy, beginning as a thoughtful, inquisitive, and friendly figure. In
Lancelot, Gawaine's friendship for Lancelot is revealed, his
later enmity, and his ultimate repentance in such a way
that his Gawaine is more favorably presented than the character in any other accounts of the intrigues which led to
the break between Lancelot and Arthur. In Tristram, the
portrait is perhaps one of the most appealing of Gawain in
modern poetry.

1341 WILDER, Amos N. The Spiritual Aspects of the New Poetry.
New York: Harper & Brothers, 1940. Robinson, p. 174
et passim. The later poems of Edwin Arlington Robinson
are of inexhaustible interest. Their significance has been
commonly missed, but they illuminate with great power the
modern situation of scrupulous and sensitive men canvassing
their failure. They are most frequently colloquies of half-
discerned souls in a twilight of damnation--clairvoyant,
acid, sometimes bitter, sometimes chastened. These are
like Dante's souls in the Inferno that suffer the slow rain

of burning flakes of fire which symbolize tormenting memories and remorse.

1342   WILDER, Thornton.  "Wilder Lauds Story Poem by Robinson:
       Matthias at the Door."  Chicago Daily Tribune, December
       12, 1931.  Pp. 17-18.  It is not a story and not an illus-
       tration:  it is poetry.  But here is a kind of poetry that
       is out of fashion.  To those who recognize the poetic ex-
       perience only in impulsive cries as arising from primary
       emotions, it has little to offer.  Little also to those who
       seek brief, miraculous notation of what the eye sees in
       nature.  To those who recognize poetry in what may hastily
       be called the grand style it brings much, though singularly
       devoid of handsome similes and frank patterns in vowels
       and consonants.

1343   WILKINSON, Marguerite.  "Review of Lancelot."  New York
       Times, April 11, 1920.  P. 170.  It has been well thought
       out, well felt and well made.  It is not a great poem, but
       no important criticism can be brought against it.  The lines
       are firm and flawless, but he can show us the color and
       texture of life and make us feel the heat of it in those old
       days of myth and magic.

1344   _____.  "A Poet Tells a Story:  Avon's Harvest."  New
       York Times, June 26, 1921.  P. 27.  He has written the
       kind of story which most writers would have made into
       crass melodrama, and he has saved it to tragedy by sheer
       intellectuality.  It is not a pleasant story, but it has the
       crispness, the conciseness and the bitter humor which makes
       such tales bearable and interesting.

1345   _____.  Contemporary Poetry.  New York: Macmillan, 1924.
       Robinson, pp. 67-72.  Prints four poems, "The False Gods,"
       "Neighbors," "The Gift of God," and "The Dark Hills,"
       with brief introductory page.  In shrewd understanding of
       mankind and as a brilliant analyst of character, Robinson
       has no superior.  He defines personality with unerring pre-
       cision and his sympathy is exquisite, his humor urbane,
       his irony wise.  By virtue of sure intellectual insight he is
       sometimes a great poet.  His technique, too, is always ad-
       mirable.

1346   _____.  "A Biographer of Souls."  Women's Press, 21 (May,
       1927), 329-331.

1347   _____.  New Voices.  New York: Macmillan, 1928.  Robinson,
       pp. 354-357.  Brief remarks based on "Richard Cory,"
       "Miniver Cheevy," and "Flammonde."  Unlike his contempo-
       raries, Robinson is a poet of intellectuals; he is not a poet
       of the people.  His humor is restrained and civil.  Even his

tragedies are urbane.  He writes with a quiet distinction of
manner that is sometimes annoying to all but intellectual
aristocrats.  He must have rubbed shoulders with life and
borne the brunt of many burdens and known life's give and
take.  For his sympathy is exquisite.  He must have been
familiar with many tragedies, for he has a rare understanding of a few.  But his poetry is far from the common earth
and from the feeling of the folk.  Even if we are unwilling
to call him a great poet, we must admit that he is an exceedingly brilliant one, with a sure sense of personal values, a rare power of discrimination between this and that,
and the essential nobleness of gesture which is part of being a gentleman.

1348  WILLIAMS, Alice Meacham.  "Edwin Arlington Robinson, Jour-
      nalist."  New England Quarterly, 15 (December, 1942),
      715-724.  Article makes use of six letters from Robinson
      and two from Edmund Clarence Stedman to Robinson on the
      subject of Robinson's attempt to publish some prose around
      1900.  Stedman urged him to do so, giving him letters of
      introduction to the New York Evening Post and the New York
      Tribune.  It is almost certain that Robinson published a piece
      on the editorial page, October 7, 1900, that filled about half
      of the fourth column, "The Balm of Custom."  On the basis
      of other letters in the Stedman Collection and an interview
      granted by Robinson in 1931, it seems likely that this edi-
      torial is Robinson's, and that it is the only journalistic
      prose which the poet ever saw in print.

1349  WILLIAMS, Stanley T.  "Edwin Arlington Robinson."  Chapter
      69 in Literary History of the United States, edited by
      Robert E. Spiller et al.  New York:  Macmillan, 1948.  Pp.
      1157-1170.  Robinson wound his solitary horn about his
      dark tower, and intellectual Childe Roland in our twentieth
      century literature.  Somber, introspective, he reminds us
      of Hawthorne, to whom he was devoted, in the scrutiny of
      delicate moral impulses and in his sensitivity to spiritual
      tragedy.  He suffered acutely under poverty, obscurity,
      and misunderstanding.  He explored the enigmas in other
      lives, recording his findings in his poems of souls warped
      by spiritual conflicts.  He saw life:  much darkness and
      a little light.  Man is betrayed less by circumstance than
      by his own character.  He absorbed into his thought and
      art the best of the old in American poetry and became the
      first of his generation to understand, however darkly, the
      new.

1350  WILLIAMS, William Carlos.  "Eat Rocks."  Nation, 167 (October
      30, 1948), 498-499.  Review of biography by Emery Neff.
      Did Robinson come at the end of a period, or was he in
      truth the great progenitor of the modern in its best sense,

and does he, rather belong to that? Neff does not really
answer the question, but seems inclined to align Robinson
with the modern era. At the beginning of his career he
stayed with the old forms and the American language, but
it did not get him very far. He would not let go of his
style. He stayed on the ball, he followed it unrelentingly.
No man has had more courage through adversity than he.
Rimbaud said, "Eat rocks," and Robinson did.

1351  WILLIAMS-ELLIS, A. "We Speak as We Can: The Man Who
Died Twice." Spectator, 132 (June 28, 1924), 1044. It is
not good enough. There must be in the actual narrative
of any poem a certain narrowness. There will be fewer
minor characters, for instance, and less worldly detail.
For this the characteristic qualities of verse--epigrammatic
and emotional--are to compensate. But in this poem we
are defrauded. Yet in prose and with all the additions
proper to a prose form the story might have been made
most acceptable.

1352  WILSON, Edmund. "Mr. Robinson's Moonlight: A Review of
Roman Bartholow." Dial, 74 (May, 1923), 515-517. Reprinted in The Shores of Light (1952), pp. 36-38. This is
one of the most arid products of a mind which has always
run much into the sands. Will grant that Robinson's shadowy world has an authentic relation to the real one, but
cannot forgive the absence of poetry. Surely a poem
should be beautiful as well as interesting: it is beauty
which makes it a poem. Roman Bartholow, though it sometimes interests, almost never rises to beauty.... Yet
Robinson has already given us enough to put us forever in
his debt. He is one of the few first-rate artists of the
older generation, and even his artistic failures are those
of a great and original mind.

1353  _____. "The Muses Out of Work: Tristram." New Republic, 50 (May 11, 1927), 319. Reprinted in The Shores of
Light: A Literary Chronicle of the Twenties and Thirties,
by Edmund Wilson. New York: Farrar, Straus & Young,
1952. Pp. 197-198. Robinson's work is discussed in article
devoted to several modern poets. Of Tristram, he says:
"... it has been extravagantly praised in some quarters,
and is undoubtedly more readable than the other two
Arthurian poems, but its lights are too low-burning and
evanescent to justify the whole of a long narrative that
reads at its worst like a movie scenario, and at its best
like a novel of adultery of the 'nineties, full of long well-
bred conversations of which the metaphysical archness
sounds peculiarly incongruous in the mouths of the heroes
of medieval legend."

1354        _____. Axel's Castle: A Study in the Imaginative Litera-
           ture of 1870 to 1930. New York: Scribner's, 1931. Rob-
           inson, passim. Treats principally the Symbolist movement
           --English, American, and French figures. Robinson was
           never identified with this group.

1355   WILSON, James Southall. "Review of Dionysus in Doubt."
           Virginia Quarterly Review, 1 (July, 1925), 311-320. Long
           article discusses eight volumes of poetry, including Robin-
           son's Dionysus ..., of which the reviewer says "an ap-
           praisal is a vaguely dangerous undertaking." If this vol-
           ume does not contain his best work, it is yet a distinctive
           and distinguished book. The sonnets prove again the poet's
           mastery of the form. Some of the longer poems are too
           coldly intellectual. It is regrettable that the very traits
           which make Robinson great are those which limit his popu-
           larity.

1356        _____. "Whirligigs of Time and Taste: Review of Collected
           Poems" [and "Cavender's House"]. Virginia Quarterly Re-
           view, 4 (January, 1930), 151-160. Article touches on a
           dozen or more books about poetry and by poets, of which
           the reviewer says he does not know which is more confus-
           ing. In general his remarks are mostly negative. The
           poets of the earlier years of the century have reached fifty.
           Those whose work is intellectual rather than "glamorous"
           continue, perhaps with a ripened wisdom, the work of their
           earlier years. Edwin Arlington Robinson's "Cavender's
           House" is a clairvoyant psychograph, but Robinson's Col-
           lected Poems may easily be one of the season's most impor-
           tant publications.

1357        _____. "Review of Selected Letters." American Literature,
           12 (January, 1941), 512-514. Book is a short collection,
           beginning in 1890 and ending in early 1935, about two months
           before he died. The outline of his life, his unchanging
           characteristics and ideas, his attitude toward his poetry
           and to life, his judgments of many contemporary poets,
           and his fundamental beliefs are all here in the mosaic that
           these selected letters build. It is a readable and also an
           amusing book; but it is also a book that builds up a clear
           and valuable total impression of a personality.

1358   WILSON, Milton. "Edwin Arlington Robinson." Canadian
           Forum (Toronto), 26 (March, 1947), 286. Review of biog-
           raphy by Yvor Winters.

1359   WINTERS, Yvor. "A Cool Master." Poetry, 19 (February,
           1922), 278-288. Has been reprinted several times, includ-
           ing Murphy, ed. (1970), pp. 8-14. This man has the cul-
           ture to know that to those to whom philosophy is

comprehensible it is not a matter of the first importance;
and he knows that these people are not greatly impressed
by the ballyhoo statement of the principles of social or
spiritual salvation. A few times he has given his opinion,
but quietly and intelligently, and has then passed on to
other things. A man's philosophical belief or attitude is
certain to be an important part of his milieu, and as a
part of his milieu may give rise to perceptions, images....
Much praise has fallen to Robinson because he deals with
people, "humanity," and this is a fallacy of inaccurate
brains. Humanity is simply Robinson's physical milieu; the
thing, the compound of the things, he sees. It is not the
material that makes a poem great, but the perception and
organization of that material. Robinson's greatness lies
not in the people of whom he has written, but in the perfect balance, the infallible precision with which he has
stated their cases.

1360 _____. "Religious and Social Ideas in the Didactic Work of
Edwin Arlington Robinson." Arizona Quarterly, 1 (Spring,
1945), 70-85. Includes remarks on "Cassandra," "Demos,"
"Man Against the Sky," "Dionysus in Doubt," and "On the
Way." Reprinted in Cary, ed. (1969), pp. 134-146. Most
of the ideas are few and vague, and they are embodied in
Robinson's weakest poetry, but they are the product of a
great poet, and must receive their share of attention.
There is already too much tendency to look for Robinson's
philosophy, and this in the long run will damage his reputation. To understand and place his religious views, one
must review the New England Calvinist tradition. His social views are generally centered in the rights of the common man. Robinson was in no sense a philosophical think-
er. He was a man with a great gift for writing certain
kinds of poetry and with a stubborn common sense which
prevented a large number of his poems on themes of the
sort which he understood from being corrupted by the
weaker side of his nature.

1361 _____. Edwin Arlington Robinson. Norfolk, Conn.: New
Directions Press, 1946. 160 pages, Makers of Modern Literature Series. Reprinted 1972. Consists of the following
chapters: Robinson's Life; New England Background; Literary Influences on Robinson's Style; The Shorter Poems;
The Three Arthurian Poems; The Other Long Poems; The
Poems of Medium Length; Conclusion, Bibliography, and
Index. Concludes that long poems are largely a waste.
Winters says: "I have always felt a certain deficiency ...
is easy to indicate but is not easy to define with any precision; it is a certain dryness, a lack of richness in the
language." The chapter "The Shorter Poems" was reprinted
in Murphy, ed. (1970), pp. 40-59. Nearly all of Robinson's

best poems appear to deal with particular persons and situations; in these poems his examination is careful and intelligent, his method is analytic, and his style is mainly very
distinguished. Robinson exhibits a taste for practical morality, a passionate curiosity about individual dramas, and
is guided by the moral and spiritual values of the general
Christian tradition. In his more philosophic poems he is
almost always careless in his thinking and equally careless
in his style.

1362 _____. In Defense of Reason. New York: Alan Swallow,
1947. Robinson, passim. This volume is a reprint of
Primitivism and Decadence (1937); Maule's Curse (1938);
and The Anatomy of Nonsense (1943). Robinson is not
discussed, but is referred to several times.

1363 _____. "Problems of a Family Man." Poetry, 70 (August,
1947), 285-286. Article is a letter to the editor regarding
a review of his book on Robinson by Mr. W. T. Scott.
Scott gives the Winters biography good marks, but objects
to a number of minor errors, most of which are misprints.
Winters defends himself, saying: "I have a fairly exacting
job, I have a family, I am active in community affairs, and
I do not live in an air-tight room. I am not a perfect proof-
reader. I realize that I should be, and I envy those who
achieve perfection."

1364 _____. Uncollected Essays and Reviews, edited by Francis
Murphy. Chicago: Alan Swallow, 1973. Reprints "A Cool
Master," pp. 3-10, and "Religious and Social Ideas in the
Didactic Work of Edwin Arlington Robinson," pp. 288-303.

1365 WISEHART, M. K. "'By Jove!' Said Roosevelt, 'It Reads Like
the Real Thing!'" American Magazine, 105 (April, 1928),
34-35.

1366 WOLF, H. R. "Edwin Arlington Robinson and the Integration
of Self," in Modern American Poetry, edited by J. Mazzaro.
New York: David McKay, 1970. Pp. 40-58. The poetry
of Robinson insists on an integrity of self, on the possibility of the mind's knowing itself fully and arranging itself
coherently. The effort and inability of Robinson's characters to achieve this integrity result in his predominant tones
and attitudes: low-keyed psychic tragedies and elegies for
undiscovered and unintegrated selves. The quest for songs
undreamed of and unknown puts him in the tradition of romance and Romantic literature, a tradition, that he uses
quite self-consciously; but, as it was for Freud, the grail
is located in the mind, and we must think of his genre finally as psychological romance and his poignancy as lying
between the lines of realism and idealism. When we consider

that he was writing of this quest at a time of idealistic
uncertainty, at the crossroads of late Victorian positivism
and psychoanalytic origins, his task becomes clear.

1367 WOOD, Clement. "Review of Lancelot." New York Call, May
16, 1920. P. 11. The poem opens at the period in the
Arthurian triangle when Lancelot, who has seen the grail,
has determined to leave Camelot and Guinevere forever,
and follow the lonely marsh-light that the knights hailed
as the true gleam. Guinevere tempts him out of this.
Arthur and his knights return, and find what the purblind
king has shut his eyes to so long. Lancelot flees, and
Guinevere is to be burned at the stake. Lancelot returns
and rescues her, taking her to his castle of Joyous Gard.
Later he surrenders her, but the poison of the situation
has raised up enemies in the king's own household, especially in his illegitimate son, Modred. Lancelot, too late,
goes to Arthur's aid and arrives after the battle in the
north, in which Arthur and Modred alike received their
death-wounds. Lancelot makes one final visit to Guinevere,
who has become a nun, and begs her to come with him.
She refuses and Lancelot disappears forever. Lancelot is
life, albeit a gray and grim vision of it. It is a great tale,
greatly told. American poetry is richer for the aching disillusionment of Robinson's art.

1368 _____. Poets of America. New York: E. P. Dutton, 1925. "Robinson: The Darkening Hill," pp. 119-141.
Mainly a biographical and family sketch. Rarely do we find
a poet whose message is so simple and unified as that of
Robinson. It is that mankind has failed: a bleak and
somber judgment. A comparison of earliest and latest volumes indicates little growth; nor was growth needed to en-
title him to the highest laurels among our living singers.
Acid drawings of human failure, a failed technique, a sense
of crashing drama, an astounding felicity of phrase, were
his from his beginning. It is worth noting that the poetic
vocabulary, long divorced from life, which still mars much
of our current piping, is eliminated at the start from this
poetry.

1369 WOODALL, Allen Earl. "Edwin Arlington Robinson." Poet-
Lore, 43 (1937), 363.

1370 WOODBRIDGE, Homer E. "A Review of Van Zorn." Dial, 58
(January 16, 1915), 47-48. The character of Van Zorn
is hazy and indistinct. The other people in the play are
human enough and the plot is simple. Into the lives of
three entangled persons, Van Zorn comes with his uncanny
powers of reading people's secrets. He enters as a potent
influence, saves one of them from suicide, persuades the

woman to break her engagement, and induces the third to
accept the situation philosophically.

1371  WOODRESS, James, et al., eds. American Literary Scholarship: An Annual Survey, 22 vols. Durham: Duke University Press, 1963-1984. Robinson represented in the
following: 1963, by Charles T. Davis, pp. 170-172. 1964,
by J. Albert Robbins, p. 138; by Ann Stanford, p. 193.
1965, by J. Albert Robbins, p. 152; by Ann Stanford, pp.
208-210, 215, 219. 1966, by Gorham Munson, pp. 189, 198-
210; by Harry Finestone, pp. 254, 263. 1967, by Brom
Weber and James Woodress, pp. 221-224, 210, 232. 1968,
by Gorham Munson and Ann Stanford, pp. 238-239, 244.
1969, by Patrick F. Quinn, p. 199; by Richard Crowder,
pp. 252-253, 261-265; by A. Kingley Weatherhead, p. 292.
1970, by Bernice Slote, p. 69; by Richard Crowder, pp.
280-287, 293-299, 304-305. 1971, by Richard Crowder, pp.
277-278, 288-290. 1972, by Alvin H. Rosenfield, pp. 312,
322-324. 1973, by Richard Crowder, pp. 304, 321-322; by
Rolf Lunden, pp. 456-457. 1974, by Richard Crowder, pp.
321-322, 332-335; by Linda Wagner, p. 348. 1975, by
Donald Stauffer, p. 45; by Margaret Anne O'Connor, p.
299. 1976, by William T. Stafford, p. 98; by Richard
Crowder, pp. 332-333. 1977, by Richard Crowder, p. 347;
by James Breslin, p. 385. 1978, by Richard Crowder, pp.
323, 325, 327-328. 1979, by Kermit Vanderbilt, p. 210;
by Richard Crowder, pp. 311, 318-319, 321. 1980, by
Paul Zender, p. 171; by Richard Crowder, pp. 357-358;
by Johnathan Morse, p. 479. 1981, None in this year.
1982, None in this year. 1983, by James K. Guimond, p.
334. 1984, by James K. Guimond, p. 348.

1372  WRIGHT, Celeste Turner. "Robinson's 'Lost Anchors.'" Explicator, 11 (June, 1953), item 57. This explanation is
largely a reply to Ellsworth Barnard, who says he does not
understand the poem, and is genuinely confused by the
imagery. To Ms. Wright, however, the symbolism seems
clear: the wrecked ship represents the sailor, the anchor
is an emblem of faith. Friends or loving women once trusted
this man; but their confidence was misplaced (their anchors
were lost). And the analogy is "old as ocean grass," for
seafaring men have long been considered unreliable.

1373  WRIGHT, Elizabeth. "Robinson's 'The Tree in Pamela's Garden.'" Explicator, 21 (February, 1963), item 47. Thinks
Marvin Klotz is essentially correct in his interpretation,
but that he comes down too strong on the "warped personality" theme. The tree could be suggestive of the Apollo-
Daphne myth, but it could refer to the tree of knowledge
in the Garden of Eden. Pamela tries to convince the townspeople that she is innocent, but she is never untrue to

herself.  She knows her claims and pretenses are really
only a cover-up for pride.  Pamela is truly one of Robinson's pathetic characters, but there is no real evidence
that she is a "morbid and warped personality."

1374  YANNELLA, Philip R.  "Edwin Arlington Robinson:  A Critical
Introduction."  Modern Language Journal, 54 (April, 1970),
293.  Review of work by Wallace L. Anderson.  Aimed at
the student and general reader, Anderson's book frankly
concedes that it owes a great deal to previous scholars.
But it also makes some important contributions to Robinson
scholarship.  The basic confusion of biography and value
remains, and sometimes the reader cringes at the author's
complete lack of grace in expression.  However, the solid
foundations of Professor Anderson's book cannot be questioned.  He clearly knows a great deal about Robinson, has
an excellent grasp of the previous scholarship, and has
done a fine job of researching some important facets of the
poet's early life.

1375  YASINSKI, William Arnold, Jr.  "Robinson, Frost, and Aestheticism:  The Imagination of Survival."  Ph.D. diss.,
Indiana University, 1978.  DA, 39 (1979), 5519A.  The
late-nineteenth-century cultural tradition of aestheticism
was profoundly important to the poetic development of
Robinson and Frost.  Both the particular and general influences of such aestheticist thinkers and writers as
Schopenhauer, Pater, Swinburne, etc. on the poetry of
Robinson and Frost illuminate specific poems, help define
the course of each poet's development, and suggest their
respective places in a large English-language tradition as
opposed to a rigidly American tradition.

1376  ZABEL, Morton Dauwen.  "Edwin Arlington Robinson."  Commonweal, 17 (February 15, 1933), 436-438.  Also published
as "Robinson in America."  Poetry, 46 (June, 1935), 157-
162.  Reprinted in Literary Opinion in America, ed.  Morton
D. Zabel.  New York:  Harper & Brothers, 1937.  "Four
Poets in America," pp. 397-406.  Also reprinted in Murphy,
ed. (1970), pp. 29-32.  He was a poet without school or
cenacle; he was fundamentally as inimitable as unapproachable; and his bleaker or more repetitive volumes might almost be interpreted as warning to the public to expect from
him none of the innovations or sensationalism that makes
literary creeds, movements, and manifestoes.  For this he
was scorned by youthful insurgents, and apparently by most
of the greater names that rival his in recent literature.
His influence was more subtle.  He brought form and tough-
ness of language into modern verse long before most of his
contemporaries, and he corrected by modest example a slow
drift toward slovenly habits and facile impressionism in
poetic thought.

1377 _____. "Robinson: The Ironic Discipline." Nation, 145
(August 28, 1937), 222-223. Review of Collected Poems.
Thinks the volume is undistinguished, and it should not be
called "complete." Many fragments are missing, and so are
the two plays. It serves, however, and will stand until a
full and definitive edition is someday printed in a style
worthy of Robinson's achievement.

1378 _____, ed. Selected Poems of Edwin Arlington Robinson,
with Introduction by James Dickey. New York: Macmillan,
1965. Reprinted Collier paperbacks, 1966.

1379 ZARDOYA, Concha. Historia de la Literatura Norteamericana.
Barcelona: Editorial Labor, 1956. Robinson, pp. 320-323.
In Spanish.

1380 ZIETLOW, Paul Nathan. "The Shorter Poems of Thomas Hardy
and Edwin Arlington Robinson: A Study in Contrasts."
Ph.D. diss., Michigan University, 1965. DA, 26 (1965),
2765. The object of this study is to show how Hardy and
Robinson, contemporary poets whose assumptions about the
origins of value in human life led them to approach poetry
from different directions, came to write works which produce remarkably similar effects. Using their verse and
statements in their letters and other writings, each chapter
attempts first to define a clear area of similarity between
them, and then to show how the similarities grew out of
basic differences.

1381 _____. "The Meaning of Tilbury Town: Robinson as a Re-
gional Poet." New England Quarterly, 40 (June, 1967),
188-211. Robinson is a regionalist writer, if by that we
mean one who through a large number of otherwise unrelated works creates the impression of a whole society in-
habiting a specific place which can be identified with a
particular part of a real country. One feels that a large
number of Robinson's poems taken together implies an even
larger whole, Tilbury Town, the home of a complete society
permeated with a definable set of values which some of its
members accept, and from which others deviate. Furthermore one recognizes in its values Tilbury Town's direct
correspondence with aspects of northern New England at
a certain stage of its history.

1382 ZIFF, Larzer. The American 1890's: Life and Times of a
Lost Generation. New York: Viking Press, 1966. "In
and Out of Laodicea: The Harvard Poets and Edwin Arlington Robinson," pp. 306-333. Extensive review of American
poetry in the 1890's, during which time James Whitcomb
Riley was the most popular poet. Robinson's first volumes
were more praised than abused by the critics. Since he

wrote in traditional forms, his work found a place in an
omnibus review which linked it with other volumes whose
pages had the same visual impact on the reader. Unlike
his contemporaries, however, Robinson had a great deal of
success in accomplishing a meaningful movement from dark
or gray or dead gods to light and color and life.

1383  ZIMMER, Giles. "Grangerford and Cory: Similar Creations."
      Mark Twain Journal, 21 (Spring, 1983), 59-60. Refers to
      a Mark Twain character. There is a striking resemblance
      between the description of Col. Grangerford at the begin-
      ning of Chapter 18 of The Adventures of Huckleberry Finn
      and Richard Cory of Robinson's famous poem. Chances
      are the resemblance is coincidental, but a comparison of the
      two passages is interesting. The remainder of the poem,
      although not closely matching Twain's description in diction
      and syntax, echoes its tone. Both writers skillfully build
      up their characters by description of physical features and
      personal qualities in such a way that the reader expects a
      satisfactory outcome on the basis of these attributes. The
      dramatic irony is identical which the reader learns that
      Grangerford has been shot to death by his enemies, and
      that Cory, with all his dignity, commits suicide.

# INDEX OF COAUTHORS, EDITORS, AND TRANSLATORS

Anderson, Wallace 1158

Bacon, Leonard 1138
Beaty, John O. 696
Benét, William Rose 522
Bloom, Harold 288
Breslin, James 1371
Brock, D. Heyward 619
Brooks, Van Wyck 306
Bulkley, Robert J. 254
Butcher, Philip 318
Bryer, Jackson R. 234

Canby, Henry Seidel 522
Condee, Ralph W. 643
Crowder, Richard 1371

Davis, Charles T. 1371
Dickey, James 1378

Finestone, Harry 1371
French, Warren 747

Gohdes, Clarence 1174
Gorman, Herbert S. 616
Guimond, James K. 1371
Gwynn, F. L. 598

Hall, Donald 1150
Heisztynski, Stanislaw 307
Henderson, Alice Corbin 891
Hill, Frank Ernest 221
Hindle, John 1018

Kirby, Thomas Austin 909
Kronenberger, Louis 473
Krzyzenowski, Julian 307

Latham, Edward C. 442
Lewis, Arthur O. 643
Lowell, Amy 819
Lunden, Rolf 1371

MacKaye, Percy 900
Mazzaro, J. 1366
Millett, Fred B. 844, 1155
Morris, Harry 1040
Morse, Johnathan 1371
Munson, Gorham 1371

O'Connor, Margaret Anne 1371
Olive, William John 909

Quinn, Patrick 1371

Rackliffe, John 862
Rickert, Edith 844
Robbins, J. Albert 1371
Robinson, E. A. 980
Rosenfield, Alvin H. 1371

Slote, Bernice 1371
Smith, Chard Powers 1138
Smith, Dave 1200
Spiller, Robert E. 1349
Stafford, William T. 1371
Stanford, Ann 1371
Stauffer, Donald 1371

Swauger, Craig G.   430


Vanderbilt, Kermit   1371
Van Doren, Mark   1149
Vinson, Esther   1138


Wagner, Linda   1371
Wasserman, Julian N.   301
Wasserstrom, William   819
Weatherford, A. Kingly   1371
Weber, Brom   1371

Whitall, William Van R.   917
Williams, Stanley T.   1151
Wilson, Edmund   281
Woodress, James   1371


Young, Thomas D.   544, 1018


Zabel, Morton D.   509, 1376
Zaturenska, Marya   626, 627
Zender, Paul   1371

Amaranth (poem by E.A.R.)   268, 326, 681, 1208
"Amaryllis" (by E.A.R.)   408
American literature (histories in which Robinson is discussed)   210,
    219, 287, 290, 300, 302, 303, 324, 328, 329, 330, 360, 412,
    418, 424, 425, 431, 440, 446, 447, 506, 507, 510, 517, 531,
    575, 627, 692, 696, 697, 722, 723, 764, 765, 803, 817, 822,
    841, 844, 850, 857, 870, 930, 937, 951, 959, 963, 1000, 1017,
    1040, 1066, 1086, 1137, 1139, 1145, 1151, 1152, 1164, 1173,
    1201, 1209, 1221, 1222, 1223, 1247, 1250, 1251, 1267, 1286,
    1287, 1316, 1317, 1318, 1321, 1325, 1349, 1368, 1382
"Annandale" poems (by E.A.R.)   597, 619, 945
Anthologies (which include poems and comments about Robinson)
    221, 270, 317, 522, 616, 645, 773, 891, 960, 979, 1204, 1234,
    1246, 1345, 1378
Arthurian legends and poems (in Robinson and others; see also
    Lancelot, Merlin, and Tristram)   37, 200, 215, 250,
    275, 288, 305, 307, 314, 319, 327, 349, 392, 409, 441, 459,
    493, 512, 543, 557, 571, 611, 675, 677, 700, 743, 788, 882,
    887, 913, 914, 968, 973, 974, 976, 977, 989, 995, 1014, 1036,
    1059, 1161, 1162, 1163, 1205, 1240, 1340
Avon's Harvest (poem by E.A.R.)   192, 334, 477


"Battle After War, The" (by E.A.R.)   1123
Bible (see also Religion)   223, 224
Bibliographic studies   234, 254, 286, 435, 538, 684, 686, 745, 784,
    785, 786, 787, 799, 805, 824, 880, 896, 898, 899, 943, 999,
    1103, 1155, 1197, 1269, 1332, 1333, 1336, 1338, 1339, 1371
Biographic and critical studies (book-length publications)   211, 229,
    240, 251, 338, 397, 448, 538, 574, 592, 648, 748, 917, 935,
    1023, 1045, 1057, 1092, 1110, 1168, 1215, 1255, 1361
Biographic (short sketches, reminiscences, anecdotes, etc.)   201,
    248, 253, 266, 269, 276, 301, 308, 310, 318, 331, 341, 344,
    347, 356, 364, 365, 383, 385, 411, 428, 434, 436, 438, 439,
    446, 473, 480, 521, 540, 542, 544, 546, 564, 579, 580, 602,
    649, 655, 661, 665, 680, 685, 698, 720, 726, 751, 774, 775,
    793, 809, 818, 819, 825, 840, 920, 921, 966, 982, 994, 999,
    1042, 1043, 1044, 1046, 1049, 1052, 1058, 1067, 1070, 1079,
    1085, 1141, 1150, 1155, 1160, 1190, 1211, 1212, 1219, 1231,
    1235, 1237, 1248, 1249, 1257, 1270, 1273, 1281, 1312, 1346,
    1368, 1369

Birthdays and other occasions (memorials, tributes, appreciations, celebrations)   44, 45, 46, 58, 60, 104, 135, 136, 137, 138, 140, 143, 144, 145, 146, 149, 376, 640, 641, 646, 652, 693, 791, 820, 829, 836, 837, 847, 848, 888, 910, 936, 978, 984, 985, 1060, 1068, 1106, 1138, 1165, 1203, 1260, 1282, 1293, 1322
Bradford, Gamaliel  306
British (comment by reviewers, etc.)   63, 64, 198, 199
"Broadway" (by E.A.R.)   384
Browning, Robert   367, 532, 795


"Captain Craig" (by E.A.R.)   949, 952, 1087, 1184, 1261, 1326
Cavender's House (poem by E.A.R.)   197, 477, 502
Characters (techniques of creation; men, women by Robinson)   453, 479, 513, 644, 660, 761, 778, 915, 1163, 1263, 1366
Children of the Night (book of poems by E.A.R.)   190, 506, 1061, 1177
"Clam-Digger, The" (by E.A.R.)   386
Collections of criticism (books, special issues of magazines, etc.)   232, 375, 387, 388, 515, 535, 541, 559, 630, 931, 950, 1283
Comedy (humor)   626, 863, 926, 1072
Courtesans (and prostitutes)   761, 909, 967, 1093, 1309
"Credo" (by E.A.R.)   589, 776
Critic (E.A.R. as)   214, 399, 801, 1101, 1108


"Dark Hills, The" (by E.A.R.)   487, 1191
Death (illness of E.A.R.; obituaries; see also biographic sketches)   125, 126, 127, 128, 129, 130, 131, 132, 265, 664, 866, 955, 1076, 1258, 1259
Dickens, Charles   370
Drama and dramatic techniques (in E.A.R.'s poetry)   256, 311, 490, 584, 682, 804, 914, 1117, 1182


Education   534, 779
Emerson, Ralph Waldo   576
"En Passant" (by E.A.R.)   1136
"Evangelist's Wife, An" (by E.A.R.)   1094


Fearing, Kenneth   747
"Field of Glory, The" (by E.A.R.)   462
"Firelight" (by E.A.R.)   237
"Flammonde" (by E.A.R.)   211, 578, 845, 879
"For a Dead Lady" (by E.A.R.)   458, 587, 634, 662, 833, 1180, 1181
"Forestalling" (by E.A.R.)   802
French (language, criticism, etc.)   293, 294, 325, 336, 389, 390-405, 671, 873, 1143, 1177, 1329
Frost, Robert   208, 256, 277, 393, 418, 583, 601, 691, 834, 1080, 1173, 1200, 1375

Gawain (also Gawaine; character in E.A.R. and others)   191, 1340
German criticism   245, 1100


Hardy, Thomas   651, 1146, 1291, 1292, 1294, 1295, 1380
Housman, A. E.   1330


Italian criticism   295, 990, 991, 992


James, Henry   1125
James, William   1169
Jeffers, Robinson   701, 1102


King Jasper (poem by E.A.R.)   442, 583, 1264


Lancelot (poem by E.A.R.)   242, 314, 327, 501, 528, 1071, 1096,
     1290
Letters of Robinson (individual and book-length publications)   218,
     241, 339, 369, 374, 380, 484, 485, 588, 628, 794, 812, 813,
     814, 852, 893, 854, 900, 1097, 1098, 1099, 1186, 1214, 1301,
     1348
Library (books and magazines owned by Robinson)   371, 377, 378,
     379, 381, 382, 702, 1187, 1188, 1306, 1310, 1331
Lodge, Henry Cabot   472
"Lost Anchors" (by E.A.R.)   437, 635, 725, 1216, 1372
Lowell, Amy   256, 393
"Luke Havergal" (by E.A.R.)   460, 529, 558, 598, 643, 832, 907,
     958, 1019, 1041


MacDowell, Mrs. Edward (includes MacDowell Colony)   340, 831, 867
Man Against the Sky, The (book of poems by E.A.R.; also title
     poem of book)   202, 249, 335, 463, 556, 683, 1020, 1088, 1144,
     1152, 1169
Manuscripts (collections of by E.A.R.; see also Research materials)
     161, 188, 239, 240, 380, 481, 539, 586, 716, 728, 1110, 1185,
     1302, 1304, 1305, 1307, 1311
Man Who Died Twice, The (poem by E.A.R.)   461
Mark Twain   358, 415, 433, 846, 1383
Masters, Edgar Lee   606, 668, 1130
Matthias at the Door (poem by E.A.R.)   503, 1342
Merlin (poem by E.A.R.)   441, 512, 976, 1118, 1162, 1207
Metaphysical poetry (relation to E.A.R.)   527, 715, 770, 1001, 1002,
     1149
Millay, Edna St. Vincent   701
"Miniver Cheevy" (by E.A.R.)   633, 877, 972
"Monadnock Through the Trees" (by E.A.R.)   645

Moody, William Vaughn   337, 366, 526, 588, 1129, 1213, 1320
"Mr. Flood's Party" (by E.A.R.)   206, 226, 320, 410, 487, 496,
     659, 719, 742, 865, 956, 957
Music (as related to E.A.R.)   475, 476, 516, 717, 797, 855


Nature (use of in E.A.R.)   246
"New England" (by E.A.R.)   209, 1266


"Octaves" (by E.A.R.)   908
"Oh, for a Poet" (by E.A.R.)   156
"Old King Cole" (by E.A.R.)   1135
"Old Story, An" (by E.A.R.)   454


Perry, Thomas S.   47, 615, 980, 1308
Philosophy (of E.A.R.)   278, 352, 368, 403, 425, 427, 465, 467,
     497, 500, 523, 621, 748, 760, 911, 944, 1132, 1265, 1284,
     1359, 1364
Poetry (General analysis of E.A.R. based on more than one poem.
     Items listed in this section are among the most important in
     Robinson bibliography.)   43, 59, 65, 76, 83, 87, 94, 112,
     133, 134, 141, 148, 150, 151, 189, 192, 203, 205, 207, 208,
     347, 349, 401, 402, 406, 407, 413, 423, 428, 445, 449, 451,
     456, 469, 492, 498, 517, 518, 519, 520, 525, 533, 558, 561,
     571, 572, 585, 591, 596, 599, 618, 633, 637, 653, 655, 663,
     666, 672, 694, 695, 696, 711, 718, 730, 736, 737, 740, 757,
     758, 766, 767, 782, 790, 791, 792, 795, 800, 806, 811, 821,
     823, 839, 842, 851, 864, 874, 875, 878, 892, 895, 901, 906,
     925, 952, 997, 1018, 1039, 1053, 1080, 1084, 1092, 1105,
     1166, 1168, 1170, 1171, 1172, 1174, 1314, 1315, 1319, 1341,
     1347, 1376
Praed, Winthrop Mackworth   699
Pulitzer prizes (won by E.A.R.)   79, 90, 92, 93, 103


Realism   277
Religion (includes Puritanism, Bible, etc.)   257, 350, 353, 354, 355,
     533, 536, 545, 617, 683, 687, 822, 835, 881, 912, 1133, 1178,
     1183, 1360
Reputation (of E.A.R.)   233, 348, 387, 452, 455, 470, 562, 640,
     641, 731, 838, 1334, 1337
Research materials (on E.A.R.)   242, 243, 284, 285, 362, 381, 382,
     416, 420, 651, 780, 794, 883, 1073, 1074, 1236, 1295, 1296,
     1297, 1298, 1299
Reviews (listed in chronological order of publication; titles listed
     here include the term "review"; items listed are by Robinson
     and major book-length studies of Robinson)

     (Books by Robinson)

The Torrent and the Night Before (1896)  1, 2, 3, 372, 373
The Children of the Night (1897)  4, 8, 9, 10, 11, 12, 13, 21,
    1061
Captain Craig (1902, 1915)  5, 6, 553, 961, 1104, 1124
The Town Down the River (1910), 14, 15, 16, 17, 18, 19, 357,
    962
Van Zorn (1914)  22, 23, 24, 32, 299, 309, 682, 815, 1370
The Porcupine (1915)  25, 26, 27, 311
The Man Against the Sky (1916)  28, 29, 30, 31, 33, 34, 35,
    36, 312, 313, 554, 673, 816, 871, 886, 1029, 1114, 1115, 1220
Merlin (1917)  37, 38, 39, 40, 41, 42, 1030, 1033, 1089
Lancelot (1920)  48, 49, 52, 603, 604, 735, 1031, 1343, 1367
The Three Taverns (1920)  50, 51, 52, 315, 605, 606, 885, 889,
    964, 1069, 1241
Avon's Harvest (1921)  53, 54, 55, 56, 316, 432, 555, 608, 889,
    905, 1006, 1242, 1344
Collected Poems (1921, 1927, 1937)  57, 61, 62, 91, 193, 244,
    258, 259, 281, 304, 422, 429, 444, 563, 570, 609, 610, 624,
    670, 678, 827, 828, 858, 872, 890, 927, 942, 954, 1037, 1055,
    1090, 1107, 1126, 1243, 1271, 1328, 1356, 1377
Roman Bartholow (1923)  66, 67, 68, 69, 70, 71, 72, 73, 260,
    524, 547, 549, 796, 918, 946, 1021, 1252, 1285, 1352
The Man Who Died Twice (1924)  74, 75, 78, 390, 612, 638, 732,
    903, 947, 1075, 1225, 1244, 1253, 1313, 1351
Dionysus in Doubt (1925)  77, 80, 81, 82, 220, 391, 426, 474,
    613, 639, 703, 904, 1022, 1032, 1091, 1127, 1128, 1140, 1224,
    1254, 1272, 1355
Tristram (1927)  85, 86, 87, 88, 89, 90, 261, 394, 508, 548,
    614, 704, 781, 893, 902, 919, 929, 988, 1007, 1024, 1245,
    1256, 1324, 1353
Sonnets 1889-1927 (1928)  96, 97, 99, 100, 395
Cavender's House (1929)  98, 101, 102, 105, 216, 227, 396, 656,
    705, 729, 752, 826, 948, 1008, 1026, 1192, 1226, 1356
The Glory of the Nightingales (1930)  106, 107, 108, 109, 262,
    321, 398, 622, 650, 671, 706, 733, 771, 772, 922, 940, 983,
    1027, 1056, 1119, 1148, 1176, 1193, 1274, 1329
Matthias at the Door (1931)  110, 111, 113, 297, 322, 565, 581,
    707, 734, 755, 894, 941, 1009, 1081, 1120, 1227, 1275
Nicodemus (1932)  114, 115, 116, 117, 118, 255, 263, 359, 400,
    505, 566, 708, 923, 933, 938, 1010, 1028, 1065, 1082, 1121
Talifer (1933)  119, 120, 122, 236, 282, 567, 709, 860, 1011,
    1194-1196, 1198, 1199, 1228, 1276
Amaranth (1934)  121, 123, 124, 264, 568, 623, 679, 688, 710,
    738, 777, 789, 924, 1012, 1035, 1062, 1229, 1277, 1278
King Jasper (1935)  139, 142, 187, 217, 222, 267, 291, 569, 689,
    712, 861, 1013, 1015, 1077, 1279, 1280
Selected Letters (1940)  147, 342, 361, 491, 499, 530, 550, 552,
    636, 674, 690, 713, 724, 763, 868, 998, 1048, 1064, 1078,
    1095, 1109, 1157, 1289, 1357
Untriangulated Stars (1948)  157, 158, 159, 160, 628, 869, 934,
    1262, 1323

Selected Poems (1965)   171, 172, 173, 298, 444, 509, 965, 1147
Letters to Edith Brower (1969)   177, 178, 180, 181, 182, 183,
    343, 754, 768, 986, 1034, 1335a

(Books About Robinson)

Hagedorn, Hermann. Edwin Arlington Robinson (1938)   20, 292,
    404, 419, 593, 625, 642, 714, 769, 807, 810, 856, 862, 1063,
    1122, 1206, 1207, 1230, 1288
Winters, Yvor. Edwin Arlington Robinson (1946)   152, 153, 154,
    155, 345, 483, 932, 1003, 1016, 1111, 1142, 1358, 1363
Neff, Emery. Edwin Arlington Robinson (1948)   162, 486, 600,
    657, 783, 1153, 1350
Barnard, Ellsworth. Edwin Arlington Robinson (1952)   163, 164,
    279, 323, 443, 488, 629, 630, 759, 1112, 1179, 1268
Fussell, Edwin S. Edwin Arlington Robinson (1954),   166, 167,
    405, 464, 537, 753, 1113, 1154
Coxe, Louis O. E. A. Robinson (1962)   235, 495, 511, 669
Smith, Chard Powers. Where the Light Falls (1965)   169, 170,
    230, 631, 673, 993, 1116
Robinson, William R. Edwin Arlington Robinson (1967)   174, 179,
    231, 494
Anderson, Wallace L. Edwin Arlington Robinson (1967)   175, 176,
    1175, 1374
Cary, Richard, ed. An Appreciation of E.A.R.: A Collection of
    Criticism (1969)   184, 185, 987
Barnard, Ellsworth, ed. Centenary Essays (1969)   186
"Richard Cory" (by E.A.R.)   346, 417, 582, 595, 749, 750, 916,
    1038, 1158, 1189, 1218
Robinson, Edwin Arlington (works by listed)   1054
Romanticism   225, 252, 288, 1335
Roosevelt, Theodore   351, 353, 658, 897, 1049, 1061, 1300, 1365


Sandburg, Carl   741
Scattered Lives (by E.A.R.)   213, 514
"Sheaves, The" (by E.A.R.)   457, 859
Social (and political concerns; includes war)   280, 421, 478, 590,
    739, 1265, 1360
Sonnets   727, 884, 953, 996, 1025, 1167, 1217
Spanish   1004, 1379
Stevens, Wallace   798


Talifer (poem by E.A.R.)   466, 468, 504
Tennyson, Alfred, Lord   974
Tilbury Town (poems by E.A.R. and other small-town references)
    238, 289, 430, 444, 667, 668, 1059, 1083, 1156, 1202, 1204,
    1381
Tocqueville, Alexis de   1144
Torrent and the Night Before, The (poems by E.A.R.)   168, 190,

332, 849, 876, 1303
Town Down the River, The  514, 765
"Tree in Pamela's Garden, The" (by E.A.R.)  741, 762, 975, 1373
Tristram (poem by E.A.R.)  195, 247, 283, 296, 319, 333, 363,
    409, 414, 450, 471, 573, 620, 654, 677, 746, 928, 969, 970,
    995, 1036, 1131, 1210
Turannos (includes poem "Eros Turannos")  632, 843, 971, 1017,
    1134, 1146


"Veteran Sirens, The"  (by E.A.R.)  228


"Wandering Jew, The" (by E.A.R.)  1159
"Whip, The" (by E.A.R.)  272, 273, 274, 981
Wright, James (modern poet)  1200